Black Women in Politics

SUNY series in New Political Science

Bradley J. Macdonald, editor

SUNY series in African American Studies

John R. Howard and Robert C. Smith, editors

Black Women in Politics

Demanding Citizenship, Challenging Power, and Seeking Justice

Edited by

Julia S. Jordan-Zachery and Nikol G. Alexander-Floyd

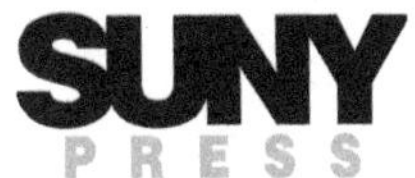

Published by State University of New York Press, Albany

Printed in the United States of America

For information, contact State University of New York Press, Albany, NY
www.sunypress.edu

Library of Congress Cataloging-in-Publication Data

Names: Jordan-Zachery, Julia Sheron, editor. | Alexander-Floyd, Nikol G. (Nikol Gertrude), editor.
Title: Black women in politics : demanding citizenship, challenging power, and seeking justice / edited by Julia S. Jordan-Zachery and Nikol G. Alexander-Floyd.
Description: Albany : State University of New York Press, 2018. | Series: SUNY series in new political science | Series: SUNY series in African American studies | Includes bibliographical references and index.
Identifiers: LCCN 2017045875 | ISBN 9781438470931 (hardcover : alk. paper) | ISBN 9781438470955 (ebook)
Subjects: LCSH: Women, Black—Political activity—Cross-cultural studies. | Women, Black—Social conditions—Cross-cultural studies. | Feminism— Cross-cultural studies.
Classification: LCC HQ1236 .B527 2018 | DDC 305.48/896073—dc23
LC record available at https://lccn.loc.gov/2017045875

10 9 8 7 6 5 4 3 2 1

I dedicate this work to my grandmothers who ploughed tirelessly to make sure that their daughters would not have to be "mules of the earth."

—Julia S. Jordan-Zachery

I dedicate this work to Melanie "Njeri" Jackson, Linda Williams, and Jewel Limar Prestage, Black women who labored tirelessly for progressive political change, and to raise up generations of scholars who would fight for social justice.

—Nikol G. Alexander-Floyd

Contents

List of Figures and Tables ix

Acknowledgments xi

Black Women's Political Labor: An Introduction xiii
Julia S. Jordan-Zachery and Nikol G. Alexander-Floyd

Section I: Black Feminists Doing Intersectionality Work / 1

1. Why Political Scientists Don't Study Black Women, but Historians and Sociologists Do: On Intersectionality and the Remapping of the Study of Black Political Women 5
Nikol G. Alexander-Floyd

2. "I Ain't Your Darn Help": Black Women as the Help in Intersectionality Research in Political Science 27
Julia S. Jordan-Zachery

Section II: Black Feminist Policy Analysis / 45

3. The Politics of Black Women's Health in the UK: Intersections of "Race," Class, and Gender in Policy, Practice, and Research 49
Jenny Douglas

4. Hiding in Plain Sight: Black Women Felons Reentering Society 69
Keesha M. Middlemass

5. Lost Tribes: An Intersectionality-Based Policy Analysis of How US HIV/AIDS Policy Fails to "Rescue" Black Orphans 97
Julia S. Jordan-Zachery

Section III: Diasporic Black Women and the Global Political Arena / 113

6. El pan, el poder y la política: The Politics of Bread Making in Honduras's Garifuna Community 117
K. Melchor Quick Hall

7. Woman Out of Place: Portia Simpson-Miller and Middle-Class Politics in Jamaica 143
Maziki Thame

8. "We Want to Set the World on Fire": Black Nationalist Women and Diasporic Politics in the *New Negro World*, 1940–1944 000
Keisha N. Blain

Section IV: Discourses, Movements, and Representation / 191

9. Morrisonian Democracy: The Literary Praxis of Black Feminist Political Engagement 195
Judylyn S. Ryan

10. Illegitimate Appetites: Michelle Obama's Anti-Obesity Campaign as Sexual Regulation 217
Grace E. Howard

11. "We Always Resist: Trust Black Women": Black Women's Reproductive Justice Activism in the Wake of Health Care Reform 237
Tonya M. Williams

Contributors 261

Index 265

Figures and Tables

Figure

2.1 Black Women as Research Subjects in Political Science, 1996–2010 00

Tables

1.1 Search Totals for Full-Length Articles (FLAs) by Titles and Abstracts, 1970–1985 10

1.2 Search Totals for Full Length Articles (FLAs) by Titles and Abstracts, 1986–2003 11

1.3 Search Totals for Full Length Articles (FLAs) by Titles and Abstracts, 2004–2008 13

4.1 Participants 77

11.1 Reproductive Justice Organizations' Constituents and Issue Niches (N=4) 249

11.2 Political Activities of Reproductive Justice Organizations before Enactment of the ACA (N=4) 250

11.3 Political Activities of Reproductive Justice Organizations after Enactment of the ACA (N=4) 252

Acknowledgments

The following chapters, "Why Political Scientists Don't Study Black Women, But Historians and Sociologists Do: On Intersectionality and the Remapping of the Study of Black Political Women," which has been slightly revised for this volume, and "'I Ain't Your Darn Help': Black Women as the Help in Intersectionality Research in Political Science," were previously published in the *National Political Science Review* (2014). "Black Women's Political Labor: An Introduction" incorporates some material from the "Guest Editors' Note" in the same aforementioned volume.

In "Black Women's Political Labor: An Introduction," Julia contributed the framing, specifically regarding the use of Zora Neal Hurston's work, and wrote the discussion of contributors' work in connection to the larger project; and Nikol wrote the section on intersectionality for the introduction. Julia wrote the introductory essays accompanying each section. Both authors coedited the volume.

We would like to thank our editor at SUNY Press, Michael Rinella, for his support of this work, as well as several anonymous reviewers whose responses strengthened the volume. We thank Judylyn Ryan, as well, for her important feedback on the introduction and book title. We would also like to thank Monica Simal and Viviane Saleh-Hanna for their thoughtful insights, which helped to frame the introduction; and Edmicelly Xavier (Julia's research assistant) for her work in helping to edit the volume. Thanks also to Laura Gillman for her contribution of sources for the introduction and to Tyson King-Meadows for a Julia R. Hight Summer Writing Fellowship that provided valuable time (for Nikol) to work on this project. Finally, we thank all of the contributors whose work is included here and for their efforts to advance social justice for Black women and communities throughout the Diaspora.

Black Women's Political Labor

An Introduction

JULIA S. JORDAN-ZACHERY
NIKOL G. ALEXANDER-FLOYD

Zora Neal Hurston's *Their Eyes Were Watching God*, widely lauded as a foundational Black feminist text, speaks to Black women's self-definition and self-actualization in the face of the interlocking and multiple forms of oppressions they confront in their daily lives. The novel foregrounds a number of recurring symbols and motifs that communicate this larger theme of Black women's self-actualization, including, for instance, the protagonist Janie Crawford's hair, which serves as a symbol and site of bodily and community control, and the mule. At the beginning of the novel, Nanny, Janie's grandmother, expounds on the complexity of race-gender politics that (some) Black women encounter. In her counsel to her granddaughter, Nanny states:

> Honey, de white man is de ruler of everything as fur as Ah been able tuh find out. Maybe it's some place way off in de ocean where de black man is in power, but we don't know nothin' but what we see. So de white man throw down de load and tell de nigger man tuh pick it up. He pick it up because he have to, but he don't tote it. He hand it to his womenfolks. De nigger woman is de mule uh de world so fur as Ah can see. (Hurston 1990, 14)

In this conversation with young Janie, Nanny offers a nuanced but incomplete understanding of Black women's often perceived role in race-gender, social, economic, and political hierarchies. Specifically, Nanny speaks to the ways in which Black women's labor is often used in the service of others. Furthermore, she speaks to a form of mistreatment and betrayal of the mule, and thus through this metaphor she speaks to how Black women are represented and treated by those both within and outside their racial group. This appropriative labor extends to emotional labor, a theme powerfully examined by Audre Lorde (2007) in her analysis of the use of Black women's emotional labor. In a similar vein, bell hooks (1995) suggests that even Black women's anger is pressed into service of the liberation of others and not themselves.

Despite its accuracy in capturing the appropriation of Black women's labor, Nanny's analysis is only partially complete, a fact that Janie recognizes at the end of her own epic journey. Whatever external exigencies constrain or coerce Black women's labor, it is evident that internal psychological, ethical, and economic commitments also propel Black women's labor. That is to say, in whatever circumstances they may labor, as self-defining and self-authorized agents, Black women are equally, if not primarily, motivated and self-directed to till their own fields. Through this largely unexplored dimension of the mule as metaphor, Hurston depicts and celebrates the process of Janie engaged in the process of self-actualization. For example, Janie's first two husbands, Logan and Joe, own mules, and these mules metaphorically embodied their treatment of Janie. Her first husband, Logan, overworked his mule in the same manner in which he overworked Janie. Joe, the second husband, treated his mule as a showpiece; similarly, Janie was used as a symbol of his stature and self-importance. In both cases, neither man valued Janie for herself. By the end of the novel, the mule disappears from the story. And what we are left with is Janie engaged in a relationship with Tea Cake, a man who values her as a partner.

The mule is often thought of as stubborn in addition to being a beast of burden. Mules, stereotypically or not, are thought of as possessing a stubborn and determined spirit. The mule is constructed as being resistant to the "master's" efforts to tame and control. As such, via this metaphor, Hurston is offering a particular view of Black womanhood—one that is stubbornly committed to realizing Black women's sense of self in spite of oppressive structures that seek to control. Within the metaphor of the Black woman as the mule who is ploughing or tilling[1] for others, Hurston offers a complex and rich analysis of the intersection of race, class, gender, and other forces in the lived realities of Black women.

As a way of critiquing and disrupting this appropriation of Black women's labor, Hurston, in the vein of Black feminists, questions the use of Black women's labor—physical, emotional and political—in liberation efforts by bringing to the forefront the positionality of Black women. Drawing on the metaphor of the mule and its use as a means of production, Black women academics and others have asked: For whom are Black women tilling? Is their labor for their liberation or solely to be used as part of the liberation efforts of others? And how do Black women envision the manifestations of their political labor?

In this collection, building on the interventions of other Black feminists who seek to highlight the appropriation of Black women's labor and Black women's responses, we deploy the metaphor of tilling to be understood in its broadest sense as the cultivation and preparation of fields or landscapes to optimize various types of production/productive processes. Specifically, we highlight tilling as a metaphor for political work, whether through formal or informal means, such as elections or grassroots organizing, respectively. This allows us to ask: How have Black women creatively responded to the challenges and opportunities with which they have been confronted in various geographical and political contexts and epochs? We also examine the ways in which scholars who examine Black political women have tilled their own intellectual fields, using their energies to question what constitutes knowledge and its various means of production and its ends, thereby creating space for investigating Black political women. In circles, especially in political science, where Political Man (Lipset 1960) and Political Woman (Kirkpatrick 1974) are still seen as White, and in the study of Black politics, where the focus is often on Black men, we examine intellectual work forged about Black Political Women in the African Diaspora (Prestage 1991).

Diasporic Black women indeed have a long history of political engagement. Although there is no one Black women's political identity, their centuries of efforts have sought to liberate Black women and other oppressed groups from economic, social, health, housing, cultural, and incarceration-related inequalities. To map and further clarify Black women's status along a number of fronts, as well as their efforts at social change, scholars across various disciplines have studied the mutually constitutive forces that shape Diasporic Black women's lives, most notably under the marker of intersectionality (see, e.g., Crenshaw 1989, 1990–1991; Berger and Guidroz 2009; May 2015; and Collins and Bilge 2016). Within political science in particular, despite a growing body of work on race and gender politics and intersectionality, extant research from both Black politics and women and politics as subfields tend to marginalize the voices of Black women. Such research, in some cases even if it relies on intersectionality—a paradigm developed by Black women and other women of color to address their oppression—pays little attention to the lives of Black women. Thus, we are left with the question: How do Diasporic Black women engage in politics? *Black Women in Politics* addresses this larger question.

In what follows, we situate *Black Women in Politics* in terms of its contributions both to the discipline of political science and to the interdisciplinary study of Black women in politics in areas such as literature and health policy as a whole. Debates concerning intersectionality are of particular relevance to the two general audiences we engage, and we first claim what we believe is our stake as Black feminist political scientists in this regard. We then extend the metaphor of tilling by turning to an examination of the ways in which the author of each chapter "tills" new intellectual ground by creating or expanding intellectual space through her chapter's contribution.

Intersectionality

Intersectionality provides a key frame for the book because of its connection to securing democratic values. Radical democratic theory presupposes substantive equality, not only on an individual level, but also for groups and communities within and among nations. This focus on substantive equality emphasizes social justice, and this commitment is one, as the chapters in this collection attest, that resounds throughout the lives and political efforts of Black Diasporic women.

In political science, scholars have explored a range of important issues that have derived from an "intersectional approach" (Berger and Guidroz 2009). We have expanded our definitions of what constitutes the political (Prestage 1991; Braxton 1994). We have examined the connections between stereotypes, symbolism, and narratives regarding Black womanhood and the production of ideology and creation of public policy (see, e.g., King 1977; Lewis 1985; Hancock 2004; Alexander-Floyd 2007; Jordan-Zachery 2009; Lewis 2016). We have explored the relationship between feminism and political consciousness (Simien 2006), as well a range of factors, such as gender, class, and sexuality, in the production of Black political ideology (see, e.g., Willoughby-Herard 2008). We have studied political movements in different times and places (see, e.g., Harris 2001; Smooth and Tucker 1999) and in and across various cultures (see, e.g, Wallace 2014). We have elaborated the operation of gender, class, age, sexuality, and other forces in the construction of institutions and the circulation of power therein (see, e.g, Smooth 2006; Brown 2014). We have examined Black girlhood and its link to prevailing ideologies and worked to maximize the visibility of the political stakes in their politicization and political potential (Brown 2007). We have worked alongside and produced research about the Black political women who operate in formal and informal political contexts and the rich range of political participation in which they engage (see, e.g., Berger 2004; Nealy 2008). We have theorized about Black women's relationships to the state, legal system, and civil society (see, e.g., Cohen 1999), as well as our claims to political values such as justice (Threadcraft 2016). And, of course, we have been engaged in articulating the ways in which intersectionality can be productively employed in the disciplinary space that is political science (see, e.g., Hancock 2007; 2016, Smooth 2006; Simien 2007; Jordan-Zachery 2007; Alexander-Floyd 2012; Lindsay 2013). Although an exhaustive survey of work produced on Black political women in political science is beyond the scope of this introduction, the preceding review nevertheless conveys the sense in which intersectionality, broadly defined, has been an important basis for remaining, in the words of Jewel Prestage, the "founder" of the field of Black women in politics in political science, "in quest" of Black political women (Prestage 1991).

Given the foregoing, it is unsurprising that intersectionality, as a research paradigm, remains a vibrant basis for research across disciplines such as political science and in multi- and interdisciplinary spaces, such as women's and gender studies and Black studies. Indeed, the number of special issues that continue to be published on the subject, most notably in *Signs* (2013), the leading journal in women's and gender studies internationally, and *New Political Science* (2015), a journal published by a left-leaning section of the American Political Science Association of the same name, as well as books and edited volumes by noted figures, such as Bonnie Thornton Dill (Dill and Zambrana 2011) and Vivian May (2015), two past-presidents of the National Women's Studies Association, among others (e.g., Berger and Guidroz 2009; Collins and Blige 2016), speak to the dynamism of the research agendas produced under the aegis of intersectionality. As Berger and Guidroz explain, "The breadth of this continued interest [in the intersectional approach] suggests robust inquiry and research, and guarantees at least another decade of intersectional research in both feminist and critical gender scholarship in traditional disciplines" (Berger and Guidroz 2009) and interdisciplinary spaces.

Despite its popularity, however, intersectionality is also in some ways at the center of an intramural debate about how and to what extent race and racialization, in particular, are relevant analytics—especially in women's and gender studies generally. For some, intersectionality anchors essentialized notions of identity and/or does not provide a means of understanding the deep imbrication of social and political forces Black women confront (see, e.g., Nash 2008). For others, it is too closely tied to Black female and other women of color's subjectivity to be useful as an analytic (Wiegman 2012). Other configurations, such as assemblages (Puar 2007), or concepts, such as fugitivity or social death, have emerged and been offered in some cases as alternatives to intersectionality. As Brittney Cooper notes, some suggest that, in its broad circulation and its justification for promoting institutional and intellectual diversity, intersectionality is a project whose time has come and gone.

The prevalence and nature of such critiques are instructive. "Intersectionality critiques," as May notes, "have become something of their own genre—a form so flourishing, at times it seems critique has become a primary means of taking up the concept and its literatures" (May 2015, 98).

> Yet, there is something about the sheer number of critiques as well as their nature that deserves consideration: *how* intersectionality is read and portrayed (and not) can be troubling, particularly when basic intersectional premises . . . are violated by a critic's operative assumptions and interpretive methods. (98) (emphasis in original).

Significantly, many of the critics of intersectionality ignore or misunderstand its emphasis on social justice. The intersectional approach has always been aimed at assessing and challenging those forces that impede full expression of political participation and facilitating personal, social, and communal well-being. The identification of intersectionality with conservative notions of identity politics that settle on essentialist foundations is problematic in that it ignores its definition by radical Black feminists, as we have argued elsewhere (Alexander-Floyd and Jordan-Zachery 2014) and on which we elaborate below. At its inception, identity politics was never suggestive of essentialist views, but rather posited social location as a function of mutually constitutive social, economic, and political forces.

As a practical matter, these critiques serve to deflect attention from addressing racialization and racism. As Brittney Cooper (2016) relates:

> [I] think that the calls to become postintersectional and to move beyond intersectionality are akin to and give false intellectual

> heft to broader political suggestions that the election of Barack Obama has thrust us into a post-racial era. These institutional and political moves index an increasing discomfort with talking about racism. (403)

Critiques of intersectionality, in other words, often accompany and/or aid and abet a turn from discussing historical and contemporary racial projects.

We claim our stake in these debates in asserting that intersectionality remains a not only useful, but also necessary approach for studying Black diasporan political women. Debates about the nature of intersectionality and its operationalization in research will likely remain, and, as we further note below, section I takes up the issue of how political science as a field in general and intersectionality research specifically has given short shrift to Black women, particularly given their importance in politics. Still, as a mode of reading the political landscapes in which Black women operate, intersectionality continues to be generative, as Alexander-Floyd points out, as both an "idea," that is, in the specific formulation offered by critical race theorist Kimberlé Crenshaw, who coined the term, and an "ideograph," that is, the broader political and intellectual project of investigating the multiple dimensions of Black political women (Alexander-Floyd 2012). As it relates to the former instance of intersectionality, political scientists in fact have been among those who have paid special attention to the key elements of Crenshaw's formulations, particularly her elaboration of various form of intersectionality—structural, political, and representational (see, e.g., Alexander-Floyd 2012; Jordan-Zachery 2012; Simien and McGuire 2014). In what follows, we link the importance of intersectionality to the metaphor of tilling and use it to illuminate the contributions of the works collected herein.

Where We Stand: Situating Black Women in Politics

At the core of this collection is the concept of power and its relationship to race, class, and gender. Power, in terms of a definition, is much contested. Although we do not seek to settle these debates, we do believe that it is important to articulate an understanding of power. Relying on Black feminist canonical texts, which include but are not limited to the Combahee River Collective (1982), Crenshaw (1989), Roberts (1997), Robnett (1997), Springer (1999, 2005), and Collins (2000), we understand power as interrelated and relational systems and processes to control or manipulate Black women's self-actualization. Additionally, we understand power as embodying both struggle, because it is unequally distributed, and the possibilities for action.

Ploughing (or *tilling*), drawing from the work of Zora Neal Hurston, is a dynamic metaphor that speaks to how Black women respond to mutually constitutive forms of oppression—that is, how they understand and respond to power. This metaphor captures the ethical and political values of liberty and justice pursued by Black women on two interrelated levels. First, it signals the efforts that Black women undertake to eliminate obstructions to their political participation and to pursue the good life. Second, in a related vein, it speaks to the efforts of scholars, particularly Black women, in carving out intellectual space for examining Black political women. With the aforementioned in mind, the works collected here address both the scholarly production of work on Black political women as well as a range of themes that capture the lived experiences of Diasporic Black women. These themes include but are not limited to unmasking power structures, Black nationalism, policy making, how the Black female body is marked, agency, activism, and democratic practices. Informed by Black feminist intersectionality theory, its understanding of power, and self-actualization, the eleven chapters comprising this edited book explore a multiplicity of Black Diasporic women's political practices and behaviors.

This collection, in enacting its own effort at expanding the field of Black women in politics in political science, emphasizes interdisciplinary research and critical methodologies and methods, as these have been important in advancing feminist research across disciplines. Specifically, *Black Women in Politics* is significant for Black women's studies as an interdisciplinary enterprise in at least two ways. First, humanistic perspectives dominate the interdisciplinary field of women's and gender studies more generally, and Black women's studies is no different in this regard. Political science scholarship that includes cultural studies, historical, and literary approaches has greatly expanded political scientists' investigations of Black women and politics. Second, political science as a discipline also has much to offer for scholarly investigators committed to the interdisciplinary integration of knowledge, including, but not limited to a focus on the state; the circulation of power within and without government institutions; issues of descriptive versus substantive electoral representation; the formation and execution of public policy; the connection among ideology, political consciousness, and public opinion; the operation of symbolic and narrative frames in ideological, institutional, and policy formation; and nonpositivistic explorations of empiricism. The chapters included herein address these issues and more.

In addition to showcasing the contributions of an interdisciplinary approach that includes political science perspectives, *Black Women in Politics* contributes to the study of Black women in politics by illuminating intersectionality's continued relevance as a research paradigm. This objective is particularly important because, as the theory/concept of intersectionality travels across various disciplines and subfields, there remains a gap in our understanding of its functioning. Particularly, there is limited research on how Black women engage intersectionality in their own political quests. Despite the fact that Black women are active political agents, there exists scant research that offers a comprehensive treatment of their political behavior and activities. This book works to fill this gap. Via a Black feminist lens, the chapters critically analyze not only Black women's engagement with conventional institutions of politics, but also how they have worked to create space outside these institutions in their efforts to demand representation and justice. Given the role that Black women play in politics—as voters, as social movement and community activists, as elected officials, and as subjects of public policy discourse—it is imperative that we expend greater energy and attention on investigating Black political women. *Black Women in Politics* provides a much-needed context for exploring recent developments in Black women in politics as a subfield of political science in its own right. It highlights three dimensions—citizenship, power, and justice—that are foundational to intersectionality theory and politics as developed by Black women and other women of color (see, e.g., The Combahee River Collective 1982; Crenshaw 1989; Berger 2004; Jordan-Zachery 2009; Alexander-Floyd 2012; Isoke 2013).

Most of the work on Black women in politics falls into two categories, namely (1) works that deal with specific geographic locations or a particular type or dimension of politics or (2) works that focus on particular time periods. Recent monographs, such as *Negras in Brazil: Re-Envisioning Black Women, Citizenship, and the Politics of Identity* by Kia Caldwell and Zenzele Isoke's *Urban Black Women and the Politics of Resistance*, which focuses on Black women's political activism in Newark, New Jersey, are examples of the former. Similarly, *Private Politics and Public Voices: Black Women's Activism from World War I to the New Deal* by Nikki Brown and Lisa G. Materson's *For the Freedom of Her Race: Black Women and Electoral Politics in Illinois, 1877–1932* serve as examples of works that provide in-depth examinations of Black women's politics in critical moments of Black political history.

Black Women in Politics builds on the extant work on black women in politics by extending beyond particular time periods, locations, or singular definitions of politics. It sets itself apart in the multidisciplinary and interdisciplinary field of women's and gender studies in three ways: (1) by focusing on contemporary Black politics not only in the United States, but also in the African Diaspora; (2) by showcasing politics along a broad trajectory, including but not limited to social movements, formal politics, public policy, media studies, and epistemology; and (3) by including a multidisciplinary range of scholars, with a strong concentration of work by political scientists, a group whose work is often excluded or limited in edited collections, a reality that diminishes attention to public policy, institutions, materiality, governance, contemporary happenings, and/or formal politics.

A central assumption of this volume is that politics operates in myriad, often overlapping, or constitutive domains. Accordingly, *Black Women in Politics* has chapters that consider the new challenges faced by this contemporary political moment, such as: How do Black women fare within raced and gendered institutions as Black female elected officials? How do African and African Diasporic women integrate political knowledge, concepts, and tactics to meet the challenges of organizing within different state regimes? How do media impact the reception of Black political figures, such as Michelle Obama, and what are the implications for our understanding of Black women, neoliberalism, and Black cultural pathology and middle-class respectability? These are just some of the questions that this collection uniquely answers.

In short, *Black Women in Politics* speaks to women's and gender studies and Black and Africana studies by providing an interdisciplinary examination of Black women in politics by Black political scientists and scholars based in other disciplines, assisting in reimagining Black women's studies as a subfield within Africana studies and women's and gender studies. The selected pieces were chosen because of the editors' commitment to scholarship that reflects and affirms Black women and politics as a subfield that overlaps with other fields within political science while standing as a separate subfield that crosses other traditional disciplines and newer ones such as women's and gender studies and Black studies. The chapters represent the best theoretical and methodological work within the subfield. Furthermore, within political science, it presents a guidebook through which scholars can understand the value of studying power using the tools, concepts, approaches, and ideas situated within political science, but deeply integrated with insights from other disciplines such as history. This collection contributes to the subfield of Black women's studies and Black/Africana studies by showcasing multi- and interdisciplinary work on Black women in politics. It expands our repertoire of methodological tools and concepts in discussing and assessing Black women's lives, the conditions under which they live, their labor, and the politics they enact to improve their circumstances.

Critical Themes in Studying Black Political Women

The contributors to this collection employ various cases and a wide range of methods to analyze how Black women, nationally and globally, are working or "tilling" in service of themselves. These approaches include critical literary analyses, narrative analysis of political frames, and interviews with previously incarcerated women, among others. Despite their different foci and methods, there are a number of common themes connecting the various chapters. Such themes include but are not limited to invisibility/hypervisibility, challenges of defining Black womanhood, agency, and citizenship. Combined, the chapters encourage us to critically think about what it means to be a Black woman in various time periods and geographic and social locations and how vectors of power mutually constitute the contours of Black women's oppression to which they respond. Although we organize the book in terms of content areas, we are mindful that there is continuity between these sections, and so we encourage the reader to engage the readings as part of a spectrum of Black women's political work and behavior as opposed to a series of separate chapters.

As an entry point into the chapters, we highlight some of the areas of convergence and divergence, but we also encourage you to use this as a springboard for discovering and critically analyzing your own themes and arguments. Doing so is in the spirit of Black feminist epistemology that recognizes there is no one "Truth." We employ the metaphor of the mule, in relation to power, to offer one reading of the chapters that constitute this collection.

Moving From Silence to Voice

In *Their Eyes Were Watching God*, Hurston traces the story of Janie's journey from silence to voice. We do not argue that Janie is voiceless, but more that others in their exercise of power are either choosing not to hear Janie's voice or are actively working to silence Janie—that is, to mute her. In her journey to voice, Janie situates her needs as central—moving from the margins to the center (hooks 1984)—and as such contradicts Nanny's assertion that Black women are the mules of the world. Hurston charts this journey of Janie's self-direction by situating Janie's lived experiences. According to hooks (1984), Black women's

> lived experience may shape our consciousness in such a way that our world view differs from those who have a degree of privilege (however relative within the existing system). It is essential for continued feminist struggle that black women recognize the special vantage point our marginality gives us and make use of this perspective to criticize the dominant racist, classist, sexist hegemony as well as to envision and create a counter-hegemony. (16)

The specific chapters included in this collection by Jordan-Zachery ("I Ain't Your Darn Help"), Middlemass (Hiding in Plain Sight), Williams ('We Always Resist'), and Hall (El pan, el poder y la política) situate the voices of Black women in their approaches to analyzing Black women in politics. By "hearing" the voices of the women who inform these studies, these authors use Black feminist theory to explore "discursive narratives and lived experiences" (Middlemass, this volume) to show how Black women's bodies are marked. Such an approach is also used to explore how Black women are rendered invisible in larger discussions of belonging and democracy. Jordan-Zachery's analysis of political science research opens with her retelling of a social event and how she was challenged when she offered a critique of the novel *The Help*. She maps this experience, coupled with her experiences at political science conferences, to explore two forms of silences that exist within political science research. According to her, the forms of silence "can be overt; this is the complete absence of Black women as research subjects and/or the recognition of their contributions." Or silence can be covert. This form of silence "allows for a form of memorializing the contributions of Black women," but still renders them omitted and or invisible in our understandings of power and democracy (this volume).

Hall situates the voices of rural Black women in Honduras to explore how they engage in "pragmatic activism" to resist land grab. Through the voices of these women, we are better able to understand not only how they organize, but, more importantly, why they organize around the production of *ereba*, or cassava bread. As she writes,

> Catalina talked about how important *ereba* is to the overwhelming majority of the village: "The only hope we have to be able to move forward is the sale of *ereba* because that is our work. And I know that if one day the moment arrives in which *ereba* has a demand at a global level, we will be able to say that the community will be able to develop because that is the agricultural work of almost 95 percent of the people in the community. (this volume)

As such, *ereba* becomes so much more than simply cassava bread; it is a means through which tradition is maintained, a means for challenging land grab, and a way for women, in particular, to advance the larger agenda of autonomy for their communities.

In "Hiding in Plain Sight," Middlemass's chapter, we are introduced to Eve and Janaye, among others, who poignantly articulate how policies consistently fail them and other previously incarcerated Black women—those who become permanently marked with the nomenclature of ex-felon. In explaining her use of personal narratives, Middlemass posits that

> quantitative methods . . . do not adequately capture reality. The prevailing methodological approaches make many women invisible in reentry discourse, and Black women are further marginalized because criminal justice scholars tend to focus on race, gender and criminal involvement as distinct characteristics and separate issues, when in fact they are not autonomous. (this volume)

The approaches used across these chapters represent one method of moving Black women from silence to voice—by situating and centering their lived experiences. By locating and giving voices to diverse Black women—ex-felon, college professor, and cassava bread–making women in Honduras—via Black-feminist approaches, these authors advance methods that deconstruct the relationships between identity and power. Through the counter-narratives of Black women, they are also advancing methods that challenge systems of power, particularly ways of knowledge production that result in the invisibility and or omission of Black women.

Invisibility and Unmasking Power Structures

This brings us to the second dominant theme running throughout the chapters—the notion of invisibility and Black womanhood. Through the metaphor of the mule, Hurston shows how power structures, within the Black community particularly, are made invisible. Consider how her two husbands treated her—neither one saw her as a woman with needs. How power structures engender the invisibility of Black women has been a longstanding research subject of Black feminist researchers. It was the impetus for Kimberlé Crenshaw's (1989) coinage of the term intersectionality, although she was not the first individual to articulate the concept. In *Black Women in Politics*, the theme of invisibility is explored differently across the various chapters. For example, Alexander-Floyd and Jordan-Zachery explore how the politics of omission, evident in political science research, results in the invisibility of Black women as research subjects. In "Why Political Scientists Don't Study Black Women, but Historians and Sociologists Do: On Intersectionality and the Remapping of the Study of Black Political Women," Alexander-Floyd, comparing political science to sister disciplines, considers the extent to which political scientists investigate the lives of Black women and issues of race, class, and gender more broadly. Using insights from Black feminist geography, she compares the production of research on Black women across four fields: political science, sociology, history, and economics. Her analysis shows the "absented presence" of Black women in political science research and how garreting can provide a means of responding to such treatment of Black women. Although some might question the utility of promoting intersectional approaches in traditional disciplines such as political science, particularly when there are interdisciplinary and other more welcoming intellectual environs, she highlights how the critiques of Black women's absented presence in political science and garreting constitute a decolonial project. Alexander-Floyd contends that to re-create the intellectual geography of political science into a space that intellectually and professionally addresses the presence of Black women would require a Perestroika-like effort to restructure the discipline. Jordan-Zachery takes up the question: How does the politics of research, specifically intersectionality research, result in the further marginalization of Black women? According to Jordan-Zachery, there is an omission project occurring in published political science research generally and within intersectionality research specifically. To explore the politics of intersectionality research, she examines the relationship between the novel *The Help* and intersectionality research to show how these cultural and academic phenomena mirror each other and reinforce and normalize the treatment of Black women. She posits that the misappropriation of intersectionality as a theory and approach to research, wherein Black women's theories are invoked only to silence their voices through exclusion in this same intersectionality research, parallels the misappropriation of Black women's voices for the advancement of the white female main character in *The Help*. In both instances, Black women's voices are muted and their quest for social justice stymied.

Williams also investigates the concept of invisibility in her exploration of Black women's reproductive justice activism. Williams sets as her purpose the interrogation of "the representational activism of black women–directed reproductive justice organizations that prioritize the political interests of intersectionally marginalized subgroups in their advocacy work, set against the backdrop of healthcare reform" (this volume). In doing such, she excavates the deep history and the extent to which Black women's organizations, located in the US South, engage in political activism on behalf of their constituents with regard to health care reform. As Williams shows, these organizations have been afforded an opportunity to engage in policy advocacy that amplifies the reproductive experiences, concerns, and subsequent political demands of intersectionally marginalized populations, the primary targets of their efforts, spanning the Clintons' attempts at health care reform through to the Obama administration's crafting and implementation of the Affordable Care Act; yet their activism remains invisible in our explorations, across multiple disciplines, on reproductive justice activism.

Invisibility, in the case of Howard's contribution, is addressed through what she terms "discursive distance" which was central to President Obama's deracialization project. As such, she argues,

> Michelle Obama's anti-obesity campaign, *Let's Move!*, allowed her to participate, from a safe, discursive distance, in debates about reproductive health and sexuality. By invoking the threat of low-income urban black pathology in the "obesity crisis," and sweeping in with a remedy couched in traditional, "True Womanhood"–style mothering, Michelle Obama was able to achieve two strategic goals for the campaign: she was able to signal a non-threatening "pro-woman" stance without substantive engagement in controversial gender issues, while simultaneously distancing herself, and the rest of the Obama family, from racialized and gendered stereotypes about black families. (this volume)

This form of discursive distancing results in the removal of some issues that are experienced by poor Black women from public discourse and the policy agenda of the Obama administration. Furthermore, via Michele Obama's discursive distancing, what becomes visible is a particular understanding of womanhood, one that is aligned with the concept of True womanhood (i.e., white womanhood) that suggests that she is committed to a specific " 'true womanhood'-style nursing, where nursing is defined as feminine care-giving, healing, and culinary skill" (this volume). Those women perceived as not fitting into this understanding of womanhood are maligned. Also, ignored in this form of invisibility is the legacy of slavery and how it continues to influence, for example, poor Black women's access to food (Howard, this volume).

Douglass's and Jordan-Zachery's analyses highlight the impact of research and policy gaps that result in invisibility. Jordan-Zachery argues that narratives of HIV/AIDS-orphaned children tend to privilege the Global South. Consequently, there are no similar narratives used in the United States to speak on the impact of HIV/AIDS and motherless children. She offers a national- and state-level analysis of policies of five areas defined as "HIV/AIDS" hotspots where HIV and AIDS disproportionately impact Black women. Specifically, she analyzes policies, or the lack thereof, targeting non-positive HIV/AIDS orphans. Extant research (although limited) suggests that these children are negatively impacted as a result of the death of their mothers, who tend to be their primary caregivers. Yet there is an absence of policies targeting these orphans. To explain this policy gap, Jordan-Zachery suggests that the absence of policy is a response to the intersectional stigma, which is mapped onto the "construction of the Black mother as 'bad.' " The bad Black mother results in these children being "out of place" and invisible to policy decision makers. In an attempt to address research and resulting policy gaps, Jordan-Zachery offers an intersectionality-based policy analysis.

The invisibility of Black women as research subjects, as activists, and as policy subjects is explored in these chapters as a means of unmasking power structures. Additionally, in unmasking these power structures the authors articulate approaches for addressing such invisibility. "For example, Douglass argues that African-Caribbean women are largely invisible in the health literature. As such, her chapter, and the others in this volume, allow for the deconstruction of negative images used in the social construction of Black womanhood. Consequently, she and other authors suggest that an intersectional approach is necessary to uncover and respond to these forms of omission as such an approach allows for an exploration of how race, class, and gender results in Black women's experiences. Doing such would allow us to better "explore the meanings, beliefs, and experiences of black women and relate this to the cultural, ethnic, economic, and demographic context of black women" (Douglas, this volume) and explain Black women's lived experiences.

Black Women's Self-Actualization and Black Masculinist Politics

Part of the challenge faced by Janie in her journey to self-actualization is that she is performing her Black womanhood in a rather masculinist setting. As Klaus Benesch (1988, 633) argues, the mule "signifies on the role of black women as well as on the male-female relationship." This is not only an intimate relationship, but it also connotes Black women's communal relationship within a hierarchy where maleness, regardless of race, is privileged and works to constrain Black women's vision of themselves. Nanny, as part of her conversation with Janie on how the black woman is the mule of the earth, tells her,

> Ah didn't want to be use for a work-ox and a broad-sow and Ah didn't want mah daughter used dat way neither. . . . Ah wanted to preach a great sermon about colored women sittin' on high, but there wasn't no pulpit for me. . . . Ah said Ah'd save de text for you. (Hurston, 1990, 15–16)

Nanny is speaking directly to how race-gender structures constrain Black women. This type of constraint, experienced as a result of patriarchy, is the third theme connecting many of the chapters in this volume.

Thame offers an analysis of the first female head of government in Jamaica. She asks: What is the meaning of "Portia Simpson-Miller in Jamaican politics," and what does her election mean for the position of Jamaican women and gendered and classed norms more broadly? Thame concludes that while the election of "Mama P" opened up potential positions for women in Jamaican politics, it did little to transform realities on the ground. This is the case because Miller-Simpson was unable to radically shift the classist and masculinist machinery of Jamaican politics.

How Black women walk a "tight line" of disrupting and/or maintaining race-gender politics vis-à-vis paternalism is also taken up by Howard. According to Howard, "[w]hile community gardening [as advocated by Obama] is a practical, perhaps even radical, solution to some of these disparities, when the suggestion comes from a person in an elite institutional position, even if their position was as institutional wife and mother, it rings more paternalistic than radical" (this volume). Keisha N. Blain, in "We Want to Set the World on Fire," explores another form of Black women's limits and tensions around self-actualization. According to her, "these tensions unfolded on the pages of the *New Negro World* newspaper" (this volume). For example, "Adelia Ireland articulated a masculinist vision of black liberation, emphasizing the absolute necessity of strong black male leadership" (this volume). Elinor White (1942) and Florine Wilkes (1944) also made such assertions. What this shows is that although these women recognized the value of their voices in the larger conversations on global oppression of Black people, they continued to maintain patriarchal structures by arguing that men must lead.

These researchers show the challenges faced by Black women in confronting Black nationalism that results in the marking of Black women's bodies and politics. What results is that some narratives are not included in public discourses, the promotion of masculinist politics, and the maintenance of stereotypes that control Black women.

Space Making and Self-Actualization

Finally, there is the theme of self-actualization and space making. The metaphor of the mule suggests Black women's resistance to conventional race-gender expectations and resulting authority. However, by the end of *Their Eyes Were Watching God*, the mule disappears. This is symbolic, as it suggests a type of self-actualization experienced by Janie. We learn that "only here, [Janie] could listen and laugh and even talk some herself if she wanted to" and that she eventually gets to the place where "[s]he got so she could tell big stories herself from listening to the rest" (Hurston, 1990, 128). This form of self-actualization, making space for her voice, is a final theme evident in all of the chapters.

Alexander-Floyd speaks of space making as a project of garreting that allows for the insertion of Black women as research subjects. More importantly, the concept of garrets and garreting affords Black women the opportunity to invert the gaze—engage an oppositional gaze—that can afford them a space for freedom. Space making can occur at multiple points for Black women and may include intellectual space, physical space, emotional space, and even spiritual space. However, space making, as detailed in the various chapters, is intimately connected to democracy, freedom, and justice.

What the chapters show is that space making is not an easy process for Black women, who must work to confront multiple and interlocking forms of oppressions. Sometimes space making can result in the reification of the negative construction of Black womanhood, as shown by Ryan, Howard, and Thame's individual chapters. However, as Hall shows, the political activity of the *ereba*-making women, vis-à-vis their efforts to preserve and actively resist the erasure of their culture, is being woven into larger political efforts by and for Afro-descendent women between sustenance farmers and urban professionals. What this suggests is that these women are crossing physical space, rural and urban, in their efforts to resist land grab. She also shows their self-actualization in their conscious decision making to identify as Black, thereby allowing them to situate themselves in global discussions of Black womanhood. This type of construction is also explored by Blain, who claims that Black US women in their writings for the *New Negro World* newspaper engaged in a politics of creating a global community to challenge the global system of white supremacy by inserting the voices of Black women in a space that was masculinist in tenor. This suggests another form of space making that transcends geographical boundaries to resist white patriarchal structures and oppressions.

Douglas, like Middlemass and Jordan-Zachery, explores exclusion policy and research and how such spaces of exclusion result in the marginalization of Black womanhood or what Douglass refers to as "intersectional invisibility." Williams's and Douglas's chapters show Black women's response to these types of spaces that result in the invisibility of Black women. In Williams's chapter, we are introduced to how Black women's reproductive activism space making is best understood as a "liberatory politic around bodily autonomy."

Jordan-Zachery and Judylyn Ryan explore space making at the intersection of culture and politics. While Jordan-Zachery explores how culture and politics are mapped onto each other and result in the disappearance of Black women, Ryan takes up the question of democracy and how it is advanced through Black women's literature. In her chapter, Ryan examines Toni Morrison's writings as a representative expression of Black feminist political engagement on the part of Black women literary artists. Morrison's novels implicitly argue and explicitly demonstrate that US democracy requires a literature whose textual strategies and discursive practices can expand democratic narrative participation, promote "narrative knowledge," sharpen the moral imagination, and provide opportunities for self-discovery. What Ryan argues, among other things, is that Morrison deploys textual strategies that revive historical thinking, thereby enabling a more meaningful analysis of both historical and current events.

The collected chapters show how Black women work on behalf of themselves to achieve self-definition and actualization, thereby articulating their visions of democracy, freedom, and justice. Combined, the chapters capture the journey, its joys and challenges, of Janie in the sense that they explore how Black women are constructed as the "mules of the earth," and as such their labor is viewed as benefiting others and not themselves, and Black women's resistance to such constructions. What the chapters show is how Black women's articulations of self, via their activism, writings, knowledge production, and so forth—in essence, their labor—is used in service of themselves and their communities.

Conclusion

Centering Black women as subjects of research has been a fundamental component of Black feminist theory and politics. *Black Women in Politics* adds to this body of research by centering the Black political woman. As the Combahee River Collective states in its classic statement of Black feminist ideology: "This focusing on our own oppression is embodied in the concept of identity politics. We believe that the most profound and potentially the most radical politics come directly out of our own identity . . ." (The Combahee River Collective 1982, 16). Significantly, whereas mainstream feminist theory views identity politics as a limited, monovocal definition of women's experiences and politics, one that attempts to speak for women as an essentialized category of difference, radical Black feminists operate from a complex and variegated framework, that captures the differences among Black women's lives and looks at a range of important factors related to oppression, as opposed to attempting to foreground one single dimension of identity. This form of identity politics, as Duchess Harris relays, is "polyvocal" (Harris 2001, 300). Furthermore, according to one of the Combahee River Collective's founders, Barbara Smith, the term identity politics was first promulgated by this Black feminist organization; as she remarks, " 'We [the Combahee River Collective] came up with the term 'identity politics' " (Smith, quoted in Harris 2001, 300). The idea of identity politics, first espoused by Black feminists in the Combahee River Collective, has been lost in the ruins of academic debate. It needs to be recovered so that we can understand identity in a sophisticated way to inform our political assessment, priorities, and action.

Analyses, as suggested in these chapters, should center Black women in our research, because in doing so we can better trace the operation of power as it manifests in this historical moment when individuals and groups cling to post–civil rights, postfeminist fantasies as opposed to the realities that people actually have to live. Given that Black women are collectively impacted by a range of structural forms of oppression, investigating their lives and the politics in which they are embedded, and that they develop, provides a window onto a multitude of contemporary political issues, including crime and punishment; public health issues, such as the HIV/AIDS crisis; labor market segregation/segmentation; discrimination in the workplace; educational access; hate crimes; geopolitical concerns; sex trafficking; and violence in intimate partner relationships and in war.

A radical Black feminist understanding of identity politics that centers Black women as political subjects moreover not only best exposes the operation of power, but it also places a priority on justice as the goal of academic inquiry and thereby disrupts the "portrait of marginality" (Prestage and Githens 1977) with which Black women have long been associated. In the midst of advanced corporatization and neoliberalization of the academy, scholars are rewarded for research focusing on apolitical aims or on individual subjectivity or questions of representation outside of any connection to macroinstitutional concerns such as public policy or legal change. Black women in politics research, from a radical Black feminist perspective, demonstrate how a scholarly focus on Black political women and the forces that impact their lives illuminates and helps to address a range of political phenomena, including, but not limited to: the production of founding narratives and political and social arrangements of the United States and beyond; the rationalizing ideologies that legitimate and sustain colonial and neocolonial relationships; the politics of cultural production, and representation and its relationship to material conditions of inequality; the sedimentation of structural inequality; and the creation of social and economic policy. This type of Black feminist research is not merely aimed at describing phenomena and outlining political happenings as ends in themselves, but is ultimately motivated by a desire to challenge and transform existing inequitable relationships and conditions in Black communities. This volume on Black women in politics thus seeks to advance an examination of identity, politics, and justice in the best tradition of radical theorizing and politics in Black communities. Each chapter makes a substantive contribution to the subfield of Black women in politics and serves as a model, methodologically and otherwise, on which future work can be based.

Notes

1. Although the term ploughing is used in Hurston's work, the term tilling is used in the introduction instead of ploughing, as the term ploughing, for some, can have negative connotations, e.g., moral corruption. See, for example, the book *Worthy Efforts* (Lis and Soly 2012) or *Border States in the Work of Tom MacIntire* (Ryan 2012, 143–45).

References

Alexander-Floyd, Nikol G. 2007. *Gender, Race, and Nationalism in Contemporary Black Politics.* New York: Palgrave Macmillan.

———. 2012. "Disappearing Act: Reclaiming Intersectionality in the Social Sciences in a Post-Black Feminist Era." *Feminist Formations* 24 (1): 1–25.

Benesch, Klaus. 1988. "Oral Narrative and Literary Text: Afro-American Folklore in *Their Eyes Were Watching God*." *Callaloo* 11 (3): 627–35.

Berger, Michele. 2004. *Workable Sisterhood: The Political Journey of Stigmatized Women with HIV/AIDS.* Princeton: Princeton University Press.

Berger, Michele, and Kathleen Guidroz, eds. 2009. *The Intersectional Approach: Transforming the Academy Through Race, Class, & Gender.* Durham: University of North Carolina Press.

Braxton, Gloria. 1994. "African-American Women and Politics: Research Trends and Directions." *National Political Science Review* 11: 121–36

Brown, Nadia. 2014. *Sisters in the Statehouse: Black Women and Legislative Decision Making.* New York: Oxford University Press.

Brown, Ruth Nicole. 2007. "Remembering Maleesa: Theorizing Black Girl Politics and the Politicizing of Socialization." *National Political Science Review* 11: 121–36.

Cho, Sumi, Kimberlé Crenshaw, and Leslie McCall. 2013. "Toward a Field of Intersectionality Studies: Theory, Applications, and Praxis." *Signs* 38 (4): 785–810.

Cohen, Cathy. 1999. *The Boundaries of Blackness.* Chicago: University of Chicago Press.

Collins, Patricia Hill. 2000. *Black Feminist Thought.* New York: Routledge.

Collins, Patricia Hill, and Sirma Bilge, eds. 2016. *Intersectionality: Key Concepts.* Cambridge: Polity.

The Combahee River Collective. 1982. "A Black Feminist Statement." In *All the Women Are White, All the Blacks Are Men, But Some of Us Are Brave: Black*

Women's Studies, edited by Gloria T. Hull, Patricia Bell Scott, and Barbara Smith, 13–22. Westbury, NY: The Feminist Press.

Cooper, Brittney. 2016. "Intersectionality." In *The Oxford Handbook of Feminist Theory*, edited by Lisa Disch and Mary Hawkesworth, 385–406. Oxford: Oxford University Press.

Crenshaw, Kimberlé. 1989. "Demarginalizing the Intersection of Race and Sex: A Black Feminist Critique of Antidiscrimination Doctrine, Feminist Theory and Antiracist Politics." *University of Chicago Legal Forum* 140: 139–67.

———. 1990–1991. "Mapping the Margins: Intersectionality, Identity Politics, and Violence against Women of Color." *Stanford Law Review* 43: 1241–99.

Hancock, Ange-Marie. 2004. *The Politics of Disgust: The Public Identity of the Welfare Queen*. New York: New York University Press.

———. 2007. "When Multiplication Doesn't Equal Quick Addition: Examining Intersectionality as a Research Paradigm." *Perspectives on Politics* 5 (1): 63–79.

———. 2016. *Intersectionality: An Intellectual History*. Oxford: Oxford University Press.

Harris, Duchess. 2001. "From the Kennedy Commission to the Combahee Collective: Black Feminist Organizing, 1960–80." In *Sisters in the Struggle: African American Women in the Civil Rights-Black Power Movement*, edited by Bettye Collier-Thomas and V. P. Franklin, 280–301. New York: New York University Press.

hooks, bell. 1984. *Feminist Theory: From Margin to Center*. Boston: South End Press.

———. 1995. *Killing Rage: Ending Racism*. New York: Henry Holt.

Hurston, Zora Neale. 1990. *Their Eyes Were Watching God*. New York: Harper & Row.

Isoke, Zenzele. 2013. *Urban Black Women and the Politics of Resistance*. New York: Palgrave Macmillan.

Jordan-Zachery, Julia S. 2007. "Am I a Black Woman or a Woman Who Is Black? A Few Thoughts on the Meaning of Intersectionality." *Politics & Gender* 3 (2): 254–63.

———. 2009. *Black Women, Cultural Images, and Social Policy*. New York: Routledge.

———. 2012. "Blogging at the Intersections: Black Women, Identity, and Lesbianism." *Politics & Gender* 8: 405–14.

King, Mae C. 1977. "The Political Role of the Stereotyped Image of the Black Woman in America." In *Black Political Scientists and Black Survival: Essays in Honor of a Black Scholar*, edited by Shelby Lewis Smith, 24–44. Detroit: Balamp Publishing.

Kirkpatrick, Jeane. 1974. *Political Woman*. New York: Basic Books.

Lewis, Brittany. 2016. "Yearning: Black Female Academics, Everyday Black Women/Girls and the Search for a Social Justice Praxis." *National Political Science Review* 17 (1): 83–88.

Lewis, Shelby, Owanah Anderson, Lucie Cheng, Arlene Fong Craig, Njeri Jackson, Isabella Jenkins, Barbara Jones, Saundra Rice Murray, Marge Rosenswig,

Patricia Bell Scott, and Bonnie Wallace. 1985. "Achieving Sex Equity for Minority Women." In *Handbook for Achieving Sex Equity through Education*, edited by Susan S. Klein, 365–90. Baltimore: Johns Hopkins University Press.

Lindsay, Keisha. 2013. "God, Gays, and Progressive Politics: Reconceptualizing Intersectionality as a Normatively Malleable Analytical Framework." *Perspectives on Politics* 11 (2): 446–60.

Lipset, Seymour. 1960. *Political Man: The Social Bases of Politics*. Garden City, NY: Anchor Books.

Lis, Catharina, and Hugo Soly. 2012. *Worthy Attitudes: Attitudes to Work and Workers in Pre-Industrial Europe*. Leiden: Brill Academic Publishers.

Lorde, Audre. 2007. *Sister Outsider: Essays and Speeches*. Berkeley, CA: Crossing Press.

May, Vivian. 2015. *Pursuing Intersectionality, Unsettling Dominant Imaginaries*. New York: Routledge Press.

Nash, Jennifer. 2008. "Re-Thinking Intersectionality." *Feminist Review* 89: 1–15.

Nealy, Lisa Nikol. 2008. *African American Women Voters: Racializing Religiosity, Political Consciousness and Progressive Political Action in U.S. Presidential Elections from 1964 through 2008*. Lanham, MD: University Press of America

Puar, Jasbir. 2007. *Terrorist Assemblages: Homonationalism in Queer Times*. Durham, NC: Duke University Press.

Prestage, Jewel L. 1991. "In Quest of African American Political Woman." *The Annals of the American Academy of Political and Social Science* 515: 88–103.

Prestage, Jewel L., and Marianne Githens. 1977. *A Portrait of Marginality: The Political Behavior of the American Woman*. New York: D. McKay.

Roberts, Dorothy. 1997. *Killing the Black Body: Race, Reproduction, and the Meaning of Liberty*. New York: Pantheon Books.

Robnett, Belinda. 1997. *How Long? How Long?: African American Women in the Struggle for Civil Rights*. Oxford: Oxford University Press.

Rustin, Bayard. 1993. "From Protest to Politics: The Future of the Civil Rights Movement." In *To Redeem a Nation: A History and Anthology of the Civil Rights Movement*, edited by Thomas West, 232–35. New York: Brandywine Press.

Ryan, Catriona. 2012. *Border States in the Work of Tom Mac Intyre: A Paleo-Postmodern Perspective*. Newcastle upon Tyne: Cambridge Scholars Publishing.

Simien, Evelyn. 2006. *Black Feminist Voices in Politics*. Albany: State University of New York Press.

———. 2007. "Doing Intersectionality Research: From Conceptual Issues to Practical Examples." *Politics & Gender* 3 (2): 264–71.

Simien, Evelyn, and Danielle McGuire. 2014. "A Tribute to the Women: Rewriting History, Retelling Herstory in Civil Rights." *Politics & Gender* 10 (3): 413–31.

Smooth, Wendy. 2006. "Intersectionality in Electoral Politics: A Mess Worth Making." *Politics & Gender* 2 (3): 400–14.

Smooth, Wendy, and Tamelyn Tucker. 1999. "Behind but Not Forgotten: Women and the Behind-the-Scenes Organizing of the Million Man March." In *Still*

Lifting, Still Climbing: African American Women's Contemporary Activism, edited by Kimberly Sringer, 241–58. New York: New York University Press.

Springer, Kimberly, ed. 1999. *Still Lifting, Still Climbing: Contemporary African American Women's Activism*. New York: New York University Press.

———. 2005. *Living for the Revolution: Black Feminist Organizations, 1968–1980*. Durham, NC: Duke University Press.

Threadcraft, Shatema. 2016. *Intimate Justice: The Black Female Body and the Body Politic*. Oxford: Oxford University Press.

Wallace, Adryan. 2014. "Influencing the Political Agenda from the Outside: A Comparative Study of Hausa Women's NGOs and CBOs in Kano, Nigeria." *National Political Science Review* 16: 67–80.

Wiegman, Robyn. 2012. *Object Lessons*. Durham, NC: Duke University Press.

Willoughby-Herard, Tiffany. 2008. "The Rape of an Obstinate Woman: Frantz Fanon's Wretched of the Earth." In *Shout Out: Women of Color Respond to Violence*, edited by Barbara K. Ige and Maria Ochoa, 264–80. Emeryville, CA: Seal Press.

Section I

Black Feminists Doing Intersectionality Work

> I believe unconditionally in the ability of people to respond when they are told the truth. We need to be taught to study rather than believe, to inquire rather than to affirm.
>
> —Septima Clark

According to Jane Junn (2016), "Women of color now make up nearly a third of female voters, and support Democratic candidates by wide margins, with African American women the stalwart of the Democratic Party." Exit polls from the 2008 and 2012 presidential elections show that Black women outvoted White women, White men, and Black men (see CWAP 2015). Black women are actively participating in the formal political process via voting. As a group, Black women have been political actors across a wide spectrum of activities, yet they remain understudied, particularly in political science. In this section, Alexander-Floyd and Jordan-Zachery take up the politics of invisibility in political science research. Alexander-Floyd considers invisibility by conducting a comparative analysis of political science versus other disciplines, namely economics, history, and sociology. Jordan-Zachery assesses intersectionality research in political science in particular as a way of unmasking how power structures within academic research result in the invisibility of Black women.

Chow, Crenshaw, and McCall (2013), as part of their efforts to define and demark the "field of intersectionality studies," offer three primary areas of research, namely the applications of an intersectional framework or investigations of intersectional dynamics; discursive debates about the scope and content of intersectionality as a theoretical and methodological paradigm; and political interventions employing an intersectional lens. What they do not necessarily engage is the larger question of whom these various research foci are "talking" about. In other words, who is being studied in the field of intersectionality studies and how? Cho, Crenshaw, and McCall (2013) assert that

> tensions . . . revolve around intersectionality's capacity to do any work other than to call attention to the particularities of Black women. The historical centrality of American Black women and Black feminism as subjects of intersectionality theory grounds reservations about intersectionality's usefulness as an analytic tool in addressing other marginalized communities and other manifestations of social power. (788)

Alexander-Floyd and Jordan-Zachery's chapters challenge whether intersectionality in fact is being deployed in a way that speaks to Black political women. In terms of political and epistemological projects, what knowledge have intersectionality and other scholarly works produced that allows us to better understand Black women as political agents? This is the implicit question addressed in this section.

Together, these authors show how Black women, while contributing much to the theorization of intersectionality and other theories and concepts, are rendered invisible in research. Alexander-Floyd and Jordan-Zachery demonstrate how Black women in scholarly research, to draw on the analogy of Janie (the protagonist in *Their Eyes Are Watching God*) in her first two marriages, are used in the service of others and are consequently silenced. This leaves us to ask: How do Black women matter in academia, particularly political science scholarly research? What knowledge is being produced that allows us to better understand Black women's political behaviors?

Academic research seems to be disappearing and disenfranchising Black women. This is particularly evident in the actual production of research that centers Black women. In her analysis of three time periods, 1970–1985, 1986–2003, and 2004–2008, Alexander-Floyd exposes a pattern that shows that, "although Black women and Black gender politics are central to U.S. political development, mainstream scholarship 'disappears' them from the production of political science as an intellectual or disciplinary space." Drawing inspiration from Ernest J. Wilson III's classic political science essay "Why Political Scientists Don't Study Black Politics, But Historians and Sociologists Do" (Wilson 1985) and his subsequent writing in the same vein with Lorrie Frasure (Wilson and Frasure 2007), Alexander-Floyd documents the profound disparity in publishing on Black women in politics among key social science disciplines. Using the lens of space and place, Alexander-Floyd asks how the epistemological and political boundaries of these disciplines can be redefined. She describes how scholars in other disciplines have created garrets or institutional spaces supportive of work on Black women. Following Johnella Butler (2001), who argues for Black studies in programs, departments, and across all disciplines, Alexander-Floyd contends that "making (inter)disciplinary trouble" requires that we invest both in interdisciplines, such as women's and gender studies and race and ethnic studies, and across disciplines. As she asks: "How can a major discipline like political science dedicated to unpacking the operation of power in society not concern itself with the fundamental role that race, gender, and other bases of social organization have played in its composition, circulation, and impact?"

Using the popular work of fiction *The Help*, Jordan-Zachery, in her analysis of four prominent political science journals for the time period 1996–2010, demonstrates how research is a political act that results in the disappearing of Black women as research subjects. Jordan-Zachery argues that there is a type of mirroring occurring between popular culture and political science research—that is, that Black women are serving as "the help" in political science, forwarding theoretical insights such as intersectionality, but being divested from the political impact in terms of scholarship by decentering Black women in intersectionality research. The discursive systems employed across these "genres" serve to reify and maintain hierarchies that dictate how Black women's labor, political and otherwise, is understood and often used in the service of others. She concludes by asking, "Will [Black women] be forgotten and left to live within the same age-old axes of oppression, as intersectionality becomes *the help* of mainstream political science?"

Why should we care about how Black women are disappearing from political science research? As Jordan-Zachery argues, "[the] politics of knowledge production influence[s] the material reality of doubly marginalized groups in general and Black women more specifically." Alexander-Floyd and Jordan-Zachery's chapters individually and collectively posit that there must be a (political) project that seeks to name, critique, and challenge the positionality of Black women in research in an attempt to continue to bring them from the margin to the center of scholarship.

The void in studying the political behaviors of Black women, particularly from their standpoint, requires that we rethink and reposition political science research. This necessitates, in part, that scholars move beyond simply acknowledging Black women in passing—often with a nod toward their contributions to intersectionality theory and voting, for instance—and recognize how ethnocentrism continues to influence how Black women are treated in and outside the academy. When researchers do engage such practices, then we are able to further and deepen our understanding of democratic practices.

References

Butler, Johnella. 2001. "African American Studies and the 'Warring Ideals': The Color Line Meets the Borderlands." In *Dispatches from the Ebony Tower: Intellectuals Confront the African American Experience*, edited by Manning Marable. New York: Columbia University Press.

Center for America Women & Politics. 2015. *Voices. Votes. Leadership. The Status of Black Women in American Politics.* http://www.cawp.rutgers.edu/sites/default/files/resources/hh2015.pdf.

Cho, Sumi, Crenshaw, Kimberlé Williams, and McCall, Leslie. 2013. "Toward a Field of Intersectionality Studies: Theory, Applications, and Praxis." *Signs: Journal of Women in Culture and Society* 38 (4): 785–810.

Junn, Jane. 2016. Hiding in Plain Sight: White Women Vote Republican. November 13. http://politicsofcolor.com/white-women-vote-republican/.

Wilson, Ernest J. 1985. "Why Political Scientists Don't Study Black Politics, but Historians and Sociologists Do." *PS: Political Science & Politics* 18 (3): 600–7.

Wilson, Ernest J., and Lorrie A. Frasure. 2007. " 'Still at the Margins: The Persistence of Neglect of African American Issues in Political Science, 1986–2003.' " In *African American Perspectives on Political Science*, edited by Wilbur C. Rich, 8–23. Philadelphia: Temple University Press.

1

Why Political Scientists Don't Study Black Women, but Historians and Sociologists Do

On Intersectionality and the Remapping of the Study of Black Political Women

NIKOL G. ALEXANDER-FLOYD
Rutgers University–New Brunswick

Recent discussions on intersectionality in political science have sparked increased attention in research to race, gender, and other identity categories, particularly in terms of "descriptive" statistical analysis (Jordan-Zachery 2007). Given that Black women and other women of color developed intersectionality as a means of assessing and confronting their own life circumstances, it behooves us to consider the extent to which political scientists investigate the lives of Black women and issues of racism, class inequality, sexism, ageism, disability, and other oppressive forces (Berger and Guidroz 2009; Dill and Zambrana 2009; Collins and Birma 2016). More specifically, what do we know about the comparative progress of scholarship on Black women and Black gender politics in the academic field of political science compared with other disciplines? What are some of the disciplinary challenges that beset the would-be Black feminist political scientist? How do the limits of research on Black political women point to deeper problems regarding political and epistemological orientations of political science?[1] In this chapter, I offer not a comprehensive multidisciplinary analysis, but a broad snapshot of four sister disciplines: political science, sociology, history, and economics. I provide a general landscape of the research on Black women in these fields both to underscore the relative dearth of literature on Black women in political science and to set the stage for a conversation about how best to influence the social production of political science as a disciplinary and intellectual "space" as well as the "place" of Black women within it.

An emphasis on space and place in this chapter helps me to better conceptualize the politics at work in the knowledge production of the discipline, and I offer here a few clarifying definitions. "Space," as we know, "is regarded largely as a dimension within which matter is located or a grid within which substantive items are contained" (Agnew 2011, 316). However, following McKittrick (2006), I see both space, the general physical and metaphorical context, and place, the specific meanings and patterns of embodiment or social, political, or other forms of relating within a given location or context, as *socially* produced and contested. Indeed, as Dorthe Possing relates, the "politics of place . . . relates to how places, such as regions, localities, nations, [or disciplines] are used to define groups of people in relation to other groups of people and is about constructing and defining the boundaries of a place, and involves negotiations about who and what is 'inside' and 'outside' that place" (Possing 2010, 2). I draw attention to the raced and gendered dimensions of political science as an academic space, and the place-making politics necessary to investigate Black political women.[2]

In addressing these issues of gender, race, space, and place as they relate to Black political women and research, I proceed along two fronts—the first is statistical, assessing the percentages of articles on Black women in political science, specifically as compared with history, sociology, and economics. The second part is interpretive/theoretical, reviewing the possible motivations for the paucity of research and suggesting how it can be counteracted. Significantly, although there are journals, such as *Politics & Gender* in political science and *Gender & Society* in sociology, that showcase work on women and gender politics, I focus on mainstream journals in these disciplines as opposed to those connected to particular subfields to highlight (as I further amplify below) the "absented presence" (Walcott 2001; McKittrick 2006) of Black political women as subjects of research in the space of mainstream political science. This allows us to account for the paradox of Black women's hypervisibility and centrality to politics, on the one hand, and Black women's invisibility or "absented presence," on the other. After surveying mainstream journals within each discipline, I use this survey to stage a conversation about the importance of centering Black political women in political science research and the place-making strategies or garreting used to illuminate Black women as subjects of research. Ultimately, I conclude that to re-create the intellectual geography of political science, a Perestroika-like effort to restructure the discipline as it relates to expanding research on Black women as political subjects and Black gender politics is required. By Perestroika, I refer to the decade-plus push in mainstream political science to "restructure" or redefine what constitutes knowledge and how to produce knowledge that is politically relevant (Monroe 2005). As it relates to Black political women and Black gender politics, we need to not only increase the amount of research, but also use a specifically Black feminist frame of reference (Alexander-Floyd 2007), one that embraces interdisciplinarity and uses a broader range of foci and post-positivist methodologies. I now turn to an examination of research on Black women to expose the raced and gendered spatial dimensions of political science relative to other disciplines.

Studying African American Women and Black Gender Politics across Disciplines

Overview and Research Design

Over thirty years ago, political scientist Ernest Wilson III provoked discussion by highlighting the relative inattention given to studying Black issues in political science relative to other "sister disciplines" (Wilson 1985). Specifically, he asked:

> Does the study of Afro-American subjects occupy a different place in our discipline from that of other traditions of inquiry, and if so, why? Why does political science seem to address questions of black political behavior with less assiduity than her sister disciplines address questions of black history or black group behavior? (Wilson 1985, 601)

Wilson addressed these questions, arguing that the "paradigmatic" approach of the discipline, its focus on elites and formal politics, mismatched the "empirical" reality of Black politics, which focused on "bottom up" politics and both formal *and* informal politics, such as social movement activity (604). His review of publications on Black issues in major journals between 1970 and 1985 across the disciplines of political science, history, sociology, and economics showed political science to lag behind history and sociology in terms of publications. Subsequent examination by Wilson and Frasure (2007) revealed a consistent pattern of relative neglect from 1986 to 2003 concerning race and Black politics in political science compared with other disciplines.

For this study, I used the same approach used by Wilson and Frasure in terms of journal selection, the database used to survey research (i.e., JSTOR), and the search for key terms relevant to the subspecialty of Black women's studies. More specifically, I reviewed the same three top journals in each discipline, namely *The American Political Science Review*, *American Journal of Political Science*, and *The Journal of Politics* in political science; *American Journal of Sociology*, *American Sociological Review*, and *Social Forces* in sociology; *The American Historical Review*, *American Quarterly*, and *Journal of American History* in history; and *American Economic Review*, *Journal of Political Economy*, and *The Quarterly Journal of Economics* in economics. Also, I used the same two time periods from this previous research, 1970–1985 and 1986–2003, and added a third, 2004–2008. The following terms were searched using JSTOR: "Black women," "African-American women,"[3] "Afro-American women," "Black feminism," and "womanism." Additionally, consistent with earlier work (Wilson 1985; Wilson and Frasure 2007), I examined totals for full-length articles for each period along three different axes—text only, title only, and abstract only. Each of the latter designations—text, title, and abstract only, yield related, but more or less detailed, levels of results. The full-length articles, as well as titles and abstracts, were determined using a search function in JSTOR, which allows terms to be searched throughout specific journals within particular time frames. In this way, the terms could be isolated across these three dimensions of inquiry (i.e., full-length articles, titles, and abstracts). Given the search terms' explicit focus on Black women, this study excludes those articles using research on Black women but framed under the rubric of "women of color." This approach promises to render those articles directly relevant to the area of study in question.

Some might suggest that the outcomes of this query will yield decidedly predictable results. After all, the relative inattention of political science compared with sociology and history is an anticipated outcome given prior research on the study of race in political science compared with other fields. This study is important, however, because it provides one means of documenting—and throwing into sharp relief—the current treatment of Black women as subjects of research in mainstream journals across key traditional social science disciplines. My purpose is to let the journals serve as markers of current conditions, telling the story of political science's suppression of work on Black political women in its own valued idiom of quantitative metrics. The paucity of research on Black women in political science, moreover, can be usefully explained by joining political science's analysis of the circulation of power with geography's concerns with the politics of space and place. This conjoining can enable us to see how dominant norms construct intellectual and material space as well as one's sense of place within disciplines. Following geography scholars such as Walcott (2001) and McKittrick (2006), I draw on the notion of an "absented presence" to explain the politics at work in the production of space in political science. For McKittrick and Walcott, Black women and Black communities, respectively, are actively omitted from the production of narratives of nation, home, and belonging. Likewise, the data I assess highlight the absence of Black political subjects in political science research.

Findings: General Numeric and Statistical Profile

The results of this examination paint a very sobering picture regarding the state of research on Black women, particularly in political science. The data discussed below similarly bespeak the absence of Black women. Although Black women and Black gender politics are central to US political development, mainstream scholarship "disappears" (Alexander-Floyd 2012) them from the production of political science as an intellectual or disciplinary space.

The first time period, 1970–1985, yielded only six, ninety-four, thirty-nine, and twenty-seven full-length articles with some mention of Black women, African-American women, Afro-American women, Black feminism, or womanism in political science, sociology, history, and economics, respectively (table 1.1 on page 10). Although sociology, history, and economics arguably produced more articles with the key terms related to Black women, they too marginalized the study of Black women in mainstream journals. From 1970 to 1985, the same political science journals published *no* articles with titles and abstracts indicating a relationship to Black women (table 1.1).

In the second time period reviewed, 1986 to 2003, all four disciplines showed progress, but political science still lagged behind sociology and history, continuing to reflect the absented presence of Black women as political subjects. Indeed, as table 1.2 on page 11 indicates, sociology and history were the two-top performers in terms of full-length articles with some mention of research terms, with 283 and 231 full-length articles, respectively. A closer look at the results connected to title- and abstract-only searches, however, reveals a less optimistic picture all around. Between 1986 and 2003, for instance,

Table 1.1. Search Totals for Full-Length Articles (FLAs) by Titles and Abstracts, 1970–1985

	Total FLA[a]	Title Only[b]	Percentage of Total FLAs (%)	Abstract Only[c]	Percentage of Total FLAs (%)
Political Science					
The American Political Science Review	0	0	0	0	0
American Journal of Political Science	3	0	0	0	0
The Journal of Politics	3	0	0	0	0
Total	6	0	0	0	0
Sociology					
American Journal of Sociology	32	0	0	3	9
American Sociological Review	33	0	0	2	6
Social Forces	29	0	0	5	17
Total	94	0	0	10	11
History					
The American Historical Review	11	0	0	NA	NA
American Quarterly	10	0	0	NA	NA
Journal of American History	18	1	6	NA	NA
Total	39	1	3	NA	NA
Economics					
American Economic Review	19	1	5	0	0
Journal of Political Economy	8	0	0	0	0
The Quarterly Journal of Economics	0	0	0	0	0
Total	27	1	4	0	0

[a]Key word search for "black women" or "African-American women" or Afro-American women" or "negro women" or "black feminism" or "womanism" in FLAs, excluding reviews, opinion pieces, and other items. Note that the FLAs, as well as titles and abstracts, were determined using a search function in JSTOR that allows terms to be searched throughout specific journals.

[b]Key word search for "black women" or "African-American women" or Afro-American women" or "negro women" or "black feminism" or "womanism" in titles only, excluding text, abstracts, author names, and captions.

[c]Key word search for "black women" or "African-American women" or Afro-American women" or "negro women" or "black feminism" or "womanism" in abstracts only, excluding text, titles, author names, and captions. Abstract information is not available for the history journals selected (except [illegible]

Table 1.2. Search Totals for Full-Length Articles (FLAs) by Titles and Abstracts, 1980–2003

	Total FLA[a]	Title Only[b]	Percentage of Total FLAs (%)	Abstract Only[c]	Percentage of Total FLAs (%)
Political Science					
The American Political Science Review	11	0	0	0	0
American Journal of Political Science	8	0	0	0	0
The Journal of Politics	15	0	0	0	0
Total	34	0	0	0	0
Sociology					
American Journal of Sociology	118	1	<1	5	4
American Sociological Review	72	0	0	10	14
Social Forces	93	0	0	6	6
Total	283	1	<.5	21	7
History					
The American Historical Review	53	0	0	NA	NA
American Quarterly	81	0	0	NA	NA
Journal of American History	97	4	3	NA	NA
Total	231	4	2	NA	NA
Economics					
American Economic Review	45	7	16	0	0
Journal of Political Economy	8	0	0	0	0
The Quarterly Journal of Economics	11	0	0	0	0
Total	64	7	11	0	0

Source: Author's compilation of JSTOR computer-generated citations by discipline, with percentages rounded to whole numbers.

[a]Key word search for "black women" or "African-American women" or Afro-American women" or "negro women" or "black feminism" or "womanism" in FLAs, excluding reviews, opinion pieces, and other items. Note that the FLAs, as well as titles and abstracts, were determined using a search function in JSTOR that allows terms to be searched throughout specific journals.

[b]Key word search for "black women" or "African-American women" or Afro-American women" or "negro women" or "black feminism" or "womanism" in titles only, excluding text, abstracts, author names, and captions.

[c]Key word search for "black women" or "African-American women" or Afro-American women" or "negro women" or "black feminism" or "womanism" in abstracts only, excluding text, titles, author names, and captions. Abstract information is not available for the history journals selected (except *American Quarterly* beginning in 2003).

political science published thirty-four full-length articles with some mention of the terms "Black women," "African-American women," "Afro-American women," "Negro women," "Black feminism," or "womanism." None of the journals, however, showed titles or abstracts related to these terms. Also, although sociology had 283 full-length articles, it had only one article with the key search items and twenty-one abstracts that contained these terms, suggesting a greater prominence of issues related to Black women in this field compared with political science, but still a relatively small number.

A review of articles with the respective terms published from 2004 to 2008 reveals little change in the general number and distribution of articles by discipline. Sociology continued to have the largest number of search terms, with seventy-three full-length articles including at least one of the primary search terms, with history following at a close second at seventy-one, and political science and economics tied at thirteen articles each. None of the journals during the period had any of the key terms ("Black women," "African-American women," "Afro-American women," "negro women," "Black feminism," or "womanism") as part of their article titles. In terms of abstracts with key terms, sociology generated eight and political science four (table 1.3).

The absented presence of Black women as political subjects reveals the inherently raced and gendered dimensions of political science as intellectual space. It undergirds a dominant politics of place that suggests that political science as a discipline is inhabited by and/or is the proper "place" of White male political subjects. Oppositional political geographies by subaltern subjects, however, have pushed back against this dominant geographic political configuration. As previously mentioned, in each of the disciplines examined, specialized journals, which address race and/or gender, arguably provide greater exposure to work on Black women as subjects. Political science, for instance, has recently seen the emergence of the *Journal of Politics, Groups, and Identities*, joining longer-standing journals such as *The National Political Science Review*, which generally deals with United States and international racial politics, and *Journal of Women, Politics, and Policy* (formerly *Women and Politics*) and the newer *Politics & Gender*, which centers women's political experiences and gender politics. Sociology's *Gender & Society* and *Race, Class, and Gender*, History's *Journal of Women's History*, and Economics' *Feminist Economics* have served as similar outlets. However, even within these forums, conventional wisdom suggests that even greater attention needs to be accorded Black women and Black gender politics. The data here are offered to provide a view of mainstream journals in these disciplines.

Table 1.3. Search Totals for Full-Length Articles (FLAs) by Titles and Abstracts, 2004–2008

	Total FLA[a]	Title Only[b]	Percentage of Total FLAs (%)	Abstract Only[c]	Percentage of Total FLAs (%)
Political Science					
The American Political Science Review	1	0	0	0	0
American Journal of Political Science	3	0	0	2	67
The Journal of Politics	9	0	0	2	31
Total	13	0	0	4	31
Sociology					
American Journal of Sociology	14	0	0	0	0
American Sociological Review	21	0	0	4	19
Social Forces	38	0	0	4	11
Total	73	0	0	8	11
History					
The American Historical Review	14	0	0	NA	NA
American Quarterly	33	0	0	NA	NA
Journal of American History	24	0	0	NA	NA
Total	71	0	0	NA	NA
Economics					
American Economic Review	6	0	0	0	0
Journal of Political Economy	2	0	0	0	0
The Quarterly Journal of Economics	5	0	0	0	0
Total	13	0	0	0	0

Source: Author's compilation of JSTOR computer-generated citations by discipline, with percentages rounded to whole numbers.

[a]Key word search for "black women" or "African-American women" or Afro-American women" or "negro women" or "black feminism" or "womanism" in FLAs, excluding reviews, opinion pieces, and other items. Note that the FLAs, as well as titles and abstracts, were determined using a search function in JSTOR that allows terms to be searched throughout specific journals.

[b]Key word search for "black women" or "African-American women" or Afro-American women" or "negro women" or "black feminism" or "womanism" in titles only, excluding text, abstracts, author names, and captions.

[c]Key word search for "black women" or "African-American women" or Afro-American women" or "negro women" or "black feminism" or "womanism" in abstracts only, excluding text, titles, author names, and captions. Abstract information is not available for the history journals selected (except *American Quarterly* beginning in 2003).

Discussion

The results of this general survey of literature published about Black women in these four disciplines is consistent with the research and scholarship of intersectionality scholars, which details the special challenges associated with producing work about Black women as political, historical, social, and economic actors (see, e.g., Dill and Zambrana 2009), such as deeply entrenched masculinist methods, a failure to support research on Black women as legitimate, and lack of access to publishing outlets, to name a few. The persistence of limitations on the amount of research on Black women, even amid progress, parallels an equally persistent paradox in the treatment of Black women in the United States, namely their hypervisibility and political centrality on the one hand and invisibility on the other.

Some might regard attention to Black women as a key point of emphasis to be misguided, either because it centers on identity or because it should be replaced by considerations of gender as a sole analytic category. But a priority on research centering on Black women as political, social, historical, and economic subjects, especially from a specifically Black feminist frame of reference, is of central importance in countering the paradox of invisibility and hypervisibility. In some respects, Black women are hypervisible in terms of the dominant cultural symbols by which they are defined, a fact that accounts for the impact of stereotypes, for instance, in the development of social welfare and family-related policy (see, e.g., Hancock 2004). Yet, at the same time, Black women's needs are largely neglected in terms of social policy (e.g., in poverty, HIV/AIDS, reproductive health, employment, and education), discrimination (e.g., in the workplace), and abuse (e.g., in terms of rape, harassment, and coercive control in domestic spaces). Black feminist scholarship centering Black women resists the hegemonic gaze invested in seeing Black women as the source of a range of difficulties as opposed to addressing the range of problems that hamper their life chances and quality of life.

Political scientists' adoption of a Black feminist orientation is consistent with the best of feminist and Black studies approaches already at work in the discipline. One of the hallmarks of Black or Africana studies research, for instance, is its emphasis on having a "centered" approach, which focuses on understanding and addressing the experiences of Blacks across the Diaspora; in keeping with this approach, Black feminist research should center on Black women as subjects and the gender politics in and/or through which Black women operate. This emphasis on centering on the Black experience holds true not only in terms of Afrocentric perspectives, but also in other liberal and progressive approaches to Black studies. This priority has been best represented in political science, moreover, by pioneering scholars in the subfield of Black politics, such as Jones (1972; 1977), Prestage (1991), and Walters (2003), among others, many of whom ventured to develop a "Black political science," that is, a political science geared toward advancing social justice in the lives of people of African descent in the United States and elsewhere (Jones 1977).

Also, in a related vein, feminists have rightly stressed the need for more research on political women and feminist research on gender. Some feminist political scientists have correctly pointed out a need to go beyond scholarship that merely adopts a "great women" approach. Research on political women can include, but must ultimately reach further than, an effort to situate individual figures that are missing from historical or political narratives and must abandon notions of a singular category marked "woman" for which we can make political claims (Carroll and Zerilli 1993). But poststructuralist and women of color critiques of the category "woman" ought not cause us to lose focus on an analysis of how Black women are oppressed or their efforts to resist such oppression. As Caribbean Black feminist Eudine Barriteau reminds us, "Shifting to gender as an analytical frame certainly does not mean that the study of women is abandoned or that one cannot maintain an exclusive focus on women in research. Neither does it mean that gender studies must automatically include men" (Barriteau 2003, 43). All scholars concerned about Black gender politics must remain, as pioneering political scientist Jewell Prestage insists, "in quest of the African American [or Black] political woman" (Prestage 1991).

Notably, the disconnect between the critical importance of Black women and Black gender politics and the relative paucity of research on Black women in mainstream political science journals represents no benign neglect, but mirrors and helps to facilitate the contentious nature of Black women's relationship with mainstream culture and politics. Although we are in a period of increased visibility for Blacks and other racial minorities in the profession (at least in terms of formal leadership roles in political science associations), the raison d'être of political science remains the same: political system maintenance, including the assertion of race, gender, and class hierarchies. As Mack Jones detailed decades ago, mainstream US political science serves first and foremost to undergird the dominant patterns and structures through which power circulates. He explains, "[A]merican education and educators in general and as a consequence American political science and political scientists are essential cogs in the wheel of oppression, for they serve to legitimate its legal and philosophical foundations" (Jones 1977, 12). The task for progressive Black political scientists, in Jones's view, is to resist the operation of oppressive political systems.

Notably, Jones's point regarding the system maintenance role of political science is underscored by the role of racist thinking as reflected in the scholarship of luminaries who founded the field and in the framing of core foci in political science research. Political scientist Jessica Blatt, in her history of racial politics in the discipline, dispels the notion that political science has "evaded" race, pointing instead to how racial politics instrumentally shaped the discipline's origins. "Founders" of the field, such as John W. Burgess, who led the first PhD granting department in political science at Columbia University, articulated central theories of political science within the racist logic of the time. Burgess, for instance, saw democracy as an important principle, but located its authority not in government, but in the state, that is, " 'the gradual and continuous development of human society . . . the gradual realization . . . of the universal principles of human nature' " (Burgess, quoted in Blatt 2012, 7).

According to Blatt, one of the principal goals of the state was to foster an "ethnically homogenous" populace and further inculcate Teutonic values within US law and politics. She also sheds a different light on conventional wisdom, which states that explicit racist ideology or race talk largely stopped after World War I. Although certain types of racial thinking, consistent with biologically based notions of race, dissipated post World War I, they were replaced by different race-based discourses "such as eugenics and mental testing" (22). Blatt explains:

> [W]hen political scientists rejected "the state" and its racial basis—they still looked to "race" to provide intellectual purchase on political life. Of course, this research program was not a fruitful one . . . But it is significant in representing early attempts by prominent political scientists to orient political science toward the measurement and evaluation of the traits of populations. This latter program has of course been enormously fruitful . . . in the fields of political psychology, opinion research, and political behavior research. Since the 1980s it has also been revived . . . in the form of attempts to link genetic traits to political attitudes. (Blatt 2012, 25)

Work on race, in others words, has left an indelible imprint on political science, particularly in terms of methods and definitions of knowledge production. The question of why political scientists do not study Black women relative to other disciplines is not one of simply methods or foci. The elements of methods and foci are critically important because they are the means through which political science "evades" Black women and politics, but they are not the reason for it. They are horses pulling a very big cart, namely a societal neglect and oppression of Black women abetted by the production of academic knowledge.

The question is: What is to be done? How can the development of a new political science, one that adopts a Black feminist frame of reference, best be developed? The answer lies in the rescripting of the terrain of struggle, both institutionally and intellectually. Indeed, drawing on Black feminist geography, I suggest that Black feminist scholarship on Black political women will thrive with the assertion and strengthening of garrets of resistance in order to respacialize the disciplinary terrain and make a place for Black feminist work. As noted Black feminist geographer Katherine McKittrick (2006) relates, the classic text by Harriet Jacobs (aka Linda Brent) *Incidents in the Life of a Slave Girl* (Jacobs 2009) provides critical insights for reorienting Black feminist thinking. Jacobs, McKittrick recalls, was able to eventually escape from slavery by holing up for seven years in a crawl space of her grandmother's attic (Jacobs 2009, 37). This space, which was nine feet by seven feet by three feet, allowed her to trick her owner into believing she had escaped and to redirect his attention and resources to apprehend her and return her to bondage while she was able to observe her family and effect her eventual permanent liberation from her condition of enslavement (Jacobs 2009, 37–44). Thus, although the garret for Jacobs was a place of confinement, it eventually secured her ultimate freedom in escaping from slavery in the South. She was positioned, in this "loophole of retreat" (Jacobs 2009, 37), in a way that gave her a special mode of insight in observing the slave community in which she was embedded (Jacobs 2009, 41–43). Even as she was located in the oppressive context of slavery, through her garreting of herself, she was able to resist it from within. So the garret points not only to the active resistance that Black women can mount politically in ways that can afford them a "loophole of retreat" by which they advance a liberating politics, but also to the way in which Black women have in fact been central, not marginal, to political development in the United States and elsewhere in the African Diaspora. Jacobs's garreting demonstrates how Black women have produced oppositional geographies. This example of garreting, I contend, also provides us with a powerful way to think about how to construct oppositional geographies in using a Black feminist frame of reference for political science.[4]

Specifically, there are two ways the concept of garrets or garreting can be important: materially, that is, in terms of the production of Black feminist scholarship on Black women; and metaphorically, that is, again, in terms of how we as Black feminist scholars analyze and assess the lives and political efforts of Black women, as constitutive of mainstream politics as opposed to residing only on the margins. As to the material issue of knowledge production, garreting occurs through creating mechanisms and spaces to authorize and facilitate work on Black women and Black gender politics. Producing journals and developing book series or other inroads at presses are, of course, significant means of directly supporting publication. Importantly, these are just examples of a broader constellation of inroads that support research and publication. Black women have supported scholars and their research, for instance, through producing edited volumes, hosting conferences, giving publication prizes, and/or developing social networks that can provide mentoring and psychosocial support necessary to thrive in the academy. The Association of Black Women Historians (ABWH) is a case in point. The ABWH has been a key institutional location for mentoring Black women historians and for authorizing and supporting research about and by Black women. Through its annual meeting, held in tandem with the Association for the Study of African American Life and History (ASALH), and its awards, which recognize scholarship for Black women, it has helped both to institutionalize the specialty of Black women's history and to support those intellectual laborers committed to such work. This has occurred alongside participation within other institutional locations. Still, the ABWH has served as a means of garreting in the way McKittrick describes, that is, a production of social space that disrupts the dominant intellectual geographic terrain. A similar process of garreting has been important for other disciplines that are more productive in terms of their work on Black women. In sociology, for instance, the American Sociological Association Section on Race, Gender, and Class, as well as specialized journals such as *Race and Ethnicity* and *Gender and Society*, facilitate the respatialization of sociology. This does not marginalize or (re)segregate Black feminist scholars. Whether they gravitate toward what are considered mainstream circles of power or favor nonhegemonic locations, they continue to operate within disciplinary matrixes.

In political science, Black women and other women of color are working to develop similar forms of garreting. Preconference meetings at the American Political Science Association for women of color have been an important means of networking and disseminating information about publication, particularly for emerging scholars. More recently, Jessica Lavariega Monforti and Melissa Michelson have co-organized and convened a biennial Women of Color in Political Science Workshop immediately prior to the American Political Science Association's Annual Meeting. The formation of the Association for the Study of Black Women in Politics is another effort. Modeled after the ABWH, the ASBWP has two missions: to facilitate the professionalization of Black women political scientists and to support progressive Black feminist research on Black women in politics in the United States and throughout the African Diaspora. Originated in 2004 and formally incorporated in 2008, the ASBWP has begun an annual awards program to recognize important research on Black women in politics. Although it has been generally welcomed, particularly by Black women political scientists who research Black women in politics, the organizers (including the author), who were junior scholars when they began this effort, have faced challenges in terms of antifeminist sentiments within the discipline, as well as the daily pressures of managing institutional racism and sexism in academe, such as putatively higher standards for research productivity and challenges to professional authority. In 2013, as a result of then NCOBPS president Wendy Smooth's Black Women's Initiative, the ASBWP formally affiliated with the National Conference of Black Political Scientists. The ASBWP has since co-organized panels and hosted a mentoring breakfast at the annual meeting of NCOBPS, and published a two-part symposium in the *National Political Science Review* (Alexander-Floyd and Willoughby-Herard 2015; 2016). In 2016, Tiffany Willoughby-Herard organized and hosted the ASBWP's first national conference, "Scandal in Real Time," at the University of California-Irvine, which brought dozens of students and junior and senior scholars together to examine the state of scholarship on Black women in politics across various fields. Efforts of organizations such as the ABWH or ASBWP help to rewrite or restructure the social production of disciplinary space.

Of course, the geographies of Black women are not all inherently oppositional. Black women can produce geographies that *do* support hegemonic geographical arrangements, both materially and metaphorically. This is arguably the case in terms of how intersectionality is currently being discussed in political science. As Julia Jordan-Zachery's chapter in this volume demonstrates, a focus on intersectionality does not necessarily provide research that illuminates Black political women and their political strivings. It just as easily gives way to descriptive research and, in some cases, research that does not focus on race but on general attributes of difference. Black women in particular and women of color more generally are "disappeared" (Alexander-Floyd 2012) as subjects and progenitors of intersectionality research.

Importantly, scholars who do seek to remap the intellectual terrain of their disciplines in oppositional ways typically do so through integrating insights from other fields and through challenging the received epistemological and methodological orientations of their disciplines. The personal accounts of some of the most noted pioneers of Black women's history demonstrate this latter point. In her contribution to her edited collection *Telling Histories* (White 2008), a compilation of firsthand accounts of Black women historians' academic lives, historian Deborah Gray White powerfully records the challenges she faced in producing Black women's history. Her first book, *Ar'n't I a Woman* (White 1985), is universally regarded as a watershed moment in Black women's history and in the study of slavery. Yet as an assistant professor she faced seemingly insurmountable challenges, stemming in no small part from a lack of understanding about the relevance of scholarship on Black women in her discipline. She explains: "I had no reason to be optimistic about finding a publisher because publishers' critiques were . . . dismissive. 'It was not complete, there was not enough work, the proof wasn't there.' And, then almost universally, publishers added, 'There is no audience for this book' " (White 2008, 96). But for a chance reading by Anne Firor Scott of the dissertation on which the book was based and Scott's subsequent offer to speak to a publisher, this pathbreaking work might not have been published. Similarly, Darlene Clark Hine (2008), eminent scholar of Black women's history, received a very traditional graduate education, generally devoid of any treatment of Black women as historical subjects. When community members prevailed on her to write a history of Black club women in Indiana, she embarked on a journey that would help her rewrite Black women's history and reshape her own trajectory as a scholar. Although earlier scholars producing groundbreaking works generally face challenges in initiating new fields of study, the resistance to doing work on Black women is persistent. Historian Mia Bay, hailing from a younger generation of scholars, notes that there was little discussion of Black women as historical subjects in graduate school and that her own entry into this area of scholarly concern was occasioned by women's studies scholars within and outside history circles post graduate school (Bay 2008, 192–93). Interdisciplinary interventions proved pivotal to the production of scholarship on Black women as historical actors, as these examples illustrate.

The same interdisciplinary push can be seen in political science. Beginning in the 1960s, scholars, particularly from Atlanta University and Howard

University, led a concerted effort to integrate Black studies approaches vis-à-vis the development of scholarship focused on Blacks and their political experiences. Indeed, the formation of the National Conference of Black Political Scientists in 1968 was birthed in this moment of intellectual commitment to producing knowledge that could effectively respond to the needs of Blacks in the United States and globally (McCormick 2009). This push for the development of a Black political science was buoyed by the activist climate of the time and the push for Black studies in the academy. One can recall *Death of White Sociology* (Ladner 1973) as a volume that marked a similar thrust in the field of sociology. Women's studies had a similar effect across disciplines, the creation of the Women and Politics subfield at Rutgers University perhaps being the most prominent example in political science. As the aforementioned text suggests, increased attention needs to be paid to interdisciplinarity and the politics of methodology in order to expand scholarship on Black women and Black gender politics in political science. To be sure, there has been progress. Further advancement, however, requires attention to the material means of scholarly production.

Of course, some might question the utility of working to advance work on Black women as political actors in the discipline of political science. Given the development of disciplines that are more open to work on Black women, including multi- and interdisciplinary spaces such as Black Studies, Ethnic Studies, Women's and Gender Studies, and American Studies, and traditional disciplines such as history, why would scholars commit to fields like political science that are arguably more conservative and restrictive methodologically and ideologically and less diverse? I think there is a better question, however, namely: *How can a major discipline like political science dedicated to unpacking the operation of power in society not concern itself with the fundamental role that race, gender, and other bases of social organization have played in its composition, circulation, and impact?* The answer to that question is critical, and it directly relates to the state of Black political women in the Diaspora and scholarship about them as political actors.

Making "(inter)disciplinary trouble" is important because disciplines are the organizing mechanism for academic work; they provide a "matrix" in which knowledge is produced, and the work of interdisciplinary enterprises such as Black women's and gender studies is to trouble or complicate and remake those formations (Alexander-Floyd 2005; 2012). Following Johnella Butler, who advocates for Black/Africana studies in free-standing programs and departments and across disciplines, Black women's and gender studies scholarship should germinate within multi- and interdisciplinary contexts as well as in traditional disciplines (Alexander-Floyd 2005). In this way, the interdisciplinary integration of Black feminist approaches in political science not only aids in restructuring the discipline of political science for more progressive ends, but also constitutes a decolonial project in the production of knowledge more generally.

Finally, in addition to place making as it relates to knowledge production, garreting is equally important in terms of the approach we take to studying Black political women. More specifically, we typically think of Black women and Black feminist politics in terms of being located at the margins. McKittrick (2006, 56–59), building on the insights of Patricia Hill Collins, who also questions the utility of situating Black women as marginal, provocatively suggests that such a framing actually reproduces the militaristic and binary formulations associated with conquest and colonization. The notion of the garret suggests that Black women's struggle against domination occurs not only from the location of the margins, but also from within the center or midst of geographic and political landscapes. In the case of Harriet Jacobs (Linda Brent), her experience of surviving in the garret of her grandmother's attic for seven years demonstrates the complicated paradox of struggle amid racial-sexual terror. Drawing on McKittrick's formulations regarding Black feminist geography for our understanding of politics yields potentially powerful results. We would find that Black women's experiences and politics might still be found in "the last place they thought of" (McKittrick 2006). However, we could also see that Black political women "are not necessarily marginal, but are central" (McKittrick 2006, 62) to politics and that investigating their efforts can transform how we define and study the operation of power.

Suggestions for Future Research

Future investigations could develop this line of inquiry on the state of research on Black political women in several ways. First, although I used the time periods 1970 to 1985, 1986 to 2003, and 2004 to 2008 to better enable comparisons with previous research, recalibrating results for each discipline along decades may yield beneficial results. Second, a fuller examination could entail a review of journals focused on gender and/or race and ethnicity, such as *Politics & Gender* in political science, *Gender & Society* in sociology, and *Feminist Economics* in economics, to understand the ways in which these subfields within disciplines have opened up research opportunities and/or positively redirected and expanded research on race and gender in mainstream journals as well. Third, we can further examine the impact of and necessity for post-positivist methodologies in examining Black political women.

The recent increased attention to intersectionality in political science, as evidenced, for instance, by special symposia in *Politics & Gender* in 2007 and 2012 as well as by preconference workshops and panels on the subject, ostensibly promises to produce a greater volume of research about Black women as political actors and Black gender politics, but there is reason to approach this expectation with some caution. As I argue elsewhere (Alexander-Floyd 2012), the interpretations of intersectionality now gaining currency are in fact a "post"–Black feminist formulation that displaces and/or deprioritizes research on Black women. Indeed, as previously indicated, research has already begun to expose the relative inattention to Black women in current intersectionality research in the discipline. I suggest further examination of the various fields to provide examples of the ways in which scholars, particularly in political science and sociology, have operationalized intersectionality in their research, including in ways that at times hinder liberatory Black feminist scholarship on Black women.

Ultimately, it is important to detail the extent and nature of the limitations on scholarship in various disciplines not only for issues of exposure, but also to provoke decisive action to substantively redirect the methodological and political priorities of the discipline. Undoubtedly, without a change of direction, the current interpretation of intersectionality within the discipline will ironically further invisibilize Black women as political actors. A truly interdisciplinary approach to intersectionality in the discipline—not one that accommodates intersectionality to prevailing paradigms, but one that truly transforms what we think we can know and the means by which we can come to know it—will be a central means of enacting the type of Perestroika-like movement that is necessary to assert a Black feminist frame of reference for political science.

Notes

1. I use the term "Black political women" to denote women of African descent in terms of their political subjectivity and engagement in formal and informal politics. It is inspired by Jewel Prestage's (1991) seminal work "In Quest of African American Political Woman."

2. For a discussion of Black feminist "home-making" and spatial politics, see Zenzele Isoke's "The Politics of Homemaking: Black Feminist Transformations of a Cityscape," *Transforming Anthropology* 19 (2): 117–30.

3. Language here, including hyphenation, reflects actual search terms used. Note: results may vary given database updates or alterations in search parameters.

4. Garrets are not flattened environments of abstract desolation in which individuals have no capacity, however limited, or where garrets are ends in and of themselves. A garret is specifically described as a "loophole of retreat," a context in which Black women as political actors and scholars can develop an "oppositional geography" in reshaping political science in particular and other contexts more generally. Others might opt for alternative analytic frames to garrets and/or intersectionality, such as fugitivity (or flight), exile, and refugeeism, in studying Black political women. These also depend on an acknowledgement of and an attempt to counteract oppressive conditions. And, significantly, they are consistent with and not oppositional to intersectionality in its ideographic dimension.

References

Agnew, John. 2011. "Space and Place." In *The SAGE Handbook of Geographical Knowledge*, edited by John Agnew and David Livingstone, 316–43. Los Angeles: SAGE.

Alexander-Floyd, Nikol. 2007. *Gender, Race, and Nationalism in Contemporary Black Politics*. New York: Palgrave Macmillan.

———. 2012. "Disappearing Acts: Reclaiming Intersectionality in the Social Sciences in a Post-Black Feminist Era." *Feminist Formations* 24 (1): 1–25.

Alexander-Floyd, Nikol G., and Tiffany Willoughby-Herard, eds. 2015. "Association for the Study of Black Women in Politics, Symposium on Black Women in Politics, Part I." *National Political Science Review* 17 (1).

———. 2016. "Association for the Study of Black Women in Politics, Symposium on Black Women in Politics, Part II." *National Political Science Review* 17 (2).

Barriteau, Eudine. 2003. "Theorizing the Shift from 'Woman' to 'Gender' in Caribbean Feminist Discourse." In *Confronting Power, Theorizing Gender: Interdisciplinary Perspectives in the Caribbean*, edited by Eudine Barriteau, 27–45. Jamaica: University of the West Indies Press.

Bay, Mia. 2008. "Looking Backward in Order to Go Forward: Black Women Historians and Black Women's History." In *Telling Histories: Black Women Historians in the Ivory Tower*, edited by Deborah Gray White, 182–99. Chapel Hill: University of North Carolina Press.

Berger, Michele, and Kathleen Guidroz, eds. 2009. *The Intersectional Approach: Transforming the Academy Through Race, Class, & Gender*. Durham: University of North Carolina Press.

Blatt, Jessica. 2012. "Race, Rights, and the Origins of American Political Science." Paper presented at the annual meeting of the Southern Political Science Association, New Orleans, LA, January.

Carroll, Susan J., and Linda M. G. Zerilli. 1993. "Feminist Challenges to Political Science." In *Political Science: The State of the Discipline*, edited by Ada Finifter, 55–76. Washington, DC: The American Political Science Association.

Collins, Patricia Hill, and Sirma Bilge, eds. 2016. *Intersectionality: Key Concepts*. Cambridge: Polity.

Dill, Bonnie Thornton, and Ruth Enid Zambrana, eds. 2009. *Emerging Intersections: Race, Class, and Gender in Theory, Policy, and Practice*. New Brunswick, NJ: Rutgers University.

Hancock, Ange-Marie. 2004. *The Politics of Disgust: The Public Identity of the Welfare Queen*. New York: New York University Press.

Hine, Darlene Clark. 2008. "Becoming a Black Woman's Historian." In *Telling Histories: Black Women Historians in the Ivory Tower*, edited by Deborah Gray White, 42–57. Chapel Hill: University of North Carolina Press.

Isoke, Zenzele. 2011. "The Politics of Homemaking: Black Feminist Transformations of a Cityspace." *Transforming Anthropology* 19 (2): 117–30.

Jacobs, Harriet. 2009. *Incidents in the Life of a Slave Girl*. Cambridge, MA: Belknap Press.

Jones, Mack H. 1972. "A Frame of Reference for Black Politics." In *Black Political Life in the United States: A Fist as the Pendulum*, edited by Lenneal Henderson Jr., 7–20. San Francisco: Chandler.

———. 1977. "Responsibility of Black Political Scientists to the Black Community." In *Black Political Scientists and Black Survival*, edited by Shelby Lewis Smith, 9–17. Detroit: Balamp Publishing.

Jordan-Zachery, Julia. 2007. "Am I a Black Woman or a Woman Who Is Black?: A Few Thoughts on the Meaning Of Intersectionality." *Politics & Gender* 3 (2): 254–63.

Ladner, Joyce, ed. 1973. *The Death Of White Sociology*. New York: Random House.

McCormick, Joseph. 2009. "NCOBPS: The First of Our Forty Years." In *Racial Americana?: Continuities and Changes in Racial Politics* (Annual Meeting Program), 27–43. Houston: National Conference of Black Political Scientists.

McKittrick, Katherine. 2006. *Demonic Grounds: Black Women and the Cartographies of Struggle*. Minneapolis: University of Minnesota Press.

Monroe, Kristen, ed. 2005. *Perestroika!: The Raucous Rebellion In Political Science*. New Haven: Yale University Press.

Possing, Dorthe. 2010. *A Politics Of Place: How Young Muslims Frame Global and Local Events in Online Communication*. Global Migration and Transnational Politics, Working Paper, George Mason University, April 11.

Prestage, Jewell. 1991. "In Quest of the African American Political Woman." *The Annals of the American Academy of Political and Social Science* 515: 88–103.

Walcott, Rinaldo. 2001. "Caribbean Pop Culture in Canada: Or, the Impossibility of Belonging to the Nation." *Small Axe* 5 (1): 123–39.

Walters, Ronald. 2003. *White Nationalism, Black Interests: Conservative Public Policy and the Black Community*. Detroit: Wayne State University Press.

White, Deborah. 1985. *Ar'n't I a Woman: Female Slaves in the Plantation South*. New York: W. W. Norton and Company.

———. 2008. "My History in History." In *Telling Histories: Black Women Historians in the Ivory Tower*, edited by Deborah Gray White, 85–100. New York: W. W. Norton and Company.

Wilson, Ernest J. 1985. "Why Political Scientists Don't Study Black Politics, But Historians and Sociologists Do." *PS: Political Science & Politics* 18 (3): 600–7.

Wilson, Ernest J., and Lorrie A. Frasure. 2007. "Still at the Margins: The Persistence of Neglect of African American Issues in Political Science, 1986–2003." In *African American Perspectives on Political Science*, edited by Wilbur C. Rich, 8–23. Philadelphia: Temple University Press.

2

"I Ain't Your Darn Help"

Black Women as the Help in Intersectionality Research in Political Science

JULIA S. JORDAN-ZACHERY
Providence College

At a social function for my daughter's fifth-grade class, I had a rather interesting interaction with another mother. Before I can get to the details of the interaction, I need to explain the context. I was engaged in a conversation with one mother; we share an interest in reading and were discussing our recent selections. As we were conversing, another mother joined us and began to speak about her "absolute love" of Kathryn Stockett's (2009) novel *The Help*. My response to her adulation was "I find the book very problematic and simplistic. I should say that this is probably because I do research on such issues."

The mother replied, "Who gives a f**k what you think! The book is brilliant." Her response left me stunned for a number of reasons, beyond the fact that it seemed inappropriate. For one, we were the only women of color among the approximate fifteen families in attendance. I was the only Black mother present—the other two were moms of Latino descent. Second, the outburst came from a woman who lived in New York City. One could suppose that this exposed her to the use of immigrant women as nannies, which could discourage disrespectful behavior toward Black women. Third, this is a woman who tells of her story of poverty and homelessness and a desire that we all treat each other with respect and dignity.

Ironically, while attending a professional conference, I had a somewhat similar discussion that diminished Black women's identities and contributions. At an American Political Science Association (APSA) conference, a White female colleague told me that I should feel proud that Black women had made such a contribution—intersectionality—to the discipline. This was in response to my questioning of the ever-expanding use of intersectionality, and more importantly, the omission of Black women in such studies. At a prior APSA meeting, I was told that should Black women attempt to exclusively hold onto the concept of intersectionality, it will go the way of the term "Holocaust," which in her imagination limited the resonance and impact of the term outside the Jewish community. Consequently, if Black academicians resisted the traveling and reimagining of intersectionality, based on the logic of her argument, then there would be less support for the specific injustices suffered by Black women.

How and why are these conversations relevant to this edited volume on Black women and politics? My conversations, separated by time and space, speak to the politics of identity. While these are individual encounters, they capture what I believe is part of a larger trend on the treatment of and response to Black women. The conversations, intentionally or not, reify and maintain discursive systems that create truth regimes, which serve as forms of regulation (Foucault 1978). The mother of my daughter's classmate and my colleagues attempted to regulate, and to some extent, mute my voice. They engaged in a project of omission. This omission project is experienced in the sociocultural, political, and academic realms. According to Sesko and Biernat (2010), Black women are being rendered invisible in a sociocultural way. In comparison with other gendered and/or raced groups, Black women tend to go both unnoticed and unheard. Black women are also "disappearing" as research subjects within our "leading" journals (see Alexander-Floyd 2012 and her chapter in this volume) and within intersectionality research.

This research note investigates how the politics of research results in the further marginalization of Black women. Generally, politics is thought to involve the relationship between social actors and the state. Ignored in such conceptualizations are other interactions and the exercise of power and use of force. Therefore, the conversations I recounted above and the ever-evolving use of intersectionality in political science research might not be thought of as politics. However, these phenomena speak to practices, systems of knowledge, and cultural norms that serve to uphold racialized-gendered hierarchies. As such, they are a form of politics.

The question guiding this analysis is: How can the politics of knowledge production influence the material reality of doubly marginalized groups in general and Black women more specifically? Researchers such as Cathy Cohen (1999), Ange-Marie Hancock (2004), and Rose Ernst (2010), address the lack of Black women's voices in policy formation and show how such omission perpetuates harm to Black women. These and other researchers critically analyze the relationship between identity and policy responses and make substantive contributions to our understanding of intersectionality; however, there remains a gap in our research efforts. Unlike these influential works, I focus on meta-questions and analyses of political science intersectionality research. As I argue below, there is an omission project occurring in published political science research generally and within intersectionality research specifically. Black women as research subjects are being omitted. Our research has not focused on how and why Black women are being omitted in social science research and specifically within intersectionality research. Alexander-Floyd (2012) offers one of the few research-length articles on this issue of the disappearance of Black women in social science research in general. This project complements hers, as I focus primarily on the discipline of political science and intersectionality research specifically. Social science research in general, and in particular intersectionality research, do not exist in a vacuum; instead, they embody power hierarchies evident in the wider society. I posit that Black women, vis-à-vis the use of intersectionality as a theory and approach, are being muted. Consequently, their movement for social justice is stymied. As a result, the purpose of intersectionality, as envisioned by Black feminists, becomes subverted and a victim of race/ethnicity, class, gender, and sexuality hierarchies.

In recent years, intersectionality as a theoretical concept has permeated various fields of study within political science. In discussing the impact of intersectionality on feminist work, Risman (2004, 442) says, "[T]here is now considerable consensus growing that one must always take into consideration multiple axes of oppression; to do otherwise presumes the whiteness of women, the maleness of people of color, and the heterosexuality of everyone." Often pitched as a theory that allows us to speak for and understand the experiences of marginalized groups, intersectionality tends to be celebrated as an all-encompassing theory. In exploring the ever expanding popularity of intersectionality, Nath (2009) suggests that intersectionality has become popular because

> (1) The analytic insights offered by theories of intersectionality are so profound and perhaps so intuitive that their widespread incorporation into feminist scholarship is, to use a colloquial phrase, a "no brainer." (2) . . . the analytic insights of intersectionality

> theorizing have been so theoretically rich and complex, that their decentering of the essential female subject has been, again, a "no brainer." (3) . . . The profundity of this type of theorization means that those affiliated with it automatically gain theoretical legitimacy. (1)

The increasing use of intersectionality as a research tool, theoretical concept, and so forth has not been without debate (see Kwan 1997 for a discussion on some perceived limitations of intersectionality). Indeed, this discussion on the merits and challenges of intersectionality theory is fascinating and thought provoking. However, what is missing from this discourse is an understanding of how such research embodies politics and power dynamics that render some groups invisible and that result in the muting of some voices. Research is a political act. The theories employed and the manners in which they are deployed and the method and methodological approaches, like a picture, tell a story. These texts "as elements of social events have causal effects—i.e. they bring about changes . . . in our knowledge . . . our beliefs, our attitudes, values and so forth" (Fairclough 2003, 8).

To explore the politics of intersectionality research and what I call an omission project, I start by examining the relationship between the novel *The Help* and intersectionality research. This allows us to contextualize what is occurring in political science. It shows how these cultural and academic phenomena at times mirror each other and also reinforce and normalize the treatment of Black women. I follow this section with the theoretical orientation of the chapter—grounded in Black feminism and group-muted theory. Next, I present the data on how Black women are treated in intersectionality research and conclude with a discussion of the findings. In my discussion, I do not seek to offer a specific theory or some comprehensive approach to addressing the omission of Black women. Instead, my goal is to explore the ways in which Black women are treated in intersectionality research with the hope of stimulating a discussion on how our politics of research might be more inclusive. At first glance, my approach may not appear to follow the typical academic mode of production: how we generate knowledge and make knowledge claims. This is because I have used this approach as a means of disrupting knowledge claims and approaches often assumed to be best suited for knowledge production. As Collins (2000, 252) asserts, "like other subordinate groups, African-American women have not only developed a distinctive Black women's standpoint, but have done so by using alternative ways of producing and validating knowledge." My approach, in conjunction with my use of first-person stories and encounters, fits with Black feminist conceptualizations of epistemology.

Black Women as Bridges: *The Help* and Intersectionality

What are the similarities between the conversations I had at the social and the one I had at the political science meeting? The parallels between the novel and my APSA conversations are not obvious until we start to look at the increasing popularity of intersectionality among scholars in political science and unpack how Black women were used in the novel. There is a parallel between the roles of Black women in *The Help* and in political science. In each instance, both sets of Black women are used to advance others' dreams and desires, even if simply to provide (cultural/theoretical) legitimacy while often remaining in the shadows. Intersectionality research, similarly to *The Help*, appears to give a nod to the voices of Black women; however, on closer inspection, Black women's voices are not necessarily heard.

The Help deploys historical narratives of the contented, silent, and "dignified" Black woman. This fictional portrayal tapped into a cultural and political moment of nostalgia—a desire for the "beauty" and "simplicity" of the past. This yearning for nostalgia requires Black women to play the role of Mammy—the docile enslaved woman who cared for and protected White interests. We cannot avoid the politics of this particular understanding of Black womanhood because "fictionalized creations of black women are not innocent; they do not lack the effect of ideological force in the lives of those represented in that black women are rendered as objects and useful commodities in a very serious power struggle" (Bobo 1995, 36).

The popularity of the novel eventually led to its adoption for the big screen. In 2011, the much anticipated movie was released. This occurred in conjunction with an intense marketing campaign designed to encourage women to not only dress like the characters, but also to eat like them. For example, the Home Shopping Network (HSN) launched a site (which coincided with the release of the movie) featuring products inspired by the movie and novel. Such products included kitchenware and clothing items designed around "Southern Belle" styles. One could aspire to dress in the fashion (out of uniform) of the maids or the more "high"-end floral ensembles of the more economically well-off women. To some extent, the lives of Black women are available for consumption with little thought of the daily lived realities of these women.

Often touted as a story of interracial, intraclass friendship, *The Help*, both film and novel versions, is really a story of White women's voice—particularly the main character's search for an alternative experience. Similarly, intersectionality as currently deployed also represents this type of search for something other—it is in part a desire to move beyond traditional understandings of identity politics. Thus, intersectionality and the voices of Black women become an avenue for others to seek freedom from the "norm." Black women serve as a bridge between both worlds. What is often neglected in this quest to seek alternatives is what happens to Black women who serve as the "help." Particularly, what is missing is how Black women's bodies, psyches, and intellects serve not for their advancement, but the advancement of others—whether in terms of tenure and promotion, other forms of job security, or simply just as a means to a more "comfortable" life.

Skeeter, the main character of the novel, was able to find her alternative—she got the job in New York that allowed her to escape the confines of White womanhood as dictated by Southern culture—by co-opting the voices of Black women. Meanwhile, Aibileen Clark, the Black maid, who served as a bridge between Skeeter and the other maids, was dismissed from her job and left to live in the South. Furthermore, although Aibileen is officially "recognized" as the author of the self-help column published in the local newspaper, she must write under a pen name of Miss Myrna. Thus, readers remain unaware of the author's true identity. Aibileen assumed "formal" authorship of this column after Skeeter left town (Stockett 2009).

Interestingly, while Skeeter was the author of this column, Aibileen's wisdom was used to respond to the readers' letters. Skeeter benefited, in multiple forms, from Aibileen's knowledge. Aibileen legitimized Skeeter as a writer. She claimed the notoriety and benefits while Aibileen went unacknowledged. The voice of this woman remained hidden behind the image of a White woman/persona. This fictitious Black woman, like her real-life counterparts, is forced to exist in the place where she is simultaneously seen while remaining invisible. Although living in the midst of the Civil Rights movement, where Black women were tormented on a daily basis, Aibileen displays no anger toward the theft of her intellect or her freedom. Maybe this is a result of no one "giving a f**k" what she thinks (in the words of the mother I spoke to at the social), or maybe it is a result of those in power choosing not to allow her to speak or choosing to ignore what she says when she does speak, thereby discrediting any critique she might offer. This is the omission project; Black women are there while not being there. It is this nebulous state that makes a critique of this project such a challenge.

Skeeter, by appropriating Aibileen's knowledge, is able to escape to the North. Aibileen is left in the South without a job, living in poverty, and having to confront sexism and racism. Although Aibileen served as the bridge that allowed Skeeter to escape the South (read: identity politics) to the North, her labor, physical, and intellectual, could not be used for her own advancement, neither could it be used for the advancement of the larger Black community (read: intersectionality as part of a freedom project). However, at the end of the novel, Stockett tells us that Aibileen's spirit is not broken. Stockett invokes the notion of the strong and often "content" Black woman—in the sense that she does not challenge multiple oppressive structures but simply focuses on getting by in the current context. This is the message I often receive from some colleagues when I question how intersectionality is used in political science research. I am told to be content and not question the politics of research.

This issue of "North"/"South" is really a question of representation and identity. It involves the politics of a "ranking" of oppression as opposed to a quest for freedom for all. When others challenge my questioning of the use of intersectionality and *The Help* by suggesting that I am incessantly angry (the trope of the angry Black woman) and that I want to claim intersectionality as only the domain of Black women, they are missing the larger issue of the politics of research and the politics of cultural representation. For me, the questioning of the use of intersectionality is not to claim it as the primary domain of Black women. Instead, it asks: Where are Black women in the excitement about intersectionality? When intersectionality loses its attractiveness, who will study Black women, and how will we study Black women? Will Black women as research subjects be left in the "South" as researchers continue their journey to the "North," as was the case with main character Eugenia "Skeeter" Phelan and Abilene Clark, her help? Will Black women be constructed simply as having a strong sprit? Will this construction, one of strength, be used as a marker of their great contribution to political science? Like *The Help*, the increasing popularity of intersectionality can be the result of a number of forces. However, if there is no questioning of power relations and how identities are constructed so that benefits are not equally distributed, then Black women and their lived experiences will be, like Aibileen Clark, left to live in the South with an unbroken sprit and a nod to their contributions.

Theoretical Foundation: Silences, Muting, and Omissions

The theoretical concept of intersectionality has as its foundation Black women's experiential knowledge—this is not to suggest that they are the only group that can claim the use of intersectionality. While some researchers take their meaning of intersectionality from Kimberlé Crenshaw's (1989, 1991) understanding of the concept, it is possible to trace a much longer history. Black women, although they might not have explicitly employed the term intersectionality, have historically expressed its core tenets. For example, in 1832 Maria Stewart spoke of the intersection of race and class in the lives of Black women (see Logan 1995). In the more recent iterations of the concept, such a history has been erased as a result of omission. Current research, beyond ignoring the early writings of Black women while citing the work of more contemporary scholars, does not necessarily, systematically, and critically engage the scholarship. In her critique of this movement, Alexander-Floyd (2012, 2) says, "[B]arely a decade into the new millennium, a new wave of raced-gendered occultic commodification is afoot, one focusing not on black female subjectivity per se, but on the concept of intersectionality."

Consequently, Black women who have theorized their experiences are treated like Aibileen of *The Help* in a substantial number of the research papers I analyze. The result is that they are simultaneously seen while remaining invisible in intersectionality research. This research invisibility is multipronged. Invisibility, in the words of M. Jacqui Alexander and Chandra Talpade Mohanty (1997, xii), occurs as a result of "token inclusion of our text." Such "inclusion" tends to be nontransformative in nature and is often done with little critical engagement. Another form of invisibility occurs as a result of who serves as research subjects. As I discuss elsewhere (Jordan-Zachery 2012), there is "a failure among researchers to recognize intra-group differences among marginalized groups." I assert,

> We tend to ignore how intersectionality is experienced and lived among different members of the same group. Furthermore we tend to concentrate our research efforts among a select group of Black women; thereby, leaving untouched the lived realities of the majority of Black women—every-day, non-elected Black women. (407)

Such invisibility results because "while the social location of racially marked otherness creates conditions of possibility for epistemic privilege in terms of intersectional theorizing, this does not necessarily foreclose the achievement of an antiracist feminist standpoint to white women and others" (Clark Mane 2012, 76). Clark Mane and others expose how Black women, while appearing to speak, are actually silenced and muted. There is an intimate relationship between silence and forgetting. As intersectionality travels, the silencing and muting of Black women in research can create a situation for forgetting why Black women–centered intersectionality as a tool for analyzing and responding to the material realties they confront on a daily basis.

Group muting theory offers a lens to understand and analyze the treatment of Black women in intersectionality research. This theory seeks to represent marginalized groups whose voices and experiences often are silenced. Being muted should not be conflated with silence. Instead, muting should be seen as the hindrance of the communicative outlets and abilities of a marginalized group at the hands of those in power. The process of muting suggests that some groups are denied representation, as they are limited in their ability to speak and to choose how they want to speak. Furthermore, some groups are denied representation based on how others choose to see them or not see them. As argued by Orbe (2005, 65–66), muted group theory is a foundational starting place for "theorizing from the margins."

Muted group theory, similarly to intersectionality, suggests that marginalized groups' perceptions and interpretations of reality are influenced by the dominant groups' constructions. This works, as argued by Kramarae (1981), because each society constructs "template structures," which are a series of beliefs, values, and opinions that collectively work to define a particular worldview. These "template structures" provide society with the "language" images, symbols, and so forth that are then used to construct and understand reality (see Ardener 1975). Template structures are relied on, explicitly and implicitly, to determine who should serve as both research subjects and producers of knowledge. Such structures can be deployed in the process of silencing some members of the community/group. They play a role in the omission project.

According to Sheriff (2000),

> Unlike the activity of speech, which does not require more than a single actor, silence demands collaboration and the tacit communal understandings that such collaboration presupposes.

> Although it is contractual in nature, a critical feature of this type of silence is that it is both a consequence and an index of an unequal distribution of power, if not of actual knowledge. Through it, various forms of power may be partly, although often incompletely, concealed, denied, or naturalized. Although the type of silence I refer to may be a more or less stable and widely shared cultural convention, it is constituted through, and circumscribed by, the political interests of dominant groups. (114)

There are two forms of silences that result from the muting process taking place in intersectionality research. One can be overt; this is the complete absence of Black women as research subjects and/or the recognition of their contributions. Another type of silence tends to be more covert in nature. Covert silence, and the resulting omissions, allow for a form of memorializing the contributions of Black women. It is the type of silence that is part of speech, thereby making it hard to identify and critique. An example of covert omission involves the citation of some works without any critical engagement of the scholarship. Regardless of the form of silence, both types ignore the narratives of Black women. Our scholarship—cultural and academic—excludes these narratives. Below, I explore how Black women are treated in intersectionality research.

Finding Black Women: Article Selection Criteria

For the period 1996–2010, I analyze four journals to determine how Black women are treated as research subjects. I focus on journal-length articles, as this allows me to identify trends and because "publications in leading journals are an important marker of professional status and a key conduit for the diffusion of ideas" (Munck and Snyder 2007, 339). The number of journal articles is considered as an indicator of the extent to which the scholarly community accepts Black women as research subjects. Beyond this, I consider how Black women are treated within these scholarly journals as another indicator of their acceptance. Combined, the count of articles and the nature of the research show the trends and status of research on Black womanhood.

Articles were selected from four journals, two of which, according to Garand and Giles (2003), are among the top-ranking journals. These journals are *The American Political Science Review* (APSR) and the *Journal of Politics* (JOP). The other two journals focus on women and/or gender. *The Journal of Women, Politics & Policy* (formerly *Women & Politics*) and *Politics & Gender* complete the journals used in this analysis.

Using a series of key words, each journal was searched and the resulting articles recorded. The key words included Black women, African American women, and intersectionality. To determine if articles on intersectionality were relevant to the study, I employed a US-based understanding of intersectionality as developed by Black women. Intersectionality, one manifestation of Black feminism in the United States, is rooted in the simultaneity and multiplicity of oppressions (race, class, gender, and sexuality, among others) and relationality (emphasis is placed on the relation between the everyday lives of Black women and socio-political and historical structures and processes). Given this understanding of intersectionality, I excluded articles that looked at women outside the United States. Furthermore, I excluded book reviews and articles in the Critical Perspective section of *Women, Politics & Policy*. This was done to ensure that the data would be comparable across the journals.

After the list of data was complied, the articles were read to determine if indeed they centered Black women and/or intersectionality. The articles were categorized using the following typology: Intersectionality (these are articles that focus primarily on the concept of intersectionality with no reference to Black women); Intersectionality and Black womanhood (these articles not only employ intersectionality, but also discuss Black women); Black women as a means (such articles are not about Black women, but employ Black women to tell a larger story); Black women (Black women are the singular focus of these articles); and Comparative (in these articles, Black women serve as a comparative group to discuss race, gender, and politics/policy).

Trends in Scholarship

Among the fifty-nine articles analyzed, the number of articles centered on Black women and/or intersectionality as the subject of the research was rather scarce. There were five articles using the concept of intersectionality (see table 1). Of these articles, three focused on Latinas, one employed intersectionality to discuss the policy-making process, and one was a comparative analysis. Further analysis reveals that four of these five articles were published in *Women, Politics & Policy* and one was published in *Politics & Gender*. In terms of research on intersectionality and Black womanhood as a singular research topic, there were two such articles and both were published in *Politics & Gender*. Articles categorized as "using Black women as a means" accounted for nine publications. In these articles, there was mention of Black women, not as part of an attempt to understand their political/policy lived experiences, but to use them to tell a larger story that often had nothing to do directly with Black women.

Black women as a singular research subject, with no explicit use of intersectionality, accounted for fifteen articles in total. Twelve of these articles were published in *Women, Politics & Policy*. *Politics & Gender* and *JOP* published two and one, respectively. The nature of these articles varied and included analyses of Black feminist thought and the impact of policies—such as the war on drugs. The major subject areas centered women either as voters, candidates, and/or representatives.

Black women, in the majority of articles (twenty-eight), were treated in a comparative manner. Again, a disproportionate number of articles were published in *Women Politics & Policy* (twenty articles). The other eight articles were published in *Politics & Gender* (five), *JOP* (two), and *APSR* (one). It is worth noting that not all comparative articles treated Black women in the same manner. Additionally, among this body of research, only one article focused on girls as a subject. The others centered Black feminist/standpoint theory, political behavior, and/or institutions. Comparative studies can be informative; however, they can also be limiting (see hooks 1991). Such studies can reinscribe differences and encourage further marginalization of Black women, as they can result in "a God trick . . . that mode of seeing that pretends to offer a vision that is from everywhere and nowhere equally and fully" (Haraway 1988, 584). Although Black women are used in some of these studies, they are employed to call attention to concerns other than the concern of the "structural sources of inequality" (Guidroz and Berger 2009, 70). Such studies can mask differentials in power relations between and within groups. This is not to suggest that all dimensions of comparative studies are inherently problematic for Black women.

[Ch 2 Figure One about here.]

Caption: Figure 2.1: Black Women as Research Subjects in Political Science, 1996–2010.]

Further examination of the trends shows that the *APSR* is apt not to publish research on Black women as singular research subjects and also is unlikely to publish work on intersectionality. The *JOP*, similarly to the *APSR*, tended not to include articles within which Black women are treated as singular research subjects. If, indeed, *APSR* and *JOP* are recognized as two of the top-ranking journals in political science, and if such rankings are key in tenure decisions, the omission of Black women among published articles sends the message that such research is not valued and, as such, should not be pursued. The other trend suggests that Black women are valuable research subjects provided they are part of a comparative study. Again, the message is that research that privileges Black women as a singular research topic is not valued in terms of published research.

Beyond the fact that Black women as singular research subjects receive minimum attention in the published articles, how they are studied can also be limiting in our understanding of their lived reality. Among the publications studied, there was minimum attention paid to Black female–centered organizations. Neither was attention paid to Black women's experiences with various public policies. During the time period analyzed, there was one article that centered Black lesbians (Fogg-Davis 2006). Finally, there were no publications that focused on Black women's public opinions. These trends suggest a rather narrow understanding of Black women's politics.

Discussion

Elizabeth Spelman (1997) discusses White women's deployment of rather vivid images of slavery to describe their own suffering. She argues that while the language of the enslaved was being appropriated, the suffering of actual slaves receded from their view and ultimately their consciousness. According to Spelman (1997, 113–17), suffragists who appropriated the language of enslaved individuals denied differences by claiming commonality of experience between themselves and the enslaved. While recognizing the utility of intersectionality, researchers seem to be engaging, consciously or unconsciously, in a similar manner to those described by Spelman. They are engaging in the same tactic used by the fictitious character Skeeter discussed above. *The Help*, in an analogous way to what is occurring within intersectionality research in political science with the study of Black women, if not challenged, is apt to treat Black women in a manner parallel to the White women suffragists described by Spelman. As a result, the experiences of Black women will remain lost while their voices become appropriated in the construction of an identity of sameness and commonality. Consequently, essentialist presumptions can become implicit in our discussions of intersectionality.

The template structures used to engage in group muting specify viable research and research subjects. Consequently, some researchers who might want to engage in certain types of research projects are discouraged and ultimately silenced. Or these researchers might be muted in the sense that they are forced, by the "rules of the game," to limit the nature of their research. Such silencing can result from covert or overt actions. I have experienced both types of silencing in my career. As a young professor, I was told by a colleague not to focus my research on Black women. According to him, I would be "pigeonholed" and my career would be stunted. Several years later, I face the challenge of finding spaces that are receptive to publishing my research and institutions that will view such work as valuable. As the data suggest, the top journals are less than likely to publish works on Black women and on intersectionality. Some institutions, implicitly or explicitly, value journal rankings and will give more "points" when hiring and during promotion and tenure decisions to research appearing in these high-ranking journals. This politics of research results in the marginalization of Black women and others who might desire to study intersectionality and Black womanhood.

This silence not only affects what happens in academia; it also has implications for how we understand politics and Black women's reality. The muting process results in some research questions going unexplored. Questions such as: How are Black women who are not elected to office engaging and grappling with issues of intersectionality? How are they defining and responding to a multitude of issues that influence their daily lives? How they are defining themselves tends to be ignored. Including Black women in our studies of politics, by centering their social, political, and cultural understandings, can broaden and (re)shape notions of how we study and ultimately understand politics. Such a framing has practical ramifications, as it allows us to further explore policies that target, directly and indirectly, Black women and their communities.

In my attempts to raise these issues, I have been dismissed. Some have dismissed my concerns about the treatment of Black women in cultural, social, and political realms by suggesting that I am not being realistic and at times appear incessantly and inappropriately angry. Such dismissals result in the failure to grasp a few critical aspects of intersectionality. One is accountability. Intersectionality requires us to be accountable in terms of how we treat the process of knowledge production and the producers of that knowledge. Beyond this, intersectionality also requires us to be accountable in terms of how knowledge is used to challenge power relations, which involves not minimizing differences and silencing the voices of those who have been "Othered." Second, to assume that Black women are to be satisfied with simply making a contribution to the larger field of political science is to lose sight of why Black women speak to the realities of living at the margins of many axes of oppression. This has long been a concern of Black women, both inside and outside the academy. Black women have long been concerned about their representation and have fought valiantly to have their voices heard.

Black women want to be more than the "help" of political science and the subfield of women and politics. While I cannot speak for all Black women, and neither do I have the requisite scientific data for support, I still make the claim that simply being satisfied with making a contribution to political science is not and has never been the goal of critical Black feminists. Faced with the possibility of the loss of voice and ultimately representation, I will not, like Aibileen, remain content dwelling in the South (read: lack of progression and equality). Instead, I will remain passionate by questioning the distribution of power and holding myself and other researchers accountable for public treatments of Black women.

At the end of *The Help*, the main character goes on to realize her dreams. She escapes. However, the Black women who helped her while risking their lives and livelihood were left to live with sexism, classism, and racism. The question that we have to confront as intersectionality traverses different spaces is: Will Black feminist theorists and by default Black women face a similar fate? Will they be forgotten and left to live within the same age-old axes of oppression, as intersectionality becomes *the help* of mainstream political science?

References

Alexander, M. Jacqui, and Chandra T. Mohanty. 1997. "Introduction: Genealogies, Legacies, Movements." In *Feminist Genealogies, Colonial Legacies, Democratic Futures*, edited by M. J. Alexander and C. T. Mohanty, xiii–xlii. New York: Routledge.

Alexander-Floyd, Nikol. 2012. "Disappearing Acts: Reclaiming Intersectionality in the Social Sciences in a Post-Black Feminist Era." *Feminist Formations* 24 (1): 1–25.

Ardener, Edwin. 1975. "Belief and the Problem of Women." In *Perceiving Women*, edited by S Ardener, 1–17. London: Malaby Press.

Bobo, Jacqueline. 1995. *Black Women as Cultural Readers*. New York: Columbia University Press.

Clark Mane, Rebecca L. 2012. "Transmuting Grammars of Whiteness in Third-Wave Feminism: Interrogating Postrace Histories, Postmodern Abstraction, and the Proliferation of Difference in Third-Wave Texts." *Signs* 38 (1): 71–98.

Cohen, Cathy. 1999. *The Boundaries of Blackness: AIDS and the Breakdown of Black Politics.* Chicago: University of Chicago Press.

Collins, Patricia Hill. 2000. "Black Feminist Epistemology." In *Black Feminist Thought: Knowledge, Consciousness, and the Politics of Empowerment*, 251–72. New York: Routledge.

Crenshaw, Kimberlé. 1989. "Demarginalizing the Intersection of Race and Sex: A Black Feminist Critique of Antidiscrimination Doctrine, Feminist Theory and Antiracist Politics." *University of Chicago Legal Forum* 140: 139–67.

———. 1991. "Mapping the Margins: Intersectionality, Identity Politics, and Violence against Women of Color." *Stanford Law Review* 43 (6): 1241–99.

Ernst, Emily Rose. 2010. *The Price of Progressive Politics: The Welfare Rights Movement in the Era of Colorblind Racism.* New York: New York University Press.

Fairclough, Norman. 2003. *Analysing Discourse: Textual Analysis for Social Research.* London: Routledge.

Fogg-Davis, Hawley. G. 2006. "Theorizing Black Lesbians within Black Feminism: A Critique of Same-Race Street Harassment." *Politics & Gender* 2: 57–76.

Foucault, Michel. 1978. *The History of Sexuality: An Introduction.* Vol. 1. New York: Pantheon Books.

Garand, James C., and Micheal W Giles. 2003. "Journals in the Discipline: A Report on a New Survey of American Political Scientists." *PS: Political Science and Politics* 36 (2): 293–308.

Guidroz, Kathleen, and Michele Berger. 2009. "A Conversation with Founding Scholars of Intersectionality Kimberlé Crenshaw, Nira Yuval-Davis, And Michelle Fine." In *The Intersectional Approach: Transforming the Academy Through Race, Class & Gender*, edited by M. T. Berger and K. Guidroz, 61–78. Chapel Hill: University of North Carolina Press.

Hancock, Ange-Marie. 2004. *The Politics of Disgust: The Public Identity of the Welfare Queen.* New York: New York University Press.

Haraway, Donna. 1988. "Situated Knowledges: The Science Question in Feminism and the Privilege of Partial Perspective." *Feminist Studies* 14 (3): 575–97.

hooks, bell. 1991. "Narratives of Struggle." In *Critical Fictions: The Politics of Imaginative Writing*, edited by P. Mariani. Seattle, 53–61. Seattle: Bay Press.

Jordan-Zachery, Julia S. 2012. "Blogging at the Intersections: Black Women, Identity, Lesbianism." *Politics & Gender* 8 (3): 405–14.

Kramarae, Cheris. 1981. *Women and Men Speaking: Frameworks for Analysis.* Rowley, MA: Newbury House Publishers.

Kwan, Peter. 1997. "Intersections Of Race, Ethnicity, Class, Gender & Sexual Orientation: Jeffrey Dahmer and the Cosynthesis of Categories." *Hastings Law Journal* 48: 1257–92.

Logan, Shirley W. 1995. *With Pen and Voice: A Critical Anthology of Nineteenth-Century African American Women.* Carbondale: Southern Illinois University Press.

Munck, Gerardo, and Richard Snyder. 2007. "Who Publishes in Comparative Politics? Studying the World from the United States." *PS: Political Science and Politics* 40 (2): 339–46.

Nath, Nisha. 2009. "Rediscovering the Potential of Feminist Theories of Intersectionality." Paper presented at the Canadian Political Science Association Conference, Ottawa, Ontario.

Orbe, Mark. 2005. "Continuing the Legacy of Theorizing from the Margins: Conceptualizations of Co-Cultural Theory." *Women & Language* 28 (2): 65–66.

Risman, Barbara. J. 2004. "Gender as a Social Structure: Theory Wrestling with Activism." *Gender & Society* 18 (4): 429–50.

Sesko, Amanda K., and Monica Biernat. 2010. "Prototypes of Race and Gender: The Invisibility of Black Women." *Journal of Experimental Social Psychology* 46: 356–60.

Sheriff, Robin E. 2000. "Exposing Silence as Cultural Censorship: A Brazilian Case." *American Anthropologist, New Series* 102 (1): 114–32.

Spelman, Elizabeth. 1997. *Fruits of Sorrow.* Boston: Beacon Press.

Stockett, Kathryn. 2009. *The Help: A Novel.* New York: Penguin Group.

Section II

Black Feminist Policy Analysis

> In order for us as poor and oppressed people to become part of a society that is meaningful, the system under which we now exist has to be radically changed . . . It means facing a system that does not lend itself to your needs and devising means by which you change that system.
>
> —Ella Baker

In 2006, Tiffany Manuel made the case for an intersectionality-informed policy analysis approach. Indeed, she argues:

> Policy scholars have not ignored the context in which people make choices, but the analytical frameworks commonly used in public policy tend to view identity characteristics like race, class, and gender as linear, static, unconnected phenomena rather than multifaceted, fluid, and intersectional. (Manuel 2006, 175)

Although there have been substantive developments in what has been commonly referred to as critical policy studies (Fischer et al. 2015) and feminist policy analysis (Marshall 1997), intersectionality as a framework/tool for policy analysis remains underutilized. Consequently, the landscape of an intersectionality-based policy analysis is undertheorized. The chapters in this section offer a framework for engaging in such an analysis.

The various chapters, with their focus on public policies in the United States and Great Britain, explore policy boundaries and how Black women respond to such. Black feminist theorists and other scholars often explore boundaries—symbolic, cultural, political, and policy oriented—to show how they exclude perceived nonconforming Black women (see King 1973;

Hancock 2004; Fogg-Davis 2006; Brown 2008; Isoke 2013). Via their intersectional analyses of boundaries, the chapters show how identity, among other factors, determines the distribution of resources, and how such identities work to create and maintain institutionalized differences. More importantly, the chapters highlight how Black women respond to these boundaries and how we might engage in practices that are responsive to such boundaries. The following chapters explore boundaries related to health care (Douglas), prison reentry policies (Middlemass), and HIV/AIDS and US Black orphans (Jordan-Zachery). Across the chapters, the authors highlight the structures and processes of exclusion/inclusion via their exploration of (a) social and collective identity; (b) class structures; and (c) gender inequalities. These authors advance Manuel's call for intersectional policy analysis in their recognition of intersectional identities.

Notably, the authors analyze the functioning of what Michelle Berger (2004) refers to as "intersectional stigma" and how it functions to constrain public policy choices; these authors also highlight how Black women who are the targets of intersectional stigma respond and work within public policy. In the vein of Black feminists, Douglas, Middlemass, and Jordan-Zachery engage themes such as identity and mobilization and visibility and invisibility in advancing an intersectionality-based policy analysis that centers the lived realities of Black women, their children, and their communities.

Similarly to the chapters in the section "Black Feminists Doing Intersectionality Work," Douglas and Jordan-Zachery examine omissions, specifically in terms of policy and research gaps. Douglas explores how African-Caribbean women in Great Britain are either "invisible in the health inequalities research" or are treated in a limited manner, and as such there is a failure to fully explore and demonstrate the extent of inequalities. She argues that invisibility or limited treatment in research may result in exacerbating the health concerns of African-Caribbean women. Beyond this, Douglas's analysis shows that in spite of discriminatory practices, these women "found time and energy to campaign for better health policies and health service provision for black communities through a range of voluntary and community organizations." Douglas demonstrates how Black political women's political agency results in a press for advancement and in ways that not only support themselves, but also their communities.

Middlemass, like Douglas, also centers Black women's agency in response to public policies. Through her analysis of "discursive narratives and lived experiences," Middlemass shows how Black women's bodies are marked as invisible vis-à-vis public policy. She centers their voices to demonstrate how they are responding—creating space within the limited confines of the narratives of a "convict." According to Middlemass,

> Lived experiences of Black women felons have value in understanding prisoner reentry . . . The personal stories allow us to understand narratives found at the intersection of race, gender and felony status and how these multiple labels simultaneously must be negotiated; how policies and status intersect in the lives of Black women felons; and despite their limited options and restricted access to social capital and money as they negotiate society, Black women felons have important stories to share about who they are and how they experience the everyday.

Like Douglas and Jordan-Zachery, Middlemass shows the value of using Black women's lived realities in analyzing and developing public policy.

Jordan-Zachery also relies on narratives to show how policy perpetuates and maintains the invisibility of Black women. Exploring both policy narratives and, in some cases, their absence, Jordan-Zachery's research illustrates how Black AIDS orphans in the United States become invisible. According to Jordan-Zachery, HIV/AIDS policy narrative frames that center orphaned children tend to privilege the Global South. As a result, in the United States there are no similar narratives that brings out of the shadows children who are orphaned as a result of HIV/AIDS. She suggests that "to understand the neglect of these children and youths, it is necessary to situate the response within the intersectional social location of their mothers." As a result of their mothers' construction as "bad," there is no space in policy to address the needs of orphans—thereby absolving government from providing care. Consequently, private charities or family members are left to address them—many of whom do not have sufficient resources to care for these children.

These chapters move us beyond chronicling the impact of the negative construction of Black womanhood within a state-centered context by detailing the mechanisms that result in marginalization and invisibility. What they suggest is that the omission of Black women's lived realities and voices can be recognized and corrected via the use of an intersectional policy analysis. Furthermore, the chapters serve as a springboard for analyzing and explaining how Black, radical women advocate for freedom and justice outside the norms of a neoliberal policy-making process and the structures of the state, which seek to eschew public concern and responses to broad-scale social needs. In doing so, the authors present different approaches from which to analyze and propose policy positions and logics. Jordan-Zachery underscores that "it is important, as advocated by Black feminists, to understand how identity is used in policy making as it advances social justice in our institutional practices and everyday lives."

References

Berger, Michele T. 2004. *Workable Sisterhood: The Political Journey of Stigmatized Women with HIV/AIDS.* Princeton, NJ: Princeton University Press.

Brown, Ruth Nicole. 2008. *Black Girlhood Celebration: A Hip-Hop Feminist Pedagogy.* New York: Peter Lang.

Fischer, Frank, Douglas Torgerson, Anna Durnová, and Michael Orsini. 2015. *Handbook of Critical Policy Studies.* Cheltenham, UK: Edward Elgar Publishing Limited.

Fogg-Davis, Hawley. 2006. "Theorizing Black Lesbians within Black Feminism: A Critique of Same-Race Street Harassment. *Politics & Gender* 2: 57–76.

Hancock, Ange Marie. 2004. *The Politics of Disgust: The Public Identity of the Welfare Queen.* New York: New York University Press.

Isoke, Zenzele. 2013. *Urban Black Women and the Politics of Resistance.* New York: Palgrave Macmillan.

King, Mae. 1973. "The Politics of Sexual Stereotypes." *The Black Scholar* 4 (6–7): 12–23.

Manuel, Tiffany. 2006. "Envisioning the Possibilities for a Good Life: Exploring the Public Policy Implications of Intersectionality Theory." *Journal of Women, Politics & Policy* 28 (3–4): 173–203.

Marshall, Catherine, ed. 1997. *Feminist Critical Policy Analysis: A Perspective from Primary and Secondary Schooling.* London: The Falmer Press.

3

The Politics of Black Women's Health in the UK

Intersections of "Race," Class, and Gender in Policy, Practice, and Research

JENNY DOUGLAS
The Open University

Introduction

In presenting an overview of black Caribbean women's health and well-being in the United Kingdom, this chapter argues that the racialized, gendered, and classed experience of black women is detrimental to their health and that they face inequalities through discrimination in education, employment, housing, health care, and social care services, which has a major impact on their health and life course. There is now a large and growing body of data on racism and discrimination in employment. In research conducted by Karlsen and Nazroo (2002), 25 percent of ethnic minority people said that they were fearful of racial harassment, and 20 percent of ethnic minority people felt that they had been refused a job for racial reasons. Fear of racial harassment and fear of discrimination have an impact on black women's psychological and emotional well-being.

The aim of this chapter is not to essentialize the experiences of African-Caribbean women, as they are diverse in terms of geography, religion, ethnicity, class, sexuality, age, and so forth, and all of these axes of oppression intersect in different ways to undermine their health and well-being. However, despite these differences, an examination of the research on health inequalities demonstrates that African-Caribbean women often are invisible in the health inequalities research. The limited data demonstrate that there are persistent and enduring inequalities in the health of African-Caribbean women compared with other groups of women in Great Britain. Hence, there is a need to examine the specificity of the experiences of African-Caribbean women. Under the umbrella of Black and minority ethnic women in the UK, there is a wide range of ethnic groups that all warrant specific attention. This chapter focuses on African-Caribbean[1] women to make their experiences visible, while recognizing that there is also a need to focus on the health experiences of other groups that are invisible in the health research literature—for example, the wide range of African ethnic/national groups in the UK.

Angela Davis, speaking at a conference in 1987 about the health of Black women in the United States, stated:

> [B]ut we have become cognizant of the urgency of contextualizing Black women's health in relation to prevailing political conditions. While our health is undeniably assaulted by the natural forces beyond our control all too often the enemies of our physical and emotional well-being are social and political. That is why we must strive to understand the complex politics of Black women's health. (1994, 55)

Although this referred to the experience of African-American women, it is still, almost thirty years later, very relevant to African-Caribbean women in the United Kingdom. This chapter aims to demonstrate this by exploring the ways in which employment and other socioeconomic and sociopolitical factors impact their health.

Starting with a brief historical overview of postwar migration of Caribbean communities in the UK, I explore racial-gender health inequalities among Caribbean women in the UK. Drawing on Black feminism (Crenshaw 1991) and intersectionality and health literature (Hankivsky 2012), I examine how the health of black women is influenced by socioeconomic factors as well as their experiences of racism and discrimination at work, and the demands of full-time work and their family life. I use the example of the British National Health Service ("NHS"), as this was the organization where many Caribbean women found employment following postwar migration to the UK. Furthermore, I argue that despite the discrimination that black women experienced in the NHS and the toll on their health, they found time and energy to campaign for better health policies and health service provision for black communities through a range of voluntary and community organizations.

The African-Caribbean Population in the UK

The main period of postwar migration from the Caribbean to the UK took place between the 1950s and 1970s. In the 1950s, the British government actively recruited workers from English-speaking British colonies in the Caribbean to rebuild Britain following the Second World War (Goulbourne 1998, 2002). Initially it was men who migrated from the Caribbean, and they were later joined by partners and children. Some children were left with extended families and joined their parents much later. Some Caribbean women migrated independently. Although various immigration acts in the UK reduced migration from the Caribbean to the UK by the early 1970s (1971, Immigration Act), Caribbean communities in the UK were not static, and there was migration from the Caribbean to the UK as well as return migration of older Caribbean people from the UK to the Caribbean (Goulbourne 2002). There is also recent migration from the Caribbean to the UK, and Reynolds (2011) argues that migration from the Caribbean in the last twenty years has been ignored by policy makers, although 44,230 Caribbean nationals were granted settlement in Britain between 1997 and 2007.

African-Caribbean people initially settled in urban communities where there were employment opportunities, such as London, Birmingham, Liverpool, and Manchester. The patterns of migration were such that individuals from particular countries and particular areas within those countries settled in specific geographic locations. In Handsworth, Birmingham, the population originated from Jamaica, while a few miles away in Edgbaston, Birmingham, the population was mainly from St. Lucia (Abenaty 2003). Patterns of settlement were based on employment opportunities and on family and social contacts and networks. Some British organizations, such as London Transport and the British Transport Commission, recruited labor directly in the Caribbean. The National Health Service was established in 1948, and, with labor shortages in crucial areas such as nursing, this led to recruitment campaigns throughout the Caribbean for workers to staff this new public service. Some Caribbean women were recruited to the NHS as nurses, but more often as auxiliaries and cleaners. Black women were often discriminated against within the NHS and were directed toward training as state enrolled nurses (SENs) rather than as state registered nurses (SRNs) (Beishon et al. 1995; Olwig 2012). This restricted their career development and progression, as SRN training was required to become midwives, health visitors, and senior nurse managers. Other Caribbean migrants were recruited to work in factories and menial jobs that the White working-class population rejected.

Overall, the African-Caribbean population has remained fairly stable since the census in 2001 in terms of its size and overall percentage of the wider UK population. In 2012 the African-Caribbean population in the UK represented approximately 1.1 percent (594,825 people) of the total population of England and Wales (ONS 2012). However, if people who classify themselves as mixed race are included, the number is much greater. In the most recent census (ONS 2012), one-third of the mixed-race group (1.2 million) had an African-Caribbean parent and a white parent. However, while the Black Caribbean and Black British population was larger than the Black African population in the UK in the 2001 census, this situation changed dramatically by the 2011 census, where the Black African population became twice as large as the Black Caribbean and Black British populations because of increased migration from Africa in the preceding decade.

There is an extensive literature on the historical experiences of discrimination and racism faced by African-Caribbean communities settling in British towns (Cottle 1978; Bryan et al. 1985; Modood et al. 1997). Caribbean migrants were forced to live in the most deprived areas and in poor housing (Brown 1984) because of the racism they experienced in housing, employment, education, and access to health and social services. This led to the setting up and development of a number of political, religious, and welfare-based community organizations in areas where Caribbean communities settled (Reynolds, 2003), providing community support. Social disadvantage, social exclusion, racism, and discrimination have all been linked to inequalities in health in Caribbean communities (Nazroo, 1997). Despite the fact that some Caribbean people have been residents of the UK for fifty to sixty years, these patterns of social disadvantage still persist.

Although census data and data from the national household survey indicate improvements in the material and socioeconomic position of some African-Caribbean people over the last fifty years, African-Caribbean families are still more likely to live in deprived neighborhoods where levels of residential concentration are high (Graham 2007; Robinson and Reeve 2006).

Although deprivation and disadvantage have been associated with residential concentration in inner cities, some researchers have reported beneficial effects for health and well-being accompanying ethnic group density (Pickett and Wilkinson 2008). They argue that although black and ethnic minority residents have lower socioeconomic status, which is associated with poor health, living in neighborhoods with other people from the same ethnic group results in fewer incidents of interpersonal racism, structural racism, and institutional racism, which is more beneficial for physical health and mental health and well-being (Becares et al. 2011; 2012). Furthermore, Reynolds (2006b) argues that for African-Caribbeans, such residential communities provide social resources and benefits despite the high levels of deprivation. Reynolds's study reports on the use of "racially defined" neighborhood resources such as black churches, black community associations, and black supplementary schools as well as transnational family gatherings and reunions to build bonding social capital. Reynolds argues that Caribbean ethnic identity is constructed and shaped by migration and settlement as well as by experiences of racial and social exclusion. It has been widely acknowledged that social context, culture, and education influence the health behavior of individuals.

One of the main reasons that people migrated from the Caribbean in the 1950s and 1960s was in search of a better life for themselves and their children. In a study designed to investigate the effects of migration, social class background, educational qualifications, and intergenerational social mobility of ethnic groups in England and Wales, Platt (2005) reported that in Caribbean communities, parents experienced downward social mobility after migration to the UK. Although the children of Caribbean migrants did obtain some upward social mobility, this was not to the same extent as children of other minority ethnic groups (e.g., Indian migrants). This was explained by the increased risk of unemployment among Caribbeans, who, despite educational qualifications, were more likely to be in marginal positions in employment. In a study by Barn et al. (2006), large differences were seen between African-Caribbean male and female employment. While 72 percent of Black Caribbean women in this study were employed, Black Caribbean men were more than three times more likely than White men to be unemployed. While the percentage of single parents was higher in African-Caribbean communities, black Caribbean single parents were more likely to be employed when compared with other ethnic groups. Even so, Barn et al. (2006) reported that Caribbean mothers were twice as likely to report financial problems as white and African mothers.

In health and social policy, black families in the United States and the UK have been portrayed as pathological and deviant (Rainwater and Yancy 1967; Lawrence 1982). This has been based on representations of matriarchal family structures (Goulbourne 2003) and absent fathers. This view has been perpetuated throughout the Caribbean diaspora (Clarke 1999). Research studies on African-Caribbean family life have reported that a greater percentage of African-Caribbean mothers are single parents (Reynolds 2005); as such, families may be vulnerable to socioeconomic disadvantage, which typically accompanies being in a single-parent household. However, African-Caribbean families often live in areas of social deprivation and high residential concentration. In these areas, there are other African-Caribbean families and an extended kinship network including grandparents who provide ongoing support (Goulbourne 1999; Reynolds 2005; Ochieng 2011). In addition, recent research on African-Caribbean fathers (Reynolds 2009; Williams et al. 2012) concluded that while black fathers may not live with their children, they were actively involved in parenting and provided additional material and social capital to their children.

Racial-Gender Health Inequalities

Early health research on African-Caribbean communities has focused on men rather than women, exploring hypertension, diabetes, and severe mental illness, particularly schizophrenia. The emphasis on research on black men is reinforced by the stereotype of black men as "dangerous" and feckless. Thus, research on black women has been sparse. There are limited studies that have pointed to inequalities in health in relation to African-Caribbean women. One notable early publication was *The Heart of the Race: Black Women's Lives in Britain* (Bryan et al. 1985). This publication documented the impact of employment, unemployment, poor housing, and deprivation on the lives and health of black communities and concluded that while black women were expected to be cleaners, nurses, and auxiliaries in the NHS, the health needs of black communities were not acknowledged or indeed addressed.

Turning to the research literature on African-Caribbean women and health, I argue that African-Caribbean women are largely invisible in the health literature. Where research has been conducted on African-Caribbean women, this has mainly been around inherited blood disorders, nutritional disorders, and reproductive and sexual health (Douglas 1992). These areas of health research have been developed because of the ways in which African-Caribbean women have been represented in the health and social care literature—as feckless and fecund. African-Caribbean women's experiences of pregnancy and childbirth received marked attention in literature of the 1980s (Larbie 1985; Phoenix 1988). Research has continued to have a major focus on the maternal role of African-Caribbean women, with most researchers viewing them primarily through the problematic lens of the "lone mother" and/or "black super woman" (Reynolds 1997a). Reviewing this literature, Reynolds (1997b) challenged essentialist representations of African-Caribbean women and the stereotypes inherent in both constructions.

A review of epidemiological studies of UK-born African-Caribbeans (Arai and Harding 2004) demonstrated that the research emphasis did not change from the 1990s to the 2000s. The researchers identified research papers on UK-born African-Caribbean men and women and found that twenty focused on mental health, three on sexual health, thirteen on autoimmune responses and other conditions, two on diet and substance misuse, and five on children's health. This review demonstrates that there is an overemphasis of research on mental ill health as a pathology of African-Caribbean communities.

There are few research studies on African-Caribbean young people and health. Despite the positive aspects of living in inner-city neighborhoods, some young people experience the effects of territoriality, which has a major impact on the health and well-being of African-Caribbean young people and young women in particular. Territoriality is performed through gang violence where young people join gangs based on their residential postcode and where someone in a neighboring street may have a different postcode and then will be a member of another gang. Young people show their allegiance to a particular gang by wearing specific clothing such as bandanas. Recent years have witnessed a rise in gang violence in British cities. In Birmingham and other cities, there has been well-documented so-called postcode gang violence (Hallsworth and Young 2008). In a study by Kintrea et al. (2008) on young people and territoriality in British cities, the researchers identified that territoriality was part of everyday life in certain inner-city neighborhoods. They demonstrated that young people (mainly young men) gained respect by representing their neighborhood and that this was an important part of their identity. However, young African-Caribbean women are largely absent from health research. Research on the health and lifestyles of young people in relation to cigarette smoking and alcohol consumption has largely excluded black and ethnic minority young people and young African-Caribbean women in particular (Douglas 2014). Furthermore, while territoriality also has a major impact on the health and well-being of young black and ethnic minority young people, it, too, is understudied.

A study on gender, ethnicity, and self-reported health among African-Caribbean populations in London (Curtis and Lawson 2000) did not focus on young women. The lack of focus of research on health stands in sharp contrast to the priority that has been given to educational concerns and issues of identity related to young black women (Phoenix 1991; Mirza 1992, 1993; Phoenix 1997; Reynolds 2004; Wright 2005). Interestingly, the lack of visibility of health-related issues in black feminist research in the UK contrasts with the situation in the United States, where black feminist research has a central focus on health (Adams 1995; Smith 1995; Bayne-Smith 1996; Roberts 1999; Schulz and Mullings 2006).

Geronimus et al. (2010) hypothesized that black women aged forty-nine to fifty-five in the US Study of Women's Health Across the Nation were 7.5 years biological older than whites. They purported that the accelerated aging in black women was due to black women experiencing stressful situations caused by interpersonal and structural discrimination in housing, employment, and other areas of their lives. Similar findings were reported by Burton and Whitfield (2006) in their study of the stress experienced by primary caregivers being associated with premature death from cancer, strokes, or cardiovascular disease. While such research evidence is not available in the UK, the African Caribbean population in the UK is similar to the African American population in the United States in relation to demographic, social, health, and economic profiles (Nazroo et al. 2007).

In terms of African Caribbean populations in the UK, African Caribbean people—men and women—are more likely to have high blood pressure and twice as likely to die of stroke under the age of sixty-five. Even though both men and women are more likely to experience a greater prevalence of hypertension, it is African Caribbean men who are more likely to receive treatment, and thus there are gender differentials that exist in relation to women receiving diagnosis, care, and treatment for this condition. In a study conducted by Higginbottom (2006), she reported that some participants linked the onset of their hypertension to particularly stressful work experiences, demonstrating the link between health and work. In the African Caribbean community, there is a tradition of working in public services such as the NHS, social services, and other forms of previously state-run organizations like British Rail. The context of employment in these services is often characterized by low pay and shortage of staff. The stressful nature of working in such organizations can be compounded by racist attitudes of coworkers and line managers, which all impact health and well-being (Carter 2000). While this is likely to have some effects on mental health and well-being, research on mental health in black communities has been on severe mental health reflective of notions of "dangerous" black men.

African Caribbean people are between three and six times more likely to be diagnosed with schizophrenia despite research highlighting the misdiagnosis of Caribbean men with schizophrenia. On the other hand, research about the extent of mental illnesses such as anxiety and depression in African Caribbean women is scant. Research conducted in 2009 suggests that the stresses of everyday living and the experience of living in a racist society may take its toll on African Caribbean women and have an overwhelming effect on their psychological well-being. Edge (2013) argues that one of the issues relating to anxiety and depression is that often black women do not wish to talk about anxiety and depression and that they do not want to discuss their personal issues with white health professionals who do not understand the social and cultural context of their lives. The national service framework for mental health in 2001 (NSF 2001) stated that the rates of depression in African Caribbean women was believed to be about 60 percent higher than that in the white population, but black women were least likely to receive treatment. Although black women may experience anxiety and depression, they do not appear to be seeking or receiving treatment. This may also be the case in relation to breast cancer, where again black women do not seek early treatment.

There has been little research on British black women and breast cancer. Rebecca Bowen and colleagues (2008) reported that black women presented with breast cancer on average twenty-one years younger than white women and that tumors were more aggressive in younger women in the black population and that black women were more than twice as likely to die of their disease. There was a large degree of academic discussion and debate about this particular paper, where many researchers (Cichowska et al. 2008; Dindyal et al. 2008; Ingleby et al. 2008) questioned whether the findings of this study are correct or whether they are an anomaly because the African Caribbean sample was younger and also the heterogeneity of the black British category. The research is comparable to the research in African American women, where again African American women are presenting with breast cancer at a much earlier age and again the tumors in young women are much more aggressive (Newman 2005).

Linking Health Research to African-Caribbean Women and Work

The health and disease experienced by African-Caribbean women may be related to their work. Work is known to impact health in both positive and detrimental ways. In a groundbreaking black feminist text, Michelle Wallace wrote about the myth of the black superwoman (Wallace 1978) and other portrayals of the "strong black woman." Reynolds (1997) argues that this image of black women has largely been constructed by the British press in correlation with the negative image of black men as irresponsible and feckless, yet many black women believe that they are able to work outside the home, bring up a family, and be the primary caregiver, often studying, being part of their communities and supporting a range of people. The research on black Caribbean women demonstrates that working full time has risen between 1992 and 2003. In 2002, black Caribbean women had the highest levels of full-time working, constituting 45 percent of all women aged nineteen to fifty-nine (Lindley, Dale, and Dex 2004). Caribbean women are also more likely to be working full time when their children are young and more likely than women in other ethnic groups to be single parents. White women have a much higher level of part-time working, In 2000–2002, white women constituted 28 percent of women aged nineteen to fifty-nine who worked part time (Lindley, Dale, and Dex 2004). In addition to representing a greater percentage of women working full time, many other African Caribbean women are also employed in unskilled, part-time, insecure jobs, and these are the very jobs that are at risk in terms of the economic downturn. This is further compounded by the discrimination that African Caribbean women experience at work, which is documented in the next section of this chapter.

African Caribbean Women in the NHS

The next section of the chapter focuses on the NHS because there is clear evidence of racism and discrimination, and it is also one of the organizations that has employed large numbers of black women since postwar migration of Caribbean communities to the UK. However, much of the data on the NHS could be relevant to many other sectors, including the higher education sector and social care. There is now a vast literature on the early discrimination that black nurses faced in the NHS (Baxter 1988; Beishon et al. 1995; Culley et al. 2001). When people first migrated from the Caribbean, women were employed in certain sectors within the NHS and often were encouraged to become SENs rather than SRNs. This put many black nurses in a position where it was very difficult to progress into the managerial sector. Although that was fifty to sixty years ago, there are still very few black women in senior management positions in the NHS. The current reorganization of the NHS, particularly the abolition of primary care trusts and replacement with clinical commission groups, has provided the opportunity for many black senior managers to be displaced.

Research also demonstrates that black health visitors and community nurses were one-third as likely as white staff to receive performance-related pay, so even when black women achieved senior positions they were getting paid less in terms of performance-related pay. Performance has much to do with the perceptions of white line managers. In a survey that was conducted of 1,200 health care visitors and community nurses, only 5 percent of black staff were awarded performance-related pay raises compared with 14 percent of their white and Asian colleagues (Carvel 2000). Thus, there are clear data to show that black senior managers in the NHS are being paid less well than their white and Asian peers.

A survey in 2008 that was undertaken by the health service journal (Santry 2008) reported that not only were black and minority ethnic workers underrepresented in senior manager positions, but they also were disproportionately involved in disciplinaries, grievances, bullying and harassment cases, and capability reviews. Discrimination at work will impact negatively on the health and well-being of black women; however, this has been underresearched. In a qualitative, exploratory study with black and minority ethnic women, Mirza and Sheridan (2008) reported that there was a gap between equality policy and legislation in the NHS and health service practice and service delivery.

Black Caribbean Women as Health Activists and Activists for Change

The aim of this chapter is not to blame black women for their own ill health, but to argue that black women must take control of their health and in so doing recognize the factors that influence their health. Poverty and income differentials lead to inequalities in health, as do poor housing, particular types of employment, racism in society, and racism and discrimination at work. Therefore, activism is needed at all levels—at the individual level to do what they can to improve their own health and the health of their families, at the community level to campaign for better health services and provisions in local communities, and at the national level to change policy and practice.

Employed in the NHS as nurses, health visitors, midwives, and community health workers, the majority of Caribbean women experienced racism and discrimination, which impacted their ability to progress into senior managerial roles in the NHS (Beishon et al. 1995). Despite this, some black women achieved senior positions in the Department of Health, becoming instrumental in establishing initiatives such as the Mary Seacole Awards (to encourage scholarship and research among black nurses) and the Breakthrough Trust (enabling leadership development). However in their private lives, many African-Caribbean women made a substantial contribution to public health, challenging racism and discrimination in health services. While working and enabling change with the NHS, black nurses were active in their local communities and churches, establishing and contributing to a range of voluntary organizations, including the Nurses Association of Jamaica, UK; the Barbados Overseas Nurses Association; the Confederation of Black and Ethnic Nurses, Midwives and Health Visitors; the Sickle Cell and Thalassaemia Association of Counsellors; the Sickle Cell Society; and Cancer Black Care, to name a few. Throughout the latter half of the twentieth century, black women were involved in campaigning for change, setting up black women's groups to challenge inappropriate, racist, and ethnocentric practices within the NHS, such as Birmingham Black Health Workers, Brixton Black Women's Collective, and the Organization of African and Asian Descent (OWAAD). Much of this work remains undocumented; however, organizations such as the Black Cultural Archive in Brixton, London, are collecting relevant reports and oral testimonies.

Developing Intersectional Research on the Health and Well-Being of African Caribbean Women

Thus, recognizing the problem with terminology, African Caribbean women are also diverse in terms of class, disability, sexuality, religion, and so forth, and all of these different axes of oppression will intersect with each other and impact their health. Theories of intersectionality (Crenshaw 1989; Hankivsky 2012) propose that these factors do not interact with health as additional and additive but cut across health in different ways and may intersect differently at different stages of the life course. What is clear is that the impact of inequalities on health is complex and changing, as are the lifestyles and experiences of African Caribbean women in the UK. Intersectionality was originally developed as a legal theory (Crenshaw, 1989) and has subsequently been used as an organizing category for feminist inquiry in many different disciplinary fields in social sciences and humanities (Lewis 2013). Lewis (2013) argues that intersectionality can be conceived as a theory, concept, methodology, heuristic, or in fact all four. More recently, intersectionality has been applied as a theory to explore inequalities and inequity in health (Hankivsky and Christoffersen 2008; Hankivsky et al. 2010; Hankivsky 2012). European feminists have questioned whether the category "race" has any relevance outside the United States and Great Britain (Lewis 2009). Some twenty-five years after Kimberle Crenshaw coined the term "intersectionality" from a black feminist perspective, some feminist theorists are developing intersectionality theory, however, by excluding and erasing black women (Alexander-Floyd 2012; Jordan-Zachery 2013. This chapter argues that when exploring and researching the health of African Caribbean women, researchers should adopt an intersectional approach that places black women at its center. Biomedical and epidemiological research does not always take account of the social, cultural, and political context of the lives of black women.

Crenshaw proposes three types of intersectionality to explain the experiences of black women: structural intersectionality, political intersectionality, and representational intersectionality (Crenshaw 1991). All three types of intersectionality relate to the experiences of black women with regard to health and health research. There is a body of research on gender and health, which focuses mainly on white women, and on "race" and health, which focuses mainly on black and minority ethnic men; and there is a body of research on inequalities in health, which focuses on poverty and class and income inequality in white communities. Hence, in all of these bodies of research, black women and specifically African-Caribbean women are absent. Carbado (2013) refers to this as intersectional invisibility. There is a need for an intersectional approach that captures and analyzes the health data on African Caribbean women across the life course. Health research needs to consider the ways in which groups' behavior differs and how this might impact results. Health research that makes pronouncements on one ethnic group is not bound to be relevant to other groups. Health status and health behavior must be understood from the social and cultural context of people's lives. Health promotion and public health research approaches should develop public health interventions in a more sustained manner from a social-determinants-of-health perspective—that is, socioeconomic and environmental factors influence health (Whitehead and Dahlgren 2006) from an intersectional social-determinants-of-health perspective. An intersectional socio-determinants-of-health approach is distinguished from a mainstream social-determinants-of health-approach (Reid et al. 2012) by the recognition that social categories are not simply additive (e.g., gender *and* "race" *and* class), but where these categories intersect, something new is created and experienced (Hankivsky et al. 2010). These categories intersect and shape and influence each other and cannot be viewed as individual, independent entities or individual variables; hence, research methodologies must capture the interconnections between variables. McCall (2005) argues that although intersectionality has emerged as a major paradigm in research, there has been limited discussion of how an intersectional methodology might work. It can be argued that intersectionality makes claims about interrelationships between different categories, but intersectional researchers rarely show how these categories are interrelated. Intersectionality is a complex phenomenon, and it is very difficult to capture complexity in social research. However, this is necessary when exploring the health of African Caribbean women in the UK. Thus, there is a need to develop quantitative research that is able to identify patterns of illness with groups of black women and compare these patterns with women of other ethnic groups. In addition, there is a need to develop and undertake qualitative research that can explore the meanings, beliefs, and experiences of black women and relate this to the cultural, ethnic, economic, and demographic context of black women. Mullings (2000, 27) calls for black feminist research methods, which are "geared toward bringing the everyday of African-American women to the forefront." Mixed methods are therefore possibly better suited to intersectional research.

This chapter presents a framework to start to examine African Caribbean women's health. The health of African Caribbean women is inextricably linked to their social and economic position, their work experience, their home life, and their experiences of everyday racism. Research studies that have examined "race" and ethnicity and health are often gender blind, while research studies that examine gender and health tend to be "race" blind, so the health needs and experiences of African Caribbean women tend to be ignored.

More research is needed on the physical, psychological, and emotional well-being of African Caribbean women that pays attention to the intersections of race, gender, and class and other oppressions and to the complexity of black women's lives. Mullings and Schulz, American researchers writing in

2006, argued that health disparities based on race, racism, class, and gender sexism are actually matters of life and death. This chapter has documented how social, economic, and political factors of living in a racialized and racist society affect the lives, health, and well-being of black women and calls for political action to ensure that black women's voices are harnessed in determining social justice in policy, practice, and research on black women's health and proposes the adoption of an intersectional approach. Furthermore, the issue of black women's health needs to be raised higher on the political agenda in terms of policy, practice, and research.

Note

1. The term "African Caribbean" has been used inconsistently by researchers in the UK (Agyemang et al. 2005), some researchers using it to refer to people who are black and of Caribbean descent and others referring to people who are of African and of Caribbean descent. This presents difficulties when comparing research findings on "African Caribbean" communities in the UK. In this chapter, I use "African Caribbean" to refer to people of African heritage who were born in the Caribbean or whose parents or grandparents were born in the Caribbean. Even this terminology is fraught with difficulties, as many terms are used, such as black British and black Caribbean.

References

Abenaty, Francis K. 2003. "Family and Social Networks among St. Lucian Migrants in Britain: The Birmingham Connection." *Community, Work and Family* 6 (1): 17–27.

Adam, Diane L., ed. 1995. *Health Issues for Women of Colour: A Cultural Diversity Perspective.* Thousand Oaks: Sage Publications.

Agyemang, Charles, Raj Bhopal, and Marc Brujnzeels. 2005. "Negro, Black, Black African, African Caribbean, African American or What? Labelling African Origin Populations in the Health Arena in the 21st Century." *Journal of Epidemiology and Community Health* 59 (12): 1014–18.

Alexander-Floyd, Nikol G. 2012. "Disappearing Acts: Reclaiming Intersectionality in the Social Sciences in a Post-Black Feminist Era." *Feminist Formations* 24 (1): 1–25.

Arai, Lisa, and Seeromanie Harding. 2004. "A Review of the Epidemiological Literature on the Health of U.K.-born Black Caribbeans." *Critical Public Health* 14 (2): 81–116.

Barn, Ravinder, Carolina Ladino, and Brook Rogers. 2006. *Parenting in Multi-Racial Britain.* York: Joseph Rowntree Foundation.

Baxter, Carol. 1988. *The Black Nurse: An Endangered Species: A Case for Equal Opportunities in Nursing.* Cambridge: Training in Health and Race.

Bayne-Smith, Marcia, ed. 1996. *Race, Gender and Health.* Thousand Oaks: Sage Publications.

Becares, Laia, James Nazroo, and Mai Stafford. 2011. "The Ethnic Density Effect on Alcohol Use among Ethnic Minority People in the U.K." *Journal of Epidemiology and Community Health* 65 (1): 20–25.

Becares, Laia, James Nazroo, Christo Albor, Tarani Chandola, and Mai Stafford. 2012. "Examining the Differential Association between Self-Rated Health and Area Deprivation among White British and Ethnic Minority People in England." *Social Science and Medicine* 74 (4): 616–24.

Beishon, Sharon, Satnam Virdee, and Ann Hagell. 1995. *Nursing in a Multi-Ethnic NHS.* London: Policy Studies Institute.

Brown, Colin. 1984. *Black and White Britain: The Third PSI Survey.* London: Policy Studies Institute.

Bryan, Beverley, Stella Dadzie, and Suzanne Scafe. 1985. *The Heart of the Race: Black Women's Lives in Britain.* London: Virago.

Burton, Linda, M., and Keith E. Whitfield. 2006. "Health, Aging, and America's Poor: Ethnographic Insights on Family Co-Morbidity and Cumulative Disadvantage." In *Aging, Globalization, and Inequality: The New Critical Gerontology,* edited by Jan Baars, 215–30. Amityville: Baywood Publishers.

Carvel, John. 2000. "NHS Pay Awards 'Riddled with Racism.'" *The Guardian,* 21 June.

Carter, John. 2000. "New Public Management and Equal Opportunities in the NHS." *Critical Social Policy* 20 (1): 61–83.

Cichowska, A. C., M. Fischbacher, A. Brock, C. Griffiths, R. Bhopal, and S. H. Wild. 2008. Letter to the editor: "Early Onset of Breast Cancer in British Black Women." *British Journal of Cancer* 98 (12): 2011.

Clarke, Edith. 1999. *My Mother Who Fathered Me: A Study of the Families in Three Selected Communities of Jamaica.* Kingston: University of the West Indies Press.

Carbado, Devon. 2013. "Colorblind Intersectionality." *Signs* 38 (4): 811–45.

Cottle, Tom. J. 1978. *Black Testimony: Voices of Britain's West Indians.* London: Wildwood House Ltd.

Crenshaw, Kimberle Williams. 1989. "Demarginalizing the Intersection of Race and Sex: A Black Feminist Critique of Antidiscrimination Doctrine, Feminist Theory and Antiracist Politics." *University of Chicago Legal Forum* 140: 138–67.

———. 1991. "Mapping the Margins: Intersectionality, Identity Politics, and Violence against Women of Color." *Stanford Law Review* 43 (6): 1241–99.

Culley Lorraine, Simon Dyson, Silvia Ham-Ying Silvia, and Wendy Young. 2001. "Caribbean Nurses and Racism in the National Health Service." *Ethnicity and Nursing Practice*, edited by Lorraine Culley and Simon Dyson, 231–51. London: Palgrave.

Curtis, Sarah, and Kim Lawson. 2000. "Gender, Ethnicity and Self-Reported Health: The Case of African-Caribbean Populations in London." *Social Society and Medicine* 50 (3): 365–85.

Davis, Angela. 1994. "Sick and Tired of Being Sick and Tired: The Politics of Black Women's Health." In *The Black Women's Health Book: Speaking for Ourselves*, edited by E. White, 18–26. Seattle: Seal Press.

Dindyal, S., M. J. Ramdass, and V. Naraynsingh. 2008. "Reply: Early Onset Breast Cancer in Black British Women: A Letter to the Editor of *British Journal of Cancer* Regarding Early Onset of Breast Cancer in a Group of British Black Women." *British Journal of Cancer* 98 (8): 1483–84.

Douglas, Jenny. 1992. "Black Women's Health Matters." In *Women's Health Matters*, edited by H. Roberts, 33–46. London: Routledge.

Douglas, Jenny, and Naomi Watson. 2013. "Editorial: Resistance, Resilience and Renewal. The Health and Well-Being of Black Women in the Atlantic Diaspora—Developing an Intersectional Approach." *Critical Public Health* 23 (1): 1–5.

Douglas, Jenny. 2014. *African-Caribbean Young Women in the UK and Cigarette Smoking*. Doctoral thesis, University of York.

Edge, Dawn. 2013. "'Why Are You Cast Down, O My Soul?' Exploring Intersections of Ethnicity, Gender, Depression, Spirituality and Implications for Black British Caribbean Women's Mental Health." *Critical Public Health* 23 (1): 39–48.

Fog Olwig, Karen. 2012. *Migrating for an Education: Family, Gender and Social Mobility among Caribbean Nurses in Britain*. Paper presented at San Diego University, November.

Geronimus, Arline T., Margaret T. Hicken, Jay A. Pearson, Sarah J. Seashols, Kelly L. Brown, and Tracey Dawson Cruz. 2010. "Do US Black Women Experience Stress-Related Accelerated Biological Aging?" *Human Nature* 21 (1): 19–38.

Goulbourne, Harry. 1998. *Race Relations in Britain since 1945*. Basingstoke: MacMillan.

———. 1999. "The Transnational Character of Caribbean Kinship in Britain." In *Changing Britain: Families and Households in the 1990s*, edited by S. McRae, 176–98. Oxford: Oxford University Press.

———. 2002. *Caribbean Transnational Experience*. London: Pluto Press.

Graham, Hilary. 2007. *Unequal Lives: Health and Socioeconomic Inequalities*. Maidenhead: Open University Press.

Hallsworth, Simon, and Young, Tara. 2008. "Gang Talk and Gang Talkers: A Critique." *Crime, Media, Culture* 4 (2): 175–95.

Hankivsky, Olena. 2012. "Women's Health, Men's Health, and Gender and Health: Implications of Intersectionality." *Social Science and Medicine* 74: 1712–20.

Hankivsky, Olena, and Ashlee Christoffersen. 2008. "Intersectionality and the Determinants of Health: A Canadian Perspective." *Critical Public Health* 18 (3): 271–83.

Hankivsky, Olena, Collen Reid, Renee Cormier, Colleen Varcoe, Natalie Clark, Cecelia Benoit, and Shari Brotman. 2010. "Exploring the Promises of Intersectionality for Advancing Women's Health Research." *International Journal for Equity in Health* 9: 5.

Ingleby, J. D. 2008. Letter to the Editor: "Early Onset of Breast Cancer in Black British Women: How Reliable Are the Findings?" *British Journal of Cancer* 99: 986–87.

Jordan-Zachery, Julia. 2013. "Now You See Me, Now You Don't: My Political Fight against the Invisibility/Erasure of Black Women in Intersectional Research." *Politics, Groups and Identities* 1 (1): 101–9.

Larbie, Jo. 1985. *Black Women and Maternity Services. A Survey of 30 Young Afro-Caribbean Women's Experiences and Perceptions of Pregnancy and Childbirth.* London: Training in Health and Race/Health Education Council/National Extension College.

Lindley Joanne, Angela Dale, and Shirley Dex. 2004. "Ethnic Differences in Women's Demographic, Family Characteristics and Economic Activity Profiles 1992 to 2002." *Labour Market Trends*, April.

McCall, Leslie. 2005. "The Complexity of Intersectionality." *Signs: Journal of Women in Culture and Society* 30 (3): 1771–800.

———. 1993. "The Social Construction of Black Womanhood in British Educational Research: Towards a New Understanding." In *Feminism and Social Justice in Education: International Perspectives*, edited by M. Arnot and K. Weiler, 32–57. London: Falmer Press.

Mirza, Heidi, and Ann-Marie Sheridan. 2003. *Multiple Identity and Access to Health: The Experience of Black and Minority Ethnic Women.* Manchester: Equal Opportunities Commission.

Modood, Tariq, and Richard Berthoud. 1997. *Ethnic Minorities in Britain: Diversity and Disadvantage.* London: Policy Studies Institute.

Mullings, Leith. 2000. "African-American Women Making Themselves: Notes on the Role of Black Feminist Research." *Souls: A Critical Journal of Black Politics, Culture, and Society* 2 (4): 18–29.

National Service Framework for Mental Health. 2001. National Institute for Clinical Excellence, Scope of Guidelines on Depression, Version 3.

Nazroo, James Y. 1997. *The Health of Britain's Ethnic Minorities: Findings from a National Survey.* London: Policy Studies Institute.

Nazroo, James Y., J. Jackson, S. Karlsen, and M. Torres. 2007. "The Black Diaspora and Health Inequalities in the U.S. and England: Does Where You Go and How You Get There Make a Difference?" *Sociology of Health and Illness* 29 (6): 811–30.

Newman, Lisa, A. 2005. "Breast Cancer in African-American Women." *The Oncologist* 10: 1–14.

Ochieng, Bertha. 2011. "The Effect of Kin, Social Network and Neighbourhood Support on Individual Well-Being." *Health and Social Care in the Community* 19: 429–37.

Office of National Statistics (ONS) (2012). 2012 Census. www.ons.gov.uk.

Phoenix, Ann. 1988. "Narrow Definitions of Culture: The Case of Early Motherhood." In *Enterprising Women*, edited by S. Westwood and P. Bachu. London: Routledge and Kegan Paul.

———. 1991. *Young Mothers*. Cambridge: Polity Press.

———. 1997. "Youth and Gender: New Issues, New Agenda." *Young* 9 (5): 2–19.

Platt, Lucinda. 2005. *Migration and Social Mobility. The Life Chances of Britain's Minority Ethnic Communities*. Bristol: The Policy Press.

Rainwater, Lee, and William L. Yancy. 1967. *The Moynihan Report and the Politics of Controversy*. Cambridge: Massachusetts Institute of Technology Press.

Reynolds, Tracey. 1997a. "Black Women and Social-Class Identity." In *Cultural Studies and the Working Class: Subject to Change*, edited by S. R. Munt, 82–96. London: Cassell.

———. 1997b. "Class Matters, 'Race' Matters, Gender Matters." In *Class Matters: "Working Class" Women's Perspectives on Social Class*, edited by P. Mahony and C. Zmroczek, 8–17. London: Taylor and Francis.

———. 1997c. "(Mis)representing the Black (Super) Woman." In *Black British Feminism: A Reader*, edited by Heidi Mirza. London: Routledge.

———. 2003. "Black to the Community." *Community, Work and Family* 6 (1): 29–45.

———. 2004. *Caribbean Families, Social Capital and Young People's Diasporic Identities*. Families and Social Capital ESRC Research Group Working Paper No. 11, London South Bank University.

———. 2005. *Caribbean Mothering: Identity and Childrearing in the U.K.* London: Tufnell Press.

———. 2006. "Family and Community Networks in the (Re)Making of Ethnic Identity of Caribbean Young People in Britain." *Journal of Community, Work and Family* 9 (3): 273–90.

———. 2009. "Exploring the Absent/Present Dilemma: Black Fathers, Family Relationships, and Social Capital in Britain." *The Annals of the American Academy of Political and Social Science* 624: 12–28.

———. 2011. " 'Birds of a Feather Stick Together'? Negotiating Community, Family and Intimate Relationships between 'Established' and 'Newcomer' Caribbean Migrants in Britain." *Journal of Community Work and Family* 6 (4): 537–53.

Robinson, David, and Kesia Reeve. 2006. *Neighborhood Experiences of New Immigration*. Sheffield: Centre for Regional Economic and Social Research, Sheffield Hallam University.

Shultz, Amy, and Leith Mullings. 2006. *Gender, Race, Class & Health: Intersectional Approaches.* San Francisco: Jossey-Bass.

Smith, Susan. 1995. *Sick and Tired of Being Sick and Tired: Black Women's Health Activism in America 1890–1950.* Philadelphia: University of Pennsylvania Press.

Wallace, Michele. 1978. *Black Macho and the Myth of the Superwoman.* New York: The Dial Press.

Williams, Robert, Alistair Hewison, Chris Wagstaff, and Duncan Randall. 2012. "'Walk with Your Head High': African and African-Caribbean Fatherhood, Children's Mental Well-Being and Social Capital." *Ethnicity and Health* 17 (1–2): 89–103.

Wright, Cecile. 2005. "Black Femininities Go to School: How Young Black Females Navigate Race and Gender." In *Problem Girls: Working with Troubled and Troublesome,* edited by G. Lloyd, 100–10. London: Falmer/Routledge.

4

Hiding in Plain Sight

Black Women Felons Reentering Society

KEESHA M. MIDDLEMASS
Howard University

Introduction

Savannah was born into one family, abandoned to the state, and adopted by another. She was raped several times by her adoptive "father," and his felonious behavior was never punished, even though it resulted in Savannah becoming pregnant before the age of twelve and in grade six. When her pregnancy became known, her adoptive parents blamed her for being a problem, as if she, on her own, willingly got pregnant. In her own words, Savannah describes her early life, with two official but different birthdates, two sets of legal names, and several authorized parents.

> My adopted father sexually abused me; when I was 12 years, 1 month and 9 days old I had twins, my first two [children] in 1990. I was in 6th grade, *6th grade* [emphasis original] and was told by my adopted mom, "we don't have none of that here"—Sheesh, as if I got pregnant by myself. They still blamed me, making it seem like it was all my fault: Who does that? To a kid? So, what did they do? They kicked me out and sent me to a group home [for teenagers]. That can eat you inside, you know, they put me out, at 12, so I grew up in predominantly

> white group homes. Lived in a group home from like 12 to 18, and I went to high school, not learning anything because I was attending different schools, got moved and stuff; no one tells me nothing, and no one is looking out for me, so I did what I could. I got a high school diploma, and wanted to go to college, you know, get out from under my past, make [my] life mine, but needed my transcripts and all those other papers [and documents] college make you have to enroll, you know, and that's when I found out the state had two files on me, with different information, one [file] was pre-adoption and the second [file] was post-adoption. My name and birth dates are different—who fucks up on someone's birthdate, the year? So, I'm 34 [at time of interview] but really, my real age beats the hell out of me. Things like that can get changed when you are adopted. One year doesn't make much difference. Oh, and the state file say I didn't have a diploma from the school I supposedly graduated from because the file had me in the dropped out category. Once I got that figured out, I now have two high school diplomas, one from the high school and one from the group home. That was all by 18; how I was raised has a big impact on me, my life, severely damaged me, because here I am trying to get my life back, go to college, but I got kicked out of the system at 18, well, you know, the state kicks you out when you age out [and reach the age of majority, with all of the attendant rights and responsibilities of adulthood], but I wasn't prepared for life. I mean, I was 18, that was a big year of shit and more shit, nothing good, wasn't prepared for life, was living on the streets, couldn't get my records, getting high and selling [drugs]. That's what I knew; I went from being a ward of the state [foster kid] to being a ward of the state [prison].[1]

In this chapter, I examine the reentry experiences of Black women convicted of a felony to explore the following research question: What happens to Black women as they attempt to reenter society after their bodies are entangled within the tentacles of the criminal justice system, they are marked as felon, and socially constructed as "other"? A felony conviction is a public and political proclamation, and, according to Foucault (1977), it has historical residue with long-reaching ramifications.

Upon returning to the community, Black women's social interactions are contextualized by this long history, the politics of being "tough on crime," and their status as felon. As a result, individuals labeled felon experience poverty and homelessness and are legally denied access to social benefits and public services.

Beginning with a discussion about the racialized gender disparities in the criminal justice system, I explore the discursive narratives and lived experiences of Black women felons and how each identity creates a uniquely criminalized, racialized, and gendered group that occupies a distinct social, political, and economic position. Using an intersectional framework, the goal is to comprehend how the dynamics of blackness, gender, and criminal status uniquely impact Black women by illustrating how race, gender, and felony status mediate relationships Black women have with the community, their families, and themselves. Intersectionality can be a theory, method of analysis, or concept applied to multiple marginalizing and intersecting identities (Berger 2004), or it can be a combination of these (see Potter 2013; Crenshaw 1989, 1991; Davis 1981; Tomlinson 2013), and this research contributes to two distinct bodies of research, intersectional criminology, and prisoner reentry.

Racialized Gender Disparities in the Criminal Justice System

Racial disparities in the criminal justice system are well documented and persist among all racial minorities; in a single generation, police tactics and policies transformed the prison population from majority White to majority minority (see Langan 1991; Western 2009), and Black men and women are disproportionately incarcerated and overrepresented in the criminal justice system (Alexander 2010). This was not an accident; rather, the historical and social context of race, the construction of blackness as criminal outside normative society (Bobo and Thompson 2010; see Schneider and Ingram 1993), and the "War on Drugs" form a collective effort to incarcerate Black bodies (King 2008; Clear 2009; Mallach 2010; Cardoso, Gaviria, and Zedillo 2009). Such ideas about blackness have been used to justify the militarization of police forces to be armed for "war" against Americans (Balko 2013; Estrada 2004).

In principle, punishment and prisoner reentry are gender and race neutral, as the laws are designed to apply equally to all people regardless of the crime, race, or ethnicity of the victim, and who is convicted, sentenced, and incarcerated. In practice, however, race neutrality does not exist; race has a long and problematic history in the United States (see Kennedy 1997), which is reflected in the policies and politics of crime. The original "tough on crime" politicians were in nineteenth-century South Carolina; they used the politics of race to keep many Blacks in servitude, enslaved, or jailed (Grossberg and Tomlins 2008; Butterfield 1996). "Tough on crime" policies in the 1980s started a new political effort to police, control, and punish racial minorities (Chin 2002), which relied heavily on long terms of incapacitation in state and federal prisons (Jacobson 2005). Certain crimes were, and continue to be, attached to race, including the crime of "being black" (Eberhardt et al. 2004) and "driving while black" (Harris 1999). Over the last thirty years, draconian drug laws have sent thousands of Black nonviolent drug offenders to prison for staggering amounts of time (see Marable, Steinberg, and Middlemass 2007).

The systematic arrangement of policies and racial animosity captured a substantially large number of women; the incarceration rate of women increased by 31 percent from 2000 to 2012 (Minton 2013). Within the female prison population, Black women comprise 22 percent of all women incarcerated in state and federal prisons, while White women represent 49 percent; however, the disparity is found in the imprisonment rate of Black women (113 per 100,000), which is twice the rate of White women (51 per 100,000) (Carson 2014). The same racial disparities appear when prisoners are released from the Department of Corrections (DOC) to return to society: approximately 95 percent of all prison inmates are released (Travis 2005), and various national estimates indicate that between 650,000 and 750,000 adults are released during any given year (US Justice Department 2013; Draine and Herman 2007; West and Sabol 2011; Rosenmerkel, Durose and Farole 2009; Carson 2014). Upon their return to society, each former prisoner is denied public benefits because of a felony conviction imposed by the criminal justice system. Of these thousands who return, Black women make up a large subgroup and are often ignored when studying prisoner reentry; yet when Black women reenter society, they face different challenges, and these differences are exacerbated because of race, gender, and felon status.

Although prisoner reentry is treated as a separate phenomenon from the criminal justice system, the two systems are intricately linked (Pinard 2006). There are a host of post-sentence penalties attached to a felony, and these secret sentences (Chin and Holmes 2002) and civil disabilities (Cohen and Rivkin 1971) are dispersed throughout statutory codes and regulations (Damaska 1968), and are not tied to a particular offense; rather, the legal provisions are tied to a felony conviction and are collectively known as the collateral consequences of a felony conviction (Chin 2002; Mauer and Chesney-Lind 2002; Travis 2005). Pinard (2006) argues that such post-sentence punishments are central to criminal justice policy, even if they are not incorporated into the "official" criminal sentence and punishment. Black women felons encounter these secret sentences and struggle to reenter because of their unique statuses are interdependent and create politicized, stigmatized, and marginalized women (Berger 2004).

In many urban communities, the convergence of race, politics, policies, and the criminal justice system has reached crisis levels, and the result is that a significant number of those released from prison return to a few concentrated neighborhoods, which plays an integral role in characterizing an entire community as criminal. Many such neighborhoods are facing high levels of social and economic disadvantage and institutional abandonment (Lynch and Sabol 2001; Mallach 2010; Wilson 1987), and these are the types of communities to which Black women felons tend to return, where society's hostility becomes a self-sustaining petite penal institution (Middlemass 2007, 2017; Russell-Brown 2004; Russell and Milovanovic 2001). Returning to communities that offer only despair to experience historical notions of infamy and civil death (Damaska 1968; Ewald 2002) while living with the public's hostility that is "integrated into the economy of the penalty," a felony conviction becomes the defining characteristic of how an individual is viewed within society (Foucault 1977, 108). Those marked as felon are no longer considered a full citizen and are conceptualized into limited spaces of existence when they are denied the assistance they need to leave the margins of society and live a productive life.

The Intersectional Dynamics of Race, Gender, and Criminal Status

The process of reentering society after serving time in prison negatively impacts women because of the unique barriers that women face, and because reentry programs tend to be male centered and fail to consider women's needs or integrate their perspectives into reentry programs (see Koski and Bantley 2013).

Criminology and the study of crime tend to be dominated by quantitative methods that do not adequately capture reality. The prevailing methodological approaches make many women invisible in reentry discourse, and Black women are further marginalized because criminal justice scholars tend to focus on race, gender, and criminal involvement as distinct characteristics and separate issues when in fact they are not autonomous. As a result, Black women felons' voices often go unheard and are ignored by the wider scholarly community (see Potter 2013). Black feminist scholars have challenged the dominant approaches, and their contributions to the field are growing in importance as they tackle important issues found at the intersection of race, gender, and status (see Bell 2012; Berger 2004; Collins 1998; Crenshaw 1989; Klein and Kress 1976; Potter 2013). Willingham (2011) argues that incarcerated Black women are triply marginalized as Black, female, and felon; Crenshaw (1989) shows how Black women experience simultaneous double-discrimination in the courts; Potter (2013) and Burgess-Proctor (2006) argue that feminist criminology necessitates embracing intersectionality; and through narratives, Richie (2001) demonstrates the challenges Black women face when they return home after being incarcerated. Such scholars' contributions have broad social, political, and functional implications for Black women felons reentering society. To capture Black women's experiences reentering society and to contribute to this rich and diverse scholarship, I take a qualitative approach using personal narratives to provide a unique gendered, racialized, and stigmatized perspective of a felony conviction.

Overcoming a felony conviction is difficult because it is constructed at multiple levels within society and is institutionalized across government procedures and programs. A felony conviction operates as an institution, with many constraining qualities and rules that are contradictory, as it (1) characterizes a specific group within the larger community; (2) endures over time and space; (3) has distinct social practices; (4) constrains the behavior of individuals; (5) imposes additional rules; (6) constitutes and reconstitutes embodied agents; (7) becomes internalized as an identity; (8) involves a particular ideology that becomes legitimate; (9) is rife with conflict; (10) changes with the passage of new laws; (11) is organized around a power structure; and (12) is mutually constituted at different and multiple levels of analysis (adopted from Martin 2004; see Lorber 1994; Risman 2004). Black women cannot escape their gender and race, and a felony is inescapable, too. Combined, the stigmatizing labels embody concepts that shape social interactions (Martin 2004; Middlemass 2017). A felony's domination over

Black women highlights the structural and institutional roots of oppression in which bodies perform in public spaces, and the labels attached to one's body signify a form of social construction (Crenshaw 1991; Brewer 1993; Berger 2004). The distinct characteristics are the result of political powers that create inequality around the issue of race, gender, and criminal status, which operate to construct marginal citizens, have profound consequences that make individuals invisible, and allow for the normalization of disparaging treatment (Middlemass 2017).

The multiplicative effects of each value-laden identity of being a Black woman felon is a lived experience, and structural barriers of inequality and forms of oppression are politicized within the larger debate about the "War on Drugs," the war on poverty, and the war against Black America (King 2008; Clear 2009). Many Black women struggle to reenter society, as a felony follows them home from prison, wields power over their relationships, cuts them off from public benefits, and shapes their decision making. Therefore, studying all three simultaneously offers critical insights in understanding how a gendered and racial framework is applicable to a felony conviction. To examine their lives, struggles, and how their felony conviction functions as an invisible stigma that becomes public when one seeks a job, applies for public benefits, or fills out an application for housing, I did extensive fieldwork in Newark, New Jersey (Middlemass 2017).

Based on ethnographic data and drawing on sociological, gender, and political insights about prisoner reentry, I employ Berger's (2004) intersectional stigma framework to situate the lives of Black women felons as they reconstitute their lives in the community. Black women felons' challenges reflect the broader concept of stigma and marginalization discussed by Berger (2004), and to understand this intersection requires direct contact with women in the community to listen to their stories and to witness their activities and aesthetics embedded in everyday practices. I spent twenty-nine months in the field, and this long-term immersion at a nonprofit organization in downtown Newark allowed me to collect first-person narratives via interviews and focus groups and by being present for long periods of time each week (Middlemass 2017). The direct and long-term engagement with participants produced a thick, detailed account of the lived experiences of Black women reentering society in the urban, downtrodden city of Newark, New Jersey (see Middlemass 2017; Penner and McClement 2008; Kleima 2004). To discover codes of meaning and cultural practices in response to the social and political environment in which Black women felons were situated (see Desmond 2014; Caughey 1982), I choose to use a phenomenological approach to analyze the data I collected.

A phenomenological approach is designed to describe a particular event or series of events as a lived experience and is a research tool that considers human subjectivity as valid while probing the data to discover the essential meaning of the phenomena under consideration (see Speziale and Carpenter 2007). In this instance, I rely on interpretive phenomenology to analyze textual data; I read and reread the narratives to identify meaning and issues of identity and applied my broader knowledge about prisoner reentry to uncover hidden gendered meanings about Black women felons reentering society (Middlemass 2017, 2015, 2014; Boxer et al. 2011, 2009). Based on the context of participants' language, and by engaging with participants personally, the analysis was designed to uncover the culture of reentry and embodied practices (Gupta and Ferguson 1997) alongside how individuals' position, agency, power, and knowledge were mediated by others (Biehl 2010). The analytical approach permitted me to recognize in the personal narratives and lived experiences of Black women individual agency, resilience, courage, and the profound spirit of each Black woman reentering society as a convicted felon.

The Discursive Narratives of Black Women Felons Reentering Society

Personal narratives of ten Black women felons returning to the community tell a holistic story that includes human emotions, struggles, and choices, which exposes how their felony conviction shapes their reentry options. More importantly, their narratives describe how being tangled in the criminal justice system, if the women served time in state or federal prison or were given felony parole, puts a great deal of strain on their health, relationships, and ability to care for their minor children. For Black women felons, from the moment they leave the courthouse or prison and return to the community, most struggle to move beyond their felony status. The narratives of the ten women are shared to illustrate how Black women felons' lives are complicated because of domestic violence, homelessness, unemployment, substance abuse, poverty, and at times hopelessness. Although all of the participants do not share each struggle and have different experiences because of their ages, which ranged from twenty-one to fifty, with a mean age of thirty-five and a half years, their respective bodies are now the focal point of punishing policies because of their intersectional stigma. Pseudonyms are used to protect participants' identity.

Table 4.1. Participants

Pseudonym	Age at time of Interview	Children	Marital Status and Caregiving Role to Children	Criminal Offense	Time Sentenced/ Time Served
Savannah	34	6	Legally separated from her husband, living in her own studio apartment. Her 6 children are wards of the state (foster care), adopted, or with their biological father.	First degree robbery Co-conspirator Conspiracy	7 years/5 years and 10 months
Eve	31	2	Never married, living with her children's father. Primary caregiver of her 2 children.	Drug distribution on school property Unlawful possession of a handgun	2 years, 6 months
Alyssa	46	3	Legally separated from her husband, living in a homeless shelter. Her 3 children are adults.	Drug possession	3 years/Out on state felony probation
Delores	50	2	Never married, has temporary housing. Her 2 children are adults.	Drug possession	55 months
Mandy	32	1	Never married, living with extended family. Primary caregiver of her son.	Drug distribution	3 years/1 year, 8 months

continued on next page

Table 4.1. (Continued)

Pseudonym	Age at time of Interview	Children	Marital Status and Caregiving Role to Children	Criminal Offense	Time Sentenced/ Time Served
Janaye	29	1	Never married, living with her boyfriend and father of her children. Primary care giver of her child.	Assault	1 year /1 year
Kimberly	42	3	Divorced, living in homeless shelter. Her 3 children live with their biological father.	Drug possession Credit card fraud Theft	5 years/2 years, 11 months
Nadina	47	0	Never married, living in a homeless shelter.	Robbery Drug distribution	4 years/3 years, 4 months
Ginger	23	1	Never married, living with friends. The child's paternal grandmother has full custody.	Assault Drug possession	8 months
Diamond	21	1	Never married, living with her boyfriend. Primary caregiver, and pregnant with her second child.	Assault	3 years felony parole (spent less than 1 week in jail)

When one knows she is breaking the law, it is an act with purpose. For Eve, she knew she was breaking the law, but knowing her actions were wrong did not stop her; she needed money to house, feed, and clothe her children. Dealing drugs is one possibility of securing financial resources, but when one is caught by the police, there are long-term ramifications. Eve was convicted of drug distribution on school property and unlawful possession of a handgun; after serving time and staying crime free for more than ten years, she is frustrated, particularly with the limited housing options for poor people convicted of a felony.

Eve's perspective on housing was summed up in two short phrases: "They must want us to be homeless. Makes no sense."[2] "They" referred to generic government officials and policies who blocked her from obtaining housing. She attempted many times to obtain Section 8 and knew she was eligible because the law states that once someone is "rehabilitated" they can obtain public housing. Despite not being rearrested since her conviction, which is now more than a decade old, the law did not apply to Eve: "I get denied. I mean they say come back [housing managers], but, look, I know, they know, we all know, it ain't goin' change. I can't get Section 8." Even though Eve and her children are eligible based on the text of law, she cannot overcome the reality of how laws are applied to the bodies of felons; there are no formal rules or state laws that prove one is rehabilitated after a felony conviction. As a result, Eve lives with her kids' father, and, by her own words: "Our stuff is shaky."[3]

Eve, like other Black women similarly situated, choose to deal with an unstable and explosive relationship rather than be homeless with her kids or go back to selling drugs. "It ain't much of a choice, you know, but I do what I gotta do to get by. I'm a felon, that's my charge, so I work under the table and try to save up, but something always needs doing, fixed, clothes for the kids, so you know, I never get ahead to get my own place."[4] Reentering society with no public support, especially a lack of housing, makes a difficult process problematic and prevents thousands of Black women from successfully reentering. The reality of reentering society as a convicted felon is that policies permanently criminalize felons, so after completing one's criminal sentence, one's access to public benefits are restricted. Such laws fail to consider the effect these policy decisions have on Black women, especially when they are custodial parents of minor children. Black women are forced to place themselves and their children in volatile situations simply to have a place to call home (see Richie 2001).

Women I interviewed and interacted with while in the field tended to have their high school diploma or its equivalency; some had earned an associate's degree, had former legal work experience in big box stores as a floor manager or in the health care industry, and wanted to work, but all of them were unable to access legal employment opportunities because of the combination of a felony conviction and criminal history background checks. Janaye was twenty-nine years old and a single mother of one minor child; together they experienced grinding poverty, and although she had been a certified nursing assistant prior to a fight with her child's father erupting into public view, she was convicted on felony assault charges, served her time, and returned home. Yet because of a state-level policy, her nursing license was automatically revoked, and she cannot get it back because of her felony conviction.

"Well, I know, and I feel as though the government is not designed for us, especially, you know, us coming home from jail. Everything is the felony charge. My charge happened at 21, you know, and I'm 29 now, and it's just so hard. I am out of the system, but I am still dealing with it. I still haven't restarted my life. Because I can't because the conviction that I have. It hinders me from employment, it hinders me from housing, from anything that's available, the charge always is that barrier if you've been convicted, you know."[5] Janaye's felony conviction for assault meant that she was unable to earn a legal income in her previous profession, so she struggled on a daily basis. "I want to better my life, the life of my kids, but I get turned down from jobs that have nothing to do with my charge or nursing. Heck, I can't even bag groceries because of my conviction."[6]

Both Eve and Janaye successfully completed their sentences and use similar language around being a felon; neither names her individual conviction, but rather the pervasive use of "my charge" means that society has taught each of them that she is a felon and not a Black woman who was convicted of a felony. The small change in language means everything: "I'm not my charge. I'm a lot of other stuff, you know?"[7]

Ginger, a twenty-three-year-old single mother, tried to lessen the gravity of her assault charge by ignoring its seriousness and using language that distracted from it; the problem, however, was that Ginger's behavior had not changed, and her tendency to fight followed her to her GED program: "I had to stop going, because they took my funding, so now it's day-to-day, you know. I just really want to get my son back." Her seemingly simple statement was contradictory and quickly shifted the topic from herself to her son. Her brilliant use of language deterred too many questions about why she had stopped going to classes, why her funding had stopped, why her life was now day-to-day, and how that related to her regaining custody of her son. The reality that Ginger was trying to hide was that she had gotten into another fight and the GED program she was enrolled in had kicked her out, which meant she lost her educational grant and a small allowance connected to her continual attendance. Without a high school equivalency certificate, it was unlikely Ginger would be able to secure a legal job, making regaining custody of her son improbable. Ginger's son's paternal grandmother had custody, and because Ginger was focused solely on getting her son back, she had lost sight of what she had to accomplish to make that possible. Ginger's story is complicated, and her anger and tendency to fight are a retort to her circumstances, and her behavior reflects what it is like to live with society's contempt; some participants respond with despair and anger to the near-impossible task of moving beyond one's felony.

Delores is a fifty-year-old former drug user who served fifty-five months in federal prison. She used to steal to get money to buy her drugs, and although she is now drug free she is unable to shake the shame of her conviction or society's disdain. Delores tells of how the stinging resentment and her anger are constant: "My conviction follows me. It was more than 5 years ago, and I ain't worked steady since. My charge was stealing, and everyone thinks I'm going to steal from them now."[8] Her resentment "at the system" sneaks into her voice: "I'm trying to better myself. I did probation, followed the rules, did their programs, but I still can't work. What am I supposed to do? I got bills to pay, rent to make. I got temp housing, but that's going to run out soon. What then? They [society] hate me, and want to, like, keep me down. I'm trying to be good. . . ." Her voice trails off and her resentment fills the room. Delores is mad at herself, too, "but I can't keep beating myself up, ok. I did wrong, I did my time, I, you know, paid my debt, but the system don't want me out, it just wants to keep me here, because of my charge, forever."[9]

Delores's words echo a common theme; she broke the law and did her time, paid her debt to society, and followed the rules of probation, yet the system of interlocking policies attached to a felony makes successful reentry problematic. Savannah eloquently describes how the single word "felon" holds so much significance in her life and the lives of other Black women like her: "Reentry is verbally and physically abusive. The name, the word, is the stupidest word on earth. Most people are entering, not (re)entering. People cannot reenter a community they've never been a part of."[10]

Five years after getting kicked out of the foster care system, Savannah was arrested and convicted in 2003 for first-degree robbery; her two codefendants committed robbery and in the process shot someone, but instead of going to trial and face thirty years in prison, they both pleaded down to fifteen years and made Savannah a codefendant by testifying that she was involved in the planning of the robbery. Savannah was sentenced as an accomplice, but because she was not involved in the actual physical robbery or the shooting, she was sentenced to seven years as a coconspirator. This is not an unusual practice in the criminal justice system; defendants are offered deals where they can reduce their time sentenced to prison if they can provide another conviction for the prosecutor. Savannah pleaded guilty and served 85 percent of her seven-year sentence; she had no defense, no other coconspirators with which to bargain with the prosecutor, and she could have served fifteen years as her codefendants. In her situation, a seven-year prison sentence sounded like the best option

> of a lot of bad ones. It's hard to tell people, I took 7 because what was I going to do? Go to trial and get 15 or more, 'cuz even though it was my first offense, the judge might be in a shitty mood and send me away for good. I did 5 years and 10 months; going away, for me, serving time [in prison] was a forced time out. I needed that; the day before I was sentenced I got high, so high, I mean *high* [emphasis original], and my plan was to do my time, get out, and get high, 'cuz that's all I knew, but I also had other goals and prison was a time out to think about those [other goals] and getting high was shifted to the side and then it wasn't even a thing, and I stopped thinking like that.

Despite a traumatic start to life, and after serving time in prison, Savannah is a productive citizen. She is completing her bachelor's degree in social work and has applied for a gubernatorial pardon to clear her criminal record so she can attend law school and work in the field of criminal justice: "No one was there for me, and I want to be there for them [and help other similarly situated Black women], those who are coming home and need an advocate to help them along their own path."[11]

One participant in need of an advocate was Kimberly, a mother of three who was dealing with mental health challenges she called "a chemical problem, my brain get the wrong signals and I feel crazy."[12] She was trying to find her voice to advocate to access mental health assistance, but as a convicted felon charged with drug possession, credit card fraud, and theft, she was unable to gain regular and continual medical assistance. She served two years and eleven months of a five-year sentence and was constantly trying to manage her mental health challenges.

> When I was [locked up] in Clinton I took my meds, all the time, really, they [guards] like to keep us high and stuff, makes it easier to do their jobs, but it was almost killing me in there. I mean I felt crazy and there ain't no help, even if you ask, it just ain't coming. That's the hard part, too, when coming home. Ain't no medical for people like me.[13]

Kimberly was describing how she was drugged while she was locked up in state prison, but the drugs did not address her mental health issues and left her feeling crazy, and upon coming home, with documented mental health illness, she was enrolled in the PROMISE Program.[14] "Everything was good, until I maxed out, then well. . . ." Kimberly's voice trailed off.[15]

Maxing out and finishing parole meant that Kimberly was no longer eligible for the PROMISE program, and because of her conviction, she is unable to acquire the needed medical and mental health help she needs. "I'm trying to make it on my own, but I'm living in a homeless shelter, and it's hard out here." When Kimberly talks of it "being hard out here," she literally is referring to her mental instability, food insecurity, and unstable living conditions.

> The shelter is bad, and I haven't had a home cooked meal, well, seems like forever. It's a set up, revolving circle, need programs for those that max out, like me. A person like me with an addictive nature and behavior—what am I going to do? Let's be honest. What am I suppose to do? I ain't got no bus card. No place to cook. Where I'm at, I can't buy food, but when you're dealing with this, your back against the wall, something gotta give. Something.

Although Kimberly did not explicitly state what that "something" was, it was implicitly shared by participants that it would be easy to revert back to their old criminal ways. Nadina, however, was explicit and explained how easy it would be to go back to the life: "To do wrong, it's one phone call away. I can call somebody right now and be back doing the do [selling drugs]." Nadina knew that if she did not secure legal employment sooner rather than later, selling drugs was a viable option to secure some money to live.

Most people convicted of a felony are denied public benefits such as housing and medical care due to the same criminal background checks; therefore, they also are unable to secure legal employment; therefore, many participants struggled to overcome their circumstances. Diamond, at twenty-two years of age, a mother of a young son, and pregnant with a second child, is working on getting her GED because she knows having a high school diploma will help her get a legal job. "My moms is always on me to get a real job, but she just don't know how hard it is, with a record and all, to do that. I be trying, but why bother; no one wants [to hire] me, and I have other stuff to worry about." The other things Diamond was referring to was her pregnancy and how she was going to manage to care for two children when she was struggling to care for one. Diamond works under the table at a grocery store and is on her feet all day, but without health care she worries about the health of her baby. She has little idea about what she is going to do when the baby comes. She is scared that her boyfriend, who is excited about the baby coming, won't be excited once the reality of a baby sets in: "He walking around like he's the man because he's going to be a dad, but he don't know. I keep on telling him it's not about bragging rights, it's diapers, food, and all the shit a kid needs, all that costs. He don't get it, and if he doesn't get it, I don't know how I'm going to care for a baby and toddler *and* [emphasis original] work at the store."[16]

The struggle to secure a legal income, health care, and stable housing creates a lot of anxiety, which creates an inescapable cycle from which the women cannot free themselves. Mandy is trapped in a cycle that she cannot get out of based on a combination of life circumstances, choices, and her charge. Mandy is a thirty-two-year-old mother of one, and her son's father is in prison serving a long sentence. "We'd get high and drink and stuff, but all that ended when I found out I was pregnant, best thing for my kid, so I just stopped. I was done." While Mandy talked, it became clear that her pregnancy and need to take care of her son changed her attitude about life in general and made getting housing, a job, and health care all the more important. "I grew up in Newark, it's all I know, lived in different places, but it's all the same," she said. Her main challenge was to find a job, but because she had only completed the tenth grade, she was "trying to do that now," but it was hard to care for her son, look for a job, and study for the GED. "You know, I never cared, working for a paycheck, didn't care, not when I could make bank on the street."[17]

Prior to getting pregnant, Mandy's life involved getting high, dealing drugs, and getting locked up in Essex County for marijuana possession while waiting for her boyfriend to bail her out and fight the charges. She always resumed drug dealing but stopped using drugs when she found out she was pregnant. Mandy made additional major changes to her life when her boyfriend was arrested with "weight."[18] When her boyfriend was incarcerated, Mandy lost her limited social capital and support system, so she started to deal heroin to make money. Yet if she were rearrested, her boyfriend would not be there to help her get out or take care of their son, which prompted her to get out of the streets and into drug court. "I stopped using, but am in drug court now, just a lot of rules to follow, two more years of rules, but it's better than being inside [prison]. I can keep my son. But it's hard to go from street to legal, hard to know stuff, being a woman, that's just extra hard. No programs for us, people like me, a mother."

Black women addicted to drugs and who are mothers face an extra burden when they are convicted of a felony, as there are few programs available for them. Alyssa captures their collective dilemma and the challenges they encounter when trying to reenter society. At the time of her interview, Alyssa was forty-six years old, separated from her husband and three adult children. "I'm homeless, in a shelter, and need to get clean before I can go home [to North Carolina]."[19] Alyssa attends Narcotics Anonymous and has a sponsor, but what she does not have is stable housing to get clean and stay clean.

> It's time, really, I need to do this, get clean, but it's hard. I mean, most addicts like me, when they go to a drug program on their own, it's because they're tired and they want to rest. I got tired, I guess, because I got clean, I can get clean on my own, did it all, worked the programs, everything, but it's staying that way. I got into a good program, got treatment, all that, I was motivated. Well, really, I was tired, so I got clean.[20]

While in the field, I spoke to many drug addicts about their lifestyle, and how it was "normal" and then would spiral out of control as their addictions took over their lives; they'd lose their jobs and housing, live on the streets, commit crimes to feed their addiction, struggle and then get tired of living a hard life on the streets, so they would find a program, work the program, and get clean. The universal problem was that the available programs had a strict time limit, and the support would be pulled out from under them just at the exact time they were getting used to being clean. Alyssa explains why she can get clean, but can't stay clean.

> I got a white collar crime, fraud, credit cards and stuff. I'm not violent, but I did what I did to get money to buy my drugs. I had jobs, but would get fired and now the conviction prevents me from getting any other jobs. So, I'm homeless and back to using. I had temporary housing, but social services not giving me anything else, and I need it, stuff, you know, to stay clean. Like 2–3 months to get clean is nothing, then it's all taken away. So, I live on a day-to-day basis. I mean, I don't even know where my next meal is coming from, you know. Um, and a job; I just want a job, the opportunity to get on my feet. I mean, it's easy for me to go out here and do something that I have no business doing that will send me back to prison, but I'm tired, you know. I mean, it's easy for me to go out here [and commit new crimes], but I don't have any more time to give [prison]. I'm just tired. I just want to be normal, but what is normal? For people like me, there is never a normal, never, just survival.[21]

Discussion

As Savannah, Eve, Janaye, Ginger, Delores, Kimberly, Nadina, Mandy, Diamond, and Alyssa reenter society, their struggles are complicated by their individual trauma and lack of social capital, but their narratives also communicate how they felt about being rendered invisible because of their identity as Black women convicted of a felony. Their narratives speak to how each participant is marginalized and stigmatized and deemed unworthy of becoming "normal." Black women's lived experiences tend to fall outside the collective social experience, but as convicted felons, they are excluded and disqualified from the type of programs and public benefits they require to lead crime-free lives; this means that they are not protected by the body politic and must make hard decisions to survive. Within each narrative, their desire to live, regardless of the obstacles, challenges, or deficits, shines through and reflects their resilience and profound spirit to survive, and it provides a rich resource about what it means to be a Black woman convicted of a felony.

Resilience is the ability to bounce back after a setback and to continually take steps forward. Resilience requires an individual to face one's adversaries, including poverty, volatile relationships, and drug addiction, and to have the strength to live a crime-free life. Participants' stories demonstrate the essence of resilience in the form of internal strength represented by their ability to resist being defeated. Savannah, in describing herself as *entering* society, captures the inherent challenge she has faced entering a society that has marked her as deviant. Savannah is a rape survivor traumatized by her abnormal childhood who continues to find new ways to rise above her circumstances. Eve is surviving by making a chaotic and at times violent relationship work so she won't be homeless. She is choosing to sacrifice her own safety to ensure that her kids have a place to stay and food to eat. "He never hits them, so I do what I have to make sure they can go to school and have stuff to eat."[22] Despite their challenges, Savannah and Eve are resilient and carry on. Kimberly knows she is "crazy" without her prescription medications, but she cannot find consistent mental health providers. Instead of falling into the abyss of "craziness" when she feels like giving up, she thinks of her kids and why she can't give up: "I love my babies, and I have to be there for them, any way I can."[23] Delores digs deep for inner strength to remain drug free, and she is proud of her accomplishment: "I ain't gone back to *that* way of life."[24] Alyssa struggles to stay drug free but is honest about her predicament, knows what she needs to be successful, and seeks out help when she needs it. Mandy, who lives a semilegal lifestyle, is slowly learning how to leave a life of crime for the good of her son. Janaye knows what type of support and services she needs to stay away from crime, and although she cannot get her nursing license back, she seeks job opportunities where she can find them. Ginger's focus is to get through another day to live for yet another one, and her singular focus on surviving from one moment to the next means that there is not a lot of planning for tomorrow or next week. However, despite having no long-term plans, her ability to resist going back to crime demonstrates her internal buoyancy.

The participants' strong desire to not return to prison means that they are slowly reclaiming their sense of self, but their lived experiences demonstrate how the rules and policies under which they must live undermine their success. For instance, if provided access to public housing, Eve would be able to remove her kids and herself from an abusive relationship; Alyssa would be able to stay drug free; and Diamond would be less stressed if she knew she had stable housing rather than having to rely on her boyfriend, which would improve her health and help provide a healthy outcome for her second child. Their narratives demonstrate that a felony is not their only identity; the mothers in the group want to be there for their kids; all of them want to do better; and despite feeling tired and on edge, their strong desire to stay out of prison means they keep pushing forward with the hope of finding a better tomorrow. Despite the negative odds, each participant was resilient, which was evident in their individual capacity to keep moving forward notwithstanding their lack of access to cash and to find small "triumphs."

Although their feats are seemingly insignificant, small gains like sobriety, reconnecting with their kids, and finding a safe place to live are important when one's life is a constant struggle, and their narratives demonstrate a class divide, as each woman would be better able to resist the dominant narratives of their "place" in society with access to capital. While economics and class status were not explicitly integrated into the analysis, the narratives of Black women demonstrate their crimes and challenges to reenter society as directly related to the lack of financial resources. Most of the participants committed crimes in search of a financial payoff, such as robbery, drug distribution, credit card fraud, and theft. Diamond and Janaye both had assault charges, and although not directly related to a financial payoff, they were in volatile relationships where the lack of money in the home was a constant stress factor. For those Black women who are primary caretakers of their minor children, they must make hard decisions because of their limited financial means, and because they are cut off from public benefits, they are always one argument or one situation away from having their entire lives fall apart again. For all of the participants, after they were convicted and incarcerated, they were worse off financially. Although the Black women are not thriving by traditional standards, none of the women were "stuck"; rather, the women may have been unhappy and resentful of how policies denied them public benefits, but their hatred of the system did not make them wilt and give up. They all demonstrated the ability to respond to a constantly changing environment, meet new challenges, and survive in uncertain conditions.

Conclusion

Lived experiences of Black women felons have value in understanding prisoner reentry, and although the small sample of lived experiences is only suggestive, it does offer some measure of what Black women felons encounter as they reenter Newark, New Jersey. The personal stories allow us to understand narratives found at the intersection of race, gender, and felony status and how these multiple labels must simultaneously be negotiated; and how policies and status intersect in the lives of Black women felons. Despite their limited options and restricted access to social capital and money as they negotiate society, Black women felons have important stories to share about who they are and how they experience the everyday. Such intersectional studies communicate important stories of those women who do not have a voice and who do not have the resources to represent themselves in the public discourse of reentry.

Black women felons' everyday lives are conditioned by the tension among their three principal identities and how the intersection of gender, race, and felony status means that Black women learn to exist with scarce economic resources, socially marginalized and isolated from mainstream society. In particular, race promotes vulnerability as a consequence of which communities Black women return to; given the subordinated position of urban residents and the institutional abandonment they experience, Black women felons face multiple risks while negotiating the economic, social, and political positions they occupy. Intersectionality allows us to explicitly connect gendered, racialized, and stigmatized identities, which is essential to understand the unique space Black women felons inhabit. By exposing the power and harm public policies place on Black women's bodies, resilience and survival become a form of resistance. As they continually adapt to different social circumstances, Black women have always found ways to survive as society is resistant to their bodies' presence, and intersectionality provides one way to challenge historical and contemporary notions of Black women and their place in society.

The discourse of race, gender, and criminality remain as permanent markers because of the social nature of a felony and the inability to change one's race and gender; explicitly studying Black women renders their resistance visible, which is critical as a sizeable number of Black women incarcerated in the late 1990s and early 2000s under the politics of being "tough on crime" and policies like the "War on Drugs" are coming home. The criminal justice system, with society's tactile approval, removes people from the community, locks them up, silences them, and then degrades them by depriving them of the ability to reenter. Upon their return, the totality of anti-felon statutes and "tough on crime" political policies makes a criminal sentence perpetual, and the hostile nature of policies connected to a felony results in notions of permanent criminality. The ubiquitous nature of policies constructs walls around female felonious bodies to limit housing options and reinforce economic injustice to create a dual society of felons and non-felons. In particular, Black women convicted of a felony operate in society with an acute awareness of being judged, and by emphasizing the basis of gender differences, the practices of women separate from men, and the types of issues and needs women care about makes their experiences visible. For Black women felons, the combination of hostile policies and "tough on crime" politics means that future studies need to focus on the reality of Black women, those convicted of a felony, and the communities they live in to understand how society makes them invisible and how they struggle every day to become visible in an effort to thrive in a hostile environment.

Felons who have returned home are treated as contemporary outlaws (Middlemass 2017). Despite being "freed" by the criminal justice system, their bodies are the main instrument in which policies are inflicted. The lived experiences of Black women convicted of a variety of felonies vary, but those experiences become a constructed political, social, and cultural phenomenon. Their social bodies have had lines drawn around them by policies as a way to segregate them out of social and economic opportunities and therefore outside of the body politic. The message is clear: social spaces are constructed for non-felons, so felons are left to struggle outside these constructed spaces, where their bodies are unnatural, contested, and stripped of societal privileges.

Notes

1. Personal interview, March 5, 2012.
2. Field notes, multiple days, 2012.
3. Ibid.
4. Ibid.
5. Personal interview, April 19, 2011.
6. Ibid.
7. Ibid.
8. Field notes, February 22, 2012.
9. Ibid.
10. Personal interview, March 5, 2012.
11. Ibid.
12. Field notes, January 30, 2013.
13. Ibid.

14. The Program for Returning Offenders with Mental Illness Safely and Effectively (PROMISE) Program is designed for offenders with mental health disorders who are reentering the community on state parole.

15. Field notes, January 30, 2013.

16. Field notes, multiple days, 2012.

17. Personal interview, February 13, 2012.

18. "Weight" refers to the weight of drugs; Mandy never disclosed how much weight her boyfriend was arrested and charged with, but said he'd be in prison until after her current two-year-old son graduated from high school.

19. Personal interview, May 9, 2011.

20. Ibid.

21. Ibid.

22. Field notes, multiple days, 2012.

23. Field notes, January 30, 2013.

24. Field notes, February 22, 2012.

References

Alexander, Michelle. 2010. *The New Jim Crow: Mass Incarceration in the Age of Colorblindness*. New York: The New Press.

Balko, Radley. 2013. *Rise of the Warrior Cop: The Militarization of America's Police Forces*. Philadelphia: Public Affairs (Perseus Books Group).

Bell, Kerryn E. 2012. "Young Adult Offending: Intersectionality of Gender and Race." *Critical Criminology* 21: 103–21.

Berger, Michele T. 2004. *Workable Sisterhood: The Political Journey of Stigmatized Women with HIV/AIDS*. Princeton, NJ: Princeton University Press.

Biehl, Joao. 2010. " 'Medication Is Me Now': Human Values and Political Life in the Wake of Global AIDS Treatment." In *In the Name of Humanity: The Government of Threat and Care*, edited by Ilana Feldman and Miriam Ticktin, 151–89. Durham, NC: Duke University Press.

Bobo, Lawrence, and Victor Thompson. 2010. "Racialized Mass Incarceration: African Americans and the Criminal Justice System." In *Doing Race: 21 Essays for the 21st Century*, edited by Hazel Markus and Paula Moya, 322–55. New York: Norton.

Boxer, Paul, Keesha Middlemass, and Tahlia Delorenzo. 2009. "Exposure to Violent Crime During Incarceration: Effects on Psychological Adjustment Following Release." *Criminal Justice and Behavior* 36: 793–807.

Boxer, Paul, Ashley Schappell, Keesha Middlemass, Tahlia DeLorenzo, and Ignacio Mercado. 2011. "Cognitive and Emotional Covariates of Violence Exposure Among Former Prisoners: Links to Antisocial Behavior and Emotional Distress and Implications for Theory." *Aggressive Behavior* 37 (5): 465–75.

Burgess-Proctor, Amanda. 2006. "Intersectionality of Race, Class, Gender, and Crime." *Feminist Criminology* 1: 27–47.

Butterfield, Fox. 1996. *All God's Children: The Bosket Family and the American Tradition of Violence.* New York: First Vintage Books.

Cardoso, Fernando, Cesar Gaviria, and Ernesto Zedillo. 2009. "The War on Drugs Is a Failure: We Should Focus Instead on Reducing Harm to Users and on Tackling Organized Crime." *The Wall Street Journal,* February 23. http://online.wsj.com/article/SB123535114271444981.html.

Carson, E. Ann. 2014. *Prisoners in 2013* (NCJ 247282). Washington, DC: U.S. Department of Justice, Office of Justice Programs, Bureau of Justice Statistics. http://www.bjs.gov/content/pub/pdf/p13.pdf.

Caughey, John L. 1982. "The Ethnography of Everyday Life: Theories and Methods for American Culture Studies." *American Quarterly* 34 (3): 222–43.

Chin, Gabriel. 2002. "Race, the War on Drugs, and the Collateral Consequences of Criminal Conviction." *Journal of Gender, Race & Justice* 6: 253–96.

Chin, Gabriel, and Richard Holmes. 2002. "Effective Assistance of Counsel and the Consequences of Guilty Pleas." *Cornell Law Review* 87 (3): 697–742.

Clear, Todd. 2009. *Imprisoning Communities: How Mass Incarceration Makes Disadvantaged Neighborhoods Worse.* New York: Oxford University Press.

Cohen, Neil, and Dean Rivkin. 1971. "Civil Disabilities: The Forgotten Punishment." *Federal Probation* 35 (2): 19–25.

Collins, Patricia Hill. 1998. *Fighting Words: Black Women and the Search for Justice.* Minneapolis: University of Minnesota Press.

Crenshaw, Kimberlé Williams. 1991. "Mapping the Margins: Intersectionality, Identity Politics, and Violence against Women of Color." *Stanford Law Review* 46 (6): 1241–99.

———. 1989. "Demarginalizing the Intersection of Race and Sex: A Black Feminist Critique of Antidiscrimination Doctrine, Feminist Theory and Antiracist Politics." *University of Chicago Legal Forum* 140: 139–67.

Damaska, Mirjan. 1968. "Adverse Legal Consequences of Conviction and Their Removal: A Comparative Study." *Journal of Criminal Law, Criminology, & Police Science* 59: 347–52.

Davis, Angela Y. 1981. *Women, Race, & Class.* New York: Vintage.

Desmond, Jane. 2014. "Ethnography as Ethics and Epistemology: Why American Studies Should Embrace Fieldwork, and Why It Hasn't." *American Studies* 53 (1): 27–56.

Draine, Jeffrey, and Daniel Herman. 2007. "Critical Time Intervention for Reentry from Prison for Persons with Mental Illness." *Psychiatric Services* 58 (12): 1577–81.

Eberhardt, Jennifer, Phillip Goff, Valerie Purdie, and Paul Davies. 2004. "Seeing Black: Race, Crime, and Visual Processing." *Journal of Personality and Social Psychology* 87 (6): 876–93.

Estrada, Felipe. 2004. "The Transformation of the Politics of Crime in High Crime Societies." *European Journal of Criminology* 1 (4): 419–43.

Ewald, Alec. 2002. " 'Civil Death:' The Ideological Paradox of Criminal Disenfranchisement Law in the United States." *Wisconsin Law Review* 5: 1045–137.

Foucault, Michael. 1977. *Discipline and Punish: The Birth of the Prison*. London: Penguin Books.

Grossberg, Michael, and Christopher Tomlins. 2008. *The Cambridge History of Law in America*. Vol. I. Cambridge: Cambridge University Press.

Gupta, Akil, and James Ferguson. 1997. "Discipline and Practice: 'The Field' as Site, Method, and Location in Anthropology." In *Anthropological Location: Boundaries and Grounds of a Field Sciences*, edited by Akil Gupta and James Ferguson, 1–46. Berkeley: University of California Press.

Harris, David. 1999. *Driving While Black: Racial Profiling on Our Nation's Highways*. New York: American Civil Liberties Union.

Jacobson, Michael. 2005. *Downsizing Prisons: How to Reduce Crime and End Mass Incarceration*. New York: New York University Press.

Kennedy, Randall. 1997. *Race, Crime and the Law*. New York: Pantheon.

King, Ryan. 2008. *Disparity By Geography: The War on Drugs in America's Cities*. Washington, DC: The Sentencing Project.

Kleiman, Susan. 2004. "Phenomenology: To Wonder and Search for Meanings." *Nurse Researcher* 11 (4): 7–19.

Klein, Dorie, and June Kress. 1976. "Any Woman's Blues: A Critical Overview of Women, Crime and the Criminal Justice System." *Crime & Social Justice* 5: 34–49.

Koski, Susan, and Kathleen Bantley. 2013. "Coping with Reentry Barriers: Strategies Used by Women Offenders." *InSight* 9 (1): 1–17.

Langan, Patrick. 1991. *Race of Prisoners Admitted to State and Federal Institutions, 1926–86* (NCJ 125618). Washington, DC: U.S. Department of Justice, Office of Justice Programs, Bureau of Justice Statistics. https://www.ncjrs.gov/pdffiles1/nij/125618.pdf.

Lorber, Judith. 1994. *Paradoxes of Gender*. New Haven: Yale University Press.

Lynch, John, and William Sabol. 2001. *Prisoner Reentry in Perspective* (Crime Policy Report, 3). Washington, DC: The Urban Institute. http://www.urban.org/UploadedPDF /410213_reentry.PDF.

Mallach, Alan. 2010. *Facing the Urban Challenge: The Federal Government and America's Older Distressed Cities*. Washington, DC: Urban Institute. http://www.brookings.edu/~/media/research/files/papers/2010/5/18%20shrinking%20cities%20mallach/0518_shrinking_cities_mallach.pdf.

Martin, Patricia Y. 2004. "Gender as Social Institution." *Social Forces* 82 (4): 1249–73.

Marable, Manning, Ian Steinberg, and Keesha Middlemass. 2007. *Racializing Justice, Disenfranchising Lives: The Racism, Criminal Justice and Law Reader*. New York: Palgrave Macmillan.

Mauer, Marc, and Meda Chesney-Lind. 2002. *Invisible Punishment: The Collateral Consequences of Mass Imprisonment*. New York: W. W. Norton & Company.

Middlemass, Keesha. 2017. *Convicted & Condemned: The Politics and Policies of Prisoner Reentry*. New York: New York University Press.

———. 2015. "The Belly of the Beast." In *The Organic Globalizer: Hip Hop, Political Development & Movement Culture*, edited by Christopher Malone & George Martinez, 213–32. New York: Bloomsbury USA Academic.

———. 2014. "War as Metaphor: The Convergence of the War on Poverty & The War on Drugs." In *The War on Poverty: A Retrospective*, edited by Kyle Farmbry, 85–104. Lanham, MD: Lexington Books.

———. 2007. "The Carceral States of America." In *Racializing Justice, Disenfranchising Lives: The Racism, Criminal Justice and Law Reader*, edited by Manning Marable, Manning, Ian Steinberg, and Keesha Middlemass, 373–80. New York: Palgrave Macmillan.

Minton, Todd. 2013. *Jail Inmates at Midyear 2012—Statistical Tables* (NCJ 241264). Washington, DC: U.S. Department of Justice. http://www.bjs.gov/content/pub/pdf/jim12st.pdf.

Penner, Jamie L., and Susan E. McClement. 2008. "Using Phenomenology to Examine the Experiences of Family Caregivers of Patients with Advanced Head and Neck Cancer: Reflections of a Novice Researcher." *International Journal of Qualitative Methods* 7 (2): 92–101.

Pinard, Michael. 2006. "An Integrated Perspective on the Collateral Consequences of Criminal Convictions and Reentry Issues Faced by Formerly Incarcerated Individuals." *Boston University Law Review* 86: 623–90.

Potter, Hillary. 2013. "Intersectional Criminology: Interrogating Identity and Power in Criminology Research and Theory." *Critical Criminology* 21: 305–18.

Richie, Beth E. 2001. "Challenges Incarcerated Women Face as They Return to Their Communities: Findings from Life History Interviews." *Crime and Delinquency* 47: 368–89.

Risman, Barbara. 2004. "Gender as a Social Structure: Theory Wrestling with Activism." *Gender & Society* 18 (4): 429–50.

Rosenmerkel, Sean, Matthew Durose, and Donald Farole Jr. 2009. *Felony Sentences in State Courts, 2006—Statistical Tables* (NCJ 226846). Washington, DC: U.S. Department of Justice, Office of Justice Programs, Bureau of Justice Statistics. http://bjs.ojp.usdoj.gov/content/pub/pdf/fssc06st.pdf.

Russell, Katheryn, and Dragan Milovanovic. 2001. *Petit Apartheid in the U.S. Criminal Justice System: The Dark Figure of Racism*. Durham: Carolina Academic Press.

Russell-Brown, Katheryn. 2004. *Underground Codes: Race, Crime, and Related Fires*. New York: New York University Press.

Schneider, Anne, and Helen Ingram. 1993. "How the Social Construction of Target Populations Contributes to Problems in Policy Design." *Policy Currents* 3: 1–4.

Speziale, Helen Streubert, and Dona Rinaldi Carpenter. 2007. *Qualitative Research in Nursing: Advancing the Humanistic Imperative*. 4th ed. Philadelphia: Lippincott Williams & Wilkins.

Tomlinson, Barbara. 2013. "To Tell the Truth and Not Get Trapped: Desire, Distance, and Intersectionality at the Scene of Argument." *Signs* 38 (4): 993–1017.

Travis, Jeremy. 2005. *But They All Come Back: Facing the Challenges of Prisoner Reentry*. Washington, DC: The Urban Institute.

United States Department of Justice. 2013. *Prisoners and Prisoner Re-Entry*. Washington, DC: U.S. Department of Justice, Office of Justice Programs. http://www.justice.gov/archive/fbci/progmenu_reentry.html.

Western, Bruce. 2009. "Race, Crime and Punishment." *Cato Unbound: A Journal of Debate*. Washington, DC: Cato Institute. http://www.cato-unbound.org/2009/03/18/bruce-western/race-crime-punishment.

West, Heather, and William Sabol. 2011. *Prisoners in 2009* (NCJ 231675). Washington, DC: U.S. Department of Justice, Office of Justice Programs, Bureau of Justice Statistics. http://www.bjs.gov/content/pub/pdf/p09.pdf.

Willingham, Breea. 2011. "Black Women's Prison Narratives and the Intersection of Race, Gender, and Sexuality in US Prisons." *Critical Survey* 23 (3): 55–66.

Wilson, William Julius. 1987. *The Truly Disadvantaged: The Inner City, the Underclass and Public Policy.* Chicago: University of Chicago Press.

5

Lost Tribes

An Intersectionality-Based Policy Analysis of How US HIV/AIDS Policy Fails to "Rescue" Black Orphans

JULIA S. JORDAN-ZACHERY
Providence College

The story of AIDS orphans in the United States typically is one framed in a discourse of crisis and the "Other." The "Other" is often viewed as those living outside the United States in unstable and/or poor nation-states, and they tend to be racialized bodies. As the narratives of HIV/AIDS and orphaned children tend to privilege the "Global South," there is no comparable narrative of pain/suffering and "rescue" applied to the cases of children orphaned by AIDS in the United States. These children, although recognized as living with the impact of motherlessness resulting from AIDS (regardless of their HIV status), seem not to be a concern for policy makers, thereby resulting in policy gaps. Policy gaps, I argue, result from these children being "out of place" in terms of a dominant social order sanctioned by some in society. This social order requires a particular format and functioning of the family, and HIV and AIDS disrupt these dominant narratives of family in general and the role of women within these structures specifically.

In this exploratory chapter, I focus on Black AIDS motherless children in the United States and how they are targeted in policy making by centering how these children are constructed as "out of place." Two groups of children are made motherless as a result of the ravishing impact of AIDS in the Black community. There are HIV-positive orphans and non-positive orphans. HIV-positive children tend to be targeted by policy for care based on their health status. Non-positive children seem to be forgotten. Desmond, Michael, and Gow (2000) argue that both groups of children can suffer from stigma, social neglect, poverty, housing instability, and psychosocial problems, which singularly or combined can result in limited futures. Yet society tends to ignore the needs of the latter group. In this exploratory intersectionality-based policy analysis (IBPA), I analyze how AIDS-orphaned Black children are marginalized in public policy. This analysis asks: Given the stigmatization of HIV/AIDS and the sociopolitical marginalization of Black women and their offspring, how are Black orphaned children, specifically non-positive orphans, constructed in and responded to by public policies? I argue that the nonresponse of public policy makers is a response to what Michele Berger refers to as intersectional stigma. "Intersectional stigma points to an understanding that women are not only *marginalized,* and socially situated (shaped by race, class, and gender), but that the category of "HIV-positive person" is loaded with effectively negative perceptions about groups of people with the virus" (Berger 2004, 24). In their response to intersectional stigma, policy makers fail to recognize non–HIV positive orphaned children. Such children are affected by intersectional stigma as a result of their socially constructed identity and as a result of their "indirect" association with HIV and AIDS. This analysis is focused on the policy efforts of the US government and communities identified as the top six "HIV/AIDS hot spots." These six communities are located in Atlanta, Georgia; Raleigh-Durham, North Carolina; Washington, DC; Newark, New Jersey; Baltimore, Maryland; and New York, New York. The rate of infection among Black women in these communities is estimated to be five times that of the national average (*Baltimore Sun* 2012).

The analysis starts with the challenge of making visible AIDS orphans in the United States. This is then followed by a review of intersectionality and IBPA. This section lays out the key questions that guide the analysis of policy responses to AIDS-orphaned Black children. In the third section, I explore the social construction of the "bad" Black mother. Section four considers the relationship between AIDS, race, gender, and public opinion. In this section, I show how the public's concern over AIDS is waning as the epidemiology changes in terms of race and gender. From there I present gaps in policy and show how such gaps influence the treatment of AIDS orphans. The paper concludes with a discussion of the impact of the invisibility of AIDS orphans on issues of social justice.

The Challenge: Making Visible AIDS Orphans in the United States

Despite the rate of infection among Black women, AIDS-orphaned children remain invisible. As a consequence of this invisibility, the number of motherless AIDS orphans is unknown. This makes this research a bit challenging—how does one analyze policy responses to a group that is not "seen" or discussed in policy? To understand policy's treatment of this group I use an indirect approach. I argue that the treatment of non–HIV positive orphans results from the social construction of their mothers. According to Hill Collins, the privileged "monolithic family type articulates with governmental structures. It is organized not around a biological core, but a state-sanctioned, heterosexual marriage that confers legitimacy not only on the family structure itself but on children born into it" (1998, 63). AIDS orphans are perceived as falling outside this monolithic family type that is sanctioned by the state. As a result of their family status—solo parent mother characteristically thought of as "bad," racialization, and/or socioeconomic status—they are typically treated as deviants and are marginalized. Consequently, the children become entangled in a narrative of dysfunction and deviance stemming from the often negative construction of their mothers, and consequently they are perceived as being "out of place."

By employing an augmented understanding of political scientists Schneider and Ingram's (1997) target population framework and Black feminist thought, this chapter shows how the social construction of Black mothers and intersectional stigma affect policy targeting Black AIDS motherless orphans. Schneider and Ingram's understanding of policy targeted populations is useful, as it helps us to understand the relationship between society's conceptualization of policy target groups, via the use of stereotypes and perceived social standing, in combination with their political power and the problem definition phase of policy making. As argued,

> The incorporation of social construction of target populations as part of policy design helps explain why public policy, which can have such a positive effect on society, sometimes—and often deliberately—fails in its nominal purpose, fails to solve important public problems, perpetuates injustice, fails to support democratic institutions, and produces an unequal citizenship. (Ingram, Schneider, and deLeon 2007, 93)

In their understanding of the functioning of target populations in politics and policy making, Schneider and Ingram offer four categories of populations. These categories include 1) the advantaged—politically strong and deserving—comprising the middle class and senior citizens, for example; 2) the contenders, who are constructed as politically strong and underserving and includes, for example, CEOs; 3) the dependents, who are thought of as politically weak and deserving—mothers and children are included in this group; and 4) the deviants—these are politically weak and underserving and include criminals and gangs. While this typology is useful for understanding the problem definition stage of policy making and the politics involved in such, it is somewhat limited, as it does not necessarily account for how race, class, sexuality, and illness might influence the social construction of mothers and their children in the United States. Critical race and gender scholars such as Dorothy Roberts inform us that race and class influence the construction of the broad category of mothers, as such identity markers are used to differentiate deserving and "deviant" mothers. She argues, "For centuries, a popular mythology has degraded Black women and portrayed them as less deserving of motherhood. . . . This devaluation of Black motherhood has been reinforced by stereotypes that blame Black mothers for the problems of the Black family" (Roberts 1997a, 950). The discourse of HIV and AIDS among this population has been mapped onto these previously existing understandings of Black motherhood. This is where intersectional stigma becomes useful for understanding not just how these women are treated, but also how their offspring are treated vis-à-vis policy.

The line of analysis pursued in this chapter builds on critical race and gender and Black women's scholarship (Berger 2004; Crenshaw et al. 1995; Hill Collins 1998; Ladson-Billings 1998; Roberts 1997b). By applying these perspectives to the case of AIDS orphans in the United States. I hope, first, to excavate and highlight the deeper problems and conflicts that are central to the neglect of motherless AIDS orphans, particularly those who are non-positive. Second, in the tradition of Black feminist thought, I seek to contribute to the larger project of social justice by unmasking power structures that work to leave some bodies out of the body politic.

Applying Intersectionality-Based Policy Analysis

To deepen our understanding of how HIV/AIDS orphans are treated by policy makers, I deploy an intersectional approach. My understanding of intersectionality is based on US Black feminists and women of color's articulations. Intersectionality, as a theoretical concept of power relations, takes into account how multiple forms of oppression, race, class, gender, and sexuality inform the lived realities of Black women and women of color. An intersectional approach allows for an interrogation of the stereotypes and images used to define Black womanhood and how they, and by extension their children, are used in the policy-making process. Additionally, intersectionality seeks to understand and explain how these women (at an individual and a communal level) respond—politically and culturally—to such oppression. (Berger 2004; Bowleg 2008; N. E. Brown 2014; R. N. Brown 2013; Combahee River Collective 1977; Jordan-Zachery 2016; Isoke 2013; Richardson 2003). This research seeks to add to this growing body of research by suggesting how intersectionality can inform policy decision making, an area that remains understudied.

An intersectionality-based policy analysis, or IBPA, is particularly useful, as it helps to contextualize how power and privilege is maintained vis-à-vis the distribution of resources. As defined by Hankivsky and colleagues (2012, 33) IBPA "provides a new and effective method for understanding the varied equity-relevant implications of policy and for promoting equity-based improvements and social justice within an increasingly diverse and complex population base." Doyal's (2009) study of Black African migrants in London shows the usefulness of IBPA for unpacking the multiple layers of discrimination experienced by these individuals. As she argues, HIV stigma cannot fully explain the extent of the discrimination faced by the migrants. Doyal, like Berger (2004), posits that HIV stigma intersects with other already existing systems of oppression such as racism, sexism, and homophobia. Consequently, we cannot only consider stigma, but our analyses also must factor in its relationship with existing systems of domination (Doyal 2009). Intersectional stigma, as defined by Michele Berger, allows for an analysis that considers how policy is a response to structural and cultural level systems and forces.

The IBPA Framework includes a set of twelve overarching questions that may be adapted to best fit the specific policy area of analysis (Hankivsky et al. 2012). For this case study, I adapt questions 3, 5, and 6. Combined, in the words of Schneider and Ingram (1993, 334), these questions allow me to explore how "the social construction of the target populations has a powerful influence on public officials" and how such constructions shape "both the policy agenda and the actual design of policy."

The questions used in this analysis are as follows:

- How have representations of the "problem" come about? (question 3)
- What are the current policy responses to the "problem"? And related subquestion: How do existing policies address, maintain, or create inequities between different groups? (question 5)
- What inequities actually exist in relation to the problem? And related subquestions: Which are the important intersecting social locations and systems? What are the knowledge/evidence gaps about this problem across a diversity of this population? (question 6)

I use these questions to guide the analysis of public policies at both the national and state levels. Doing so provides insights into how Black AIDS orphans, particularly non-positive orphans, are described in policies and how their social locations influence their treatment. Combined, these questions allow me to ask how the mothers of these children and by extension their children are conceptualized as deserving or undeserving citizens in HIV and AIDS policy decision making.

Intersectionality and Intersectional Stigma: Race, AIDS Orphans, and Visibility

The intersection of race, class, gender, and sexuality constructs, produces, and disciplines the parameters of the discourses on AIDS orphans in the United States. Consequently, making sense of the public and policy responses to AIDS orphans requires a determined unpacking of the social construction of Black women in general and Black women who are HIV positive specifically. Doing so allows for a deeper exploration of how policy constructs citizens and their relative power and privileges based on their social location. As I argue, the treatment of orphans is related to the social construction of their mothers as "deviants" and as "undeserving." These children do not rise to the status of the "innocent" not because of anything they have done, but simply because of who their mothers are. AIDS orphans, like the "crack babies" of the 1980s and 1990s, are constructed as the offspring of the "bad" Black mother. Both sets of children signal the perceived breakdown of the Black family, as the construction of both populations tend to turn to individual-level factors for explanations of the troubles these children face and the potential trouble they will pose to the wider society as opposed to structural factors such as poverty and patriarchy. Thus, policy tends to focus on risk behaviors of the individual while minimizing the context that makes some hypersusceptible to some illnesses.

Images of the "crack mother" and "crack baby" embody the racing-gendering process of crime policy decision making (Jordan-Zachery 2009) and a continuation of the narrative of the "damaged" Black family. According to Patricia Williams (quoted in Bower 1995, 144), "the signifying power of the black single mother . . . as poor, drug addicted, and natally absent . . . is integral to the public articulation of fetal harm and abuse." Consciously or unconsciously, AIDS orphans are similarly constructed—vis-à-vis their mothers. The (non) policy response to Black motherless AIDS orphans is a result of the signifying power of the "bad" Black mother. These women are debased because of their perceived immoral sexual activity; their known or unknown experiences with substance abuse; their connection, real or perceived, with sex work; their race; and their economic status. They are "bad" as a result of the stigma of AIDS and the previously existing social construction of Black womanhood as the antithesis of the "good" woman.

Reliance on such a construction of HIV-positive Black women and those who have AIDS prevents the public and policy makers from considering how the social location of these women heightens their susceptibility to the virus. The spread of HIV and AIDS among African American women is related to their experiences with multiple and intersecting oppressive structures including race, gender, and social class. The intersectionality of racial discrimination, poverty, racial segregation, high incarceration rates, low-sex ratios, fractured gender identity, gender roles, stigma, and high levels of illicit drug use results in Black women's disproportionate exposure to HIV and later AIDS (see Adimora and Schoenbach 2002, 2005; Connors 1996; Feist-Price and Wright 2003; Krieger 1999; Logan, Cole, and Leukefeld, 2002; Pequegnat and Stover, 1999; Whitehead, 1997; E. M. Wright, 2003; E. R. Wright and Martin, 2003). These are factors that are external to the individual and individual-level behaviors. However, policy, such as the Ryan White Care Act and the ABC approach (abstinence, be faithful, use a condom) seems more concerned with medical responses for people living with HIV/AIDS and their sexual behaviors than with the structural inequities they face that make them susceptible to HIV and AIDS. To focus on the structural factors would require that policy makers think of HIV and AIDS as a civil rights or human rights issue. Such a frame has not been systematically used in the United States. This, in part, helps us to understand why this group of motherless children remains invisible in the United States.

Although there is a similarity in the use of the "bad" Black mother in constructing these children, there is a substantive difference in how the children are seen or not seen. Unlike the "crack baby," who was very visible in the media and among policy makers, the AIDS orphan, regardless of status, remains relatively invisible in the United States. Motherless AIDS orphans, unlike the "crack baby," seem to elicit no moral panic. It is possible that these children fail to elicit such a response because there is no perceived threat particularly of violence and economic costs associated with these children that targets the White community. There is no threat that these children will leave their communities and cause harm. Also, there does not seem to be much political capital associated with them in the way that the "crack baby" was used politically.

AIDS: Race, Gender, Epidemiology, and Public Opinion

Why Black AIDS motherless children and youths? I focus on motherless children, as it is the definition used by the Centers for Disease Control (CDC), the World Health Organization, and the United Nations Children's Fund. Additionally, the mother is often the primary (or sole) caregiver of the children who are impacted. In 2011, the United Nations Programme on AIDS estimated that there were approximately 79,000 (i.e., 63,000–100,000) AIDS orphans aged zero to seventeen in the United States (UNAIDS). As of the writing of this chapter, there are no available data on the number of Black children who have been orphaned as a result of HIV/AIDS. As the epidemic enters its third decade, women and girls of color—especially Black women and girls—bear a disproportionately heavy burden of HIV/AIDS (CDC 2010). According to the CDC (2013), in 2010, "[t]he estimated rate of new HIV infections for black women (38.1/100,000 population) was 20 times as high as the rate for white women, and almost five times as high as that of Latinas." As of 2007, "HIV was the ninth leading cause of death for all blacks and the third leading cause of death for black women and black men aged 35–44" (CDC). Conceivably these individuals have left children behind. Some researchers argue that this is a difficult population to track primarily as a result of stigma (Lichtenstein 2008). Consequently, it is difficult to ascertain the impact of the spread of AIDS among this group. However, given the epidemiology of the virus, one can extrapolate that, regardless of status, a substantial number of those orphaned are Black and Latino. Yet policy does not explicitly address the needs of these children.

As the disease has spread into minoritized and marginalized poor communities and communities of color, the public has shown decreasing concern over HIV/AIDS. As reported by the Kaiser Family Foundation 2011 survey, "In 1987, two-thirds of Americans named HIV/AIDS as the most urgent health problem facing the country." In 2011, 7 percent counted HIV/AIDS as an urgent health problem. Comparatively, in 2004, seven in ten reported having heard, seen, or read about the HIV/AIDS epidemic; in the most recent survey, four in ten said that they had such exposure (Kaiser Family Foundation, 2011). During the 2012 presidential election, neither candidate, Barack Obama nor Mitt Romney, discussed HIV/AIDS and its relation to race, gender, class, or sexuality during the three presidential debates. This trend of not substantively addressing HIV/AIDS was also apparent in the 2016 presidential election. In the presidential debates between Hilary Clinton (Democrat) and then-candidate Donald Trump (Republican), HIV/AIDS was mentioned once (in the final debate by Clinton). Furthermore, HIV/AIDS and its relationship to race, gender, and socioeconomic status was not centered. It has been argued that the public's declining concern over HIV/AIDS is a result in part of medical advances in treating the disease, as the availability of drugs has moved the disease to a "chronic illness" as opposed to a death sentence (Valdiserri 2004). The declining concern over HIV/AIDS, particularly as the diseases spreads to Black communities, has implications for federal and local government's policy responses.

A number of social scientists have argued that there is a relationship between public opinion and government policy and politicians' behavior (Burstein 1998; Manza and Cook 2002). Researchers such as Galston (2007) and Kaid et al. (2007) suggest that there is a feedback loop between public opinion and health policy. They argue that an informed and educated public can influence opinion on health and policy issues, and this in turn can encourage and promote support and advocacy on behalf of these issues. An informed public can articulate and at times better organize for particular policy priorities. The general public's waning concern about HIV and AIDS appears to have contributed, in part, to the general lack of a policy response to this growing problem. Consequently, not only are these women invisible, but their children are also invisible in our construction and understanding of the impact of HIV and AIDS. Specifically, those Black children who have been left orphaned—motherless—as a result of AIDS are ignored in our discourses about the impact of the disease. Lichtenstein

(2008, 54) suggests that this is the result of the challenges faced in finding and identifying these children, as "their identity and whereabouts will be unknown to most service providers."

Policy Gaps

Currently, the United States does not have a national HIV/AIDS policy. The Ryan White Comprehensive AIDS Resources Emergency (CARE) Act, originally enacted in 1990, remains the cornerstone of the federal government's response to HIV/AIDS. The Bureau of the Health Resources and Services Administration is responsible for the administration of the CARE Act. The CARE Act provides funding to states, territories, and other public and private nonprofit organizations to develop, organize, coordinate, and operate programs to effectively and efficiently deliver health care and support to those living with HIV/AIDS and their families. In 2000, as part of the renewal of the CARE Act, Title 1 was amended in part to target communities of color in highly impacted areas with increased funding. Some of this increased funding was designated to assist children orphaned by AIDS. President Obama, as part of his response to HIV/AIDS, developed a National HIV/AIDS strategy. This strategy set as policy priorities (1) reducing HIV incidences, (2) increasing access to care and optimizing health outcomes, and (3) reducing HIV-related health disparities (Office of National AIDS Policy 2009). While attempting to offer a comprehensive approach to addressing HIV and AIDS, the National AIDS Policy does not directly target orphans.

In terms of the six HIV/AIDS identified hot spots: Atlanta, Georgia; Raleigh-Durham, North Carolina; Washington, DC; Newark, New Jersey; Baltimore, Maryland; and New York, New York; there are no agencies that provide special care for AIDS-orphaned children—those who are not positive. In these states, there are no agencies that work to identify these children and ensure that they can access protective laws, such as the American Disabilities Act (ADA). The ADA protects a variety of health, educational, housing, and legal rights of disabled citizens, including HIV-positive children or those whose caregivers are HIV positive. However, many of these children often do not access these services because "the lack of knowledge about the cause of a parent's death may preclude orphaned children [whether HIV positive themselves or not] from being identified as a special population" (Lichtenstein 2008, 66). Most of these states rely on Part D funding of the CARE Act that is designed to target children, women, and families. To date, there are no identifiable organizations that have as their primary mission the service of AIDS orphans and especially those who are non-positive. There needs to be more research done in this area to determine how such organizations might be filling the policy gaps in these AIDS hot spots.

There are a number of shortcomings in public policy that contribute to the invisibility of AIDS orphans in the United States. Policy shortcomings are in part a result of the language used to frame the disease. As Adam (1989) posits,

> The strength of AIDS language is not due to imminence, reason, or inevitability, but to concrete political forces. In the mid-1980s, legislative bodies in the United States . . . have been moving to guarantee a particular AIDS story through formal regimes of censorship and through funding the educational agencies which would promote the official story. (9)

The "official story" of HIV/AIDS in the United States has not provided space to discuss motherless orphans. Subsequently, public policy's (on the specific issue of AIDS orphans) shortcomings include, but are not limited to, limited services to kin caregivers, improper and inadequate means of "tracking" these orphans, and failure to confront structural inequities as a means for addressing the widespread impact of HIV/AIDS—particularly among non-positive orphans.

Discussion

This exploratory case study reveals how policies at both the national and state levels fail to protect motherless AIDS orphans who are non-positive. The fact is that they appear not to be directly targeted by HIV/AIDS policies. To understand the neglect of these children and youths, it is necessary to situate the response within the intersectional social location of their mothers. Policy is predicated on the construct of the "bad Black mother." Society traditionally has not offered a positive response to these women and their children (Roberts 1997b). Consequently, if we are to offer a substantive response to the issues experienced by AIDS orphans, it is important to examine how policies serve to further marginalize these women and subsequently the children they leave behind. As we analyze policy's treatment of motherless Black AIDS orphans,

> We need to deconstruct the industries of . . . policy making from the perspectives of culture, gender, and socioeconomic status and enquire as to the reasons for their hegemony and practice. [We have to ask:] Are they . . . achieving equity? Do they enable the goals of social inclusion and well-being to be reached? Do they respect the breadth of citizenship in a country, and do they enhance or hinder the inspirations of all citizens? (Waldegrave 2009, 97)

Assumptions and constructions of Black women and their children perpetuated within HIV and AIDS discourses challenge policy's capacity to address the contexts and factors influencing Black women's susceptibility to HIV and AIDS. This can limit research, policy, and practice efforts to adequately address the processes of power that intersect with the social location of the targeted group to shape health, health behavior, and health care. As a consequence, policy, or lack of policy, could lead to the further marginalization of women and subsequently their orphaned children.

The challenge facing policy makers at both national and state levels is to design policy that is more equity oriented. This can be achieved by using intersectionality theory and its attendant principles to inform policy proposals and policy choices. Accordingly, policy makers must be willing to meaningfully incorporate the input of these women's voices and their experiences in their understanding of the policy problem. Such initiatives would shift the frame for understandings of HIV and AIDS toward intersectionality and social justice and, in so doing, disrupt discriminatory discourses that have impeded equitable policies and practices, thereby making visible what seems to be a forgotten population—Black AIDS orphans. Future research is needed to bring to the center those children who are orphaned as a result of HIV/AIDS. Such research is needed to help make visible their lived realities and those of their caregivers. Furthermore, future research is needed on how communities, organizations, and individuals in those communities are addressing this issue of HIV/AIDS orphans. When we are able to see what is being done, we will be better situated to address policy gaps. Such research will help to further develop the value of using an intersectional approach to policy making. Finally, it is important, as advocated by Black feminists, to understand how identity is used in policy making as it advances social justice in our institutional practices and everyday lives.

References

Adam, Barry D. 1989. "The State, Public Policy, and AIDS Discourse." *Contemporary Crises* 1: 1–14.

Adimora, Adaora A., and Schoenbach, Victor. J. 2002. "Contextual Factors and the Black-White Disparity in Heterosexual HIV Transmission." *Epidemiology* 13 (6): 707–12.

———. 2005. "Social Context, Sexual Networks, and Racial Disparities in Rates of Sexually Transmitted Infections." *The Journal of Infectious Diseases* 191 (s1): s115–s122.

Berger, Michelle. 2004. *Workable Sisterhood: The Political Journey of Stigmatized Women with HIV/AIDS.* Princeton, NJ: Princeton University Press.

Bower, Lisa. 1995. "The Trope of the Dark Continent in the Fetal Harm Debates: "Africanism" and the Right to Choice." In *Expecting Trouble: Surrogacy, Fetal Abuse, and New Reproductive Technologies*, edited by Patricia Boling, 142–55. Boulder, CO: Westview Press.

Bowleg, Lisa. 2008. "When Black+Lesbian+Woman ≠ Black Lesbian Woman: The Methodological Challenges of Qualitative and Quantitative Intersectionality Research." *Sex Roles* 59 (5): 312–25.

Brown, Nadia. E. 2014. "Black Women's Pathways to the State House: The Impact of Race/Gender Identities." *National Political Science Review* 16: 81–96.

Brown, Ruth Nicole. 2013. *Hear Our Truths: The Creative Potential of Black Girlhood.* Urbana: University of Illinois Press.

Burstein, Paul. 1998. "Bringing the Public Back in: Should Sociologists Consider the Impact of Public Opinion on Public Policy." *Social Forces* 77 (1): 27–62.

Centers for Disease Control and Prevention. 2010. *National Women & Girls HIV/AIDS Awareness Day*. March 7, 2010. http://www.cdc.gov/Features/WomenGirls HIVAIDS/.

Centers for Disease Control and Prevention. 2013. "HIV among African Americans." Accessed March 5, 2015. http://www.cdc.gov/hiv/topics/aa.

Centers for Disease Control and Prevention. n.d. "HIV among African Americans." Accessed March 5, 2015. http://www.cdc.gov/hiv/topics/aa/.

Cohn, Meredith. 2012. "Black Women in City Infected with HIV at Higher Rate than National Average." *The Baltimore Sun*, March 8, 2012. Accessed April 10, 2015. http://articles.baltimoresun.com/2012-03-08/health/bs-hs-aids-women-20120308_1_black-women-cases-of-hiv-infection-aids-awareness-day.

Combahee River Collective. 1977. *The Combahee River Collective Statement.* Accessed April 8, 2016. http://circuitous.org/scraps/combahee.html.

Connors, Margaret. 1996. "Sex, Drugs and Structural Violence: Unraveling the Epidemic among Poor Women of Color in the United States." In *Women, Poverty, and AIDS: Sex, Drugs, and Structural Violence,* edited by Paul Farmer,

Margaret Connors, and Janie Simmons, 91–123. Monroe, MD: Common Courage Press.

Cook, Judith, Andrew Boxer, Jane Burke, Mardge Cohen, Kathleen Weber, Proshat Shekarloo, Heidi Lubin, and Lynn Mock. 2004. "Child Care Arrangements of Children Orphaned by HIV/AIDS." *Journal of HIV/AIDS & Social Services* 2 (2): 5–20.

Crenshaw, Kimberlé, Neil Gotanda, Gary Peller, and Kendall Thomas, eds. 1995. *Critical Race Theory: The Key Writings That Formed the Movement.* New York: The New York Press.

Desmond, Chris, Karen Michael, and Jeff Gow. 2000. The Hidden Battle: HIV/AIDS in the Household and Community. *South African Journal of International Affairs* 7 (2): 39–58.

Doyal, Lesley. 2009. "Challenges in Researching Life with HIV/AIDS: An Intersectional Analysis of Black African Migrants in London." *Culture, Health & Sexuality* 11 (2): 173–88.

Draimin, Barbara, Ivy Gamble, Amy Shire, and Jan Hudis. 1998. "Improving Permanency Planning in Families with HIV Disease." *Child Welfare League of America* 77, no. 2 (March–April): 180–94.

Feist-Price, Sonja, and Lynda Brown Wright. 2003. "African American Women Living with HIV/AIDS: Mental Health Issues." *Women & Therapy* 26 (1/2): 27–44.

Galston, William A. 2007. "Civic Knowledge, Civic Education, and Civic Engagement: A Summary of Recent Research." *International Journal of Public Administration* 30 (6/7): 623–42.

Hankivsky, Olena, Daniel Grace, Gemma Hunting, Olivier Ferlatte, Natalie Clark, Alycia Fridkin, Melissa Giesbrecht, Sarah Rudrum, and Tarya Laviolette. 2012. "Intersectionality-Based Policy Analysis." In *An Intersectionality-Based Policy Analysis Framework*, edited by Olena Hankivsky, 33–45. Vancouver, BC: Institute for Intersectionality Research and Policy, Simon Fraser University.

Hill Collins, Patricia. 1998. "It's All in the Family: Intersections of Gender, Race, and Nation." *Hypatia* 13 (3): 62–82.

Ingram, Helen, Anne Schneider, and Paul deLeon. 2007. "Social Construction and Policy Design." In *Theories of the Policy Process*, edited by Peter A. Sabatier, 93–126. Boulder, CO: Westview Press.

Isoke, Zenzele. 2013. *Urban Black Women and the Politics of Resistance.* New York: Palgrave Macmillan.

Jones, Jenny. 2004. "Permanency Planning for HIV/AIDS Affected Children: Options for Care." *Journal of Human Behavior in the Social Environment* 9 (1/2): 57–68.

Jordan-Zachery, Julia S. 2016. "Learning from the Doers: Women of Color AIDS Service Organizations and Their Understanding of Intersectionality." *National Political Science Review* 18: 141–60.

——. 2009. *Black Women, Cultural Images, and Social Policy.* New York: Routledge.

Lynda L. Kaid, Monica Postelniu, Kristen Landreville, Hyun Jung Yun, and Abby Gail LeGrange. 2007. "The Effects of Political Advertising on Young Voters." *American Behavioral Scientist* 50 (9): 1137–51.

Kaiser Family Foundation. 2011. "HIV/AIDS at 30: A Public Opinion Perspective at 30, A Report Based on the Kaiser Family Foundation's 2011 Survey of Americans on HIV/AIDS." June 1, 2011. Accessed March 10, 2016. http://www.kff.org/kaiserpolls/upload/8186.pdf.

Krieger, Nancy. 1999. "Embodying Inequality: A Review of Concepts, Measures, and Methods for Studying Health Consequences of Discrimination." *International Journal of Health Services* 29 (2): 295–352.

Ladson-Billings, Gloria. 1998. "Just What Is Critical Race Theory and What's It Doing in a Nice Field Like Education?" *International Journal of Qualitative Studies in Education* 11 (1): 7–24.

Lichtenstein, Bronwen. 2008. "Little Needles, Big Haystack: Orphans of HIV/AIDS in the Deep South." *Journal of HIV/AIDS Prevention in Children & Youth* 9 (1): 52–69.

Logan, T. K., Jennifer Cole, and Carl Leukefeld. 2002. "Women, Sex, and HIV: Social and Contextual Factors, Meta-Analysis of Published Interventions, and Implications for Practice and Research." *Psychological Bulletin* 128 (6): 851–85.

Manza, Jeff, and Fay Lomax Cook. 2002. "A Democratic Polity? Three Views of Policy Responsiveness to Public Opinion in the United States." *American Politics Research* 30: 630–67.

Mason, Sally, and Nathan Linsk. 2002. "Relative Foster Parents of HIV-Affected Children." *Child Welfare League of America* 81 (4): 541–69.

Office of National AIDS Policy. 2009. *National HIV/AIDS Strategy*. Office of National AIDS Policy. December 15, 2009. Accessed March 15, 2016. http://whitehouse.gov/administration/eop/onap/nhas/.

Pequegnat, Willo, and Ellen Stover. 1999. "Considering Women's Contextual and Cultural Issues in HIV/STD Prevention Research." *Cultural Diversity and Ethnic Minority Psychology* 5 (3): 287–91.

Richardson, Elaine. 2003. *African American Literacies*. New York: Routledge.

Roberts, Dorothy. 1997a. "Unshackling Black Motherhood." *Michigan Law Review* 95 (4): 938–64.

———. 1997b. *Killing the Black Body: Race, Reproduction, and the Meaning of Liberty*. New York: Pantheon Books.

Schable, Barbara, Theresa Diaz, Susan Y. Chu, M. Blake Caldwell, Lisa Conti, Ollie M. Alston, Frank Sorvillo, et al. 1995. "Who Are the Primary Caretakers of Children Born to HIV-Infected Mothers? Results from a Multistate Surveillance Project." *Pediatrics* 95 (4): 511–15.

Schneider, Anne. L, and Helen Ingram. 1993. "Social Construction of Target Populations: Implications for Politics and Policy." *American Political Science Review* 87 (2): 334–47.

———. 1997. *Policy Design for Democracy*. Lawrence: University Press of Kansas.
UNAIDS. n.d. *United States of America*. Accessed March 2, 2015. UNAIDS.org.

Valdiserri, Ronald O. 2004. "Mapping the Roots of HIV/AIDS Complacency: Implications for Program and Policy Development." *AIDS Education and Prevention*, 16 (5): 426–39.

Waldegrave, Charles. 2009. "Cultural, Gender, and Socioeconomic Contexts in Therapeutic and Social Policy Work." *Family Process* 48 (1): 85–101.

Whitehead, Tony. 1997. "Urban Low-Income African American Men, HIV/AIDS and Gender Identity." *Medical Anthropology Quarterly* 11 (4): 411–47.

Wright, Ednita. M. 2003. "Deep from Within the Well: Voices of African American Women Living with HIV/AIDS." In *African American Women and HIV/AIDS: Critical Responses*, edited by Dorie J. Gilbert and Ednita M. Wright, 29–50. Westport, CT: Praeger.

Wright, Eric R., and Tiffany N. Martin. 2003. "The Social Organization of HIV/AIDS Care in Treatment Programmes for Adults with Serious Mental Illness." *AIDS CARE* 15 (6): 763–73.

Section III

Diasporic Black Women and the Global Political Arena

> "Be not discouraged black women of the world, but push forward, regardless of the lack of appreciation shown you."
>
> —Amy Jacques-Garvey

Crenshaw (1991) suggests that intersectionality manifests in three theoretical understandings: political, structural and representational. K. Melchor Quick Hall, Maziki Thame, and Keisha N. Blain's chapters address both political and structural intersectionality in an international context. Political intersectionality reflects the different (and sometimes conflicting) political agendas of the various groups to which an individual may belong or within which they "define" their identity (Crenshaw 1991, 357). Structural intersectionality centers the operation of systems and structures in society that result in the marginalization of individuals—in terms of their social needs and legal status. Crenshaw (1991, 358) offers the following claim to demonstrate the functioning of structural inequality: "Intervention strategies based solely on the experiences of women who do not share the same class or race will be of limited help" because individuals operate from (and are treated differently in) different social locations that are influenced by race, gender, class, and sexuality identities. For Crenshaw, both forms of intersectionality influence the lived realities of Black women in multiple and diverse ways.

Hall, in "El pan, el poder y la política: The Politics of Bread Making in Honduras' Garifuna Community," analyzes the voices of rural Black women in Honduras to show their engagement in "pragmatic activism," a form of political intersectionality, to resist land grab, a form of structural intersectionality. In her analysis, Hall articulates that through the politics of bread making, the women are able to engage "resistance to cultural erasure and displacement." The Garifuna women's resistance is executed on many fronts, including organizing co-ops for making *ereba*, which are simultaneously social and political spaces; maintaining ancestral practices; and via the socialization of women. She concludes her chapter by showing how these rural women are mobilizing beyond their immediate communities and therefore influencing urban women's political organizing by engaging in what she refers to as "nontraditional political activities."

Thame's analysis moves us from the realm of Black women engaging in nontraditional political activities to show how Black women (at least one), in the context of Jamaica, engage structural intersectionality. In "Woman Out of Place: Portia Simpson-Miller and Middle-Class Politics in Jamaica," Thame shows how the first elected female prime minster of Jamaica operates in a masculinist system. She argues that "Simpson-Miller's place in Jamaican politics raises questions about how black women's leadership can be nurtured within party politics, particularly because those women come from outside traditional networks of power." Thame shows how Simpson-Miller at times creates space and how such efforts are limited in the political structures she navigates. Finally, Blain, similarly to Thame, explores Black women's functioning within a raced-masculinist structure. As she argues, Black women in the international arena had to fight to have their voices heard; moreover, their voices were often constrained by a male-dominated understanding of freedom and liberty.

In "We Want to Set the World on Fire," Keisha N. Blain takes up the general topic of the means by which Black women make space in seemingly masculinist spaces. Using Black women's 1940s writings in the *New Negro World* newspaper, Blain offers us a critical analysis of the political ideas of Black nationalist women. Blain argues that Black women had to fight for space to articulate their vision of freedom. She states, "Despite the masculinist and patriarchal orientation of the Universal Negro Improvement Association (UNIA), the *New Negro World* provided a crucial platform for nationalist women to engage in national and international political discourses." Black nationalist women advocated for Pan-Africanism as a means of addressing White supremacy and oppression, countering negative stereotypes often used to describe Blacks. Although they engaged in activism around global Black liberation, Blain shows how their writings were filled with tension resulting from their intersectional identities. For instance, she states that as "community feminists," they challenged sexism and sought to empower Black women globally. Yet they walked a fine line between advancing women's opportunities and supporting Black men's leadership.

These researchers show the challenges faced by Black women in confronting the sociocultural marking of Black women's bodies and how their politics involves challenging norms even while working within an existing system. As a result, some narratives are not included in public discourses, masculinist politics are promoted, and stereotypes that can control Black women are maintained. Hall, Thame, and Blain, individually and collectively, through their use of intersectionality afford us an opportunity to reconceptualize race and gender and political behavior. They show how Black women craft their political responses to political and structural intersectionality, which often results in their being rendered invisible and silenced. Such political strategizing is in response to the Euro-American oppression of Black women and is also a function of the Black community's internal structuring. Although recognizing that these two processes are distinct but intimately connected, the authors bring to the forefront how Black women create space and use their voices against exclusion and marginalization—both internal and external to Black communities.

Reference

Crenshaw, Kimberlé. 1991. "Mapping the Margins: Intersectionality, Identity Politics, and Violence Against Women of Color." *Stanford Law Review* 43 (6): 1241–99.

6

El pan, el poder y la política

The Politics of Bread Making in Honduras's Garifuna Community

K. MELCHOR QUICK HALL
Brandeis University Women's Studies Research Center

Introduction

The unique language and music of the Afro-descendant and autochthonous Garifuna community has been recognized as a masterpiece of oral and intangible heritage by the United Nations Educational, Scientific and Cultural Organization (López 2001). The ancestral villages of this transnational community span the Caribbean coast of Central America and include small towns in Belize, Nicaragua, Honduras, and Guatemala. Of these Central American states, Honduras has the longest-standing and largest villages that continue to maintain the Garifuna language and culture today. In fact, the villages in the other Central American countries were formed by Garifuna people who migrated from Honduras after being forcibly exiled from the island of Saint Vincent by the British in 1797 (Gonzalez 1988). In these Honduran Garifuna ancestral villages, it is possible to find long-standing traditions including the production of *ereba*.

Ereba—a Garifuna word translated into English as cassava bread—is the staple food in these ancestral Garifuna villages of Honduras. Baked exclusively by women, it has been studied as a culturally significant food staple in the Garifuna community, often with a focus on the laborious processing of the cassava plant (Gold 2009, 50; Gonzalez 1969, 46; Gonzalez 1988, 107–8). In recent years, a number of scholars have studied the Garifuna community's political resistance in response to the encroachment on Garifuna ancestral lands (Anderson 2009; Brondo 2013). However, the link between women's production of *ereba* and political resistance has gone unexplored. As a response, this chapter focuses on organizations linked to the *ereba* tradition that are engaging in nontraditional political resistance—a discussion well suited to an anthology that aims to uncover ways in which Black women of the African Diaspora engage in politics, even when others fail to recognize it. Prestage (1991) wrote about the paucity of information on African American women's nontraditional political activity, which is shaped by the "legal and cultural circumstances they faced at the time" (89). Marginalized in the larger Honduran society, the Garifuna women of Honduras are engaging in nontraditional political activity through both the ancestral culinary tradition of *ereba* making in rural communities and the articulation of political alternatives in urban centers that highlight connections to both rural and urban Black Honduran communities.

The Naming/Labeling of Blackness

Before discussing the *ereba* production of the Garifuna women of Honduras, it is important to clarify two reasons why this is, in fact, appropriate to an anthology about Black women and politics. The first issue is related to the question of naming and identity: "Are the Garifuna women Black?" The second question to which I respond is "Can women's bread making, which does not directly engage the government, be considered political?" Ultimately, I have answered both of these questions in the affirmative. Below, I briefly explain how and why I came to these conclusions.

As Alexander-Floyd and Simien (2006) have articulated, the very exercise of naming a group is an important one, replete with political implications. Thus, it is noteworthy that today most Garinagu do not refer to themselves as *negro*, or the Spanish translation of Black. Moreover, throughout history the Garifuna community has taken various positions in relation to other Afro-descendants. The group's unique historical heritage can be traced to slaver shipwrecks off the coast of Saint Vincent around 1675 and the miscegenation of Africans with the Carib indigenous people (Fabel 2000, 145; Gonzalez 1988; Johnson 2005, 45). British occupiers of the island removed the Garinagu, or Black Carib, as they called them, from the island in 1797 following a series of land disputes (Johnson 2006, 42). Thus, Garinagu were not enslaved in the Americas. The distinctive history of the Garifuna people with regard to both bondage and language (i.e., speaking the indigenous Garinagu language) led many Garifuna to resist affiliation with other Afro-descendants throughout much of their history until the 1950s (Gonzalez 1997, 200–1; Johnson 2007, 102).

In spite of this resistance, during the 1800s, the Garinagu were classified as Negro by the Republic of Central America (Bateman 1998). Throughout the 1960s, they continued to be classified by outsiders as *moreno*, a term often used as the Latin American equivalent of Black (Euraque 2007, 92–93). The term *moreno* has been used at times as a more polite racial term than Black, as England (2010) describes: "It places one on the colour continuum somewhere near the bottom but with the suggestion that there is some mixture on the way to whiteness" (201). However, starting in the 1970s, *negro* was used by Garifuna people as a "conscious political, cultural, and racial identification with the African diaspora" (England 2010, 202). In the 1980s and 1990s, with increased Garifuna migration to the United States to work in the service economy as well as increased visibility of indigenous movements in Honduras, there was a tendency for Garifuna people to identify themselves as simply Garinagu, focusing on ethnic, rather than racial, identity: "This identification as Garifuna (rather than simply *negro* or *moreno*) was strategic because it removed the Garifuna from the colour continuum and placed them alongside indigenous peoples as a group that is culturally and racially distinct from the *mestizo* majority and intends to stay so" (England 2010, 203).

In recent years, Garifuna organizations have held meetings of Afro-descendants in Honduras, clearly marking an intentional political link between Afro-descendants in Honduras and those in other parts of the Americas (ODECO 2010). This chapter is rooted in ten months of fieldwork in Honduras during the 2011–2012 academic year funded by a Fulbright research grant. When I entered the Garifuna villages, I was not certain that the explicitly pan-African sentiments of the urban, mobile elite of the Garifuna community would be echoed in the rural communities. However, I found that villagers connected with me as part of an African Diasporic community, engaging me in discussion about Black politics in the region, especially regarding the first Black president of the United States, Barack Obama. It is in this context of explicit and direct communication with the Garifuna women of Honduras that I discuss their identity as Black women in the Americas. Furthermore, this chapter advances a Black feminist agenda, understanding Black feminism as

> *an embodied, positioned, ideological standpoint perspective that holds Black women's experiences of simultaneous and multiple oppressions as the epistemological and theoretical basis of a "pragmatic activism" directed at combating those social and personal, individual and structural, and local and global forces that pose harm to Black (in the widest geopolitical sense) women's well-being.* (McClaurin 2001, 63 emphasis in original)

Thus, it is important to understand the simultaneously Black and indigenous identity of Garifuna women. It is only after these simultaneous and multiple identities are understood that the specific types of oppressions that challenge Garifuna women can be analyzed.

Indigenous Identity and Matrifocality in the Context of Land Politics

Garifuna women's indigeneity is an important aspect of their connection to the land. Historically, the Garifuna people have faced considerable challenges in being recognized as an indigenous group because of their skin color, or racial identity; in fact, it was not until 1992 that the World Council of Indigenous Peoples admitted the Garifuna people (Taylor 2012, 158). Further, the recognition of the Garifuna as an indigenous group has been important to political claims to communal, ancestral lands. As Anderson (2009) writes, "Indigeneity thus provided a language through which collective claims could be made and heard; it made a collective subject that the state and other actors could recognize as legitimately distinctive" (134).

While indigeneity is central to land claims, it is also resisted by many Garifuna people as an ethno-racial category. Instead, the term "autochthonous" is preferred: As Gordon and Anderson (1999) write, "The careful use of the term *autochthonous (autóctono)* as opposed to *indigenous (indígena)*—with its connotations of biological Indianness—allows Garifuna to make primordial claims while maintaining a racial distinction" (291). In this way, the ethno-racial identity of the group is deemphasized. In addition to the group's autochthonous identity, Garifuna matrifocality is also an important element of understanding the social and political connections to land.

Matrifocality has been described as "a kinship system in which women, as mothers, serve as the foci of households, extended kin groups, and ritual" (England 2006, 67). The matrifocality of Garifuna society is well documented by scholars (England 2006; Gonzalez 1969; Kerns 1983). One way in which this matrifocality manifests is through consanguineal households, or homes in which women related through their mother assist each other with household and childcare responsibilities (Kerns 1983, 120). Not only are older women the focal point of ritual and affective relations in these households, but they are also the primary redistributors of goods (including food) and money (England 2006, 68; Kerns 1983, 120). Another important manifestation of Garifuna matrifocality is the matrilineal inheritance of land. The combination of women's primary role as redistributors of goods and money with their ownership and inheritance of land makes women's agricultural and food production (i.e., the production of *ereba*) central to the discussion of land politics, as explored below.

The Race, Gender, and Class of Honduras's Land Policies

Jordan-Zachery (2009) has discussed the *racing* and *gendering* of policy in the United States. In this section about the politics of *ereba* making, I discuss how the laws that govern the land on which cassava production takes place are both raced and gendered. Given this important historical context and contemporary reality, it will be demonstrated that the continuation of the culinary tradition of *ereba* making is a form of political resistance that responds to discriminatory land-grabbing policies.

In 1974, Honduras passed an agrarian reform law that targeted the ancestral lands of the Garifuna for redistribution. As a result, Honduras's National Agrarian Institute (INA) encouraged peasants seeking farmland to migrate to the North Coast, where the Garifuna ancestral villages are located. Although the land was inhabited and cultivated by the Garifuna people, the government did not consider the way in which the land was being used as a productive and efficient use of the land. England (2006) described the characterization of the land use as follows: "INA categorized the subsistence agricultural practices of the Garifuna (and indigenous peoples) as summarily unproductive, failing to give the land a 'social function'—that is, agricultural production for the market, cattle ranching, or resource extraction. In the end, both large landowners and *colonos* on the North Coast used the agrarian reform of 1974 as a way to expropriate Garifuna agricultural land" (112). Not only did this policy privilege wealthy landowners, but it was also a direct attack on the social and cultural context of Garifuna farming. It represented a pernicious and discriminatory devaluation of the Garifuna method of farming.

Historically, the Garifuna have used a mixed-crop swidden agricultural style in which there are periods of time when plots of land are resting (i.e., not being cultivated) while other plots are in use (England 2006, 48). The government reform allowed outsiders to claim these "resting" plots of land and title them, even though there were Garifuna families who had been cultivating the land for generations. During this period, there were some individuals who cleared these (temporarily) unused plots and sold them to large landowners (England 2006, 116). In this way, Honduran government officials, ambitious farm workers, and large-scale capitalists worked in collaboration to rob Garifuna families of their land. The impact of the policy was targeted; the target was the Black and indigenous Garifuna woman who was the traditional landholder in Garifuna society.

When Jordan-Zachery (2009) discusses the raced and gendered nature of policy, she identifies specific societal consequences: "For one, the practices and processes of politics and policy making create and maintain race, gender and other divisions in society" (3). The Honduran land reform policy was intended to maintain the social hierarchy that privileged wealthy landowners and to further marginalize economically those Garifuna communities that were already physically marginalized at the coastal edges of the country. According to Jordan-Zachery (2009), "[t]he goal of Black feminist politics is to theorize about and strategize to address the various manifestations of intersecting oppressive structures and ideologies" (1–2). The Garifuna community, existing at the intersection of a Black racial identity and an indigenous—or autochthonous—ethnic identity, has long navigated the challenges of being oppressed and marginalized by multiple, intersecting systems. In relation to land rights, the group has often allied with other indigenous groups to make important political advances.

Under pressure from Garifuna and other indigenous organizations, in 1994 the Honduran government ratified convention number 169 of the International Labor Organization, which provided protection for the collective rights of indigenous groups, including the protection of territory used for crop cultivation, hunting, collecting medicinal plants, and sacred sites (England 1999, 20). With this added protection under the watch of the international community, the Garifuna worked to title more of the communal lands. However, by 1995, only fourteen of the forty-eight Garifuna communities had received definitive land titles (Brondo 2013, 45). The land titles that did exist neither covered the historical landholdings of communities nor addressed past encroachments (Brondo 2013, 45; England 2006, 230–31). Using collective action, including an organized march of thousands of Garinagu on the capital city of Tegucigalpa in 1996, the Garifuna community was able to have additional money allocated to land titling, resulting in most Garifuna communities receiving titles for land by 2002 (Thorne 2004, 25).

Because the Garifuna society is matrifocal and land is inherited through matrilineal lines, government actions to obtain and exploit coastal lands have had a disproportionate impact on Garifuna women (Brondo 2013, 81). Anderson (2009) describes the transfer of land away from Garifuna women as follows: "More Garifuna women own homes than Garifuna men and familial usufruct rights for communal lands tend to pass from women to their daughters. Therefore, the transfer of land into private property involves a significant resource loss for Garifuna women to mestizo men and, to a lesser extent, Garifuna men" (56). The Garifuna women's loss of land stood in sharp contrast to the headway that non-Garifuna women were making in terms of the acquisition of private land titles (Brondo 2013, 81). To analyze this varied impact on "women," one should engage in an intersectional analysis. More specifically, one might analyze what Crenshaw (1991) calls structural intersectionality, which highlights the ways in which the location of women of color at the intersection of race and gender makes our experiences different from the experiences of women of the majority (1245).

In the absence of an intersectional approach, this transfer of land away from the Garifuna minority to the mestiza majority might be interpreted as simply an increase in the private ownership of land by women. However, as Yuval-Davis (2009) reminds us, "Social divisions are about macro axes of social power but also involve actual, concrete people" (46). In this context, the lived experience of the Garifuna woman is quite different from that of the *mestiza* woman. To evaluate the gendered impact while neglecting the ethnic and racial impact would be a mistake and would provide an incomplete and inadequate picture. As Crenshaw (1989) so aptly writes, "Because the intersectional experience is greater than the sum of racism and sexism, any analysis that does not take intersectionality into account cannot sufficiently address the particular manner in which Black women are subordinated" (140).

It is especially important to analyze the impact on indigenous women who have held communal land titles. As Brondo (2013) describes, "Legislation thus focuses on the issuance of private land titles as opposed to communal land titles with matrilineally based use rights" (81–82). This emphasis explains why land ownership trends have moved in different directions for Garifuna and non-Garifuna women. These encroachments on Garifuna land cannot be understood simply in terms of gender (i.e., women and men as landowners) or ethnicity (i.e., indigenous and nonindigenous landowners); they must be contextualized in a racialized history of land (re)distribution: "The massive impoverishment of the majority of African peoples today, as well as millions in Asia and Latin America—normalized as a question of development—is not simply a humanitarian tragedy, but, in part, the product of a racialised international order, a form of global structural racism" (Jones 2008, 924–25). Thus, the land transfer represents an action that is both economic and political with gendered, ethnicized, and racialized implications. This example thus highlights the critical importance of an understanding of how race and ethnicity interact with gender, class, and other factors when governments enact policies. In other words, an intersectional approach is required to understand fully the implications of state policies.

By examining the issue of land rights with an intersectional lens, we are able to see how the empowerment of one group of women (i.e., mestiza women) can be directly linked to the disempowerment of another group of women (i.e., Garifuna women): "While Honduran women in general are making some headway in terms of receiving private land titles in their names, Garifuna women's land loss has accelerated under neoliberal land titling programs" (Brondo 2013, 81). These varying impacts have been forecast and highlighted by Michelle Fine (2009), who says the following: "I want to point out a political space where I believe intersectional analyses are critical and underexplored. This has to do with gender, class, and race as women negotiate the neoliberal state; that is, how girls and women from very different political and demographic life spaces survive when the State refuses to attend to the needs of communities and families" (Guidroz and Berger 2009, 69). It is in this context that we examine the policies of the Honduran state and their impact on marginalized communities.

Brondo (2013) has characterized Honduras's neoliberal land policies as follows: "The decades-long processes of privatization have moved land from a largely Garifuna women's resource to that of mestizo and foreign men. The 'gender-blind' neoliberal land policies of the 1990s served to expand land displacement and gender inequality, especially in the tourism boom on Honduras's coastline" (81). Consequently, there is no such thing as gender-blind or race-blind policy; there are only single-axis analyses that fail to engage the complex realities.

Further, the persistence of Garifuna women engaging in the centuries-old tradition of *ereba* making is a form of resistance to the people and policies that intend to displace them. The tradition continues to bring together large groups of women for the peeling, grinding, and straining of cassava. These spaces are both political and social. Organizations called *galpones casaberos* have been created around the production of *ereba* to mechanize and modernize the process for faster and more efficient production, often with a larger non-Garifuna market in mind. These organizations are a source of cultural and economic strength in the community. In the section below, I discuss how these organizations are engaging in a politics of resistance.

Galpones Casaberos as Political Bodies of Resistance and Wealth Redistribution

The villages that the 1974 agrarian reform targeted for resettlement were (and are) known as the heart of Honduran Garifuna culture. Whereas in the cities, children might grow up speaking only Spanish, on the northern coast the primary language is Garifuna. You can find men engaging in the artisanal fishing for which they are known, and women baking *ereba*. In examining the social status of Garifuna women in these ancestral villages, Sutton (1997) wrote the following: "They articulate a conscious aim of preserving and transmitting Garifuna culture as it comes under threat from the commercial values of tourism and the sale of coastal land. . . . They draw on their long history of working together to form cooperatives that have proven to be economically successful" (xiii–xiv). It is with this political consciousness that the *galpones casaberos* organize the production of *ereba*.

During the 2011–2012 academic year, I worked in three villages with four *galpones casaberos* (hereafter referred to as *galpones*). In this chapter, the names of villages, organizations, and farmers have been changed to provide anonymity. In Cuenca, I worked with "Women's Traditions" and "Community Cassava." "Community Cassava" was the first *galpón* (singular of *galpones*) in Cuenca. It was started with the cooperation of all the families in the village and was intended to serve the entire community. "Women's Traditions" developed later, when a group of women within the community felt they would be better served by opening their own *molino,* or cassava-grinding house; it is an all-women's organization. At the time of my fieldwork (2011–2012), the groups were working together, alternating days when their *molinos* were open, so that the *ereba* makers always had a place to grind and strain cassava daily. Further, members from one organization often took advantage of services at the other organization's *molino* because of the proximity to their cassava field or some other convenience. In addition to working with the *galpones* in Cuenca, I also worked in the nearby villages of Zafra and Carmona. In Carmona, I worked with the mixed-gender *galpón* "Fish to

Cassava" that was cooperatively run by a group of cousins. Finally, in Zafra, I worked with "Women Warriors," which was an all-women's organization.

A common thread among these groups was that they organized families, and more specifically women, who were engaging in the production (and sometimes commercialization) of *ereba*. While sociologists often acknowledge the important impact of families in politics, the role of families is often neglected in the mainstream discourse of political science and international relations. However, when we examine the role of the *galpones* in the organization of *ereba*—the principal agricultural product of many Garifuna villages—we can not ignore the political significance of families or the organizations that mobilize their collective labor.

Haney and Pollard (2003) describe the ways in which states have evoked the image of families and called for the action of families to various political ends: "Sometimes the family has been deployed as a metaphor for imagining the state; at other times, the family has been used in more concrete terms as a model for state-building. At still other times, the family has been used to move state policies in new directions or as a vehicle for state goals" (Haney and Pollard 2003, 1). As mentioned earlier in this chapter, the Honduran government historically has considered the presence of Garifuna families on the northern coast as a barrier to the country's development; these families stood in the way of the expansion of capitalist production by large landholders. Contrastingly, the *galpones* organize the activity of families in ways that are central to grassroots community development—past, present, and future.

The sale of *ereba* is the primary source of income for many of the Garifuna women of the villages. Although there are spikes in *ereba* sales during holidays, when there is an influx of Garifuna people returning to the ancestral homes from the cities or from abroad, what the *ereba* makers wanted was a steady market. Many villagers envisioned a strong *ereba* market as a path out of poverty, and described an unreliable market as a constant source of frustration. As an example, Alejandro said, "We are vigorously searching for a market for our product because right now there is a lot of cassava to pick to process *ereba* and we don't have sales demand because we don't have a market that demands of us, asks of us, the quantity of *ereba* that we can produce."

Catalina talked about how important *ereba* is to the overwhelming majority of the village: "The only hope we have to be able to move forward is the sale of *ereba* because that is our work. And I know that if one day the moment arrives in which *ereba* has a demand at a global level, we will be able to say that the community will be able to develop because that is the agricultural work of almost 95 percent of the people in the community." Zoe spoke to the importance of *ereba* for the single mother: "Right now, what I would want, as a producer of *ereba*, as a single mother, I would want my community in general to have a good market for the production and sale of *ereba* because there is always production. And if we had a good market, with the product that exists, our product would be in that market." Simply put, the *galpones casaberos* are the organizations that were driving the development work that stands in stark contrast to the state's suggestion that Garifuna people's use (or lack of use) of land was an impediment to development. By promoting the culinary tradition of *ereba* making as a means to an alternative form of development—not the development imagined by the state—the *galpones* are central to the politicization of this agricultural activity. Moreover, this politicization was accomplished through the galvanization of families in the service of the cooperative and collaborative *ereba*-making processes.

Waltner and Maynes (2004) recognize that families are critical to the political projects of states and that "family relations have the capacity to uphold or undermine social and political order" (56). The authors link global development to family activities:

> World historical change involves the activities of families—that is, small groups linked by ties of marriage, descent, or adoption, normally constituting fluid coresidential households. Global encounters and major processes of global development are structured by systems of kinship—that is, socially recognized relationships between people in a particular culture who are (or are held to be) biologically related or who are given the status of relatives by marriage, adoption, or other ritual. (Waltner and Maynes 2004, 48)

What this statement highlights is that the family is not outside or beyond the boundaries of state policies and politics; instead, family relations are integral to those politics and policies. When we consider the centrality of the consanguineal household to the matrifocal Garifuna societal structure, the important role of women in agricultural production and food redistribution is clear. The Garifuna households—and more specifically the women in these households—are the drivers of community development. Further, when it comes to the production of *ereba* in Honduran villages, the *galpones* are the organizational structure at the heart of the villages' most important agricultural product.

Apart from the coordination of agricultural labor, the *galpones* are also promoting communal sharing and the redistribution of wealth in the villages. Valentina, one of the members of "Community Cassava," said the following: "We work united. We work united when we pick cassava. We unite to peel that cassava. We help one another mutually. Almost all the Garifuna work is done communally. It is united, communal." Within the *galpones*, members find tremendous support. Samantha said, "In the cooperative, we are all united." Diego emphasized collective work: "There is a lot of collective work. The people always help one another do things for the benefit of the community's development." And Julia talked about living peacefully with mutual understanding: "We live peacefully and united. . . . We get along well. We understand one another." For each of these villagers, the *galpón* is central to collective work and communal sharing.

One of the ways that the *galpones* advance the communal values of sharing is by promoting Garifuna mutual assistance through support of *galpón* members in times of financial crisis. The organizations often lend money to members for personal medical expenses or for the burial of a family member. They provide support to individuals however and whenever needed, if at all possible. In spite of the general aversion to accepting loans, including micro-loans, from nongovernmental organizations, there was the sense that the *galpones* provided a more caring and understanding form of financial support. Whereas many nongovernmental organizations that discover that a borrower spent a business loan burying a family member might judge that individual harshly for mixing business and personal funds, the *galpones* understand family as the base for community development, and support the care of one's family. In this way, the *galpones* are central to the redistribution of resources among families in the villages. While most (three of the four) *galpones* did not have significant profit during my 2011–2012 fieldwork, "Women Warriors" regularly redistributed profits among its members. The organizations continued to grow because of the contributions of their members; further, those members benefited from the profitability of the organization. The *galpones*, thus, engage in the politically significant redistribution of wealth at the scale of the village. *Ereba* production also has a significant social role, as described below.

Socialization in the Production of Ereba

As mentioned above, in the mid-1970s, Honduras's National Agrarian Institute targeted Garifuna land for resettlement because of a supposed lack of "social function." In contrast to the suggestion that the Garifuna agricultural work lacks social function, *ereba* production has a deep historical and social significance for the community. The economic value of the product is only part of the benefit. During interviews with Garifuna villagers, it became clear that producing *ereba* provided an important connection to ancestral heritage, early socialization for young girls, and a supportive network for Garifuna women.

The villagers expressed tremendous pride in doing work that connected them to their ancestors. People regularly shared stories about learning to work the land with their mothers and grandmothers. Women often talked about how they had been learning to work the land from the days of their childhood. As an example, Julieta shared the following information about her family's cassava cultivation: "Right now, my father has died. My mother is already old. She can't do much. But from the time I've been a girl, they taught me to do this work. So, I am taking care of the land for all of us. I am taking care of it all." Women typically had stories of learning to work in the fields, and bake *ereba*, at a young age. They enjoyed sharing memories of these traditions passed down.

Maria Jose said, "As [*ereba*] is from our ancestors, from it we live. So, for my part I wouldn't want our culture to disappear. From [*ereba*], we are living. Because even though we don't have money, from it we survive. So, it is important in our lives." Samantha also spoke of the Garifuna ancestors, saying, "We are accustomed, acclimated to the life of our ancestors. We are acclimated to our land, our work, our culture." Through the work in the fields, women kept alive the connection to their ancestors. Although these feelings were strongest among the middle-aged women in their forties and fifties, younger women also talked about the importance of agricultural work as their inheritance.

Gabriela, who was sent to the city to live with relatives when she was a little girl, shared her childhood thoughts about returning home: "I am going to return to my village. I am going to work [the land] with my mother because I like to eat cassava. I like to eat yam. I like to eat everything the land produces." Gabriela's statement highlights a rare enthusiasm among younger women for the agricultural labor that defines life in the villages. Whereas many young adults prefer the employment opportunities of the city to the sustenance farming of the villages, Gabriela loved the agricultural work from the time she was a young girl. While all the villagers I interviewed would agree that agricultural work is an important link to ancestral heritage for the entire community, specific activities were designated according to gender roles and identities.

Thorne (2004) describes Garifuna culture as having "a particular set of subsistence activities and a related gendered division of labor" (23). She describes that division of labor as follows: "In agricultural production, men are usually responsible for soil preparation as well as slashing and burning, while both men and women are involved in the sowing, harvesting and storage of the crop. Women cultivate and grate yucca, dry it, and then bake it over hot coals into the finished product, cassava bread, some of which is reserved for local market consumption" (Thorne 2004, 23). This description is consistent with what I observed during my time in the villages. It is also consistent with how members of the *galpones* described their own work.

Characteristic of sentiment throughout the villages, Diego, a member of "Community Cassava," described *ereba* production as women's work:

> I do not mean to say that the work is exclusively done by women. . . . Culturally, true enough, the one who does more is the woman. But the role of the man from the preparation of the land, meaning the clearing of land and chopping of trees, this is the most direct work of the man. . . . Everything is distributed [among men and women] with the woman being more dedicated to the processing of the cassava that would be the preparation of the *ereba*. But the role of the man is also integral. It is all distributed. The man is involved in the preparation of the land all the way through the planting of the cassava. Afterwards, the rest of the work is more cultural and is the function of the woman.

As evidenced in the passage above, *ereba* belongs culturally to the women in spite of the participation of men in cassava cultivation.

In this way, there is both gender complementarity and ownership of *ereba* production by women. Women have long taken cultural ownership of *ereba* making in Garifuna communities, as one of the early pioneers in the study of Garifuna culture, Nancie Gonzalez (1969), describes:

> It was traditional in Black Carib culture for the women to be the primary agricultural producers. Men contributed in this sphere

> by clearing and burning the land in preparation for planting, but after that the women took over and completed the cycle of cultivation and harvesting. A woman's responsibility did not end with the harvest—she also processed the foods and produced and converted them into edible form. For bitter manioc, this involved the laborious task of expressing the poisonous acid, and the manufacture of *areba*, or cassava bread, the main staple. (46)

Women, through the baking of cassava flour to produce *ereba*, are at the center of *ereba* production. They represent the apex of this multistage process involving multiple family and community members.

The matrifocality of Garifuna society means that the history of encroachment on Garifuna lands has a direct impact on women's agricultural work. Gargolla (2005) writes about the threat to Garifuna women from global forces that impose increasingly hierarchical gender structures: "Garifuna women are presently in danger of having their role devalued in their community as a result of the loss of coastal land and the shift from a rural economy, that valued their role, to a market-based economy" (137). Both the economic and social functioning of Garifuna women is severely impacted by attempts to displace communities from their land. It can also be psychologically damaging, as *ereba* work is something about which Garifuna women are quite proud, and losing access to land means losing access to a treasured ancestral food tradition.

As an example of the pride evoked in *ereba* production, we can consider how the women who do this work contrast themselves with modern-day urban professionals. Camila described herself as follows: "I'm not a professional, but I'm a professional when it comes to using a machete." Similarly, Sofia described an alternative understanding of what it means to be a professional: "I don't have a profession. I'm not a professional, but I'm a professional at working the land." There is a significant amount of pride associated with *ereba* making, at least among the principal *ereba* makers.

By and large, the women who would describe their primary vocation as *ereba* making are mothers in their forties and fifties. They tend to be the heads of their households; they often have spent most of their lives in the villages; and they have relatively little formal education (i.e., between a second- and sixth-grade education). In thinking about the political, social, and economic power of these women, it is useful to contrast the experiences of women of different ages. Such contrasts are easily explored in relation to the younger, college-bound women of the villages.

Although the older women pooled resources to educate both young men and women of the village at urban universities, young men were able to have children with relatively little social stigma, while young women who became pregnant before finishing their studies were often shamed. While initially considered good investments, these women were blamed for wasting the resources of their families. If a young woman returns to the village pregnant (or with a young child), she is no longer considered a good investment. Instead, she is required to work the land with the older women. In this sense, for many young women, *ereba* making was the backup plan for those individuals who were unsuccessful in the city. These women felt ashamed for having failed their families.

One young woman, Guadalupe, opened up about returning to the village pregnant: "I am struggling for my daughter; that is why I am baking *ereba*. I didn't have the intelligence to succeed when my mother sent me to school. I failed. I left the city pregnant. That is why I am no longer studying. However, I am working with my mother, baking *ereba* and clearing fields to move ahead, to fight for the future of my daughter." Because men are not expected to care for children on a daily basis, having children in no way complicates a young man's career or education in the city. For young women, however, it changes their life path.

The shaming of young women comes largely from the middle-aged women. As Khan (1987) notes, the older women have significant power and independence in the community: "In Garifuna as in other societies, there are certain cultural expectations that distinguish and separate individuals belonging to different stages of the life-cycle. Behavioral standards and expectations for post-reproductive women often change, and this new stage is marked by freedom from many of the cultural restrictions on their earlier behavior" (184). While the older women, *as a group*, certainly hold significant political, economic, and social power in the community, they have created a standard that is difficult to meet for the younger women who follow in their footsteps.

That this creation of an infallibly chaste female student ideal hurts the opportunities of young Garifuna women to access education is an example of representational intersectionality, or "the cultural construction of women of color" (Crenshaw 1991, 1245). As Crenshaw (1991) writes, "Controversies over the representation of women in popular culture can also elide the particular location of women of color, and thus become yet another source of intersectional disempowerment" (1245). Certainly the controversy over how young women sent to the city to further their studies should "represent"

Garifuna community values has resulted in decreased educational access for young Garifuna mothers.

Garifuna Women and the Future of Politics

Above I have outlined the centrality of *ereba* production to community development and land politics of the ancestral Garifuna villages. My decision to focus on rural development and politics was motivated by what I identified as a sometimes narrow focus on urban development, professionalization, and formal national politics. In a country where an estimated 48 percent of the population lives outside the urban centers (US CIA World Factbook 2011), I thought it important to explore the realities and possibilities for development in more remote areas and to understand how that grassroots development is politicized. Within the Garifuna community, there is considerable tension, especially among organizations vying for political leadership, about the best way to move forward in terms of development and politics. Through an analysis of Garifuna political organizing, it is possible to examine the third type of intersectionality discussed by Crenshaw (1991), political intersectionality. Political intersectionality highlights how the politics of groups singularly focused can often have the effect of further marginalization of individuals at the crossroads, or intersections, of those issues.

The two major Honduran Garifuna organizations—ODECO and OFRANEH—have represented very different, gendered political approaches: "Among the Garifuna of Honduras, there is clearly a rivalry and tension between the two major organizations, OFRANEH, a grassroots supported organization led by women, and ODECO, a nongovernmental organization led by a man, but largely staffed by women and serving a large female constituency" (Safa 2006, 229). ODECO has had stronger international support and has worked closely with the Honduran government and the Garifuna population in the United States while building alliances with Afro-descendants internationally. OFRANEH has been more deeply rooted in local Honduran Garifuna communities and historically has emphasized alliances with other indigenous groups. In addition to being distinguished by emphases on different aspects of the Garifuna identity and having very different capacities for international collaboration, there also has been a deep gendered distinction between the groups' political approaches. (It remains to be seen how the April 2016 passing of ODECO's leader, and the transition to a female president, might impact the gendered nuances described below.)

ODECO had been a more patriarchal organization, led by the same charismatic leader since its inception, while OFRANEH has been more matriarchal and feminist in its approach to politics. Brondo (2013) describes these characteristics of OFRANEH as follows:

> OFRANEH, for instance, a matriarchal organization, offers a counternarrative of development, falling into the "alternatives to development" perspective, which takes a critical stance against the discourse of modern development models and puts faith in grassroots social mobilization efforts to overcome the structures and discourses of modern development. OFRANEH's approach can also be characterized as informed by feminist critiques of development in highlighting the differential experiences that Garifuna women face as a result of national development policy. (172)

OFRANEH also resists much of the large-scale tourist development that ODECO has embraced, and when ODECO held a summit for Afro-descendants in La Ceiba in August 2011, OFRANEH organized a concurrent countersummit. Crenshaw (1991) writes, "Ignoring difference *within* groups contributes to tension *among* groups" (1242). Certainly, in the context of Honduran (and global) politics, vying for a position as the voice of the Garifuna people has created considerable tension between these two national organizations. Given the tension between ODECO and OFRANEH, it is no wonder that a number of Garifuna political women have explored a third alternative for active political engagement.

As mentioned above, the *galpones casaberos* are one avenue through which Garifuna women in their forties and fifties have considerable access to political status and economic resources. Building on the social status already granted them as mothers and heads of household in a matrifocal society, these women are well positioned to enact change. However, the physical mobility of these rural women is often restricted by economic constraints. As such, I have been particularly interested in urban-based political initiatives that link directly to the *ereba*-making work that has so much potential for the mobilization of rural communities. On a return trip to Honduras in January 2015, I was pleased to meet with an organization that was developing this link between urban professionals and rural sustenance farmers.

During my initial fieldwork in Honduras from October 2011 to August 2012, I had the opportunity to work with a woman who had been purchasing *ereba* from the villages to make flavored cassava chips, which were widely marketable outside the Garifuna niche market. Lina Hortensia Martinez had been working for years to sell and distribute these flavored cassava chips in markets and restaurants throughout Honduras, as well as to Garifuna clients in the United States, through her company, Wabagari Distribution. Her commitment to the preservation of Garifuna culinary traditions, as well as her commitment to women's empowerment, resulted in a number of initiatives that had the goal of increasing the economic, political, and social capital of the *ereba* makers of Iriona with whom she worked so closely.

Martinez and a small group of other Afro-descendant women started an organization to address the multidimensional health, political, social, economic, and cultural needs of Afro-descendant women in Honduras. The organization was named Sasamu, a Garifuna word that means a trusted and respected decision maker or elder in the community who gives advice and guidance to others. It was created for Afro-descendant women to work together to improve the living conditions of the Afro-Honduran woman through various means. When I found out that Hortensia Martinez had started this organization, I asked if she could arrange for me to meet some of the members of Sasamu. During my January 2015 visit, I met with four members—Lina Hortensia Martinez, Karen Vargas, Noelmy Balbina Arzú, and Isabel Virgen Bonilla. They shared their separate yet related visions for the important political work of this emerging organization. Below I share some of their thoughts about the path forward for the Afro-Honduran woman.

Hortensia Martinez started the meeting by talking about the importance of the Black woman having a voice. She described women as the owners of the land and talked about their direct connection to the land as growers and cultivators of various crops, including cassava. She talked about the primary resources of land and sea, which are typically understood in gendered terms, with women cultivating crops and men fishing. In urging a return to a time when there was a deeper connection to these resources, she talked about her hope for an organization that will educate and motivate women to make their own decisions about how to live in connection with these important resources. (While Martinez has left the country to pursue economic opportunities abroad since my visit, she continues to contribute to women's economic development through her business endeavors.)

Balbina Arzú is a medical doctor who has an interest in addressing public health issues. She talked about the importance of state support for positive health outcomes and the role of nongovernmental organizations in the management of health services. She linked the prevention of various illnesses to environmental factors, and faulted the government for not providing better protection for Garifuna lands. Threatened by narcotraffickers, the villagers need the support of the government, she said. She talked about the vast differences in opportunities based on race and gender, and named political participation as key to obtaining better economic and health outcomes for Afro-Honduran women. Describing a politics of exclusion as part of the problem, she lamented the vast differences in quality of life and discussed the concentration of resources in Honduran cities as compared to rural towns. Advocating for a distribution of resources better aligned with need, she discussed the broad impact of women's health challenges on the entire community. Speaking to the women gathered, she said, "We know and feel the need." The connection among women that she evoked is the foundation for political solidarity. Balbina Arzú intended to contribute to the well-being of Afro-Honduran women in rural and urban communities. While at the time of the meeting, she resided in the city, she hoped to someday return to the village where she was raised. As of March 2017, she was in the running for political office with the National Party of Honduras (*La Tribuna* Online 2017).

Vargas is a lawyer who discussed the relationship of the Afro-Honduran to the state and the challenges for Afro-Honduran women seeking leadership in politically active organizations. She envisioned a role for Sasamu in advocating for the Afro-descendant and indigenous person who has been neglected and marginalized by the state. She described the organization's focus on women's empowerment along multiple dimensions, including economic, cultural, and academic empowerment. She distinguished Sasamu as an organization that had an explicitly gendered identity. Similar to Balbina Arzú, she stressed the importance of a shared cultural experience among Afro-descendant women.

Virgen Bonilla is an aspiring entrepreneur who was working as the assistant to Hortensia Martinez in the operation of Wabagari Distribution. As a woman in her twenties, she was the youngest person at the table. Initially reluctant to talk, she shared her desire to work with other women to advance community development because of the obvious need in the community. During my visit, Virgen Bonilla accompanied me to the ancestral Garifuna villages in Iriona; it was her first trip to the area. She remarked that in the *galpones* that were led by men, the women seemed afraid to take charge of their own organizations. She said that the work she was doing (to impact women's empowerment) felt like an important mission. (Since Martinez's departure from Honduras, Virgen Bonilla has taken on considerable responsibility in running Wabagari, and as of April 2017 she was continuing to advance her education through weekend courses.)

Although these women were at the very beginning stages of developing Sasamu, they appeared to be filling a vacuum in the political terrain when it comes to the Garifuna woman of Honduras. They were privileging the Afro-descendant identity in a way that mirrors ODECO, but not discounting the indigeneity embraced by OFRANEH. They were based in the city, but embraced deep connections to the rural community. They embodied a diverse range of feminist critiques of the state, adopting different political affiliations. In spite of these political differences, they remained committed to the common goal of Afro-Honduran women's empowerment. While they were focused on national collaborations, similar to OFRANEH, they were a mobile group of professionals well equipped to call on international and transnational allies with reach similar to ODECO.

When I returned from my trip, I planned to follow the development of this nascent women's group that appeared to have found an important and underserved political niche in their commitment to Afro-descendant women, across political, geographical, and economic boundaries. Since my return to the United States, I have learned that the organization has already folded, its preservation complicated by the many personal challenges to survival in Honduras. However, each of the women individually continues to be committed to improvements for Afro-descendant women in the country.

Conclusion: Black Political Women

This chapter began with a discussion of the Black and indigenous identities of Garifuna women, who are the focus of this Black feminist exploration of *el pan, el poder y la política*—or bread, power, and politics—in Honduras. Centering Garifuna women's experiences, I was able to discuss how the Honduran policies impacting Garifuna communities are racialized, gendered, and classed, employing a structural intersectional analysis. The *galpones casaberos* that organize women's *ereba* production resist these structural oppressions. In spite of that resistance, a representational intersectional analysis highlights the ways in which the cultural construction of the chaste Garifuna woman often disadvantages young Garifuna mothers in their educational pursuits. Finally, through a political intersectional analysis, I discussed how contentious national politics have created an opening for new political organizations. I highlight the nascent organization, Sasamu, which attended to the challenges of rural Afro-descendant women even as it engaged urban politics. Crenshaw (1989) writes, "It seems that placing those who currently are marginalized in the center is the most effective way to resist efforts to compartmentalize experiences and undermine potential collective action" (167). Sasamu engaged those Black Honduran women on the coastlines and at the margins of Honduran society.

Inextricably linked to the *ereba* work of rural Garifuna women, and committed to the empowerment of Afro-descendant women, broadly speaking, Sasamu was one example of the nontraditional political activities of Black women. Sasamu, attentive to the power structures that aim to oppress Afro-descendant women, was committed to the empowerment of Afro-descendant women in rural and urban areas. The group highlighted a social justice orientation that embodied the " 'pragmatic activism' directed at combating those social and personal, individual and structural, and local and global forces that pose harm to Black (in the widest geopolitical sense) women's well-being," as McClaurin (2001, 63) so aptly describes as the goal of Black feminist work. Although the organization has ceased to exist since the original writing of this chapter, its presence, however fleeting, is evidence of the desire of Black political women to advocate on their own behalf. I look forward to following these women and others like them in future writings.

References

Alexander-Floyd, and Evelyn M. Simien. 2006. "What's in a Name?": Exploring the Contours of Africana Womanist Thought. *Frontiers: A Journal of Women Studies* 27 (1): 67–89.

Anderson, Mark. 2009. *Black and Indigenous: Garifuna Activism and Consumer Culture in Honduras.* Minneapolis: University of Minnesota Press.

Anderson, Mark. 2009. *Black and Indigenous: Garifuna Activism and Consumer Culture in Honduras.* Minneapolis: University of Minnesota Press.

Bateman, Rebecca B. 1998. "Africans and Indians: A Comparative Study of the Black Carib and Black Seminole." In *Social Dynamics and Cultural Transformations.* Vol. 1: Central America and Northern and Western South America, edited by Norman E. Whitten Jr. and Arlene Torres, 200–22. Bloomington: Indiana University Press.

Brondo, Keri Vacanti. 2013. *Land Grab: Green Neoliberalism, Gender, and Garifuna Resistance in Honduras.* Tucson: The University of Arizona Press.

Crenshaw, Kimberlé. 1989. "Demarginalizing the Intersection of Race and Sex: A Black Feminist Critique of Antidiscrimination Doctrine, Feminist Theory and Antiracist Politics." *University of Chicago Legal Forum* 1: 139–67.

Crenshaw, Kimberlé. 1991. "Mapping the Margins: Intersectionality, Identity Politics, and Violence against Women of Color." *Stanford Law Review* 43 (6): 1241–99.

England, Sarah. 1999. "Negotiating Race and Place in the Garifuna Diaspora: Identity Formation and Transnational Grassroots Politics in New York City and Honduras." *Identities: Global Studies in Culture and Power* 6 (1): 5–53.

England, Sarah. 2006. *Afro Central Americans in New York City: Garifuna Tales of Transnational Movements in Racialized Space.* Gainesville: University Press of Florida.

England, Sarah. 2010. "Mixed and multiracial in Trinidad and Honduras: Rethinking Mixed-race Identities in Latin America and the Caribbean." *Ethnic and Racial Studies* 33 (2): 195–213.

Euraque, Dario. 2007. "Free *Pardos* and Mulattoes Vanquish Indians: Cultural Civility as Conquest and Modernity in Honduras." In *Beyond Slavery: The Multilayered Legacy of Africans in Latin America and the Caribbean*, edited by Darién J. Davis, 81–122. Lanham, MD: Rowman & Littlefield.

Fabel, Robin F. A. 2000. *Colonial Challenges: Britons, Native Americans, and Caribs, 1759–1775.* Gainesville: University Press of Florida.

Gargolla, Francesca. 2005. "Garifuna: A Culture of Women and Men." Translated by Carlos Montoro. In *The Garifuna: A Nation Across Borders: Essays in Social Anthropology*, edited by Carlos Montoro, 137–58. Belize: Cubola Productions.

Gold, Janet N. 2009. *Culture and Customs of Honduras.* Westport, CT: Greenwood Press.

Gonzalez, Nancie L. 1988. *Sojourners of the Caribbean: Ethnogenesis and Ethnohistory of the Garifuna.* Urbana: University of Illinois Press.

Gonzalez, Nancie L. 1997. "The Garifuna of Central America." In *The Indigenous People of the Caribbean*, edited by Samuel M. Wilson, 199–205. Gainesville: University Press of Florida.

Gonzalez, Nancie L. Solien. 1969. *Black Carib Household Structure: A Study of Migration and Modernization.* Seattle: University of Washington Press.

Gordon, Edmund T., and Mark Anderson. 1999. "The African Diaspora: Toward an Ethnography of Diasporic Identification." *The Journal of American Folklore* 112, no. 445 (Summer): 282–96.

Guidroz, Kathleen, and Michele Tracy Berger. 2009. "A Conversation with Founding Scholars of Intersectionality: Kimberlé Crenshaw, Nira Yuval-Davis and Michelle Fine." In *The Intersectional Approach: Transforming the Academy through Race, Class, and Gender*, edited by Michele Tracy Berger and Kathleen Guidroz, 61–79. Chapel Hill: University of North Carolina Press.

Haney, Lynne, and Lisa Pollard, eds. 2003. *Families of a New World: Gender, Politics, and State Development in a Global Context.* New York: Routledge.

Johnson, Paul Christopher. 2005. "Migrating Bodies, Circulating Signs: Brazilian Candomblé, the Garifuna of the Caribbean and the Category of Indigenous Religions." In *Indigenous Diasporas and Dislocations*, edited by Graham Harvey and Charles D. Thompson Jr., 37–51. Burlington, VT: Ashgate.

Johnson, Paul Christopher. 2006. "Joining the African Diaspora: Migration and Diasporic Religious Culture among the Garífuna in Honduras and New York." In *Women and Religion in the African Diaspora: Knowledge, Power, and Performance*, edited by R. Marie Griffith and Barbara Dianna Savage, 37–58. Baltimore, MD: Johns Hopkins University Press.

Johnson, Paul Christopher. 2007. *Diaspora Conversions: Black Carib Religion and the Recovery of Africa.* Berkeley: University of California Press.

Jones, Branwen Gruffydd. 2008. "Race in the Ontology of International Order." *Political Studies* 56: 907–27.

Jordan-Zachery. 2009. *Black Women, Cultural Images, and Social Policy.* New York: Routledge.

Kerns, Virginia. 1983. *Women and the Ancestors: Black Carib Kinship and Ritual.* Urbana: University of Illinois Press.

Khan, Aisha. 1987. "Migration and Life-Cycle among Garifuna (Black Carib) Street Vendors." *Women's Studies* 13: 183–98.

La Tribuna Online. 2017. Resultados preliminares: 58 mujeres se alzan a la cabeza en el PN. March 15, 2017. Accessed April 30, 2017. http://www.latribuna.hn/2017/03/15/resultados-preliminares-58-mujeres-se-alzan-la-cabeza-pn/.

López, Asbel. 2001. "Preserving the Magic: A Tangible Debut." *The UNESCO Courier* (September): 43.

McClaurin, Irma. 2001. "Theorizing a Black Feminist Self in Anthropology: Toward an Autoethnographic Approach." In *Black Feminist Anthropology: Theory, Politics, Praxis and Poetics*, edited by Irma McClaurin, 49–76. New Brunswick, NJ: Rutgers University Press.

Organización de Desarrollo Étnico Comunitario (ODECO). 2010. Cumbre Mundial Afrodescendientes. September 21, 2010. Accessed April 3, 2015. http://odecohn.blogspot.com/2010/09/cumbre-mundial-afrodescendientes.html.

Prestage, Jewel L. 1991. "In Quest of African American Political Woman." *The Annals of the American Academy of Political and Social Science* 515: 88–103.

Safa, Helen I. 2006. "Questioning *Mestizaje*: The Social Mobilization of Afrodescendant Women in Latin America." In *Inclusion and Exclusion in the Global Arena*, edited by Max Kirsch, 225–41. New York: Routledge.

Sutton, Constance R. 1997. "Foreword." In *Women and the Ancestors: Black Carib Kinship and Ritual.* 2nd ed., edited by Virginia Kerns, ix–xvi. Urbana: University of Illinois Press.

Taylor, Christopher. 2012. *The Black Carib Wars: Freedom, Survival, and the Making of the Garifuna.* Jackson: University Press of Mississippi.

Thorne, Eva. T. 2004. "Land Rights and Garífuna Identity." *NACLA Report on the Americas* (September/October): 21–25.

US Central Intelligence Agency (CIA) World Factbook. 2011. Last modified November 17, 2017. https://www.cia.gov/library/publications/the-world-factbook/geos/ho.html.

Waltner, Ann B., and Mary Jo Maynes. 2004. "Family History as World History." In *Women's History in Global Perspective*. Vol. 1, edited by Bonnie G. Smith, 48–91. Urbana: University of Illinois Press.

Yuval-Davis, Nira. 2009. "Intersectionality and Feminist Politics." In *The Intersectional Approach: Transforming the Academy through Race, Class, and Gender*, edited by Michele Tracy Berger and Kathleen Guidroz, 44–60. Chapel Hill: University of North Carolina Press.

7

Woman Out of Place

Portia Simpson-Miller and Middle-Class Politics in Jamaica

MAZIKI THAME
Clark Atlanta University

This chapter examines the importance of Portia Simpson-Miller in the postindependence politics of Jamaica. That politics has been shaped and dominated by middle-class men, and Simpson-Miller was Jamaica's first female, grassroots prime minister. In these respects, her rise to the top suggests a digression from the main character of political life and an opening to power for women of the society and for those at the bottom. Simpson-Miller is of interest not only because of her role as a political leader, but also because of her meaning in the context of a Black feminist interrogation of the intersectional oppressions that women face—of gender, race, and class—and how we might understand terrains of power given these intersections. This chapter is thus situated within the charge of Nikol Alexander-Floyd that political scientists and students of Black politics adopt a frame of reference that accounts for gender and points to the usefulness of Black feminist intersectionality as a means to account for race, class, and gender as mutually constitutive and productive (Alexander-Floyd 2007, 17). Simpson-Miller is to be studied as a way to understand those dynamics through a Caribbean lens as part of a conversation between diasporic Blacks about the diasporic experience. The chapter therefore also responds to Eudine Barriteau's call for Caribbean feminist theorizing to interrogate both the relations of power within relations of gender and how the experiences of gendered identities are grounded in asymmetrical practices of power (Barriteau 2003, 4). Barriteau argues that a distinguishing feature of Caribbean women's lives is the absence of power (ibid). How therefore is Simpson-Miller's leadership to be understood given Barriteau's assessment that Caribbean women's lives are characterized by the absence of power? How should we understand Simpson-Miller given the relations of power within gender relations in Jamaica? How, using intersectionality as a frame of reference, should Black women's power be understood in a Black-governed society? Within US Black feminist thought, it is understood that Black women's subordination occurs within intersecting oppressions of race, class, gender, and sexuality (Collins 2009, 26). Black feminist thinking is a means to deepen knowledge of the status of Black women relative to other groups and among Blacks (Lindsay 2015, 28) and by extension how hierarchies are built and power distributed. A study of Portia Simpson-Miller, a Black woman of the grassroots who comes to power in Jamaica, helps us to understand the status of Black women in a global Black experience marked by anti-Black racism that is gendered and classed.[1] In the case of Jamaica, this frame of reference helps us to expose the nature of power in political life, who it privileges, and how it creates, and challenges, injustices in that society.

The Jamaican political system evolved out of British parliamentarism. It is a two-party system in which the two main political parties, the Jamaica Labour Party (JLP) and the Peoples National Party (PNP), became dominant given their connection to the labor movement of the 1930s and the process of decolonization. The PNP and especially its leader, Norman Manley, were at the forefront of the bid for self-government from the 1940s to independence in 1962. It was known as the party of intellectuals that flirted with the political left, especially in the 1970s under the leadership of Michael Manley. Simpson-Miller has been in its leadership since 1978, when she was the only woman elected vice president of the party. She was elected president of the party in 2006 when she was among the 13 percent of female parliamentarians. A year after her assumption of leadership of the PNP and the nation, Simpson-Miller lost the general elections. Hope inspired by her candidacy and victory gave way to disappointment and lowered expectations for her capacity to change the politics of and prospects for the Jamaican people. Those expectations, however, were not in line with the realities of political life and Simpson-Miller's place in it. Specifically, Simpson-Miller's place as a grassroots woman who is seen to represent the interests of the poor and of women is determined by the view of poor Black women within the society and her own participation in the masculinist machinery of Jamaican politics. According to Alexander-Floyd (2007, 1), masculinist gender power is the exercise of influence and control by men to delineate institutional boundaries, establish patterns of leadership, and produce identity. Simpson-Miller does not command the type of power that could pose a serious threat to the exercise of power by middle-class men over the Jamaican state and therefore could not transform the race, class, and gendered dynamics of power in Jamaica.

The state is taken here as the main site for exploration of Jamaican politics and as a site of middle-class power in Jamaica. Rupert Lewis notes that it is the site of middle-class elite mobilization of the people and that it has been their role to take control of the state by evolutionary or revolutionary means throughout the region (Lewis 2001, 127, 128). That class has ruled with the collaboration of a traditional economic non-Black elite that finances political parties and networks with the political elite (Lewis 2001, 130). Of concern in this chapter is the nature of the role played by the middle class in Jamaican politics and how and why Portia Simpson-Miller's emergence represents a symbolic shift, rooted in the failures of the political agendas of the Jamaican middle class. I argue that it is only symbolic because it does not carry with it a politics of change, at least not around the question of whose interests are served by the state. C. L. R. James wrote very scathingly of the West Indian middle classes, arguing that much of the political middle class were beneficiaries of the mass movements of the 1930s and were seeking primarily to be admitted to the largely non-Black elite ruling class (James 2013, 250).[2] He posited that they saw themselves as separate and distinct from the masses of the people, and among the powerful qualifying distinctions was their education. It was "a form of social differentiation. It put you in a different class" (James 2013, 254). He believed the middle class had no confidence in the abilities of the masses of the people, who, like the slave owners before them, if told, "Why not place responsibility for the economy on the people?," replied, "You will ruin the economy, and further what can you expect from people like these?" (James 2013, 256).

While there have been shifts in the character of the Caribbean middle classes since James's writing at the beginning of independence, such as the expansion of Blacks' presence in that group and a reduction in their attachment to colonial ideas, especially among those radicalized in the late 1960s and 1970s, there continues to be significant contempt for the masses and little confidence in their abilities for self-determination. This is seen in responses to Simpson-Miller as representative of that group. Lewis argues that the political relationship between the Black middle class and the underclass is "characterized by sterile dependency and political subordination, as is evident in the garrison constituencies of the urban poor communities or welfarism" (Lewis 2001, 139). Within garrison constituencies, systems of patronage tied whole communities of the inner city to one of the two main political parties. Support to politicians (usually middle-class men) was guaranteed in exchange for spoils, but the state has been less able to provide clientelistic benefits given its impoverishment and the turn to neoliberalism. Such constituencies had a local political leader called a don who would represent the party's interest at the local level, control the distribution of spoils, and organize violent defense of the constituency against threats from the opposing party.[3] Simpson-Miller rose through the ranks in that system, but was different from other politicians because she hails from the constituency itself. Indeed, her ascendancy and leadership would be impacted by anti-Black and sexist sentiment within the society and also, critically, contempt for the poor from which she hails; that is, given the norms of Jamaican politics, she would not have been expected to rise to the top. Her position as leader of the Jamaican nation may therefore be seen as challenging the status quo because she was "out of place." Her rise points to shifting expectations of politics as a politics that could accommodate the rise of a Black woman from the bottom and who was self-proclaimed as pro-poor. At the same time, she has not deployed a different form of politics and is in that sense part of the existing mechanism of middle-class rule in Jamaica. Her characterization as mother of the nation, "Mama P," is tied to her rise through violent, "garrison," paternalistic politics, but also to her empathetic characteristics that have identified her with the plight of the poor. I argue that this representation has been important to the PNP insofar as it obscured the class character of the party, and Mama P could be deployed symbolically to distract the nation from its conservatism, neoliberalism, and masculinism. Simpson-Miller's leadership was both constrained by masculinism, shaped by her subjective position as a Black woman from the base of society and she is a participant in it.

Middle-Class Politics and Its Gendered Norms

In terms of Caribbean women and their place, it is important to note that while Caribbean gender systems are patriarchal, they are not always rigid. Barriteau reminds us that Caribbean society will "permit women to take on responsibilities essentially constructed as masculine, as long as these do not produce a corresponding shift in the gendered relations of power" (Barriteau 1998, 192). This was rooted in a colonial experience in which, according to Linnette Vassell, colonial ideology stressed women's service while warning against the promotion of their rights. It did not, she says, embrace calls that questioned or sought to change power relations between men and women (cited in Lewis 2000, 275). Linden Lewis argues that there was considerable collusion of Caribbean men with the colonial authorities to reproduce colonial hierarchies in that they did not contest the colonial gender order, participated in it, and benefited from the patriarchal rule of colonizers and the system, which assured them leadership roles, access to power, and valued resources (Lewis 2000, 274).

To understand the roles that were ascribed for women but that produced gender norms more broadly, we can turn to the politics of respectability, which was an important dimension of colonial and then middle-class politics in Jamaica. Evelyn Brooks Higginbotham shows how a politics of respectability was a means for Black Baptist women to oppose the social structures and representations of white supremacy in the late nineteenth and early twentieth centuries in the United States. Respectability, she says, assumed political dimensions for these women insofar as it became a means to contest racist images and structures (Higginbotham 1994 186–87). It "emphasized reform of individual behavior and attitudes both as a goal in itself and a strategy for reform of the entire structural system of American race relations" (Higginbotham 1994 187). Similar strategies emerged in the Caribbean out of the colonial project's civilizing mission, presumed able to "turn those believed incapable of rule into reliable rulers." Socialization into British norms, manners, parliamentary modes of governance, conjugal marriage, and the science of domesticity effectively socialized the colonized into respectability (Alexander 2013, 263). This was tied to the question of who should rule, and its answer was definitive at Jamaican independence: Brown middle-class men, because they were believed to have best assimilated British norms and culture, rather than Whites, who were not seen as legitimate rulers of the postcolonial nation. Anthony Bogues notes, however, that included in the middle-class project, which came to be understood as Creole nationalism, was the civilization of Blacks: the construction of the respectable Black (Bogues 2002, 15). That project sought to construct citizenship in terms of Caribbeanness and Creoleness, one that would accept middle-class leadership and values, develop a nuclear family, labor, vote, "speak properly [English] and softly, listen to good music, comport themselves with proper gestures, respect authority and uphold Christian values" (Bogues 2002, 15).

Alexander posits that nationalist parties mobilized consensus for nation building in terms of a "neutered invocation to citizenship," but the creation of women's wings of the political parties showed a gendered call to patriotic duty. She says:

> Women were to fiercely defend the nation by protecting their honour, by guarding the nuclear conjugal family, "the fundamental institution of the society," by guarding "culture" defined as the transmission of a fixed set of proper values to the children of the nation, and by mobilizing on the party's behalf into the far reaches of the country. She was expected to represent and uphold a respectable femininity and, in so doing, displace the figure of the white Madonna. Patriotic duty for men, on the other hand, consisted in rendering public service to the country, and in adopting the mores of respectability. (Alexander 2013, 263–64)

This, she says, involved the symbolic triumph of the nuclear family over the extended family and other family forms (Alexander 2013, 264).

Marriage has factored critically as the institution that was meant to build better families and a better nation. In parliamentary debates on the Matrimonial Causes Act of 1988, which sought to ease the process of divorce, the state's preoccupation with and privileging of marriage was expressed. Several speakers showed a concern for the perpetuation of marriage. J. A. G Smith concluded his introduction of the bill by stating: "I do expect that this Bill will necessarily make marriage more continuous but I sincerely hope it will do nothing to necessarily abbreviate or bring the institution into anything other than we would really like for that institution which we regard so highly" (Jamaica Hansard 1989, 10). The House noted its approval with applause. Similarly, A. Johnson held that he hoped publicity would be given to the bill so that "people would get out of the whole habit of being afraid of marriage and not entering into it in the numbers which are needed if we are to have more and better families properly speaking in our shores" (Jamaica Hansard 1989, 10). The fact that the nuclear unit has not been consolidated as a norm is treated as a national failure because it is understood as having been replaced by insecure families, mainly female-headed ones, which are not able to bring up "good" citizens.

Tracy Robinson argues that "notwithstanding the gender neutrality of many citizenship laws in the Caribbean and the language of equality implied in Caribbean constitutions, men remain the paradigm of a citizen and in a significant measure, women are included as citizens through their relationship to men" (Robinson 2003, 232). As a result, marriage becomes an important source of women's inclusion as citizens. Robinson argues further that "being able to define oneself socially and legally by reference to a man through marriage provides a distinct form of legitimacy and acceptance for women in the eyes of the community." She goes on to say that this legitimacy is nonetheless constrained because it depends on the performance of femininity-based dependence (Robinson 2003, 248). Simpson-Miller has identified with this characterization of women's dependence on men. Early in her first term as prime minister, questions were raised about whether she was using public funds for personal consumption on her travels abroad. She responded that her husband, as her caregiver, afforded her the means to spend as she wished; he had indeed provided her with his credit card (cited in Heron 2008 89). Simpson-Miller's representations of her married life reinforced middle-class respectability as an ideal.

On the other hand, Simpson-Miller has shown a sensitivity to the stereotyping of the underclass not shared by her fellow parliamentarians. In discussions on the Sexual Offences Act, there was an attempt to include wording that would make it an offense where an adult in authority causes a child to watch a sexual act. Member of Parliament Ronald Thwaites responded, "Chairman, I am fully sensitive to the consciousness of the member, but if you put in that subsection the whole of Central Kingston will go to jail." There was laughter in the House. He continued, "When you live in one room children are introduced to the sight of sex helplessly at an early age." Simpson-Miller's response showed an understanding of the very problematic representations undertaken by her colleagues. She interjected, "These things do not occur without precautions being taken by adults" (Jamaica Hansard 2009, 358–59).

It is especially middle-class men who benefit from representations that vilify working-class parenting and idealize the male breadwinner because they enjoy patriarchal status as the head of the nuclear family. Men's presence in the nuclear unit gives them power over women but also over those men, usually those in the Jamaican underclass, who do not marry and do not enjoy status as responsible males within the larger society partly because of their absence from the nuclear unit. In the present moment of perceived threat to male power, women who are unmarried and procreating share a significant amount of burden in explanations of "national crises" in Jamaica. Failing mothers and absent fathers of the working class are singled out, but generally all men who are not perceived as living up to patriarchal standards, such as homosexuals, are seen as a part of the problem. Single mothers are seen as bringing up violent criminals who create disorder in the nation. Barriteau points out that public discourse holds women "responsible for the destruction of families, high rates of divorce, male economic and social marginalization, and the comparatively poorer performance of boys and men at every educational level" (Barriteau 2003, 326). Alexander-Floyd notes that in the case of African Americans, the public focus on young, endangered Black men has reinforced the tendency to see Black families (especially the single female–headed ones) as the source of their own social and economic problems (Alexander-Floyd 2007, 6). Conservative politics, including that of Black nationalism, redirected attention from Blacks' social, economic, and political inequality as manifestations of racism to redefining Black male-female roles in line with patriarchal models (Alexander-Floyd 2007, 25–26). In the Jamaican case, the discourse similarly distracts from the structural causes of marginalization of poor Black men and women. The promotion of the nuclear family thus becomes important to the consolidation of men's power in general, but the stigmatization of non-nuclear families is specifically important to consolidating middle-class status and middle-class men as the right type of people for rulership; that is, it discredits the type of leadership that Simpson-Miller represents.

The Significance of Portia Simpson-Miller

Coming to Power

How was Portia Simpson-Miller as head of government to be understood in the context of Jamaican politics and the norms of middle-class power? The Creole nationalist project, which brought Jamaica to independence, is seen to have collapsed or is collapsing given its failure to fulfil the expectations of the masses of the population. Simpson-Miller came to the fore at a period in which political life could not be seen simply or only in terms of Creole nationalism. Indeed, her rise could be seen as part of its collapse. Meeks argues that the political moment of Jamaica in the 2000s is defined by hegemonic dissolution. In it, the pre- and postindependence ruling bloc is moribund; there is insurgent questioning from below, manifested in culture wars on the appropriateness of the Jamaican language, on new assertions of blackness, and in the dance hall and its music (Meeks 2014, 163–64). He argues that the nation is presently in the advanced stages of hegemonic dissolution, and while "the Jamaican state and the social bloc that operates within its circles, is still firmly in power," its hold is increasingly tenuous (Meeks 2014, 166). Simpson-Miller's relationship to the collapse of Creole nationalism and to hegemonic dissolution is grounded in her relationship to the civilizing mission, which constructed the citizen as the respectable Black.

Simpson-Miller fails to fulfill the expectations of leadership in Creole nationalism. She is not seen as the respectable black by virtue of the fact that she had not risen through the ranks via education and the professions. She rose through the ranks from the lowest level of representation in the PNP and developed her career within the garrison structures, which depended on violence and patron-client relations to maintain party loyalty in communities. Simpson-Miller represents one of the long-standing garrison constituencies (Saint Andrew South Western), which shifted allegiance to the PNP in the 1976 general elections by a significant majority. The constituency was a safe JLP seat up to that point. The shift is explained by Barry Chevannes as both the product of changes in constituency boundaries and more significantly by the pushing out method, in which known JLP supporters were forced to leave the area (cited in Sives 2010, 92).

Negative portrayals of Simpson-Miller in the public domain occur within the frame of Creole nationalist expectations of leadership and are in line with stereotypes of Black women of the Jamaican ghettos. They are constructed as uncontrolled women who are loud, vulgar, have children with no regard for their maintenance and with multiple "baby fathers"; as people who prioritize their personal enjoyment and material needs over those of their offspring and who are good for sex but not necessarily wifehood. These women are deemed inferior on all counts, except in sexual matters in relation to their Brown-skinned, middle-class counterparts.[4] Specifically, Simpson-Miller is seen to be vulgar, low-class, lacking in proficiency in the English language, and incompetent given her low educational achievement. For her part, it is important to note that Simpson-Miller attempts to secure middle-class respectability, which is evidence of the contradictions of the present political moment in Jamaica, specifically relating to the hold of the middle and upper classes over formal politics. She herself maintains a commitment to the English language, represents herself as a wife who depends on her husband, invokes Christian moralizing as an indication of her decency, and most cogently self-identifies as the mother of the nation, the type who can save the nation, especially its poor.

Simpson-Miller's battle for leadership of the PNP and the nation occurred within this frame of reference. She twice vied for the presidency of the party and in both instances came up against middle-class leadership. She would lose in her first bid to P. J. Patterson, who originates from the rural peasantry, had established himself as middle class through the legal profession, and would rest his legitimacy on the rise of a certain type of Black respectability and Black nationalism. In that case, Simpson-Miller was presented as unsuited to the task given her failure to qualify herself in education. In her second bid for the presidency in 2006, Simpson-Miller says she took the message from her 1992 defeat and got her certification (Ritch 2006, A9). Despite this move, she continued to face questions around her qualification to rule from within the PNP, from the opposition JLP, and in popular assertions regarding her command of the English language and general deportment. In those elections, Simpson-Miller defeated the Brown and Black middle-class men of the PNP who satisfied the expectations of Creole nationalist citizenship and would defeat the JLP, thought of as most representative of non-Black elite interests in the 2011 general elections. Her victories were indicative of a shift in understandings of politics, of who should rule and what qualified them. In those elections, race, class, and gender considerations were of significance. Patterson's "Black Man Time" had narrowly focused on the enrichment of a Black bourgeoisie, and the JLP (perceived as Brown) failed to alleviate conditions of the poor. Because middle-class men could not address their needs, the public advanced that it was now time for the [Black, grassroots] woman. In 2006, Don Anderson polls showed that women in the public favored Portia. Of the 51.4 percent who favoured her candidacy, the majority were women, and she also had high support at the lower socioeconomic level (Brown 2006, 1). In explaining the JLP loss in 2011, commentator Kevin O'Brien Chang argued that the opposition leader Andrew Holness, "as someone from the bowels of the people" (Holness has since risen to the ranks of Brown middle class) must reconnect the JLP with the working class, because many of the urban poor viewed the party as "a rich uptown party unconcerned with the less fortunate" (Chang 2012, F3). The JLP misread the political moment as one in which they could rely on middle-class understandings of suitability for rule as shaped by Creole nationalist visions of citizenship. Both the JLP and PNP segments that did not support Simpson-Miller deployed an elitist politics of language that continues to see the Jamaican language as illegitimate and played on Simpson-Miller's lapses in English as a disqualifying characteristic. They presented her as a vulgar, low-class woman, lacking in the trappings of respectability.[5] This position mobilized women and the poor, who, one could argue, saw the assaults as directed both at Simpson-Miller and at the demographic she was seen as representing. Simpson-Miller's popular base is among the poor, and her victories indicated the increasing confidence of the Black poor, given their previous commitment to middle-class power and their participation in politics as defined by that class. As Meeks argues, they no longer take it for granted that Browns and the middle class should lead them. PNP delegates, he says, "elected a president whom the poor and dispossessed perceive to be their own" (Meeks 2014, 167).

In considering the significance of Simpson-Miller in the 2006 campaign for leadership of the PNP, sociologist Don Robotham argues that there was an emerging left trend in Jamaican politics. He posits that this was not a clear-cut ideological form of the left but that it was manifesting in charismatic personality politics, that there was a "deep desire for a political leader who is 'caring' and who shows 'compassion,' as the campaign slogans of Minister Simpson-Miller proclaim." He notes that there was strong popular mass support for her and that her appeal transcended the PNP (Robotham 2006, G8). Indeed, Simpson-Miller styled herself as the people's choice (Ritch 2006, A9), noting her significance in the milieu of middle-class politics. Robotham contends that Simpson-Miller was tapping into the deep current of political and social discontent that was current in Jamaica and that was independent of her. This he ties to the neoliberal economics pursued by Michael Manley in the 1990s, which intensified poverty and alienation in Jamaica and which Jamaicans felt unequally benefited a small minority. He concludes that the people desired a leader who identified with their suffering and who would bring about change (Robotham 2006, G8).

Fixing Gender Matters

When Simpson-Miller first assumed the leadership of the PNP, it was celebrated as a victory for women. Because she was a woman, Black, and grassroots at a moment of Jamaican political life that distrusted middle-class men's efforts up to that point, she was able to rise to leadership even while these characteristics gave cause for her to be policed. Her position was aided by racial, class, and gender norms embedded in Creole nationalism in that poor Black women's reputations can be redeemed through self-sacrificial motherhood. Tracy Robinson points out that motherhood is the mechanism through which Caribbean women do service for the nation and is the basis for citizenship (Robinson 2003, 246). This idea has a history in Black nationalist constructions of the role of women in defending the race and is attached to wider notions of women's role in nationalism

(Anthias and Yuval-Davis 1989; Alexander-Floyd 2007; Mitchell 2004). Simpson-Miller's signification as Mama P is an important dimension of the gendered construction of Black women, but in this case, it is a stereotype that was useful in the prevailing understandings of citizenship and allowed her to compete with the respectable Black or Brown male. The view of working-class Black men does not similarly give them legitimate access to the formal political sphere. Mothering represents the ultimate expression of womanhood and femininity, even for women who are not biological mothers. Portia Simpson-Miller's representation in politics as Mama P is reflective of those expectations of the roles of women.[6] Simpson-Miller would in this vein declare to applause in her Women's Day statement to parliament that surely the men would join her in saluting Jamaican women, "bearing in mind that when things are difficult and the men do not even know how the children will be fed, mamma will find a way to ensure that both man and children are fed" (Simpson-Miller, 2011). She is of course relating to her own role as Mama P but also to generally accepted ideas about the type of mothers deemed valuable.

In addition to legitimizing her place, the identifier Mama P is important to understanding the relationship between the poor and politics and the gendered nature of this relationship. Middle-class politics is built on a dependent relationship between those at the bottom and their representatives in parliament. Posturing as "defender of the poor," without a power base for empowerment of the poor, Simpson-Miller's politics remained wedded to the paternalism of the political arena. In that arena, the poor are seen to be in need of redeemers, and the political process is presumed to offer their redemption. The paternalism of political life and the dependence of those it purports to save are especially evident in garrison politics and the patron-client relations within it. Garrison politics constructed a form of dependence in which the political party and reference to it were seen as the only means to access resources of the nation for those living in garrison communities. Simpson-Miller established strong credentials within garrison politics, including in its construction of a violent politics. In being in control of a garrison constituency, Simpson-Miller would have had to establish her credibility among gunmen of the underclass, especially in the ideologically inspired and intense violence of the 1970s when she came to prominence in the party. Her legitimacy as a ruler in that arena demanded that she show control over the violence, those who performed it, and her community at large. Mama P thus could play a dual role of nurturer and disciplinarian. Indeed, garrison politics presented Simpson-Miller with an alternative to rising through the professions. While paving a path for her advance, however, it also brought her into a process that would perpetuate the power of the middle class over the political arena and over those at the bottom. Indeed, it brought her into power relations that empowered men and emphasized masculinism, especially violence, control, and discipline.

Simpson-Miller's place at the head of the patriarchal state thereby did not shift the context of gender power even while there is space for women's inclusion within it. Her power and that of other women continues to be curtailed by virtue of their status as women, based on their class and color and the roles they have been required to play to advance in politics. In her 2011 statement to parliament on International Women's Day, Simpson-Miller stated that women in parliament "are always held to a different standard and a higher standard than our male counterparts are judged. We're under more scrutiny than our male counterpart" (Simpson-Miller 2011). Simpson-Miller argued that women needed to be more involved at all levels of the political process, but that they suffered constraints to their involvement. When MP Natalie Neita-Headley responded that women were in need of greater financial support to facilitate their involvement, a member declared "go a family court fi dat" (House of Parliament 2011). The metaphor of the family court invokes women's dependence—it reminds us of the need for the state to intervene to ensure men's participation in caregiving and thus the outburst from the member diminished Simpson-Miller's and Neita-Headley's claims, and more generally women's vulnerabilities, especially those that emerge because of familial responsibility. The member's response invoked women's dependent place in the home. It calls our attention to the ways that women's power is circumscribed even when they are at the "negotiating table."

In other gender matters, Simpson-Miller showed potentially transformative leadership when she expressed a willingness to review the state's position on homosexuality in political debates, leading to the victory of Simpson-Miller over Andrew Holness in the December 2011 general elections. The leaders of both political parties were required to respond to a question on the status of homosexuality in Jamaica. Simpson-Miller contended that persons should not be discriminated against on the basis of sexual orientation, that the state should reconsider the buggery law, and that she personally opposed the position of former Prime Minister Bruce Golding that homosexuals did not have a place in his cabinet. Simpson-Miller's own politics of respectability may have prevented her from making meaningful strides in this arena, but the climate of political life is also limiting. Given popular antihomosexual sentiments in public discourse, Simpson-Miller may have chosen to follow an electoral tide as opposed to a position of principle in this case.

Portia and the Poor

As with her status as a woman and representative of women, Simpson-Miller's mandate from the poor would also be challenged from the outset. Meeks notes that she would "have to rely on many persons who were lukewarm or openly hostile to her ascendancy to power" to manage the machinery of government (Meeks 2014, 167). Indeed this disunity and a failure to bring funding to the party were seen to be critical to her loss in general elections in 2007 (Sives 2010, 171). The fulfillment of a mandate from the Jamaican masses would face tremendous constraints given the character of political life. She would of necessity come up against middle-class control of the state and the fact of their contempt for the groups that Simpson-Miller represents. Simpson-Miller would not have the benefit of an organizationally strong support base. The dispossessed, her main support, remain distant from the operation of government and have not developed any organizational form that could seriously contend with the power of the state. Meeks argues that "whereas the Jamaican working people have shown the ability to mount impressive, spontaneous community mobilizations around local concerns . . . there is little evidence of deep, layered community-based organization building from the local level to address national and global issues" (Meeks 2014, 167).

Under Simpson-Miller, the PNP maintained a neoliberal vision of the market as king and of trickle-down, growth-oriented "development" and favor to the business class. In her inaugural address after her 2011 electoral victory, Simpson-Miller posited that the government's "policies are based on the principle that the private sector is a major participant in shaping the economy of the country." She promised: "Let me say emphatically to our business community at home and overseas: we will pursue a tight fiscal policy, reduce our debt-to-GDP ratio, maintain key macro-economic fundamentals and be careful and prudent in our debt management." With respect to *the people*, she called:

> On all Jamaicans to take responsibility for our lives. Be the best student you can be; the best parent; the best teacher; doctor or nurse; politician, public servant or private business person; athlete or entertainer; designer, dressmaker, hairdresser or barber;

> and strive to improve ourselves by reinvesting in our personal development. That is how people ultimately make progress. This government can provide the context and the opportunity. That is the partnership I want.

In a concession that sought to address the concerns of those outside the resource-owning economy, she proclaimed that "in a time of crisis, government must act to stimulate growth and to restore confidence in the country's ability to pay its way. Hence, in the short and medium term, we will use state resources to stimulate employment through the Jamaica Emergency Employment Programme (JEEP)" (Simpson-Miller 2012). JEEP created employment for "those in the lower socio-economic stratum: persons with special needs; those with low skill levels and those from under-served communities" (Jamaica Budget 2013/2014, 908). Under JEEP, members of parliament were given an allocation to carry out projects, mainly in roadwork (Davies 2015). Unemployment data did not, however, improve in the four years of the Simpson-Miller administration, moving from 12.4 percent in 2011 to 13.2 percent in 2015 (Statin 2011, 2015).

There was no indication that the government under Simpson-Miller would digress from its neoliberal path or pursue policies that were pro-poor. Therefore it is unclear what the context and opportunity for the peoples' development would be. If, at all, problems of poverty were to be addressed, they would be as short-term measures (JEEP) or would be resolved through the prevailing market logic, despite the fact that neoliberal economics had itself imposed burdens on the Jamaican people. If the government sought to stimulate growth, as opposed to equity and development, the people should seek their fortunes through "reinvesting in [their] personal development," through taking responsibility for themselves, and this would serve as the basis for a partnership between government and citizen. Indeed, the state under the PNP and in the Simpson-Miller years was increasingly business friendly. The IMF reported in 2015 that "over the last five years, there has been a welcome revenue shift from income to consumption taxes" (International Monetary Fund, 2015, 9). Government revenue from the General Consumption Tax (GCT) shifted from 27 percent of total tax revenue in fiscal year ending March 2011 (FY2011) to 34 percent in FY2015, while corporate taxes remained at 12 percent of total tax revenue for the period (Central Government Operations Table, FY2011–FY2015). Other initiatives, which favored the private sector, included the passing of the Employment (Flexible Work Arrangements) (Miscellaneous Provisions) Act, 2014, which among other measures, amended the definition of overtime work. Overtime work would no longer be calculated daily after eight hours of work, but weekly after forty hours of work have been done, effectively denying workers the previous arrangement. Trade unionist Lambert Brown, in submissions to parliament, argued that:

> "The trade union concern is about the removal of overtime occurring on a daily basis. As it stands now in the Minimum Wage Act, after eight hours in a day, you get overtime," Senator Brown said. "What the new arrangement in this Bill says is that if you work 13 or 16 hours in a day you will not get overtime, unless you work for a total of 40 hours-plus during the week. We prefer to maintain the arrangement where overtime is calculated on a daily basis." (cited in Waugh, 2014)

The exploitation of cheapened labor remained the path to stimulating the economy under Simpson-Miller. In new manifestations of free zone areas, the government also pursued the establishment of a Special Economic Zone Act that would allow local and foreign investors to take advantage of investment opportunities in Jamaica. Presumably these would operate under better labor conditions than older Free Zone arrangements, but there is little question that investments were meant to be secured through access to cheap labor and attractive tax incentives. The PNP's bid for investment also controversially included the decision to lease the Goat Islands for the development of a logistics hub by the Chinese. This decision raised concerns from environmental groups about damage to the Portland Bight protected area and to fisher-folk who operate there.[7] At stake is the future and well-being of Jamaicans. Such decisions mirror familiar practices of privatizing public goods to private interests (such as beaches to hoteliers) to exploit as they wish and to the exclusion of ordinary Jamaicans. The PNP's phase of neoliberal economics under Simpson-Miller was no doubt a factor in their electoral loss of 2016, fewer than five years after her first electoral victory.

Defeat

In the 2016 general elections, the opposition JLP campaigned with two significant promises that suggested a break from the austerity measures employed by the PNP. They promised to remove income taxes from Jamaicans earning less than J$1.5 million and to remove auxiliary fees from schools across the nation. The PNP maintained that it had passed eleven IMF tests and would continue on a path of austerity as the sure route of "progress." In the short election period, Simpson-Miller's leadership came under direct scrutiny through her refusal to participate in electoral debates. It confirmed for the public, who distrusted her competence (especially in relation to her command of English, which they believed to be a sign of intellectual capacity), that she was not up to the task of the position of prime minister. Simpson-Miller's silence on a range of public policy issues had emerged as problematic throughout the period of governance. Her silence has, however, to be considered in terms of her silencing and the silencing of what she represents, the intersectional oppressions facing Black women. Her political career marks the ways in which Black women are subordinated, but it also points to ways in which those women fashion their own triumphs through inverting the stereotypes used to oppress them. It is of importance that women like Simpson-Miller show up in the first place.

The attacks on Simpson-Miller have no doubt impacted her confidence to speak on behalf of the people. She became increasingly silent after assuming the position of prime minister, possibly giving in to public, especially the middle-class public, cry that she was an embarrassment whenever she spoke and that she did not and could not represent them. That public was keen to remind her of her place below them and certainly not belonging to the high office of prime minister. Newspaper cartoons and popular discourse routinely represented her as a virago, and that representation was core in the JLP campaign against her and the PNP in the 2011 elections. At that time, the public took Simpson-Miller's side; in 2016, they did not. The 2011 elections were a vote against the JLP and its message but also an indication that ordinary Jamaicans now felt that they had the right to be in power (as represented by Simpson-Miller as leader).

The PNP's 2016 loss therefore should be seen as part of a crisis of middle-class politics steeped in its failure to address the concerns of those at the bottom and to continue on the message of empowerment of the poor, Blacks, and women, all of whom Simpson-Miller represented. The PNP failed to create an environment in which that could thrive, especially because Simpson-Miller herself was not empowered to rule. In 2016, it was no longer credible to think of Simpson-Miller or the PNP as the hope of the poor, because their achievements together spoke nothing of a kind of politics that would center those Jamaicans most disadvantaged in the nation. Her loss at the polls confirms the reading that her stewardship was largely symbolic and therefore could not be sustained. She faced sustained and significant opposition within her party and the middle class and was unable to fulfill an agenda that could secure the continued support of her base among the Jamaican Black poor or among women.

Conclusion

Viewing Portia Simpson-Miller's place in Jamaican politics through a Black feminist lens means interrogating the ways in which her candidacy was embattled from the start and reveals the ways in which Black women's relationship to power is curtailed by anti-Black racism and its intersections with sexist and classist ideas, current even within states governed by Black men. Her leadership exposes the hierarchies of blackness that exist within the Black diaspora and the ways in which new elitisms captured the postcolonial nation. It therefore also reveals issues of social justice facing the Jamaican society at large. Racist, classist, and sexist ideas are deployed to create hierarchies of power that elevate specific groups of men and marginalize others and women in general. All societies are marked by specific conditions that determine who is privileged, but Black women typically do not fall within those groups in the Black diaspora. The ascent to power in political life therefore requires strategic engagement with and exposure of the dynamics of masculinist power if Black women are to have success in empowering not only themselves but also those groups whom they represent or those who are marginalized with them.

There is no doubt that Simpson-Miller's rise to the top of the PNP and the Jamaican government is a great personal achievement. She advanced against the odds, being a Black woman from the grassroots in a political climate that rewards and empowers middle-class men. In this sense, she has shattered the status quo. This is especially important given the ways in which citizenship and leadership have been narrowly defined as being based in British, then middle-class, respectability and given that the woman known variously as "Portia," "Sista P," as "Mama P" does not emerge from that ilk and is out of place in it. Since 1976, support from her constituency had been unwavering, and she is one of the few politicians who had appeal across party lines. She has at points represented a unifying force across parties but not along class lines. She had not served to bridge the divide between the masses and those in and above the middle classes, and consequently she had not been able to move Jamaica on a path of consensus among these groups. The conditions of the poor in Jamaica demand attention, and a vote for Simpson-Miller was a vote to address the problems of injustice and exclusion that many in the nation face. Like those at the bottom, however, Simpson-Miller would face the contempt of the upper classes. Like those at the bottom, she was not empowered to tackle the problems of the state and nation, and by virtue of this, she was immobilized in her place in the gendered, raced, and classed contours established by middle-class, masculinist, and anti-Black politics. Simpson-Miller is a product of this politics, her rise an indication of a shifting political moment but one lacking in the force required to transform realities on the ground. Her own strategic engagement with these forces has meant inverting popular stereotypes about black women (as specific to her identity as Mama P) as a way to self-empowerment. Her engagement should, however, be interrogated, because it depended on problematic understandings of the groups she represents and reinscribed their subordination. Through Simpson-Miller, we can rethink the types of strategies that black women may use to gain and reorder power.

Simpson-Miller's place in Jamaican politics raises questions about how Black women's leadership can be nurtured within party politics, particularly because those women come from outside traditional networks of power. It also implores us to consider how change can occur, when the desire for change comes from those marginalized groups, in this case, Black women from the bottom and poor Blacks. Political leadership, especially the type that does not represent the status quo, cannot afford to leave its base behind. Indeed, if it is to be fortified, the base must be similarly empowered to make demands on leadership when leaders divert from the course. Women who rise to the top must lay on the table and address head-on those challenges they face—of race, class, and gender—as part of the normal business of governance and seek ways to change societal values as a way to effect social justice and to secure their own power when they choose to step out of their places.

Notes

1. Keisha Lindsay similarly examines how anti-Black racism is gendered and ethnicized in her study of black immigrants and African American men and women.

2. C. L. R. James, "The West Indian Middle Classes," in *Caribbean Political Thought: Theories of the Post-Colonial State*, ed. Aaron Kamugisha (Kingston: Ian Randle Publishers, 2013), 250.

3. The idea of garrison politics was coined by Jamaican political scientist Carl Stone. He distinguishes it from other clientelistic politics by the added role of violence in maintaining allegiance to political parties. Amanda Sives explains how the

character of the garrison has shifted over time and in relation to the increasing power of dons via their capacity to distribute spoils through the gains of the drug trade.

4. Dancehall entertainer Beenie Man sings of this dynamic in his 1995 song "Slam."

5. See political campaign ads for the periods. Also see Heron.

6. For a discussion of how similar representations of Simpson-Miller exist in the media, see Taitu Heron, "Political advertising and the portrayal of gender, colour and class in Jamaica's general elections 2007," *IGDS Working Paper Series* 5—Gender and Governance (2008): 59–104.

7. See savegoatisland.org.

References

Alexander, M. Jacqui. 2013. "Not Just (Any) Body Can Be a Citizen: The Politics of Law, Sexuality and Postcoloniality in Trinidad and Tobago and the Bahamas." In *Caribbean Political Thought: Theories of the Postcolonial State*, edited by Aaron Kamugisha, 257–73. Kingston: Ian Randle Publishers.

Alexander-Floyd, Nikol. 2007. *Gender, Race, and Nationalism in Contemporary Black Politics*. New York: Palgrave Macmillan.

Anthias, Floya, and Nira Yuval-Davis. 1989. *Woman-Nation-State*. New York: Palgrave Macmillan.

Barriteau, Eudine. 1998. "Theorizing Gender Systems and the Project of Modernity in the Twentieth-Century Caribbean." *Feminist Review* 59: 186–210.

———. 2003. "Confronting Power, Theorizing Gender in the Commonwealth Caribbean." In *Confronting Power, Theorizing Gender: Interdisciplinary Perspectives in the Caribbean*, edited by Eudine Barriteau, 3–24. Kingston: University of the West Indies Press.

———. 2003. "Requiem for the Male Marginalization Thesis in the Caribbean: Death of a Non-Theory. In *Confronting Power, Theorizing Gender: Interdisciplinary Perspectives in the Caribbean*, edited by Eudine Barriteau, 324–55. Kingston: University of the West Indies Press.

Bogues, Anthony. 2002. "Politics, Nation and PostColony: Caribbean Inflections." *Small Axe* 6 (1): 1–30.

Brown, Rudolph. 2006. "Portia: PNP's First Female PM." *The Gleaner*, February 26.

Chang, Kevin O'Brien. 2012. "Can Portia Be Jamaica's Lula?" *The Gleaner*, January 8.

Collins, Patricia Hill. 2009. *Black Feminist Thought*. New York: Routledge.

Davies, Omar. 2015. "Statement on the Major Infrastructure Development Programme/Jamaica Emergency Employment Programme." Jamaican Ministry of Transport, Works, and Housing. May 26.

Government of Jamaica. *Estimates of Expenditure 2013/2014: For the Financial Year Ending 31 March 2014* (Jamaica Budget).

Government of Jamaica. FY2011–FY2015. *Central Government Operations Table.*

Heron, Taitu. 2008. "Political Advertising and the Portrayal of Gender, Colour and Class in Jamaica's General Elections 2007." *IGDS Working Paper Series—Gender and Governance* 5: 59–104.

Higginbotham, Evelyn Brooks. 1994. *Righteous Discontent: The Women's Movement in the Black Baptist Church, 1880–1920.* Cambridge: Harvard University Press.

International Monetary Fund. 2015. *IMF Country Report* No. 15/343.

Jamaica Hansard. 1989. Vol. 14, No. 3, January 4–April 26.

———. 1995. Vol. 20, No. 3, January 24–March 28.

———. 2009. Vol. 34, No. 3, March 31.

James, C. L. R. 2013. "The West Indian Middle Classes." In *Caribbean Political Thought: Theories of the Post-Colonial State*, edited by Aaron Kamugisha, 249–56. Kingston: Ian Randle Publishers.

Lewis, Linden. 2000. "Nationalism and Caribbean Masculinity." In *Gender Ironies of Nationalism: Sexing the Nation*, edited by Tamar Mayer, 261–82. New York: Routledge.

Lewis, Rupert. 2001. "Reconsidering the Role of the Middle Class in Caribbean Politics." In *New Caribbean Thought: A Reader*, edited by Brian Meeks and Folke Lindahl, 127–43. Kingston: University of the West Indies Press.

Lindsay, Keisha. 2015. "Beyond "Model Minority," "Superwoman" and "Endangered Species": Theorizing Intersectional Coalitions and Black Immigrants, African American Women, and African American Men" *Journal of African American Studies* 19 (1): 18–35.

Meeks, Brian. 2014. *Critical Interventions in Caribbean Politics and Theory.* Jackson: University Press of Mississippi.

Mitchell, Michele. 2004. *Righteous Propagation: African Americans and the Politics of Racial Destiny after Reconstruction.* Chapel Hill: University of North Carolina Press.

Ritch, Dawn. 2006. "Portia, Superior By Far." *The Gleaner*, February 19.

Robinson, Tracy. 2003. "Beyond the Bill of Rights: Sexing the Citizen." In *Confronting Power, Theorizing Gender: Interdisciplinary Perspectives in the Caribbean*, edited by Eudine Barriteau, 231–61. Kingston: University of the West Indies Press.

Robotham, Don. 2006. "Jamaican Politics and Latin America." *The Gleaner*, February 5.

Sives, Amanda. 2010. *Elections, Violence and the Democratic Process in Jamaica, 1944–2007.* Kingston: Ian Randle Publishers.

Simpson-Miller, Portia. 2011. *Statement to Parliament on International Women's Day.* March 8.

———. 2012. *Inaugural Address.* January 5.

Statistical Institute of Jamaica (STATIN). 2011. 2015. *Labour Force Statistics.* Accessed October 12, 2015. http://statinja.gov.jm/LabourForce/NewLFS.aspx.

Thomas, Deborah A. 2011. *Exceptional Violence: Embodied Citizenship in Transnational Jamaica.* Durham, NC: Duke University Press.

Waugh, Soren. 2014. "Upper House Passes Flexi Work Bill." November 3. http://www.bessfm.com/upper-house-passes-flexi-work-bill/.

8

"We Want to Set the World on Fire"

Black Nationalist Women and Diasporic Politics in the *New Negro World*, 1940–1944

KEISHA N. BLAIN
University of Pittsburgh

Introduction

In January 1942, Josephine Moody, a Black nationalist, wrote an impassioned article titled "We Want to Set the World on Fire," which appeared in the *New Negro World*, a Pan-Africanist newspaper based in Cleveland, Ohio.[1] In the article, Moody called for an immediate overthrow of the global White power structure in order to achieve universal Black liberation. Reflecting the ethos of the "New Negro Movement"—the antiracist political and cultural awakening that swept the nation and the world during the 1920s and 1930s—Moody demanded a militant and urgent response to global White supremacy (see Huggins 1971; Lewis 1979; Baker 1987; Baldwin 2007; Baldwin and Makalani 2013). "The bleeding wound of Africa is wide open," Moody argued, "and the nations of the world keep the wound from healing, and we, the Negro must be our own physician to effect a healing of that wound." The liberation of Africa, Moody continued, would only come by force: "We want to set the world on fire, we want freedom and justice and a chance to build for ourselves. And if we must set the world on fire . . . we will, like other men, die for the realization of our dreams" (Moody 1942).

Moody's statements capture the sense of urgency brought on by World War II, a period in which "anticolonial issues acquired a new prominence and stood side by side with domestic demands" for Black political and social equality (Von Eschen 1997, 7). In the aftermath of Germany's attack on Poland in September 1939, and the immediate military response from the British and French, it was apparent to Moody that a global crisis was at hand—one that would forever change the world in which she lived. Notwithstanding the fear and anxiety felt by Americans during this period, World War II signaled to Moody, and many others, that the disruption of the global color line was imminent. At its core, the global color line—which described both European colonialism in Africa and Asia and US expansionism in places like Haiti and the Dominican Republic—appeared to be fixed in place despite the persistent struggles and protest movements that had emerged in the United States and abroad (see Du Bois [1903] 1994; Marable and Agard-Jones 2008). Still, for Black nationalists like Moody, the 1940s was a moment of possibilities; one in which Black activists in the United States could forge new political alliances with people of color across the world to eradicate the global system of White supremacy and seize their individual and collective freedom.

This chapter examines the political ideas of Black nationalist women during the 1940s, based on their writings in the *New Negro World* newspaper. Modeled after the *Negro World*, the official periodical of Marcus Garvey's Universal Negro Improvement Association (UNIA)—the dominant Black nationalist organization in the United States and worldwide in the immediate post–World War I era—the *New Negro World* was established by James R. Stewart, Garvey's successor in the UNIA.[2] Following Garvey's death in London on June 10, 1940, Stewart was elected the new president general of the organization, which he led from his base in Cleveland, Ohio. He established the *New Negro World* in October of that year, providing a vehicle for UNIA members to address various issues ranging from racial violence in the Jim Crow South to decolonization in Africa. Reflecting the Black masculinist and patriarchal orientation of the UNIA, Stewart carefully monitored the newspaper and relied heavily on men in the organization to submit articles. As a result, Black nationalist male writers dominated the newspaper.[3]

Despite this limitation, the *New Negro World* provided a public platform for women in the UNIA to address the political and social challenges of the era and to offer critical insights into how people of African descent should respond to these developments. With limited access to the formal political process, these women, mostly rank-and-file activists, used the *New Negro World* as a space in which to engage in national and international political discourses. Through an array of writings including editorials, reprinted speeches, and poems, Black nationalist women articulated a global vision of Black emancipation and endorsed Pan-Africanism—the belief that African peoples, on the continent and in the diaspora, share a common past and destiny (Adi and Sherwood 2003). Moreover, these women championed the establishment of a Black nation-state in West Africa as a legitimate response to racial discrimination and global White supremacy.

By examining Black nationalist women's writings in the *New Negro World*, this chapter deepens our understanding of twentieth-century US history, Black women's history, and the history of the modern African diaspora. Since the 1970s, a number of scholars have examined the role of the Black press in US history, paying particular attention to how newspapers have functioned as key sites for Black political engagement since the early nineteenth century (see La Brie 1970; Pride 1997; Simmons 1998; Vogel 2001; Washburn 2006). By the 1940s, a plethora of Black newspapers existed, representing a wide range of political perspectives on Black life in the United States and other parts of the African diaspora. While much of the scholarly works on this period have emphasized mainstream newspapers such as the *Chicago Defender*, the *Baltimore Afro-American*, and the *Pittsburgh Courier,* this chapter uncovers the history of the Pan-Africanist newspaper, the *New Negro World,* which circulated in Black communities across the United States and other parts of the African diaspora during World War II.

At a moment when federal authorities were amplifying their efforts to censor Black journalists and editors, the *New Negro World* represented an alternative voice to the popular periodicals that dominated the Black public sphere (Alkebulan 2014). One of the few militant diasporic newspapers in circulation during the 1940s, the *New Negro World* functioned as a counterhegemonic response to global White supremacy, endorsing a range of policies aimed at bolstering Black political and economic self-determination on a national and global scale (Gramsci 1971). By addressing developments taking place in the Black diaspora and by including editorials written by activists across the globe, the newspaper provided a bridge between Blacks in the United States—particularly those in Chicago, Cleveland, Detroit, and New York—and other peoples of African descent in places like Canada, South Africa, and Cuba (Hill 1983, 694).

This chapter is the first essay that utilizes the previously understudied newspaper to show how Black nationalist women—a subordinate group within the global racial and gender hierarchies—asserted their political agency and demanded equal recognition and participation in global civic society. Paying particular attention to Black nationalist women—a group that has been largely absent in the scholarly discourse on Black life during the 1940s—this chapter departs from studies by Kevin Gaines (1996), Merline Pitre (1999), Jonathan Scott Holloway (2002), Lee Sartain (2007), Touré F. Reed (2008), Felix L. Armfield (2012) and others, which privilege Black middle-class activism within mainstream civil rights organizations, such as the National Association for the Advancement of Colored People (NAACP) and the National Urban League (NUL). By centering the political ideas of mostly working-class activists in the UNIA, this chapter underscores the wide-ranging ideological and organizational work among Black men and women during the 1940s.

In addition, it expands on the scholarship on twentieth-century Black women's intellectual, social, and political history. Since the publication of Karen Tucker Anderson's seminal article "Last Hired, First Fired: Black Women Workers during World War II" (1982), a number of scholars have examined the experiences of Black women during the 1940s, emphasizing how they served the nation during the war. Most recently, Martha S. Putney (1992), Maureen Honey (1999), Megan Taylor Shockley (2004), Martha J. Bailey and William J. Collins (2006), Cheryl Mullenbach (2013), and others have delineated the opportunities and obstacles Black women found in the army and labor force during this period of transition and turmoil. While these works have offered key insights into the lives of Black women during this era, much work remains to be done to understand fully the lived experiences of Black women in these years. Thus, this chapter shifts focus from much of the scholarship that examines Black women's lives primarily through the prisms of war and labor and instead explores Black nationalist women's complex engagement with national and global political discourses during the 1940s.

While much of the literature on Black nationalism in the United States centers on the ideas and activities of Black male theorists, activists, and leaders, this chapter gives visibility to Black women's political agency in an arena in which they have been marginalized (see Moses 1989; Adeleke 1998; Robinson 2001; Taylor 2010). Joining the scholarly works of E. Frances White (1990), Ula Taylor (2002), Charise Cheney (2005), Patricia Hill Collins (2006), Nikol Alexander-Floyd (2007) and others, this chapter foregrounds women's voices and explores the gendered contours of Black nationalist thought and praxis. It reveals that gender issues—including ideas about feminism, manhood, and womanhood—are central to the theories and practices of Black nationalism in the United States and other parts of the African diaspora.

Moreover, the chapter captures the continued salience of Black nationalism as a driving force in Black women's politics during an era that historians of Black nationalism have largely overlooked. While scholars typically focus on the Garvey movement of the 1920s or Black Power of the 1960s and 1970s, this chapter centers on the intermediate period between these two movements (see Martin 1976, Stein 1986, Lewis 1987, Ogbar 2004, Joseph 2006, Johnson 2007). In so doing, the chapter underscores how this era provided fertile ground for Black nationalist women to enter the public political sphere and engage in national and international political discourses.

Black Nationalism and the UNIA during the 1940s

The 1940s were an era of significant transformation in the lives of Black men and women across the United States and other parts of the globe. The outbreak of World War II, more than any other development during this period, marked a turning point in global history (Polenberg 1980; Brandt 1996; Wynn 2000). Concerned about the future of millions of people of color across the globe whose lives would be greatly impacted by the Second World War, Black activists across the diaspora amplified their efforts to end global racism, White imperialism, and colonialism (Von Eschen 1997; Meriwether 2002; Swindall 2014; Anderson 2014). On the home front, many Black Americans were ambivalent about supporting American military aspirations given the persistence of racial violence, disenfranchisement, and Jim Crow segregation. A. Philip Randolph's plan for a March on Washington (1941) and the "Double V" campaign (1942), which called for an end to fascism abroad and Jim Crow at home, exposed the racial grievances concerning United States foreign policy (Bynum 2010; James 2013; Lucander 2014). These developments coincided with the formation of the Congress of Racial Equality (CORE), a multiracial political organization that helped to launch the modern Civil Rights Movement and the Second Wave of the Great Migration, in which an estimated one million Black Southerners relocated to the North and West (Meier and Rudwick 1973; Grossman 1989; Wilkerson 2010).

For Black women in particular, the 1940s was an era of hope and possibility marred by the persistence of racial and gender inequality. When the United States entered World War II on December 8, 1941, women entered the labor force in record numbers to replace the men who had gone to battle. Certainly the rapidly expanding labor force improved socioeconomic conditions for many Black women, who constituted six hundred thousand of one million Black workers during World War II (Honey 1999, 2). A significant number of Black women who entered the army—an estimated four thousand—joined the Women's Army Corps (WAC), and more than three hundred became members of the Army Nurse Corps (Treadwell 1954; Earley 1989; Moore 1996; Honey 1999). Notwithstanding the significance of these opportunities, Black women's experiences during the 1940s were shaped by racial and gender discrimination. On the war front, African American WACs were relegated to segregated living quarters and endured, on a daily basis, gender and racial prejudice in an army dominated by White male officers (Buckley 2001, 295–304). In the workplace, Black women encountered a racialized and gender-based hierarchy, which consistently placed them at the bottom (Anderson 1982, 84).

Amid the socioeconomic upheavals of this era, many Black men and women turned to the Universal Negro Improvement Association (UNIA) as a significant site for political engagement. Originally established in Kingston, Jamaica, in 1914, the UNIA attracted an estimated six million members in more than forty countries around the world. By the mid-1920s, the UNIA's Cleveland chapter boasted an estimated five thousand members. However, in the immediate aftermath of Garvey's deportation in 1927, a host of factors, including financial difficulties, fragmentation, sexism, and ethnic tensions, facilitated the UNIA's decline in Cleveland (McDuffie 2011a). During the years of the Great Depression, local UNIA divisions also experienced a decline in membership as a host of other Black protest groups emerged, such as the Future Outlook League (FOL), a militant alternative to mainstream political organizations like the NAACP (Leob 1947; Philips 1999).

In October 1940, when James R. Stewart moved the UNIA's main headquarters from Harlem to Cleveland, local Black residents developed a renewed interest in Garveyism—Marcus Garvey's race-based philosophy of Black pride, African redemption, economic self-sufficiency, racial separatism, and political self-determination. An insurgent global political movement aimed to combat White supremacy, Garveyism appealed to Black men and women in Cleveland and other parts of the United States and African diaspora during the 1940s. Black Clevelanders, as historian Erik S. McDuffie has argued, "came to see themselves through Garveyism as inextricably connected to the African diaspora" (2011a, 164). Stewart's establishment of the *New Negro World* in 1940 certainly strengthened these transnational ties.

Published monthly from 1940 to 1944, the *New Negro World* had a modest distribution of an estimated fifteen hundred copies per issue. However, it appealed to a very diverse group of Black activists in places like Costa Rica, Cuba, Jamaica, and South Africa (McDuffie 2011a; Hill 1983, vol. 10: 694).

In addition to providing a bridge between Blacks in the United States and other parts of the African diaspora, the *New Negro World* was a platform from which Stewart and other Garveyites articulated a masculinist and patriarchal vision of Black liberation. During a period in which masculine ideals and images dominated the public discourse, *New Negro World* writers promoted what historian Martin Anthony Summers refers to as the "spirit of manliness"—a term that Garvey himself referenced in a 1920 speech. The "spirit of manliness," which Black middle-class men exhibited during the early twentieth century, signified a "modern ethos of masculinity . . . that characterized a society dominated by Victorian values" (Summers 2004, 8; Hill 1983, 616). Along these lines, the *New Negro World* featured an array of writings—articles, reprinted speeches, sermons, and poems—and images that constructed Black men's identities "within the paradigms of providership, production, and respectability" (Summers 2004, 26). Moreover, the newspaper endorsed a repressive and gendered ideology of Black leadership—one in which men occupied positions of power and authority while women were relegated to secondary, subordinate positions. In this way, it underscores the masculinism and misogyny of what theorist Wahneema Lubiano (2002) refers to as the "romanticized Black Nationalist subject." "Black nationalism," Lubiano argues, "produces a nonstate romanticized subject but not necessarily a critique . . . that would lead to the global overthrow of capitalism and/or homophobic patriarchy" (2002, 163).

Reflecting the ideal of Victorian manliness, writers of the *New Negro World* characterized men as the vigilant protectors of Black women and children. Writing in the newspaper in May 1942, Stewart reminded Black men in the organization that "the protection of our womanhood" was paramount. Describing his vision of the future Black nation-state, Stewart insisted that "[t]he women of Africa must not be exposed as our women in America, under the pretense of total war and Democracy" (Stewart 1942). In another editorial titled "Man's Inhumanity," Stewart lamented the deplorable conditions of people of color in the United States and across the globe, insisting that "countless men, women and children are sacrificed because *there are yet men who believe that might makes right*" (Stewart 1942, emphasis added). Nathaniel C. Patton, who served as assistant editor and circulation manager for the *New Negro World*, expressed similar sentiments in an article titled "Courage!—Gentlemen" (Patton 1942). Appealing directly to men in the UNIA, Patton reminded readers of their sole purpose: to serve as "natural leaders of millions of Negroes in their physical [and] spiritual redemption." "The Negro fast approaching MANHOOD," Patton continued, "is demanding his share of the family wealth and opportunities" (ibid.). Patton's statements underscore how Black nationalists envisioned strong male leadership as fundamental to universal Black liberation. Significantly, his statement also underscores the patriarchy inherent in Black nationalist discourses. As political scientist Nikol Alexander-Floyd (2007) argues, "The requirements of patriarchal manhood are key components of the cultural background through which hegemonic and counter-hegemonic nationalisms are imagined, pursued, and maintained" (2007, 31).

Black Nationalist Women, Gender, and Diasporic Politics

While the *New Negro World* became a platform for Black nationalist men to promote the "spirit of manliness," it was also one of the few public platforms available for nationalist women to articulate their views on a range of issues. Within the constraints of a male-dominated newspaper, Black nationalist women could not directly challenge masculinist discourses in print, but they certainly challenged Black patriarchal authority.[4] These women practiced what historian Ula Y. Taylor refers to as "community feminism," a "territory that allowed [women] to join feminism and nationalism into a single coherent, consistent framework." "At times," Taylor asserts, "community feminism resembled a tug-of-war between feminist and nationalist paradigms, but it also provided a means of critiquing ideas of women as intellectually inferior" (Taylor 2002, 2). Black nationalist women during the 1940s practiced "community feminism" by engaging in various political and social activities that sought to advance racial uplift and empower Black women in the organization and in the broader community.

Despite the inability to directly challenge Black patriarchy on the pages of the *New Negro World*, nationalist women found a space in the newspaper in which to engage in national and global political discourses. Moreover, the newspaper afforded a national and global audience to Black nationalist women, thereby bolstering their political platform. Indeed, many Black activists across the African diaspora turned to the *New Negro World* to keep abreast of contemporary developments. David Wilson, a Garveyite residing in St. Andrew, Jamaica, credited the newspaper for providing encouragement and crucial information about Black nationalist efforts across the globe: "It is my joy and gladness that we can encourage each other thru the organ which is the official mouth piece of the Head Quarters [sic]. I am very thankful to see so many divisions and branches from different parts, which are doing their best to keep the Faith of this wonderful program alive . . ." (Wilson 1942). In similar fashion, Joseph A. Todd, an activist residing in Havana, Cuba, praised the newspaper for publishing the "most stimulating articles . . . [that] give us food for thought" (Todd 1942). Moreover, he credited the newspaper for reawakening the political consciousness of Afro-descended people—especially "the stray ones of the flock" (Todd 1941). Writing to the newspaper in December 1941, Todd continued to praise James Stewart and others for launching the newspaper: "We the officers and members of the Havana Division . . . congratulate you for the reappearance of our 'indispensable mouth-piece,' the *New Negro World*" (ibid.).

Through this periodical, Black nationalist women brought international attention to worsening economic conditions and growing political uncertainty in the United States, situating these developments within a larger global struggle for Black freedom. Reminiscent of nineteenth-century journalist Ida B. Wells-Barnett, Black nationalist women during the 1940s used their political writings to advocate the end of lynching. In a 1943 poem titled "My Race," Florine Wilkes, a frequent writer for the *New Negro World*, expressed deep frustration over the mistreatment of Black men and women in the United States:

> In the depths of a long dark corridor
> Stands the remains of a Noble Race
> They've butchered, lynched and hanged us
> Because we wanted better place
> We've been kicked, shunned and segregated
> And looked upon as an outcast,
> We've suffered under the foot of the white man
> How long will this terror last?

Wilkes's poem captured the mood of frustration that many African Americans felt during the 1940s (Wilkes 1943). As the global war for democracy waged on, these men and women were engaged in a seemingly never-ending struggle for freedom and equality at home. Therefore, Wilkes's question—"How long will this terror last?"—was certainly one that countless Black activists were pondering.

For many women writers of the *New Negro World*, there appeared to be no end in sight. In her article "The Real Solution," Theresa E. Young upheld this point of view. An activist from Cincinnati, Ohio, Young served as the UNIA's assistant secretary general and an associate editor of the *New Negro World*. While much of her work centered on assisting Stewart with the publication of the newspaper, Young sometimes included her own articles, which addressed social issues of the day. In her editorial, Young described White mob violence and racial discrimination as part of the very fabric of American society. "Discrimination has extended to every phase of racial life," she argued, "In every city, state, and town, Negroes are restricted from white residential areas and forced to live in undesirable sections." "Negro children must attend separate and inferior schools," she continued, "and where school opportunities are available nothing of the history of the Black Man is taught, but in every instance the race is reminded that it [cannot] successfully aspire to a social and personal relation on the same level as whites" (Young 1943). Young's editorial cited racial prejudice as the ultimate failure of American democracy. Similarly, activist Edith Allen condemned racial injustice and offered a scathing critique of American democracy in a 1941 editorial: "[I]n America the land where Democracy IS SUPPOSED to be in evidence . . . a human being was shackled to a tree in the public square in the state of Georgia by a law enforcement officer." "Even the beast[s] are not mistreated," Allen declared, "and yet such action is unchallenged and such perpetrators go unpunished." "Is this democracy?' " she rhetorically asked (Allen 1941).

Despite the political gains of the early 1940s—most notably, the passage of FDR's Executive Order 8802 in 1941 to prohibit discrimination in the defense industry—many Black activists were frustrated with the slow pace of political change in the United States. Similar to Black women in US leftist groups during this period, Black nationalist women used their writings to bring attention to the persistence of racial inequality in the United States and abroad (Davies 2007; Harris 2009; McDuffie 2011b; Gore 2011). In her 1940 master's thesis at Fisk University, titled "The Negro Woman Domestic Worker in Relation to Trade Unionism," Communist Party activist Esther Cooper Jackson decried the exploitation of African American women along the lines of race, sex, and class (McDuffie 2011, 115). Cooper Jackson's writings were consistent with those of other Black women in the Communist Party, including Claudia Jones and Grace P. Campbell, who framed "black women domestics as the most vulnerable and exploited women and workers in the U.S. political economy" (McDuffie 2012, 8).

While Black nationalist women were not oblivious to the class dimension of their political struggle, their writings in the *New Negro World* centered on challenging all forms of racial oppression (Bush 1998). In January 1942, Ethel M. Collins, a veteran activist from Jamaica who had joined the UNIA during the early 1920s, called on Black men and women across the globe to demand their God-given rights. "As far as humanity goes," she wrote, "all men are equal. . . ." "It is true," she continued, "that economically and scientifically certain races are more progressive than others; but that does not imply superiority." Rather than sit idly by as the ideology of White supremacy continued to spread throughout the world, Collins appealed to *New Negro World* readers to take a definitive stance toward racial progress. Employing masculine language, Collins declared, "Our appeal to the world today is [this]: Let us have justice, let us have fair play and we shall prove ourselves as *real men* should" (Collins 1942, emphasis added).

In another article, Eustance G. Campbell, an activist residing in Newark, New Jersey, decried White supremacy and called for an immediate response from Black activists across the globe. "There is no time to lose," she explained in a July 1942 editorial. "There is a lot of work to be done. We can't wait until the War is over to be free; the time is now, right now" (Campbell 1942). Similar to nationalist leaders Marcus Garvey, and Edward Wilmot Blyden before him, Campbell drew inspiration from the Zionist movement for Jewish self-determination (Hill 1998). During the 1940s, as news of the Holocaust spread across the globe, Zionist groups attempted to secure international support for the creation of a Jewish state. Campbell insisted that, like Jews, Black men and women deserved support, specifically an army of their own: "Don't you see what the White Race is doing? He is speaking about giving the Jews an Army in Palestine, then, where will OUR Army be[?]." Emphasizing the urgency of the situation, Campbell implored "Brothers and Sisters of the African Tribe" to join the struggle for Black liberation and political self-determination. "This is the only chance we have," she explained, "and if we let this chance pass us, we will not get it again for a thousand years more" (Campbell 1942). Campbell's editorial underscored the heightened sense of urgency and awareness of global racial politics among people of the African diaspora during this period. It also illustrates how Black nationalists constructed what scholars Sidney J. Lemelle and Robin D. G. Kelley (1994) have described as a "transnational and racialized 'imagined community" (1994, 7). Viewing herself as a member of a diasporic community of Black activists across the globe, Campbell emphasized the need for sustained political alliances and collaborations across geographical boundaries.

Campbell was certainly not alone in her diasporic political vision. From miles away, Black nationalists in Cuba lent their support to US-based activists and embraced a diasporic identity that transcended the nation-state. In a 1942 letter to the newspaper, Cuban Garveyites empathized with their fellow comrades in the struggle for Black liberation: "The members of the Marianao Division of the Universal Negro Improvement Association, and well wishers, join our down-trodden brothers the world over, in wonderment about the present day happenings. We see that Democracy is facing a supreme test." Expressing some optimism about the inevitable liberation of people of African descent, Cuban Garveyites remarked, " 'He that soweth to the wind, shall reap in a whirlwind.' The law of evolution is seemingly unchangeable, and if the ruling Governments do not incline their hearts toward Justice to four hundred million Negroes, the world over, then their task will be hard" ("Democracy is Facing a Test" 1942). In another letter to the editor, members of the same Cuban division praised the UNIA's efforts in the United States, expressed enthusiasm for the revived Garveyite newspaper, and extended a warm welcome to active members in the organization. "Our doors are always open to receive you," they promised, "Our failures are your failure [and] likewise our success is yours" (Todd 1941).

Through the pages of the *New Negro World*, Black nationalist women grappled with questions about citizenship, identity, and national belonging. At a moment when race leaders like W. E. B. Du Bois called on African Americans to join the war effort to improve their political standing in the United States, nationalist women emphasized the need to create a Black nation-state elsewhere. As "transcultural Afrodiasporic subjects," these women, from wide-ranging cultural backgrounds and identities, envisioned themselves as members of a diasporic polity and hoped to facilitate the unification of people of African descent (Guridy 2010, 4). For these women, the Black struggle for full citizenship and equal participation under the law appeared futile. "America knows the story of our 300 years of suffering," Ethel Collins explained, "We have watered her vegetation with our tears. We have built her cities and laid the foundations of her materialism with the mortar of our blood and bones. We have fought in all wars, and die[d] courageously . . ." Yet, Collins lamented, the struggle to "solve the race problem" persisted (Collins 1942).

Viewing West African emigration as the ultimate solution to eradicating global White supremacy, Collins explained: "We want the right to have a country of our own . . . Africa is the legitimate, moral, and righteous home of the Black peoples of the world." Insisting that people of African descent needed to "create their own destinies" and build the "culture and civilization of their own," she went on to emphasize the importance of reclaiming Africa: "[W]e of the Universal Negro Improvement Association have made up in our minds to work for the restoration of human liberty and the land of our fathers" (ibid.). Elaine Cooper, secretary of the UNIA's division in Montreal, Canada, expressed similar sentiments, arguing that "Negroes should be more determined today than they have ever been, to protect their own interests." Emphasizing the need for Black men and women to establish their own nation, Cooper implored readers of the *New Negro World* to "realize that the time is coming when every man and every race must return to its own 'vine and fig tree'" (Cooper 1942; Marano 2010).

Echoing the sentiments of earlier Black nationalist thinkers—Martin Delany, Edward Blyden, and Henry McNeal Turner among them—women writers for the *New Negro World* championed Black emigration, arguing that Africa is the homeland for people of African descent. "Africa is calling us Home to our Native Land," Eustance G. Campbell explained, "Africa, where we can enjoy Peace and Happiness for ourselves . . ." (Campbell 1942). Other women writers embraced this point of view. Writing in a 1943 editorial, Theresa Young reasoned that West African emigration was a viable response to the persistent challenges of racial segregation, Black disenfranchisement, violence, and terror. "The conditions of life that Negroes have faced and are still facing in America," Young argued, "are conducive in the highest degree to a nationalistic spirit." "At every point in their social evolution," she continued, "opposition presents persistent discrimination to show that the Negro . . . will be tolerated only in the capacity of menials." "The Negro must learn," she concluded, "that if he is to take his rightful place, he too must have a government of his own" (Young 1943). Without mincing words, activist Edith Allen endorsed this point of view, informing readers that racial acts of violence would only cease to occur if—and when—Black people "had a country of [their] own" (Allen 1941). Writing in a 1942 editorial titled "Liberty," Jamaican-born activist Ethel Collins asserted, "The Pilgrim and colonists did it for America, and the New Negro can do it for Africa" (Collins 1942). These statements underscore how the rights of self-determination, belonging, and autonomy were essential themes in Black nationalist women's political writings.

During the 1940s, Black nationalist women—like their male counterparts—used the pages of the *New Negro World* to promote the Greater Liberia Bill. Introduced in 1939 by Mississippi senator and White supremacist Theodore G. Bilbo, the congressional bill called for millions of dollars in federal aid to relocate African Americans to West Africa (Fitzgerald 1997). While many race leaders across the country openly denounced the Bill and its controversial author, Black nationalist men and women found it to be a glimmer of hope. Indeed, the Bill stirred long-held nationalist aspirations of establishing an autonomous Black nation-state. Moreover, many Black Americans of all political persuasions rallied behind the controversial senator and his bill, hoping to escape the racial injustice and economic hardship they faced during the Great Depression.

When the bill failed to pass in 1939, Pan-Africanist feminist Amy Jacques Garvey—Marcus Garvey's second wife—attempted to revive it during World War II (Goldthree 2010). From her base in Jamaica, Jacques Garvey launched a massive campaign to promote the bill with the backing of Black activists across the diaspora. In April 1944, Jacques Garvey wrote to Jamaican doctor and civic leader Harold Moody, who served as president of the League of Colored Peoples—a London-based Pan-Africanist organization (Marable 1998, 106). In this letter, she laid out her arguments in support of Bilbo's bill, describing it as "the best plan" that would "ease the . . . problems" of Black Americans and other people of African descent.[5] Moreover, Jacques Garvey envisioned the bill as an opportunity for the United States to "develop West Africa from Gambia to Equatorial Africa . . . [and] send experts in all branches of government and for security, to teach and train Africans and Colonists from America to take over their country eventually." She believed that skilled Black emigrants from the United States would play a crucial role in making West Africa "a progressive, Democratic nation."[6]

While she envisioned the Greater Liberia Bill as a means of bolstering Black political and economic autonomy, Jacques Garvey—like other men and women in the UNIA—subscribed to a civilizationist view of Africa that was characteristic of nineteenth-century Black nationalist thought (Adeleke 1998, Moses 1989). Indeed, she and other UNIA activists supported the bill despite its inclusion of a clause that would grant the United States government military control over the West African territories. These activists also laid claim to African land and envisioned relocation to West Africa as an opportunity to control and Americanize native Africans. Their perspectives illustrate how, as E. Frances White (1990) argues, Black nationalism "can be radical and progressive in relation to white racism and conservative and repressive in relation to the internal organization of the black community" (1990, 76–77). Political scientist Dean E. Robinson (2001) concurs with this assessment, arguing that Black nationalist movements "have reproduced some of the most conservative ideas in U.S. history on issues of race, economic disparity, and social mobility" (2001, 133).

On the one hand, Black nationalists were deeply committed to Pan-Africanism as a "direct response to the imperialist annexation of Africa and Eurocentrism" (Bush 1999, 14). On the other hand, they subscribed to a civilizationist view of racial uplift that mirrored the same practices they rejected. Reflecting the imperialist aspirations of these activists, Florine Wilkes, a frequent writer for the *New Negro World*, declared in a poem, "No man shall successfully rule my people, [b]ut a man who looks like me" (Wilkes 1943). Wilkes's statement, and Jacques Garvey's writings, underscores what Stephanie Batiste (2011) describes as the "uneven, inconclusive, and sometimes contradictory" nature of "black manifestations of imperial discourses" (2011, 258).

Through the pages of the *New Negro World*, Black nationalist women also sought to "counter [the Black] experience of cultural and temporal dispossession, and to furnish the black American community with a usable past" (Dubey 1994, 25). Rejecting the negative images and stereotypical depictions of Black history culture that dominated mainstream mass media, women wrote articles that emphasized African beauty and exalted the nobility of African civilizations. In an editorial titled "Arise," Adelia Ireland, a Black nationalist residing in St. Louis, Missouri, reminded *New Negro World* readers of their rich African heritage: "We are the Sons and our Father left us a great heritage, for in the days of old, there were Kings and Princes. They had a civilization. . . . The City of our Forefathers was traveled by Cesar, and who can forget Hannibal, who scalled the Alps and marched on Rome [sic]. His Nobility shall never die" (Ireland 1942). Subscribing to a romanticized view of precolonial Africa, Ethel Collins expressed similar sentiments: "Stand beneath the colossal Pyramid of Egyptian civilization from the books of the dead. Walk along the banks of the Niger and listen to the solemn voice of Nineveh's ashes and Babylon's decay; they all tell that the Black Sons of Ham gave to the World its civilization" (Collins 1942). These examples underscore how, as Wahneema Lubiano (2002) has argued, Black nationalism "articulates a desire—always unfillable—for complete representation of the past and a fantasy for a better future" (2002, 157).

Similar to earlier Black nationalists, women writers of the *New Negro World* embraced the philosophy of Ethiopianism, evoking biblical verses as a prophetic reminder of inevitable Black redemption (Shepperson 1953; Drake 1970; Moses 1978; Moses 1998). Reflecting Ethiopianist discourse of the eighteenth and nineteenth centuries, women writers for the *New Negro World* endorsed the belief that the "redemption" of Africa—the complete liberation of peoples of African descent—was divinely ordained. As Mrs. J. P. Giddings, an activist from Virginia, expressed it, "Let us ask Him to hasten the day the Princes shall come out of Egypt, and Ethiopia shall stretch forth her hand to God; let us tell Him that we know now that our house is occupied by strangers, but are willing to take a chance to fight, yes even die, for a part of His house that He gave to the Black Race . . ." (Giddings 1942). Ethel Collins agreed, urging readers to hold fast to Psalm 68:31: "Princes shall come out of Egypt, and Ethiopia shall stretch out her hands unto God." "We have accomplished much . . . through Unity of purpose," she added, "but we shall not stop . . . for there is much more to be done to reach our objective" (Collins 1942). Collins's statements, along with those of Mrs. J. P. Giddings, illustrate how women drew upon earlier Pan-Africanist traditions to refine their political strategies and ideologies during the 1940s.

The global visions of African redemption that appeared in Black nationalists' writings during this period were intertwined with the question of gender roles. Whereas Black women on the Communist Left embraced a progressive gender politics—by pursuing a "black left feminist" agenda that was attentive to the intersecting dimensions of race, gender, and class—women in the UNIA endorsed a more conservative point of view (McDuffie 2011b, 3–4; Robinson 2001, 34–38). Indeed, as historian Asia Leeds (2013) has argued, "the political philosophy of [Black nationalism] held women's bodies and behavior under heavy surveillance," promoted "respectable" Black womanhood, and emphasized women's responsibility to "mother the race through the biological and cultural reproduction of successful black offspring" (2013, 1). Writing in the *New Negro World* in 1942, Cuban Garveyite James A. Todd remarked, "LET OUR WOMEN AWAKEN TO THE FACT THAT 'NO RACE CAN RISE HIGHER THAN ITS WOMEN' " (Todd 1942). Aaron Rivers, an activist residing in Cincinnati, Ohio, expressed these sentiments in a 1942 editorial: "Without womanhood, this world would be as one vast desert unpeopled . . . True womanhood loves her offspring far dearer than her life" (Rivers 1942). "The [perseverance] of womanhood to give the earth prosperity," he wrote, "shall always be a beacon light to the glory of her maker and the joy of heaven" (ibid.). Much like the earlier poetry of Marcus Garvey, Rivers's writings revealed a veneration of Black womanhood particularly in relation to motherhood (Bair 1996, 42). Black nationalist women certainly celebrated motherhood but also envisioned themselves as leaders in their communities.

As "community feminists," they challenged sexism and sought to empower Black women globally. Yet they walked a fine line between advancing women's opportunities and supporting Black men's leadership. These tensions unfolded on the pages of the *New Negro World* newspaper. In an article published in July 1941, Adelia Ireland articulated a masculinist vision of Black liberation, emphasizing the absolute necessity of strong Black male leadership. "Arise Black men," Ireland declared, "and come out in the light and let the world know their sense of duty" (Ireland 1942). Speaking before a crowd of UNIA supporters in 1942, Elinor White, state commissioner for Illinois, elaborated on this point: "If the *men* of the Black race in Africa, West Indies, South and Central America and the United States of America, would work together on this great program given us by the late honorable Marcus Garvey, there is no reason why we cannot present to the world . . . a race of self-respecting and able people" (White 1942, emphasis added). Florine Wilkes expressed similar sentiments in a poem, calling on Black men across the globe to "wake from [their] slumber . . . and fight for [the] MOTHERLAND" (Wilkes 1944). These examples exemplify how Black nationalist women envisioned men's roles in the global struggle for liberation and within the imagined future Black nation-state. Like Garvey and other Black men in the UNIA, nationalist women often endorsed a masculinist view of leadership.

At the same time, women also found ways to challenge male patriarchy. The actions of longtime Garveyite Ethel Collins exemplify this point. In 1943, Collins found herself in a precarious situation when chief editor James Stewart openly denounced her in a series of articles in the *New Negro World*. Despite Collins's more than twenty years of service to the UNIA, Stewart quickly dismissed Collins, describing her as "being totally disloyal" (Stewart 1943). Collins had exerted authority by openly challenging Stewart's leadership and questioning his 'executive' decisions (McDuffie 2011a, 176). Unwilling to accommodate Collins's defiance, Stewart went to great lengths to discredit Collins's standing in the movement. Because she was unable to address the issue in the newspaper, Collins launched a letter-writing campaign shortly thereafter in an effort to defend her actions and clear her name. Writing on August 15, 1943, Collins attempted to set the record straight: "No doubt you have read the articles written by Mr. James R. Stewart, president general of the UNIA in Cleveland, Ohio; and published in the *New [Negro] World* . . . quoting me and others as being disloyal to the association. In this act of his, I am compelled to make a reply and give some enlightenment on the matter . . ." After reminding readers of her twenty-three-year service to the organization, Collins denounced Stewart's actions, noting that it was "wicked for anyone at this late hour to style me as being disloyal." "It is too late now for me to change," she added, "You can count on me to be the same in life and in death—my work for good shall never cease."[7] Despite her inability to challenge Stewart's leadership directly in the *New Negro World*, Collins's actions demonstrate her refusal to accept Stewart's behavior and exemplify the ways in which Black nationalist women in the UNIA sought to resist male patriarchy within the male-dominated organization. Importantly, her story provides yet another glimpse into the richness and complexities of Black nationalist women's ideas and praxis during the 1940s.

Conclusion

The *New Negro World* newspaper, despite its endorsement of a repressive and gendered vision of universal Black emancipation, provides one of the most significant archival accounts of Black nationalist political ideas during World War II. Though the newspaper was relatively short-lived—it folded in 1944 largely as a result of financial troubles and growing factionalism in the UNIA—it functioned as one of the few US-based Pan-Africanist newspapers circulating in global Black communities during the 1940s. During this period of economic and political turmoil, the *New Negro World* provided a medium for Black nationalist women, including many rank-and-file activists, to address national and global concerns. With limited access to the formal voting process during the 1940s, the *New Negro World* afforded Black nationalist women, from a range of socioeconomic backgrounds and from various parts of the diaspora, a public forum from which to actively participate in political discourse and thus operate in activities beyond the confines of home and family (Baker 1984).

By recovering the history of the newspaper and foregrounding the writings of the women who graced its pages, this chapter deepens our understanding of the diverse political strategies and tactics people of African descent have employed in their struggles against racial discrimination, inequality, and global White supremacy. In addition, it offers a glimpse into how Black nationalists skillfully used their political writings in the newspaper to galvanize activists during World War II. Their efforts, which have been previously overlooked in the historical record, helped to usher in a transformative era of social reform and activism. Indeed, the political work of these men and women set the stage for a new generation of militant activists during the Civil Rights–Black Power era who were determined to secure universal Black liberation—"by any means necessary" (see X 1970, Taylor 2010).

Notes

1. This chapter is an edited version of my article: Keisha N. Blain, " 'We Want to Set the World on Fire': Black Nationalist Women and Diasporic Politics in the New Negro World, 1940–1944," *The Journal of Social History* 49, no. 1 (Fall 2015): 194–212. In this chapter, I use the term "Black nationalism" to describe individuals who embraced the political view that Black people constituted a "separate group or nationality by virtue of their African heritage, their shared historical experiences (slavery, segregation, ghettoization and other forms of oppression), and their distinct culture." Black nationalists generally emphasized African heritage, Black economic self-sufficiency, political self-determination, and racial separatism, which often, though not always, meant West African emigration (See West 1999, 83, Moses 1978, 17).

2. Founded by Marcus Garvey, with the assistance of Amy Ashwood, in Jamaica in 1914, the UNIA was the largest and most influential Pan-Africanist movement of the twentieth century—promoting racial pride, African redemption (from European colonization), economic self-sufficiency, racial separatism and political self-determination. From Kingston, Jamaica, Garvey oversaw UNIA affairs before relocating to Harlem, New York, where he incorporated the organization in 1918. At its peak, from 1919 to 1924, the organization attracted an estimated six million members in more than forty countries around the world. In 1927, Garvey was deported after spending time in prison for alleged mail fraud.

3. These writers include individuals such as Charles James, Ruben Starling, and Zebedee Green.

4. Although the majority of those on staff were men, a few women did help with the production and distribution of the newspaper. Theresa E. Young, a Garveyite from Cincinnati, Ohio, was an associate editor while Jamaican-born activist Ethel M. Collins worked as the newspaper's secretary general.

5. Amy Jacques Garvey to Harold Moody, April 17, 1944, Box 2, Marcus Garvey Memorial Collection, Fisk University, Nashville, Tennessee.

6. Jacques Garvey to Moody, April 17, 1944, Box 2, Garvey Memorial Collection.

7. Ethel Collins to Officers, Members and Friends of the UNIA and of the Race, August 15, 1943, Box 1, Garvey Memorial Collection.

References

Adeleke, Tunde. 1998. *UnAfrican Americans: Nineteenth-Century Black Nationalists and the Civilizing Mission.* Lexington: University Press of Kentucky.

Adi, Hakim, and Marika Sherwood, eds. 2003. *Pan-African History: Political Figures from Africa and the Diaspora since 1787.* London: Routledge.

Alexander-Floyd, Nikol. 2007. *Gender, Race, and Nationalism in Contemporary Black Politics.* New York: Palgrave Macmillan.

Alkebulan, Paul. 2014. *The African American Press in World War II: Toward Victory at Home and Abroad.* Lanham: Lexington.

Allen, Edith. 1941. "Ga. Prisoner Chained to Tree." *New Negro World,* October.

Anderson, Carol. 2014. *Bourgeois Radicals: The NAACP and the Struggle for Colonial Liberation, 1941–1960.* New York: Cambridge University Press.

Anderson, Karen Tucker. 1982. "Last Hired, First Fired: Black Women Workers during World War II." *Journal of American History* 69: 82–97.

Armfield, Felix L. 2012. *Eugene Kinckle Jones: the National Urban League and Black Social Work, 1910–1940.* Urbana: University of Illinois Press.

Baker, Houston A. 1987. *Modernism and the Harlem Renaissance.* Chicago: University of Chicago.

Baker, Paula. 1984. "The Domestication of Politics: Women and American Political Society, 1790–1920." *The American Historical Review* 89: 620–47.

Bailey, Martha J., and William J. Collins. 2006. "The Wage Gains of African-American Women in the 1940s." *The Journal of Economic History* 66: 737–77.

Bair, Barbara. 1996. "'Ethiopia Shall Stretch Forth Her Hands Unto God': Laura Kofey and the

Gendered Vision of Redemption in the Garvey Movement." In *A Mighty Baptism: Race, Gender, and the Creation of American Protestantism,* edited by Susan Juster and Lisa MacFarlane. Ithaca: Cornell University Press.

Baldwin, Davarian L. 2007. *Chicago's New Negroes: Modernity, the Great Migration, and Black Urban Life.* Chapel Hill: University of North Carolina Press.

Baldwin, Davarian L., and Minkah Makalani, eds. 2013. *Escape from New York: the New Negro Renaissance Beyond Harlem.* Minneapolis: University of Minnesota Press.

Batiste, Stephanie. 2011. *Darkening Mirrors: Imperial Representation in Depression-Era African American Performance.* Durham: Duke University Press.

Brandt, Nat. 1996. *Harlem at War: The Black Experience in WWII.* Syracuse: Alfred A. Knopf.

Buckley, Gail Lumet. 2001. *American Patriots: The Story of Blacks in the Military from the Revolution to Desert Storm.* New York: Random House.

Bush, Rod. 1998. *We Are Not What We Seem: Black Nationalism and Class Struggle in the American Century.* New York: New York University Press.

Bush, Barbara. 1999. *Imperialism, Race, and Resistance: Africa and Britain, 1919–1945.* New York: Routledge.
Bynum, Cornelius. 2010. *A. Philip Randolph and the Struggle for Civil Rights.* Urbana: University of Illinois Press.
Campbell, Eustance G. 1942. "Wake Up Negro." *New Negro World*, January
Cheney, Charise L. 2005. *Brothers Gonna Work It Out: Sexual Politics in the Golden Age of Rap Nationalism.* New York: New York University Press.
Collins, Ethel M. 1942. "Liberty." *New Negro World*, January
———. 1942. "A Tribute to the Late Marcus Garvey." *New Negro World*, July.
Collins, Patricia Hill. *From Black Power to Hip Hop: Racism, Nationalism, and Feminism.* Philadelphia: Temple University Press.
Cooper, Elaine. 1942. *Untitled. New Negro World*, January.
Davies, Carole Boyce. 2007. *Left of Karl Marx: The Political Life of Black Communist Claudia Jones.* Durham: Duke University Press.
"Democracy Is Facing a Test." 1942. *New Negro World*, March.
"Divisional News, Mariana Division 203." 1942. *New Negro World*, July.
Drake, St. Clair. 1970. *The Redemption of Africa and Black Religion.* Chicago: Third World Press.
Dubey, Madhu. 1994. *Black Women Novelists and the Nationalist Aesthetic.* Bloomington: Indiana University Press.
Du Bois, W. E. B. [1903] 1994. *Souls of Black Folk.* New York: Dover.
Earley, Charity Adams. 1989. *One Woman's Army: A Black Officer Remembers the WAC.* College Station: Texas A&M University Press.
"Elinor White, State Commissioner of Illinois, Make Stiring [sic] Appeal to Black Women and Men All Over the World." 1942. *New Negro World*, May.
Fitzgerald, Michael. 1997. "'We Have Found a Moses': Theodore Bilbo, Black Nationalism, and the Greater Liberia Bill of 1939." *Journal of Southern History* 63: 293–320.
Gaines, Kevin. 1996. *Uplifting the Race: Black Leadership, Politics, and Culture in the Twentieth Century.* Chapel Hill: University of North Carolina Press.
Giddings, J. P. 1942. "Have I a Place in My Father's House?" *New Negro World*, March.
Goldthree, Reena N. 2010. "Amy Jacques, Theodore Bilbo, and the Paradoxes of Black Nationalism." In *Global Circuits of Blackness: Interrogating the African Diaspora*, edited by Jean Muteba Rahier, Percy C. Hintzen, and Felipe Smith. Urbana: University of Illinois Press.
Gore, Dayo F. 2011. *Radicalism at the Crossroads: African American Women Activists in the Cold War.* New York: New York University Press.
Gramsci, Antonio. 1971. *Selections from the Prison Notebooks of Antonio Gramsci.* Translated by Quintin Hoare and Geoffrey Nowell-Smith. London: International Publishers.
Guridy, Frank. 2010. *Forging Diaspora: Afro-Cubans and African Americans in a World of Empire and Jim Crow.* Chapel Hill: University of North Carolina Press.

Harris, LaShawn D. 2009. "Running with the Reds: African American Women and the Communist Party during the Great Depression." *The Journal of African American History* 94: 21–43.

Hill, Robert A. 1983. *The Marcus Garvey and Universal Negro Improvement Association Papers.* Berkeley: University of California Press.

———. 1988. "Black Zionism: Marcus Garvey and the Jewish Question." In *African Americans and Jews in the Twentieth Century: Studies in Convergence and Conflict,* edited by V. P. Franklin. Columbia: University of Missouri Press.

Holloway, Jonathan Scott. 2002. *Confronting the Veil: Abram Harris, Jr., E. Franklin Frazier, and Ralph Bunch.* Chapel Hill: University of North Carolina Press.

Honey, Maureen, ed. 1999. *Bitter Fruit: African American Women in World War II.* Columbia: University of Missouri Press.

Huggins, Nathan Irvin. 1971. *Harlem Renaissance.* London: Oxford University Press.

Ireland, Adelia. 1942. "Arise." *New Negro World,* July

James, Rawn. 2013. *The Double V: How Wars, Protest, and Harry Truman Desegregated America's Military.* New York: Bloomsbury Press.

Johnson, Cedric. 2007. *Revolutionaries to Race Leaders: Black Power and the Making of African American Politics.* Minneapolis: University of Minnesota.

Joseph, Peniel E. 2006. *Waiting 'Til the Midnight Hour: A Narrative History of Black Power in America.* New York: Henry Holt and Co.

La Brie, Henry G. 1970. *The Black Newspaper in America, A Guide.* Iowa City: Institute for Communication Studies, University of Iowa.

Leeds, Asia. 2013. "Toward the 'Higher Type of Womanhood': The Gendered Contours of Garveyism and the Making of Redemptive Geographies in Costa Rica, 1922–1941." *Palimpsest: A Journal on Women, Gender, and the Black International* 2: 1–27.

Lemelle, Sidney, and Robin D. G. Kelley, eds. 1994. *Imagining Home: Class, Culture and Nationalism in the African Diaspora.* London: Verso.

Leob, Charles. 1947. *The Future Is Yours: The History of the Future Outlook League, 1935–1946.* Cleveland: Future Outlook League.

Lewis, David Levering. 1979. *When Harlem Was in Vogue.* New York: Penguin.

Lewis, Rupert. 1987. *Marcus Garvey: Anti-Colonial Champion.* London: Karia Press.

Lucander, David. 2014. *Winning the War for Democracy: The March on Washington Movement, 1941–1946.* Urbana: University of Illinois Press.

Marable, Manning. 1988. *Black Leadership.* New York: Columbia University Press.

Marable, Manning, and Vanessa Agard-Jones, eds. 2008. *Transnational Blackness: Navigating the Global Color Line.* New York: Palgrave Macmillan.

Marano, Carla. 2010. " 'Rising Strongly and Rapidly': The Universal Negro Improvement Association in Canada, 1919–1940." *Canadian Historical Review* 91: 233–59.

Martin, Tony. 1976. *Race First: The Ideological and Organizational Struggles of Marcus Garvey and the Universal Negro Improvement Association.* Dover: Majority Press.

McDuffie, Erik S. 2011. "Garveyism in Cleveland, Ohio and the History of the Diasporic Midwest, 1920–1975." *African Identities* 9: 163–82.

———. 2011. *Sojourning for Freedom: Black Women, American Communism, and the Making of Black Left Feminism.* Durham: Duke University Press.

———. 2012. "'For the Full Freedom of . . . Colored Women in Africa, Asia, and in these United States . . .': Black Women Radicals and the Practice of a Black Women's International." *Palimpsest: A Journal on Women, Gender and the Black International* 1: 1–30.

Meier, August, and Elliot Rudwick. 1973. *CORE: A Study in the Civil Rights Movement, 1942–1968.* New York: Oxford University Press.

Meriwether, James. 2002. *Proudly We Can Be Africans: Black Americans and Africa, 1935–1961.* Chapel Hill: University of North Carolina Press.

Moody, Josephine. 1942. "We Want to Set the World on Fire." *New Negro World,* January.

Moore, Brenda L. 1996. *To Serve My Country, To Serve My Race: The Story of the Only African American WACS Stationed Overseas during World War II.* New York: New York University Press.

Moses, Wilson Jeremiah. 1978. *The Golden Age of Black Nationalism, 1850–1925.* New York: Oxford University Press.

———. 1989. *Alexander Crummell: A Study of Civilization and Discontent.* New York: Oxford University Press.

———. 1998. *Afrotopia: The Roots of African American Popular History.* Cambridge: Cambridge University Press.

Mullenbach, Cheryl. 2013. *Double Victory: How African American Women Broke Race and Gender Barriers to Help Win World War II.* Chicago: Chicago Review Press.

Ogbar, Jeffrey O. G. 2004. *Black Power: Radical Politics and African American Identity.* Baltimore: Johns Hopkins University Press.

Patton, Nathaniel C. 1942. "Courage!—Gentlemen." *New Negro World,* November–December.

Philips, Kimberley L. 1999. *Alabama North: African-American Migrants, Community, and Working-Class Activism in Cleveland, 1915–1945.* Urbana: University of Illinois Press.

Pitre, Merline. 1999. *In Struggle Against Jim Crow: Lulu B. White and the NAACP, 1900–1957.* College Station: Texas A&M University Press.

Polenberg, Richard. 1980. *War and Society: The United States, 1941–1945.* Westport, CT: Greenwood Press.

Pride, Armistead Scott. 1997. *A History of the Black Press.* Washington, DC: Howard University Press.

Putney, Martha S. 1992. *When the Nation Was in Need: Blacks in the Women's Army Corps during World War II.* Metuchen: Scarecrow Press.

Reed, Touré F. 2008. *Not Alms but Opportunity: The Urban League and the Politics of Racial Uplift, 1910–1950.* Chapel Hill: University of North Carolina Press.

Rivers, Aaron. 1942. "Womanhood." *New Negro World*, July.
Robinson, Dean E. 2001. *Black Nationalism in American Politics and Thought.* New York: Cambridge University Press.
Sartain, Lee. 2007. *Invisible Activists: Women of the Louisiana NAACP and the Struggle for Civil Rights, 1915–1945.* Baton Rouge: Louisiana State University Press.
Shepperson, George. 1953. "Ethiopianism and African Nationalism." *Phylon* 14: 9–18.
Shockley, Megan Taylor. 2004. *We, Too, Are Americans: African American Women in Detroit and Richmond, 1940–54.* Urbana: University of Illinois Press.
Simmons, Charles A. 1998. *The African American Press: A History of News Coverage During National Crises, With Special References to Four Special Newspapers, 1827–1965.* Jefferson: McFarland and Company.
Stein, Judith. 1986. *The World of Marcus Garvey: Race and Class in Modern Society.* Baton Rouge: Louisiana State University Press.
Stewart, James. *Untitled. New Negro World.*
———. 1942. "Man's Inhumanity." *New Negro World*, November–December.
———. 1943. "To the Officers, Members and Friends of the Association and of the Race." *New Negro World*, March.
Summers, Martin Anthony. 2004. *Manliness and Its Discontents: The Black Middle Class and the Transformation of Masculinity, 1900–1930.* Chapel Hill: University of North Carolina Press.
Swindall, Lindsey R. 2014. *The Path to the Greater, Freer, Truer World: Southern Civil Rights and Anticolonialism, 1937–1955.* Gainesville: University Press of Florida.
Taylor, James. 2010. *Black Nationalism in the United States: From Malcolm X to Barack Obama.* Boulder: Lynne Rienner Publishers.
Taylor, Ula. 2002. *The Veiled Garvey: The Life and Times of Amy Jacques Garvey.* Chapel Hill: University of North Carolina Press.
Todd, Jos. A. 1941. "Greetings from Mariana Div. No. 203." *New Negro World*, December.
———. 1942. "The Negro and the Color Question." *New Negro World*, May.
Treadwell, Mattie E. 1954. *The Women's Army Corps.* Washington, DC: Government Printing Office.
Vogel, Todd, ed. 2001. *The Black Press: New Literary and Historical Essays.* New Brunswick, NJ: Rutgers University Press.
Von Eschen, Penny. 1997. *Race Against Empire: Black Americans and Anticolonialism, 1937–1957.* Ithaca: Cornell University Press.
Washburn, Patrick S. 2006. *The African American Newspaper: Voice of Freedom.* Evanston, IL: Northwestern University Press.
West, Michael O. 1999. "'Like A River': The Million Man March and Black Nationalist Tradition in the United States." *Journal of Historical Sociology* 12: 81–100.
White, E. Frances. 1990. "Africa on My Mind: Gender, Counter Discourse and African-American Nationalism." *Journal of Women's History* 2: 73–97.
Wilkes, Florine. 1943. "My Race." *New Negro World*, February.

———. 1943. "Our Condition." *New Negro World*, March.
———. 1944. "To Black Men Everywhere." *New Negro World*, November
Wilson, David. 1942 (July). "Divisional News, St. Andrew Division." *New Negro World*, July.
Wynn, Neil A. 2010. *The African American Experience during World War II*. Lanham, MD: Rowman and Littlefield.
Young, Theresa E. 1943. "The Real Solution." *New Negro World*, September.
X, Malcolm. 1970. *By Any Means Necessary: Speeches, Interviews, and a Letter by Malcolm X*. New York: Pathfinder Press.

Section IV

Discourses, Movements, and Representation

> If they don't give you a seat at the table, bring a folding chair.
>
> —Shirley Chisholm

> I need to work outside government, on my own.
>
> —Marian Wright Edelman

How do discursive practices, through institutions, civil society, and constructions of embodiment, support and maintain hegemonic understandings of Black womanhood, and how do Black women resist? This is a central question that links the chapters in these sections. The chapters in this section examine Black women's oppositional gaze in response to the institutionalization of discourses, practices, and structures. According to bell hooks,

> the capacity of [B]lack women to construct ourselves as subjects in daily life the extent to which [B]lack women feel devalued, objectified, [and] dehumanized in this society . . . those [B]lack women whose identities were constructed in resistance, by practices that oppose the dominant order, were most inclined to develop an oppositional gaze. (1992, 127)

By exploring and documenting Black women's oppositional gaze to oppressive social and political narratives, through storylines, scripts, or other means, the authors demonstrate how Black women envision and work toward their desired current political condition and engagement.

Literary critic Judylyn Ryan shows how Toni Morrison's work is representative of Black women writers who write politically engaged and transformative work. Ryan demonstrates how Morrison's writings constitute an ongoing and profound meditation on the meaning of US democracy. As Ryan explains: "Morrison's focus on expanding representation, participation, interpretive competence, and moral agency, expresses her commitment to democracy and to the type of social relationships it postulates." Morrison's work stages a context for readers to become educated about and grapple with trauma and its political implications, and to do so in a way that facilitates "emotional engagement" and "revive(s) historical thinking."

In "Illegitimate Appetites: Michelle Obama's Anti-Obesity Campaign as Sexual Regulation," Grace Howard explores the concept of discursive distance to show how Obama's anti-obesity campaign, *Let's Move!*, allows her to participate in debates about reproductive health and sexuality. According to Howard, discursive distancing is shown in how the *Let's Move* campaign is organized. As she argues,

> That *Let's Move!* is not just another government program is an essential facet of the campaign's use as a deracialization strategy communicating the message of self-sufficiency, self-control, and individualism vital to Obama's respectability performance. This is not a program encouraging the kind of irresponsibility associated with Welfare Queens—if you are hungry but cannot afford food, *Let's Move!* would encourage you to get your hands in the dirt to grow your own solutions. . . . Obama's book does not mention public assistance as a resource. (Howard, this volume)

Howard demonstrates how Obama's initiatives authorize patriarchal gender norms and support notions of respectable gender behavior.

Similarly to the chapters that make up the section Black Feminist Policy Analysis, Howard shows that the "nonprototypical" Black woman will be responded to with nontransformative policy suggestions. Howard shows "there is power in looking" (hooks, 115) to name "what we see" (hooks, 116). In so doing, Howard is able to expose the functioning of stereotypical representations, thereby showing the hegemonic constructions of race and gender in Obama's *Let's Move!*

Tonya M. Williams's "'We Always Resist: Trust Black Women': Black Women's Reproductive Justice Activism in the Wake of Health Care Reform" demonstrates how the "nonprototypical" Black woman who often is not taken up in policy discussions creates space for her representation. She refers to this space as "liberatory politic around bodily autonomy." Williams demonstrates how Black women respond to the politics of health care reform by engaging in a case study of the "representational behavior of black women–directed reproductive justice organizations within the political milieu of health care reform." She shows the particular valence that reproductive justice has within the broader context of health policy.

These analyses help us to better understand Black female bodies' materiality as a site for the intersection between the political and cultural realms. By considering discursive structures and rhetorical devices, the authors offer insights into structures of ideology and power that might simultaneously converge and diverge in the political and cultural spheres. Central in this section is how Black women accord order and meaning to the materiality of their lives. The authors in this section, to use the story of Janie Crawford from Zora Neale Hurston's *Their Eyes Were Watching God*, exhibit Black political women's journey to autonomy. Consequently, we are offered a greater comprehension of Black women's political behavior in general. In short, the authors in this section especially showcase Black women's narratives of democracy and justice.

Reference

hooks, bell. 1992. "The Oppositional Gaze: Black Female Spectators." In *Black Looks: Race and Representation*, 155–31. Boston: South End Press.

9

Morrisonian Democracy

The Literary Praxis of Black Feminist Political Engagement

JUDYLYN S. RYAN
Ohio Wesleyan University

> If anything I do, in the way of writing novels (or whatever I write) isn't about the village or the community or about you, then it is not about anything. . . . which is to say yes, the work must be political.
>
> —Toni Morrison 1984, 344

It will come as no surprise to readers of Black women's fiction that Black women literary artists have made significant contributions to the project of Black feminist political engagement. For Black women literary artists—poets, novelists, essayists, playwrights, and short fiction writers—political engagement has cohered around a deep concern for representation and participation as they relate to a complex view of humanity and to the dictates of democracy, informed by an acute awareness of the Janus character of US democracy. It is worth noting, however, that their approach and strategies differ from more familiar modes of political engagement. The political engagement of Back women literary artists is instead characterized by several distinct features. First, it typically engages the society of readers—not institutional agents—whose defective social literacy it exposes and seeks to transform. Second, it is equally interested in mapping the intersections of (sociopolitical) jeopardy and the intersections of (intellectual and moral) insight that condition Black women's lives and that simultaneously authorize their discursive authority. Third, it frequently seeks to promote political, pedagogical, and therapeutic objectives. Finally, to the extent that it seeks to enhance cognitive competencies, it is contiguous with aspects of affect theory, but more fully consonant with the emerging field of narrative medicine, as I discuss below.

The cohort of US Black women writers whose careers overlapped with the Civil Rights movement of the mid-twentieth century (among them Zora Neale Hurston, Gwendolyn Brooks, and Ann Petry), as well as those who came of age during that period (including Maya Angelou, Toni Morrison, Nikki Giovanni, Audre Lorde, June Jordan, Paule Marshall, Lorraine Hansberry, Lucille Clifton, Sonia Sanchez, Alice Walker, Toni Cade Bambara, and Ntozake Shange), and whose works were central to the newly established Black studies curriculum in the 1960s and to women's studies in the 1970s and 1980s, fully illustrate the literary praxis of Black feminist political engagement. Of them, none better exemplifies its complexities and achievements than the Nobel laureate Toni Morrison. Perhaps none has had a more profound cultural impact or greater intellectual and political influence.

In essays as luminous as her fiction, Morrison has directed a studied gaze at several quarters of the US landscape—literary, historical, cultural, and political. While the phenomenon of intellectual double-voicing—through both literary fiction and nonfiction essays—is not new to American letters, Morrison has enlarged the parameters for collective self-examination designed by literary predecessors such as William Carlos Williams, Zora Neale Hurston, Langston Hughes, T. S. Eliot, Richard Wright, James Baldwin, and Ralph Ellison in the scope, cadence, conclusions—and openings—her works offer.

Of these literary ancestors, Ralph Ellison displays the closest affinities to Morrison in his literary preoccupation with US democracy. In fact, his 1960s essay "The Novel as a Function of American Democracy" provides a useful context for examining the type of political engagement that Morrison's oeuvre reflects and advances. In it, Ellison writes, "I do happen to feel that in this country the novel . . . found a function which it did not have in any of the nations where it was developed by artists who made it resound so effectively with their eloquence" (Ellison 1986, 308). "The novel," Ellison continues, "was not invented by an American, nor even for Americans; but we are a people who have, perhaps, most need of it—a form which can produce imaginative models of the total society if the individual writer has the imagination, and can endow each character, each scene, each punctuation mark with his own sense of value" (Ellison 1986, 319). Elsewhere in the essay, Ellison clarifies why US Americans are most in need of the novel. As he further explains,

> On many, many levels we don't know who we are, and there are always moments of confrontation where we meet as absolute strangers. Race is by no means the only thing which divides us in this still-undiscovered country. We're only a partially achieved nation, and I think this is good because it gives the writer of novels a role beyond that of entertainer. (Ellison 1986, 317–18)

Revisiting Ellison's mid–twentieth-century assessment today, one must ask the question: Does US democracy require a particular type of literature? Looking beyond the literary opportunities that Ellison sees in the country's status—or condition—as a "partially achieved nation," one has to wonder at the causes of this delayed maturation. By what forces or factors is US democracy underdeveloped? Given its arrested development, exactly what kind of literature does US democracy—do US Americans—need? As a critical component of her Black feminist political engagement, Morrison's fiction and nonfiction writings position readers to engage and respond to these questions.

The Perils of US Democracy

Among the several perils threatening the health of US democracy—as a philosophical and ethical commitment and as social and political practice—and responsible for its condition as "a partially achieved nation," the most urgent are collective historical occlusion, inept historical thinking, social illiteracy, defective moral reasoning, defective (public policy) decision making, and self-endangering voting behaviors. To varying degrees, these are all (historically) rooted in the practice of racism. In an earlier essay, "Language and Narrative Technique in Toni Morrison's Novels," I argued that Morrison's "teacherly vision is a conscious response to the racialized gaze that has informed the discursive practices, interpretive habits, and moral competence of the society-as-readers, and that has been the root cause of particular failures of democracy" (Ryan 2007, 151–52). That is to say, the defective interpretive habits of the "society-as-readers" and "particular failures of democracy" can be attributed to a national addiction to looking at oneself and at others through the prism of race. The most lasting (and latent) effect is a profound and widespread emotional detachment from, and a profound lack of empathy for, people who are not only dispossessed but also viewed as disposable.

Consistent with this history, popular definitions of disposable people in the United States have traditionally focused narrowly on racial minorities. In fact, however, institutional behaviors target a diverse range of people: working- and lower-class Whites, low-wage workers, immigrants, the unemployed, people with mental disorders, incarcerated people, the homeless, and, more recently, Muslims. Emotional detachment toward people defined as disposable accounts for the massive expansion of the prison industrial complex that has made the United States, since 2003, the world leader in incarcerated populations, the opposition to health care reform initiatives, the opposition to "big government" and its mediating role in balancing the social contract to preserve the rights and interests of propertyless people, the vitriol of the (anti-Mexican/Latino) immigration debate, the progressive disempowerment of working Americans, and the profound lack of responsiveness to the widening disparities between the (working) poor and the wealthy.

The perils of defective historical thinking, social illiteracy, and emotional detachment are particularly apparent in the mainstream public responses to proposed policy initiatives such as health care reform that have been widely opposed by some of the very constituencies of dispossessed and disposable people they are meant to benefit. Indeed, one notable feature of the current manifestations of defects in historical thinking and moral reasoning is the increasing numbers and visibility of people who, in the words of the writer Ayi Kwei Armah, have become "prejudiced against [their] own survival" (Armah 1971, xiv), supporting those economic policies that undermine their socioeconomic well-being and opposing those policies that would secure and stabilize their well-being.

Given her numerous analyses—most pointedly in the essay "Home" (Morrison 1997)—of the ways in which race and racism imperil the society of readers, it is no surprise that Morrison's novels implicitly argue and explicitly demonstrate that US democracy requires a literature whose textual strategies and discursive practices can expand democratic narrative participation, promote "narrative knowledge," sharpen the moral imagination, and provide opportunities for self-discovery.

In "Outing the Black Feminist Filmmaker in Julie Dash's *Illusions*," I first identified the concept "democracy of narrative participation" as a feature of Black women's cinema (Ryan 2004). That analysis was in part prompted by the work of legal scholar Lani Guinier. In *Lift Every Voice:*

Turning a Civil Rights Setback into a New Vision of Social Justice, Guinier insists that "participation matters, after all . . . Participation among and with others offers more than simple survival. It nourishes and reinforces both the individual and the community. . . . And democracy demands the ability to participate, the opportunity to act in close association with others, and the right to a hearing" (Guinier 1998, 18). Based on my reading of Guinier, I concluded that while the (human) rights—of representation and of participation—asserted in the US Declaration of Independence "had been given extensive consideration in relation to structures of governance and electoral processes, . . . a genuine commitment to democracy requires . . . representation and participation in national cinema . . . national history" (Ryan 2004, 1321) and national literature.

As I later described it, the work that promotes or achieves a democracy of narrative participation can use several different approaches, all informed by a threefold commitment to providing a more expansive presentation of characters who would otherwise—or elsewhere—be considered marginal, to endowing them with their full human complexity, and to allowing them to occupy the narrative foreground (Ryan 2005, 22).

Accordingly, in each of her novels Morrison creates a fictional universe populated with both major and minor characters who are all allowed to occupy the narrative spotlight. For a society of readers conditioned by literary, cinematic, social, and political practices to accept the "convenience" of "major" characters portrayed with complex humanity and "minor" characters diminished and flattened, entering Morrison's populous and democratic narrative universe is challenging. Nevertheless, the technique creates several important effects. First, it avoids the danger of "othering" by structuring readers' access to the interior world of both "minor" and "major" characters. Second, it generates an epistemology that enables readers to know each character from within his or her own particularized psychological universe. Third, it allows for an exchange of multiple gazes between the characters and readers. Dismantling the "binary casting of central and marginal characters" "enables the artist to expand the narrative to reveal that even individuals whose presence is temporally or socially limited have full personalities and unlimited human agency" (Ryan 2005, 22). In so doing, the novel both relies on and increases readers' "narrative knowledge."

"Narrative knowledge" is the term used by narrative medicine pioneer and medical educator Dr. Rita Charon to describe a set of critical competencies instilled by literary reading. Although not widely known, the field of narrative medicine developed out of a conviction that literary readings and literary reading competence can restore empathetic abilities that may become atrophied in the medical education process. In *Narrative Medicine: Honoring the Stories of Illness*, Dr. Charon, an internal medicine specialist who later earned a PhD in English, notes that "despite . . . impressive technical progress, doctors often lack the human capacities to recognize the plights of their patients, to extend empathy toward those who suffer, and to join honestly and courageously with patients in their struggles toward recovery, with chronic illness, or in facing death" (Charon 2006, 3). Restoring these capacities is the primary objective of narrative medicine, one of the most significant innovations in medical education. "If narratives are stories that have a teller, a listener, a time course, a plot, and a point," says Charon, "then narrative knowledge is what we naturally use to make sense of them. Narrative knowledge provides one person with a rich, resonant grasp of another person's situation as it unfolds in time, whether in such texts as novels, newspaper stories, movies, and scripture or in such life settings as courtrooms, battlefields, marriages, and illnesses" (Charon 2006, 9).

Dr. Charon's listing of the "life settings" in which narrative knowledge is essential can and must be expanded to include the many other social and professional arenas, such as neighborhoods, K-through-12 classrooms, airports, restaurants, playgrounds, police precincts, newsrooms, legislative chambers, and corporate boardrooms, in which citizens interact in our democracy. Equally important, the benefits uncovered by Dr. Charon and other narrative medicine theorists accentuate the efficacy of the strategies for political engagement developed by Toni Morrison and other Black women literary artists. As Charon (2006) observes,

> Medicine can benefit from learning that which literary scholars and psychologists and anthropologists and storytellers have known for some time—that is, what narratives are, how they are built, how they convey their knowledge about the world, what happens when stories are told and listened to, how narratives organize life, and how they let those who live life recognize what it means. Using narrative knowledge enables a person to understand the plight of another by participating in his or her story with complex skills of imagination, interpretation, and recognition. (9–10)

The narrative knowledge that supports both interpretive and ethical competence in medical practice is equally important to rehabilitating the range of social and professional interactions that has been impaired by a long history of racist socialization.

Empathy and the Moral Imagination

Morrison's focus on expanding representation, participation, interpretive competence, and moral agency expresses her commitment to democracy and to the type of social relationships it postulates. In the Afterword to the twenty-fifth anniversary edition of *The Bluest Eye*, Morrison reveals that she tried to have the characters "transfer . . . the problem of fathoming [the causes behind the "insignificant destruction of a black girl" (Morrison 1993, 214)] to the presumably adult reader, to the inner circle of listeners" (Morrison 1993, 214). By her own estimate, the results were unsatisfactory. As she describes it, she succeeded only in "lead[ing] readers into the comfort of pitying [Pecola Breedlove] rather than into an interrogation of themselves" (Morrison 1993, 211). Despite her careful deployment of narrative strategies, "many readers remain touched but not moved" (Morrison 1993, 211). This retrospective assessment of the novel's "failure" underscores what has been a primary commitment for Morrison from the inception of her literary career, that is, the ethical competence and agency of her readers. Indeed, no comment is as revealing of Morrison's vision of the role of the writer in a democratic society as her assessment in the essay "Peril." There, Morrison writes,

> Certain kinds of trauma visited on peoples are so deep, so cruel, that unlike money, unlike vengeance, even unlike justice, or rights, or the goodwill of others, only writers can translate such trauma and turn sorrow into meaning, sharpening the moral imagination. (Morrison 2009, 4)

These and similar reflections attest to Morrison's aspiration to move readers to a level of emotional engagement and investment, a commitment that is emblematic of Black feminist political engagement. In her view, the community of readers is responsible for getting to the root of particular trauma and of reflecting on their own roles in and/or relation to that trauma. Significantly, Pecola is not only a representative trauma victim but also typifies those groups of disposable people toward whom our society prefers, maintains, and prescribes an absolute detachment. It is therefore doubly significant that this first novel, the one that arguably has the most abundant affective cues, is the one that Morrison judges a failure in terms of the specific concern with orchestrating an emotional investment. In terms of engineering emotional engagement, it appears that providing *fewer* affective cues might be *more* efficacious.

Given her stated commitments and her own estimation of the failures of *The Bluest Eye*, it is not surprising then that Morrison's fiction has been increasingly crafted—in content and in form—to generate a reading process that seeks to activate or reactivate readers' emotional circuits: First, she chooses to explore the interior world of characters belonging to groups from which the society has historically remained emotionally detached; second, she purposefully withholds narrative details—especially what I call an affective infrastructure—that would encourage a type of emotional surrogacy. Culminating with her novel *A Mercy*, Morrison requires and positions readers to undergo what she describes as a type of absorbed reading, an immersion that facilitates empathetic access to the characters.

Morrison's insistence that writers are uniquely positioned to respond to this and other trauma in ways that "sharpen the moral imagination" is especially significant given the broad spectrum of impairment and disability caused by racism.[1] Her emphasis becomes more meaningful when viewed in relation to Antonio Damasio's observation of the role of emotion and feeling in moral judgment. In *Descartes' Error*, Damasio, the renowned neuropsychologist, first proposed that "certain aspects of the process of emotion and feeling are indispensable for rationality" (Damasio 1994, xiii) and "that the *absence* of emotion and feeling is no less damaging" than emotional biases (Damasio 1994, xii). Damasio's clinical findings on the critical importance of emotions in moral decision making raise a host of questions about the possibility that ideologies—and in particular, the ideology of race (to the extent that it conditions socialization)—can impair neurological functions in ways similar to brain injury or disease. Can "impaired feelings" be caused by factors other than disease or physical injury to the brain? Can race or gender socialization deactivate emotional systems of the brain in general or with regard to specific individuals or groups? Conversely, are there deficits in neural processing in a healthy—i.e., noninjured—brain that can be attributed, broadly speaking, to cultural socialization? What is the role of emotion and feeling in public policy decision making? To what extent might defective public policy decision making be attributable to emotional detachment toward dispossessed and disposable constituencies? To the extent that emotion is essential to moral reasoning, how might emotional detachment affect historical thinking, social literacy, and the practice of democracy, all of which involve moral reasoning? And can literature respond therapeutically to reverse socialized emotional detachment and impaired feelings?

Several studies have now confirmed Damasio's clinical findings. One of the most instructive was a 2001 study by an interdisciplinary team of investigators led by Harvard professor Joshua Greene, at the time a doctoral student in Princeton's philosophy department. In an article titled "An fMRI Investigation of Emotional Engagement in Moral Judgment," Greene and his colleagues describe using functional magnetic resonance imaging, or fMRI, to observe the neural activity of test subjects faced with a variety of decision-making scenarios involving "moral-personal conditions," "moral-impersonal conditions," and "non-moral conditions" (Greene et al. 2001).[2] The study focused on two moral dilemmas representing moral-impersonal and moral-personal conditions, respectively. One involved a runaway trolley, the other a footbridge, with the following conditions:

> A runaway trolley is headed for five people who will be killed if it proceeds on its present course. The only way to save them is to hit a switch that will turn the trolley onto an alternate set of tracks where it will kill one person instead of five. . . . [In] a similar problem, the footbridge dilemma . . . a trolley threatens to kill five people. You are standing next to a large stranger on a footbridge that spans the tracks, in between the oncoming trolley and the five people. In this scenario, the only way to save the five people is to push this stranger off the bridge, onto the tracks below. He will die if you do this, but his body will stop the trolley from reaching the others. (Greene et al. 2001, 2105)

Using the classification described above of moral-impersonal and moral-personal conditions, the researchers predicted the absence of what they called "emotional interference" for the former conditions as measured by both neural activity and faster response times. As predicted, Greene and his colleagues found that most respondents said yes to redirecting the trolley onto an alternate track in the first dilemma, while most respondents said no to pushing a stranger off the footbridge in the second dilemma.

Looking more closely at the study, however, one notices that the "impersonal" character—or framing—of the trolley dilemma seems to rest on the empathetic ability or social consciousness of particular respondents and not on the dilemma itself. What would happen if one were to reframe the dilemma by reimagining the unknown person on the alternate track and allowing that person to attain the same human distinction as the stranger on the footbridge whom test subjects have to touch? Would test subjects be as emotionally detached in reasoning about the runaway trolley scenario if the person on the alternate track were an acquaintance—whether liked or disliked? Would they be as emotionally disengaged if "the five" were five North Koreans and "the one" were a US diplomat? Or if the "trolley" were a grenade misfired from a US military launcher and "the five" were five Syrian civilians and "the one" were a single US soldier? Or if the "runaway trolley" were the subprime mortgage crisis, "the five" were five million low-income homeowners facing foreclosure, and "the one" were an investment bank (and its wealthy managers and investors)?

Under these different frames, test subjects in the United States would probably make different judgments about resolving the trolley dilemma. More importantly, to the extent that the variations suggested above elicit a more intense emotional engagement with the dilemma, they also reveal the degree of abstraction regarding the person on the alternate track and hence the degree of detachment with which test subjects engage that dilemma.

Although not its intended objective, the Greene study offers a preliminary understanding of the ways in which a particular socialization—whether shaped by race, class, gender, or any other ideology—might lead to the type of emotional detachment that prevents the neurological engagement and activity essential for healthy decision making about other people's lives. This is important because racially informed responses, behaviors, actions, and misreadings are in some sense an accumulation of emotionally detached or hyperattached moral misjudgments about particular groups and individuals. A significant detail of the Greene study is the neural similarity between moral-impersonal and non-moral decision making they observed. If emotions are essential to moral reasoning, then the noninvolvement of emotion circuits in the trolley dilemma would suggest that these decisions are *neurologically* defective. The researchers' reference to, and perhaps preference for, the absence of "emotional interference" is revealing. Second, to the extent that neural and behavioral responses to the moral-impersonal trolley dilemma are (socioculturally) representative, they may indicate a significant pattern of emotional disengagement in moral-impersonal decision making, the type of decision making that medical and other professionals—as well as voters in a democratic society—must routinely perform. Their finding that neural responses to "non-moral" dilemmas (for example, deciding whether to travel by bus or by train) and "moral-impersonal" dilemmas (for example, deciding whether to raise the current minimum wage to fifteen dollars) involve similar types of emotional disengagement is particularly troubling because professional and public policy decision making tends to occur in intellectual spaces that resemble the conditions of moral-impersonal decision making.

If emotions are essential to effective moral reasoning and moral judgment, there can be no sharpening of the moral imagination without emotional engagement. Indeed, emotional engagement appears to be critical to the process of sharpening the moral imagination. Since social identities are charged—positively and negatively—with different emotional valences, moral judgment about those lives will inevitably be influenced and perhaps determined by preset valences. These judgments are particularly fraught in professional and public policy deliberations about those lives. And it is this peril that Toni Morrison's fiction—as a mechanism for prompting emotional engagement, expanding narrative knowledge, and generating narrative thinking—prepares readers to safely negotiate.

In *Beloved*, for example, readers' moral reasoning about Sethe's "rough choice" will depend on their reading of the emotional quality of her life, in the discernment that the killing has left her, like Baby Suggs, holy in a suspended psychological state (Morrison 1987a). Here Morrison reverses her self-described failure in *The Bluest Eye*, successfully transferring to adult readers the responsibility of fathoming the causes behind the characters' choices and prompting a critical examination of their own. Readers' experience of having to activate and involve emotion systems in the process of making moral judgment will prepare them for more urgent extratextual responsibilities. Sethe's or, if you will, Margaret Garner's, "rough choice" is not the only historical or current event with which US Americans must come to terms. Completing this task is a mere starting point for critically examining rougher choices in the present as well as those littered throughout US history that require interrogation and understanding.

Historical Thinking and Narrative Knowledge

In addition to demanding a significant degree of emotional engagement, Toni Morrison's fiction is carefully crafted to revive historical thinking. In fact, of the eleven novels she has written, several might be described as historical novels, works that seek to revive historical consciousness and/or disrupt patterns of "collective amnesia." Morrison's construction of a "usable past" is unusual because her novels never offer a specific public historical narrative or history. Instead, they carefully sidestep known historical figures and events. In *Beloved*, for example, the focus is not on the historical Margaret Garner—who inspired Morrison's literary excursion—but on an imagined Black mother, Sethe. In *A Mercy*, the narrative gaze follows the fictional Jacob Vaark, not the historical Jonathan Bacon, who spearheaded the seventeenth-century event known as Bacon's rebellion that is also referenced in the novel. These narrative choices serve to redefine readers' interpretive and ethical responsibilities. Instead of being distracted by the quest to assess resemblances, other challenges emerge. What they offer, even insist on, is an opportunity for readers to engage in historical thinking, an act that requires *active* composition—literally piecing together dismembered and disremembered fragments.

Like arterial circuits that have been obstructed by plaque deposits, historical thinking in the United States is in many ways "blocked"—by collective historical occlusion, emotional detachment, and risk-averse perceptions of the past. Throughout her fiction, Morrison uncovers and makes available to readers new pathways of inquiry and insight. Among other significant effects, these bypass circuits can enable readers to more successfully negotiate contemporary perils by regenerating the flow of historical thinking and increasing social literacy.

Although history itself is not a behavioral science, educational psychologist and cognitive scientist Samuel Wineburg offers a behavioral analysis of public attitudes toward history in the United States that illuminates Morrison's artistic explorations. In *Historical Thinking and Other Unnatural Acts*, Wineburg differentiates between historical knowledge and historical thinking, noting that "to engage in historical thinking [is to be] called on to see human motive in the texts we read; called on to mine truth from the quicksand of innuendo, half-truth, and falsehood that seeks to engulf us each day; called on to brave the fact that certainty, at least in understanding the social world, remains elusive and beyond our grasp" (Wineburg 2001, 83). For Wineburg, the ability to engage in historical thinking is an essential component of "social literacy," "a literacy not of names and dates but of discernment, judgment, and caution" (Wineburg 2001, ix). For Morrison, as for Wineburg, social literacy is a necessary precondition for, and a critical component of, a healthy democracy.

Behavioral approaches such as Wineburg's provide new ways of interrogating US attitudes toward the past. Equally important, they facilitate a greater appreciation of Morrison's fiction as a therapeutic and performance-enhancing application meant to reactivate emotional circuits of the brain to generate more extensive and effective historical thinking in line with the responsibilities of democratic citizenship.

In 2004, Morrison published *Remember: The Journey to School Integration*, a history book for adolescent readers. In the commanding but protective tone of the book's grandmotherly narrator, Morrison designs a model for historical thinking that prefigures the positioning crafted for readers of *A Mercy*. In its opening sentences, the narrator confides,

> This book is about you. Even though the main event in the story took place many years ago, what happened before it and after it is now part of all our lives. Because remembering is the mind's first step toward understanding, this book is designed to take you on a journey through a time in American life when there was as much hate as there was love; as much anger as there was hope; as many heroes as cowards. A time when people were overwhelmed with emotion and children discovered new kinds of friendships and a new kind of fear. As with any journey, there is often a narrow path to walk before you can see the wide road ahead. And sometimes there is a closed gate between the path and the road.
>
> To enliven the trip, I have imagined the thoughts and feelings of some of the people in the photographs chosen to help tell this story. (Morrison 2004, 3)

The emotional engagement Morrison scripts for juvenile readers is no different from the one she envisions for adult readers of her historical fiction. In describing that process in the article "The Site of Memory," she admits that "memories and recollections won't give me total access to the unwritten interior life of these people. Only the act of the imagination can help me" (Morrison 1987b, 104). Perhaps the most important innovation in Morrison's writing is her restraint in mapping the path and pointing to the open gate without disclosing what her own excursion to the territory has revealed.

Intersectional Identities and Founding Narratives

Of her several novels, *A Mercy* perhaps most fully displays Morrison's Black feminist political engagement. In it, she uses several techniques to prompt readers' emotional engagement: a minimalist affective infrastructure; the unfamiliar and initially alien language of the principal narrator, Florens; deliberate omissions; intersectional portraits of the unfamiliar victims of the US socioeconomic and political order; and an extended thematic exploration of self-invention as both an individual and a national project. As she announced decades ago in the essay "Rootedness," "to have the reader work with the author in the construction of the book—is what's important. What is left out is as important as what is there" (Morrison 1984, 341). As such, whatever historical insight or recovery readers achieve is what they will have worked to create and for which they can claim both authorship and ownership.

Like *Beloved, A Mercy* revisits those human experiences and group interactions—not just events—lost to collective historical occlusion. As previously mentioned, events like Bacon's Rebellion and the seventeenth-century witch hunts are referenced in the novel, but are not its main concern. Instead, the novel focuses on the interactions among a racially diverse cast of characters who have not yet come to define themselves solely or primarily in racial terms, and for whom a range of intersectional identities generates different life circumstances and outcomes.

In discussing *A Mercy*, Morrison has said that she wanted to examine the world before slavery becomes racialized.[3] What happens to class as a social category, one might ask, and as an aspect of self-definition when slavery becomes racialized? Two major effects occur. First, class becomes invisible for those who are not enslaved and/or are raced as White. The second and perhaps unexpected effect is that class simultaneously disappears for those who are raced as non-White and/or enslaved. Thus, the seventeenth-century colonial world to which Morrison's readers are transported is one in which conventional group identities—and with them, collective memory and certain master narratives—have been reframed. In colonial America, all the Natives are not "savages," and all the savages are not Natives. All the slaves are not Blacks, and all the Blacks are not slaves. All the White men are not free, and all the White women are not prized and protected. In presenting US readers with a view of the society before slavery becomes racialized, Morrison allows them to rediscover the operation of class categories and class hierarchies in this geopolitical landscape and to see the types of configurations this recognition allowed then and can allow still.

The novel introduces several distinct characters—whom the narrator describes as "orphans, each and all" (Morrison 2008a, 59)—in the household and service of Jacob Vaark, himself a "ratty orphan become landowner" and, later, farmer turned financier. There is the Native American woman Messalina, called Lina, orphaned by an epidemic that wiped out her entire village, she and two boys the sole survivors. There is Florens, the black teenaged girl whose mother begs Jacob to take her child in payment for a bad debt owed by her Catholic master, Senor D'Ortega, because she "saw the tall man see you as a human child, not pieces of eight" (Morrison 2008a,166). The transaction, readers learn, was motivated by the mother's desperate attempt to save her daughter from the predatory sexual abuses of D'Ortega *and* his wife. There are the two White male indentured servants, Willard and Scully, a seventeenth-century version of a gay couple—one still working to pay his passage after the "original seven years stretched to twentysome," the other indentured to fulfill his deceased mother's contract and who had been "schooled, loved and betrayed by an Anglican curate" (Morrison 2008a, 153) by age twelve. There's Sorrow, the half-witted, red-haired girl, rescued from a wrecked ship. And, finally, there's Jacob's wife, Rebecca, a mail-order bride sent to the "New World" by working-class English parents anxious to be disencumbered of responsibility for an unmarried daughter.

While it foregrounds class identities and structures, *A Mercy* also critiques one of the concepts that has been central to US democracy, that is, the myth of self-invention, the notion that anyone—with certain well-defined exceptions—can make something of him- or herself, regardless of socioeconomic status or circumstances of their birth, and that the nation itself developed sui generis.

In fact and in fiction, the myth of self-invention has been firmly attached to ownership, to a vision of the self defined and constituted by the acquisition of property. In *The Bluest Eye*, Morrison describes Black people's connection to this mythology, a reflection of their self-invention as US American subjects "looking forward to the day of property" (Morrison 1993, 18).

Founding myths of self-invention are never simply rejected in Morrison's novels. Instead, they are juxtaposed with alternative processes of self-invention. In *A Mercy*, Morrison explores the hidden psychological origins, consequences, and dangers of self-invention, showcasing different and competing modes. Jacob Vaark, the "ratty orphan" become landowner who emerges from the primeval fog of a seventeenth-century Virginia coast, sees "forests untouched since Noah" (Morrison 2008a, 12) only because the Native American presence and claim have been voided. For Jacob, this land is a tabula rasa, a "disorganized world" where "rank tremble[s] before courage" (Morrison 2008a, 25), a blank slate on which he can unmake and remake the social identity assigned in Europe. While he sneers at the diminished

Portuguese aristocrat D'Ortega, he refuses to acknowledge even to himself what the reader immediately recognizes—that his ambition is driven by and fashioned from that of his former continental rival.

For Lina and Florens's mother, a minha mãe, by contrast, the social geography extends no easy promise of self-invention but the threat of dispossession. The difference is captured in Lina's confession to the trees: "You and I, this land is our home, but unlike you I am exile here" (Morrison 2008a, 59). Sharing a similar experience of exile and dispossession, a minha mãe recalls, "It was there I learned how I was not a person from my country, nor from my families. I was negrita. Everything. Language, dress, goals, dance, habits, decoration, song—all of it cooked together in the color of my skin" (Morrison 2008a, 165).

Lina responds to this threat with a very distinct mode of self-invention:

> [L]onely, angry and hurting . . . she decided to fortify herself by piecing together scraps of what her mother had taught her before dying in agony. Relying on memory and her own resources, she cobbled together neglected rites, merged European medicine with native, scripture with lore, and recalled or invented the hidden meaning of things. Found, in other words, a way to be in the world . . . The shame of having survived the destruction of her families shrank with her vow never to betray or abandon anyone she cherished. (Morrison 2008a, 48–49)

In its deepening excavation of the nation's class-informed and multicultural past, *A Mercy* functions as a type of prequel to *Beloved*. There is, however, a more complex relationship between the two works. In looking more closely at the novel *Beloved*, one notices Morrison's attention not simply to the various lacunae in historical knowledge but also to exploring the characters' attitudes toward both personal and collective memory. Sethe, Paul D, and the various men and women who make up the social milieu of the novel's late nineteenth-century setting all display varying degrees of risk aversion regarding the choice of whether to preserve and/or engage both personal and collective memory.

The fictional portraits in Morrison's *Beloved* constitute a behavioral assessment of attitudes toward the past, one that mirrors a much larger and more ubiquitous pattern of risk aversion toward history on the part of contemporary US Americans. And it is readers' response to collective history and disabling patterns of risk aversion that is Morrison's principal concern.

Behavioral research has shown that individuals tend to be risk averse when a risky choice is framed in relation to the prospect of gain and risk seeking when the same choice is framed in relation to the prospect of loss. This psychological tendency perhaps accounts for the characters'—and society's—attitude toward engaging and revisiting a collective past that is routinely framed as a risk that carries the prospect of gain. That is say, the prevailing assumption is that if you expand historical thinking, you gain a greater knowledge and understanding of past events but with the accompanying risk of increased feelings of guilt or shame. To a large extent, the narrative works to replace this with a different frame, one that defines the choice of revisiting personal and collective memory in relation to the prospect of loss: if you don't engage and preserve historical thinking, you lose or jeopardize your ability to fully understand or make decisions about your economic and political well-being and miss out on the opportunity to become free of crippling guilt and shame.

In a similar vein, Morrison's representation of *A Mercy*'s seventeenth-century setting is carefully designed to remind readers that many of the twenty-first century's most urgent crises have their roots in the nation's pre-Slavery, colonial, and multinational beginnings. The novel provokes renewed inquiry into the role of religious authorities in the sexual exploitation of children; the incipient mind-set that would eventually lead to the twenty-first century's environmental disasters; the class oppression and ideology in Europe that were transported, along with European arrivants, to the Americas; the insight and blindness of the free African; the double-consciousness of working-class Whites; the exploitation of indentured and enslaved workers; the absence of legal protections or recourse for the poor and for women; the cross-cultural community of women and the "hidden transcripts" underlying and informing their relationships; and the defects of self-invention as an act of survival on the part of individual orphans and for the nation, a land claiming no antecedent or prototype.

Morrison's commitment to displacing myths of innocence generates plots that foreground the characters' culpability: Sethe's for the killing of her infant daughter in *Beloved* (Morrison 1987a), Joe Trace's and her aunt Alice Manfred's for Dorcas's death in *Jazz* (Morrison 1992), and Frank Money's unspeakable violation in *Home* (Morrison 2012). In confronting and exploring their own repressed failings, Morrison's characters achieve new levels of self-discovery, acquire new interpretive competence, begin to make more enabling choices on their own behalf, and provide an essential model for US readers. For Morrison's characters, having a moral foundation or framework never ensures interpretive competence. Paradoxically, the reverse is true. Through this reversal, Morrison expresses her view of the relationship between interpretation and ethics, or, more specifically, of the ways in which interpretive competence increases ethical competence and supports ethical agency.

Conclusion

Although concealed for most of the novel, *A Mercy*'s narrative structure is governed by a single, iconoclastic, and multivalent event: an enslaved Black woman writing by candlelight on the walls of a vacant mansion built for, but never occupied by, a now-deceased White man—the private space of mourning, analysis, interpretation, invention, and prophecy. A booming echo of the biblical handwriting on the wall that Daniel must interpret, this event signifies on both the latent vacuity of US democracy and the Black women writers who have sought to fill it with meaning. (Like theirs, Florens's discursive authority emanates, on the one hand, from the intersections of jeopardy that delimit her experiences as an enslaved Black woman and, on the other hand, from intersections of moral and intellectual insight contoured by the same identity coordinates.) When she invites her audience to enter this discursive space at the beginning of the novel, Florens explicitly links moral judgment and interpretive competence:

> Don't be afraid. My telling can't hurt you in spite of what I have done . . . You can think what I tell you a confession, if you like, but one full of curiosities . . . One question is who is responsible? Another is can you read? (Morrison 2008a, 3)

Here the question of who is responsible can have two distinct meanings—one focused on the cause, the other on a possible solution. Still, Florens's questions underscore a more important point. Whether the issue is our failing public schools, our high rates of incarceration, our involvement in foreign wars, our policing practices, our failure to respond to ongoing climate change, our dysfunctional elections, our failure to ensure competent and affordable health care for all, or any other critical issue, the question of who is responsible can only be discerned if the answer to the second question—"can you read?"—is affirmative.

By design, the only certain audience for Florens's text is Morrison's twenty-first century reader. The same is true of the insight her absent mother longs to share with her:

> [T]o be given dominion over another is a hard thing; to wrest dominion over another is a wrong thing; to give dominion of yourself to another is a wicked thing. (Morrison 2008a, 167)

For those twenty-first century US voters actively committed to supporting candidates, platforms, and economic and social policies inimical to their own survival interests, this last warning has an urgent resonance. For Florens and for Morrison's readers, the future depends on an understanding of not just the politics but also the ethics of self-possession, the sine qua non of a healthy democracy.

As a political thinker and literary artist, Toni Morrison belongs to that genealogy of Black women activists that includes Maria Stewart, Sojourner Truth, Ida B. Wells-Barnett, and Shirley Chisholm. Like so many other Black women writers, Morrison's fiction and nonfiction writings fully display the force of their ethical, intellectual, and political authority. As she declares in the essay "Peril," "A writer's life and work are not a gift to mankind; they are its necessity" (Morrison 2009, 4). Through the many innovative textual strategies she employs in her recurring portraits of US American lives in various regional and temporal settings, Morrison's novels equip readers with tools for strengthening the practice of democracy.

Notes

1. In "Racism's Uprooting: White Racial Jeopardy and Democracy"—forthcoming in *Black Renaissance Noire*—I examine the concrescence of White racial jeopardy and White racial privilege and explore the possible neural correlates of racism's (psychological) uprooting of Whites.

2. According to Greene and his colleagues, "Typical examples of non-moral dilemmas posed questions about whether to travel by bus or by train given certain time constraints and about which of two coupons to use at a store" (Greene et al. 2001, 2106).

3. In an October 2008 interview, Morrison explained, "I wanted to separate race from slavery . . . to see what it was like, what it might have been like, to be a slave without being *raced*. Because I couldn't believe that was the natural state of people

who a) were born and people who came here; that it had to be constructed, planted, institutionalized, and legalized." See "Toni Morrison discusses *A Mercy* with NPR's Lynn Neary," NPR, October 27, 2008, http://www.npr.org/2008/10/27/95961382/toni-morrison-a-mother-a-stranger-a-mercy.

References

Armah, Ayi Kwei. 1973. *Two Thousand Seasons.* Oxford: Heinemann.

Charon, Rita. 2006. *Narrative Medicine: Honoring the Stories of Illness.* New York: Oxford University Press.

Damasio, Antonio R. 1994. *Descartes' Error: Emotion, Reason, and the Human Brain.* New York: G. P. Putnam's Sons.

Ellison, Ralph, ed. [1967] 1986. "The Novel as a Function of American Democracy." In *Going to the Territory.* New York: Random House.

Greene, Joshua D., R. Brian Sommerville, Leigh E. Nystrom, John M. Darley, and Jonathan D. Cohen. 2001. "An fMRI Investigation of Emotional Engagement in Moral Judgment." *Science* 293: 2105–8.

Guinier, Lani. 1998. *Lift Every Voice: Turning a Civil Rights Setback into a New Vision of Social Justice.* New York: Simon & Schuster.

Kahneman, Daniel, and Amos Tversky, eds. 2000. *Choices, Values, and Frames.* Cambridge: Cambridge University Press.

Morrison, Toni. [1970] 1993. "Afterword." In *The Bluest Eye* (20th anniversary ed.). New York: Knopf.

———. 1984. "Rootedness: The Ancestor as Foundation." In *Black Women Writers (1950–1980): A Critical Evaluation*, edited by Mari Evans, 340–44. New York: Anchor/Doubleday.

———. 1987a. *Beloved.* New York: Knopf.

———. 1987b. "The Site of Memory." In *Inventing the Truth: The Art and Craft of Memoir*, edited by William Zinnser, 106–9. Boston: Houghton Mifflin.

———. 1992. *Jazz.* New York: Knopf.

———. 1997. "Home." In *The House that Race Built*, edited by Wahneema Lubiano, 3–12. New York: Random House.

———. 2008a. *A Mercy.* New York: Knopf.

———. 2008b. "Toni Morrison Discusses *A Mercy* with NPR's Lynn Neary." NPR. October 27, 2008. http://www.npr.org/2008/10/27/95961382/toni-morrison-a-mother-a-stranger-a-mercy.

———. 2009. "Peril." In *Burn This Book: PEN Writers Speak Out on The Power of the Word*, edited by Toni Morrison, 1–4. New York: HarperCollins.

———. 2012. *Home.* New York: Knopf.

Ryan, Judylyn S. 2004. "Outing the Black Feminist Filmmaker in Julie Dash's *Illusions.*" *Signs* 30 (1): 1319–44.

———. 2005. *Spirituality as Ideology in Black Women's Film and Literature*. Charlottesville: University of Virginia Press.

———. 2007. "Language and Narrative Technique in Toni Morrison's novels." In *The Cambridge Companion to Toni Morrison*, edited by Justine Tally, 151–61. New York: Cambridge University Press.

———. 2017. "Racism's Uprooting: White Racial Jeopardy and Democracy." Forthcoming in *Black Renaissance Noire* 17: 2.

Wineburg, Samuel. 2001. *Historical Thinking and other unnatural acts*. Philadelphia: Temple University Press.

10

Illegitimate Appetites

Michelle Obama's Anti-Obesity Campaign as Sexual Regulation

GRACE E. HOWARD
University of Southern Indiana

"The physical and emotional health of an entire generation and the economic health and security of our nation is at stake."

—Michelle Obama, at the 2010 launch of *Let's Move!*

Michelle Obama was often called the president's secret weapon. Highly intelligent and well educated, she is also a loving mother and a stylish dresser with humble beginnings. In the midst of the heated 2012 election season, where issues of sex and reproduction were front and center, Michelle Obama was conspicuously absent from the "War on Women" debate. And yet Michelle Obama's image proved invaluable for the Obama campaign. Though Michelle Obama was in some ways constrained by racist black family pathology stereotypes, what Nikol Alexander-Floyd calls the "Black Cultural Pathology Paradigm" or BCPP (2007), I argue that Obama was often able to overcome or shift these stereotypes onto others by aligning herself with an elite class-specific model of familial and sexual respectability.

Michelle Obama's anti-obesity campaign, *Let's Move!*, allowed her to participate, from a safe, discursive distance, in debates about reproductive health and sexuality. By invoking the threat of low-income urban black pathology in the "obesity crisis," and sweeping in with a remedy couched in traditional, "True Womanhood"–style mothering, Michelle Obama was able to achieve two strategic goals for the campaign: she was able to signal a nonthreatening "pro-woman" stance without substantive engagement in controversial gender issues while simultaneously distancing herself, and the rest of the Obama family, from racialized and gendered stereotypes about black families.

In making this argument, first I discuss the role of the first family as a nationalist institutional model or prototype, where women are presented in terms of their function as mothers, wives, and keepers of the moral code. I also discuss some of the challenges that first ladies in general, and Michelle Obama in particular, have faced in fulfilling this symbolic role, bringing intersectionality to bear on the first lady both as a national symbol and as a political agent. Next I discuss the Obama campaign's deracialization strategy for overcoming these obstacles using the former first lady's updated, hip version of republican respectability and the cult of true womanhood in the *Let's Move!* campaign to distance herself from the perceived threat of the unbridled black appetite, now embodied as a fat, black social menace. Finally, I spell out the implications of Obama's strategy for black women engaging in politics and for those who are unable to conform to Michelle Obama's example.

First Ladies and the Nation

In her role as first lady, Michelle Obama was part of a nationalist family model. Her official position was literally the *First* Lady, the self-proclaimed Mom-in-Chief (*NPR* 2012). Anne McClintock notes that the discourse about nation is "constituted from the very beginning as a gendered discourse, and cannot be understood without a theory of gender power" (1993). Likewise, Lisa Guerrero writes that first ladies "influence conceptions of 'American' for all women . . . [They] become 'sites' for the symbolic negotiation of female identity" (Guerrero 2011, 68). Politically, the first lady must walk the line between wife/mother and political asset, which Guerrero suggests erases the identity of the actual woman playing the part (Guerrero 2011, 70). Women are deployed as symbols of the nation but are systematically excluded from full participation in the nationalist project (McClintock 1993 62; Yuval-Davis 1997). Women in nationalist projects are often limited to reproductive roles, including pregnancy and birth, the reproduction of national boundaries, and the reproduction and transmission of ideology and culture (Yuval-Davis and Anthias 1989).

As a member of the National Family model, Obama performed the role of the president's moral center, grounding the president's image as a moral and virtuous man capable of exerting and maintaining control, an image rarely applied to black men in US political discourse. For example, in 2012, Michelle Obama told *People Magazine* about her bedtime routine: "We have a ritual where [Barack] tucks me in, because I'm usually in bed before anybody [. . .] He'll come and turn the lights out and give me a kiss and we'll talk. He's like, ''Ready to be tucked?' I'm like, 'Yes I am' " (Jules 2012). At the 2012 Democratic National Convention, Michelle Obama gave a speech in which, after invoking the greatness of the United States with images of veterans, founding fathers, immigrants, suffragettes, Martin Luther King Jr., and gay marriage, she said, "I say all of this tonight not just as a First Lady . . . and not just as a wife. You see, at the end of the day, my most important title is still 'mom-in-chief' " (NPR 2012).

First ladies often face a negative public response when they are perceived as stepping too far into an overtly political role—even when this political role grows out of republican family values. First ladies have always struggled to enact the perfect public performance, balancing notions of republican respectability and family norms with their public visibility and attachment to powerful political men (Parry-Giles and Blair 2002; Williams 2009). When Michelle Obama was not being compared to Jackie Kennedy for her youth, fashion sense, and Camelot-style romance, she was often compared to Hillary Clinton. Obama and Clinton were unique among first ladies for holding law degrees and having had careers as lawyers before coming to the White House. Both Obama and Clinton struggled to fit into the traditional first lady role because of their overt political engagement and career experience. Clinton's political participation was far more formalized than Obama's, having been appointed to head the task force on health care reform (Friedman 1993). Of Hillary Clinton, McGinley writes, "The public perceived her as arrogant and condescending, masculine and too rough around the edges. Distancing herself from her feminine side in order to demonstrate her strength, Clinton was the butt of ridicule and scorn" (McGinley 2009). She continues, "Hillary Clinton, therefore, found herself in a double bind: Either act more feminine and be judged incompetent or act masculine and be considered unlikeable" (McGinley 2009).

Bringing Intersectionality to the Mother-In-Chief

If Hillary Clinton was in a double bind, Michelle Obama was in a triple bind. Obama's blackness changed the dynamics of the masculine/feminine, competent/incompetent binary. As such, an intersectional analysis of Michelle Obama, both as a black political woman and as a national symbol, is necessary to demonstrate her strengths, weaknesses, the intricate precariousness of her position, and the possible paths toward security.

As Guerrero notes, the first lady role begins with a "naturalized assumption of whiteness," suggesting that in the process of navigating the naturalized whiteness of the First Lady role and in walking the domestic/political asset line, the person who is Michelle was all but forced to disappear (Guerrero 2011). Guerrero offers the fallout from Obama's February 2008 speech in Wisconsin as evidence for the difficulty that she faced as first lady because of her race. At this appearance, Obama said, "For the first time in my adult lifetime, I'm really proud of my country, not just because Barack has done well, but because I think people are hungry for change" (Guerrero 2011, 72). Guerrero writes that because of Obama's blackness, "any statement that was critical of any aspect of the American Nation was interpreted by detractors, the majority of whom were white, as ungrateful or elitist" (Guerrero 2011, 72). Her qualified pride in her country melted the assimilated black woman image into the image of an "angry black woman who carries a racial grudge" (Guerrero 2011, 74). Obama's ability to mother, her shopping habits, food choices, body, and clothes, among other things, were all scrutinized in ways that were unimaginable for prior first ladies. Even playful comments about the president's family life came under scrutiny. As Williams notes, "her critics also focused on such benign comments as Mrs. Obama's complaints about her spouse's failure to pick up his socks or return the butter to the refrigerator—going so far as to suggest she was "emasculating" her man (Williams 2009, 834).

In her position as first lady, it was imperative for Michelle to anticipate and respond to this scrutiny in her image production, from her fashionable yet frugal dresses bought at Target and Old Navy, to her constant reassurance to the public that she was first and foremost a mom, to her perfectly toned arms. Thus, political strategy necessitated a softer, more domestic version of Michelle Obama—one whose pride in her country was not qualified, one who performed an ever more domestic version of the first lady role. Near the end of her husband's second term as president, Obama somewhat candidly acknowledged the pressures of navigating this terrain at a commencement address to Tuskegee University graduates. She recalled how she was subject to a different set of questions than typical prospective first ladies because of her race: "Was I too loud, or too angry, or too emasculating?" (The White House 2015). She shared derogatory media statements, including one that said she exhibited "a little bit of uppity-ism" and another that called her "Obama's Baby Mama" (The White House 2015).

Guerrero's analysis importantly describes the constraints placed on Obama, but it also leaves Obama as a passive victim of racialized patriarchy. While the social maze she describes *is* deeply problematic, Guerrero's focus on Obama as a passive symbolic presence for the Obama administration obscures much of Michelle Obama's actual exercise of political power. Obama is an exceptional woman. She attended Princeton and Harvard. She had a career as a powerful lawyer, and then, the wife of a president, Michelle Obama rather successfully ventured into the traditionally feminine, traditionally white housewife position for one of the world's most powerful patriarchs. She opened up about this in her Tuskegee address:

> now, some folks criticized my choices for not being bold enough. But these were my choices, my issues. And I decided to tackle them in the way that felt most authentic to me—in a way that was both substantive and strategic, but also fun and, hopefully, inspiring. (The White House 2015)

Domesticity, Responsibility, and Deracialization

As a part of the Obama family respectability act, Michelle Obama joined a hip, modern, and increasingly domestic performance of "true womanhood" that had an impact on both social discourse and on policy. This softened image, while politically advantageous throughout election campaigns and the Obama administration in general, was most dramatically deployed in the midst of the so-called "War on Women" during the 2012 presidential election. Indeed, it is difficult to imagine how Michelle Obama, who as a black woman must contend with pervasive racist hypersexuality stereotypes, could successfully make public statements about her husband's plan to increase access to contraceptives while performing the necessary respectability politic. The combination of her discursive silence on overtly sex-related issues with the use of her high-publicity domestic performance is worthy of analysis.

In 2012, Obama for America launched a series of online ads featuring a pearl-clad, smiling Michelle Obama, including a Mother's Day ad. In the months approaching the 2012 presidential election, Obama competed in a push-up contest on *The Ellen DeGeneres Show*; sack raced through the White House with Jimmy Fallon; appeared on *The Biggest Loser*, *The Colbert Report*, and the children's television show *iCarly*; and released a cookbook (which I discuss below) titled *American Grown: How the White House Kitchen Garden Inspires Families, Schools, and Communities*, all to promote her *Let's Move!* initiative.

Ramping up Michelle Obama's public appearances for her anti-obesity campaign was good election strategy, as she often reported more favorable ratings than her husband. Melissa Harris-Perry describes the special place that Michelle Obama occupies in many people's hearts, including her own. She writes, "Michelle Obama is the living, breathing possibility of sister citizenship" (Harris-Perry 2011, 299). Echoing Harris-Perry, Beyoncé's handwritten note to Michelle Obama, posted on Twitter, praises her for being "the ULTIMATE example of a truly strong African American woman" because "she is a caring mother, she's a loving wife, while at the same time, she is the First Lady!!!!" ("Michele Obama" 2012). Despite her exceptionality, many laud Michelle Obama as the face of black womanhood. Though she was largely silent on substantive political debates on sex and sexuality, her image gave the Obama campaign ample political mileage.

Obama did not, and could not, contribute to a great many issues in her husband's campaign for presidency and throughout his two terms, but the way she navigated the limitations on her participation during the surge in political discourse on sex during the 2012 election, from Sandra Fluke's testimony on contraceptive access, to Mitt Romney's foot-in-mouth "binders full of women" comment, to Todd Aiken's assertion that women cannot become pregnant from the "legitimate rape," is most illustrative (Jaco 2012). Rather than publicly engaging in the discourse surrounding the "War on Women," Michelle Obama's image, that of an athletic yet fashionable, highly educated yet family focused, simultaneously progressive and traditional woman, was strategically employed to signal "pro-woman" in a politically expedient way. This is an example of what Joseph McCormick Jr. and Charles E. Jones refer to as "deracialization," a political strategy used to gain support with white voters by "avoiding explicit references to [Black or] race-specific issues, while at the same time emphasizing those issues that are perceived as racially transcendent, thus mobilizing a broad segment of the electorate" (McCormick and Jones 1993, 76). Her anti-obesity campaign, *Let's Move!*, focused on the need for personal responsibility, moderation, self-control, and family values—many of the themes shared in debates on contraceptives, sex, and gender roles. Tamar Mayer discusses the ways that the interplay of multiple identities and nation "often pressures people to negotiate their identities in complex ways" (Mayer 2000, 1). Indeed, while her image production shifted considerably toward a traditional domestic role, I suggest that she was not "backseat driving" at all, but rather, that she was participating in the political discourse in her own right through the veneer of traditional domesticity.

The set of myths encompassed by the BCPP have implications for public policy, including welfare cuts, forced sterilizations, and marriage-promotion policies. Social scientists have noted that the Moynihan Report of 1965, the 1996 Personal Responsibility and Work Opportunity Act (PRWORA), and the 1998 fatherhood legislation are related policy attempts to reformulate the family. Julia Jordan-Zachery, for instance, writes that Moynihan places the blame for a plethora of social ills on the supposed pathologically dysfunctional black family, which included an emasculating black matriarch and an absent black father (Jordan-Zachery 2008). The PRWORA and the 1998 fatherhood legislation were designed to complement one another, the PRWORA redefining the state's relationship to the mother, and the fatherhood legislation attempting to reinstate absent fathers to their traditional leadership position in the home under a specific and formalized nuclear family structure (Jordan-Zachery 2008). Likewise, Nikol Alexander-Floyd underlines that the PRWORA made substantial cuts to the provision of public assistance to poor families, while fatherhood initiatives served as a response to the social, economic, and political ills that stem from the putative breakdown in families (Alexander-Floyd 2007). They replaced public support with greater enforcement of paternity support (see also Haney and March 2003). Jordan-Zachery's analysis of congressional hearings concerning these policies reveals a bipartisan belief that pathological fatherlessness in African American communities was the cause of widespread substance abuse, delinquency, illegitimacy, and poverty (Jordan-Zachery 2008). Indeed, the Obama administration also touted and expanded fatherhood legislation and programming, including its highly publicized National Responsible Fatherhood Clearinghouse attempting to replace female dependence on the state with a more respectable female dependence on the male-spouse-as-breadwinner.

The absence of strong fathers in black families is accompanied by a number of images of flawed black mothers, including the obese Mammy and the sexually voracious Jezebel, which culminate in the Welfare Queen figure (Jordan-Zachery 2008). Deborah Gray White notes the inverted nature of the two figures, which allowed southern whites to flip the stereotype to suit their rhetorical needs: "On the one hand there was the woman obsessed with matters of the flesh, on the other was the asexual woman. One was carnal, the other maternal. One was at heart a slut, the other was deeply religious. One was a Jezebel, the other a Mammy" (White 1999, 46). This two-sided coin also allowed Michelle Obama to invoke the threat of illegitimate appetites for food (in the obese Mammy figure) and illegitimate appetites for sex (in the promiscuous Jezebel figure).

Welfare Queens are considered costly social abominations that weaken and destabilize the state. Not only do they take money they do not deserve from decent tax payers, but they also make no effort to care for their many children. Jordan-Zachery describes the Welfare Queen as a symbolic compilation of the Jezebel and the Mammy outside the context of slavery. Like Jezebel, the Welfare Queen is tricky, selfish, and sexually depraved, breeding the culture of poverty, spawning more and more children to receive a larger welfare check (Jordan-Zachery 2008). Like Mammy, she is fat and an inadequate mother. As such, Roberts writes, "Decadent black mothers, then, were responsible for the menace that Blacks posed for American order" (Roberts 1999, 12). Roberts continues, "Poor Black mothers do not simply procreate irresponsibly; they purposely have more and more children to manipulate taxpayers into giving them more money" (Roberts 1999, 17).

The Welfare Queen's size reflects that she is well cared for, although now it serves as an indication not of her hard work, but of her laziness and greed (Jordan-Zachery 2008). Jordan-Zachery reports Heritage Foundation senior researcher Robert Rector's criticism of the poor under the welfare state, proposing that " '[t]he biggest dietary problem of people living in poverty is obesity, not hunger,"' implying that the problem is overconsumption and not deprivation (Jordan-Zachery 2008, 44). According to Ange-Marie Hancock's empirical analysis of images of black women in congressional hearings on the PRWORA, "the ten most frequent dimensions of the 'welfare queen' in public identity include: *Don't Work, Overly Fertile, Teen Mothers, Illegitimacy, Single-Parent Family, Crime, and Culture of Poverty*" (Hancock 2004). Obama's narrative of decline followed this same line of thinking: bad fat black women are responsible for the moral and material decline of America.

Black Cultural Pathology Paradigm Meets the Anti-Obesity Campaign

The overarching narrative of the *Let's Move!* campaign invoked many of the same images at work in the BCPP without explicitly naming them—an example of what Alexander-Floyd and other social scientists, following Ross and Levine, call a "stealth urban policy"—a policy aimed at urban areas without seeming to aim at urban areas (Alexander-Floyd, *Gender, Race, and Nationalism* 2007; Persons 2004). Obama invoked the idea of fatherlessness in black communities by repeating the importance of the father's presence at the dinner table. She mentioned urban convenience store grocery shopping and food deserts as limiting *convenient* access to healthy foods, as though poor urban families do not eat well as a matter of inconvenience. Many of the photographs in *American Grown* contain images of non-white children visiting the White House gardens from schools in Washington, DC, the increasingly gentrified and increasingly white "Chocolate City," where they learn about waiting for seeds to grow and fruit to ripen before it is eaten. They learn that the best things are the things you do for yourself. Michelle Obama writes on a popular medical web site:

> We have a set of routines and rituals that help us not just from a health perspective, but to stay strong as a family. Ultimately, that's what "Let's Move" is all about too: not just making kids healthier, but strengthening families. And the beauty of it is that it's not just another government program. ("Michelle Obama Takes On Childhood Obesity")

The importance of that last sentence should be noted. That *Let's Move!* is not just another government program is an essential facet of the campaign's use as a deracialization strategy, communicating the message of self-sufficiency, self-control, and individualism vital to Obama's respectability performance. This is not a program encouraging the kind of irresponsibility associated with Welfare Queens—if you are hungry but cannot afford food, *Let's Move!* would encourage you to get your hands in the dirt to grow your own solutions.

At $30 a copy, and containing very little practical information about nutrition or gardening, it is unclear how *American Grown* is meant to help communities suffering from lack of adequate nutrition to actually start their own successful gardens. The *Let's Move!* web site includes interactive and educational information on exercise, nutrition, making a good grocery list, and even a gardening guide. The "Eating Healthy on a Budget" page lists three resources, the "3 P's—Plan, Purchase, and Prepare Food on a Budget," "Smart Shopping for Veggies and Fruits," and a weeklong healthy sample menu ("Eat Healthy"). Tips include "Find quick and easy recipes online," "Buy groceries when you are not hungry," and "Be creative with a fruit or vegetable and use it in different ways during the week."

What little information is offered is vastly oversimplified. Obama noted that the White House vegetable garden, complete with a fig tree, Thomas Jefferson's heirloom seeds, and soil modifiers, *only* cost $200, yet it produced enough surplus food to supply the White House's kitchens and a local food charity. While it is dubious that the entirety of the gardening materials, including gardening tools, were purchased for only $200, and while for many individuals $200 is no small sum, Obama also failed to account for the labor and time cost of the team of experts and groundskeepers under her employ who made her garden so productive and beautiful.

As a piece of strategic election propaganda, The *Let's Move!* program was not intended to provide practical instruction. It was designed to speak to the image of dysfunctional black families who lack self-control and abuse government assistance out of distaste for honest work. Obama's book does not mention public assistance as a resource. None of the primary web links on the *Let's Move!* website contain information about food insecurity or public assistance for food—this information can only be accessed by using the site's search function. The repetition of the words *hard work, sacrifice,* and *responsibility*, and the recollection of her own urban upbringing in *American Grown* suggest that Obama's focus on obesity was a political strategy, allowing her to grapple with many of the same issues that make up the controversial national debates about women's health and sexual respectability without ever mentioning sex. The obesity crisis becomes a proxy for personal responsibility and self-control—all a part of Obama's deracialization strategy.

Deflecting the Image of the Bad Black Mom

Through her anti-obesity work, Obama's presentation as an "ultimate" in black womanhood—a beautiful, sensible, caring, and healthy mother, the mother of the nation—allowed her to deflect some of the pathology stereotypes from herself and her own family. Mayer contends, "because the nation is often constructed by elites who have the power to define the nation in ways that further their own interests, the same elites are also able to define who is central and who is marginal to the national project" (Mayer 2000, 12). In doing so, Obama invoked the constructed threat of the pathological black family while offering the self-regulation and self-surveillance of her *Let's Move!* program as a neoliberal solution. She simultaneously aligned herself and her family with responsible, bootstrap-pulling Americans and created distance between herself and the bad women of the BCPP.

This strategy, however, comes at a price. By establishing herself as an "ideal," capable of defining national security threats and policing the behavior of others, Obama exercised what Ange-Marie Hancock calls "maternalist paternalism" (Hancock 2004). Not only was Obama deflecting the stereotype from herself and onto others, but she also was helping to maintain and produce those damaging stereotypes. E. Frances White contends that the use of respectability and conservative gender roles to debunk white nationalist narratives about black family pathology ultimately reveals "ideological ties to other nationalist movements, including European and Euro-American bourgeois nationalists over the past 200 years" (White 1990, 507). By engaging in a nationalist republican respectability norm, lines of inclusion and exclusion, legitimacy and illegitimacy, respectability and pathology, are drawn. *Let's Move!*'s promotion of individual responsibility and traditional republican family models, hard work, and moderation of appetite could even be seen as an attempt at the symbolic destruction of the Welfare Queen and the national security threat that is her wanton *sexual* appetite.

Narrative of Decline

Michelle Obama's *American Grown* is an instructive example of her nationalistic respectability performance. In her book, Obama takes care to remind the reader of a simpler, healthier time, constructing a "narrative of decline" (Alexander-Floyd 2007, 64). Among other things, narratives of decline "note a fall from a previously better era" and may feature villains, victims, and statistics "to shore up the nature of the impending doom or crisis" (Alexander-Floyd 2007, 64). Pictures of the WWII-era Chicago Southside serve as evidence of a time when black families in Chicago took responsibility for their nutrition and for their communities. A black-and-white picture of a vegetable truck where her father worked as a child, and another of a group of Chicago victory gardeners in 1942, accompany a story about how her mother incorporated vegetables into every dinner and how the kids had to clean their plates "no matter what." Parents sent their kids out to play without worry of crime or violence. Dessert was only served on Sundays, and, unless her father was working the night shift, he said grace and ate dinner with his family at the kitchen table. She takes care to pay tribute to her parents' hard work and selfless sacrifice. Her reconstruction of the past even romanticizes Thomas Jefferson's gardening efforts, with Obama going so far as to name multiple White House garden plots containing heirloom seeds from Monticello "Jefferson Beds," a curious move considering Jefferson's slave ownership. Obama's focus on Jefferson's gardening work portrays Jefferson as a hardworking outdoorsman who never relied on others to meet his needs, with no mention whatsoever of the hundreds of slaves working on his plantation, doing the labor of garden maintenance.

While Obama's praise and romanticization of Monticello likely was meant to do the political work of showcasing her patriotism and was a nod to her own historic past, it also does the political work of furthering a historical narrative that defines a plantation owner as an everyman, a rugged individualist. Obama's refusal to mention either slavery in the context of Jefferson's gardens or pervasive racism in the context of the WWII Chicago victory gardeners obscures the inequalities and disadvantages that have created the current crises in access to healthy food, leisure exercise, and health care. As McClintock notes, this harkening back to idealized versions of a largely invented past with rigid gender constructions is a typical element of nationalist authority (McClintock 1993) and helps to reaffirm Michelle Obama's place as the nation's moral compass.

In contrast to the *simple, healthy* times of the antebellum South and the segregated North, Obama presents us with an ugly contemporary reality of a rising tide of obesity, a crisis that threatens our children's futures and even our national security. Double-dutch was replaced with video games, and healthy meals fresh from the farm were replaced with greasy fast food meals eaten on the go. Dining as a family at the kitchen table has become a thing of the past. She notes that one in three American children is overweight or obese and that in the last thirty years, childhood obesity rates have tripled. She suggests that the mere presence of overweight, nonathletic children is to blame for the increase of bullying in schools, childhood depression, and low self-esteem (Obama 2012).

Obama shares her own journey toward her now enlightened position in *American Grown*. She tells readers that *Let's Move!* was inspired by concern for the health of her two daughters after her pediatrician asked her what she had been eating. The pediatrician went on to warn Obama about skyrocketing childhood obesity rates and weight-related illness, which Obama refers to as "lifestyle diseases." She laments the damage she had unknowingly been doing to her own daughters' futures by occasionally picking dinner up at a fast food restaurant or "popping something into the microwave while finishing up a conference call." Though Obama acknowledges that we cannot "turn back the clock," she does remind the reader that "we still have the power to make good choices about what we feed our families."

In Obama's narrative, the power to make good, responsible choices is not only essential for ending the obesity crisis—the future of American hegemony is also at stake. In *American Grown,* Obama describes the obesity epidemic as a literal threat to national security, citing its impact on the economy and military recruitment, echoed by the quote at the beginning of this article from the 2010 launch of *Let's Move!* Of economic impact, she states, "we currently spend $150 billion a year to treat obesity-related health conditions"—taxpayer money being wasted on the undisciplined (The White House 2010). She discusses the impact of obesity on employee absenteeism and worker productivity, invoking laziness. She goes on to lament that obesity is one of the most common disqualifiers for military service and cites an Army lieutenant's concerns over the financial cost of extensive dental work and bone fractures for military recruits. No mention is made of the relationships between poverty, military recruitment, and health. Instead, a call is made for drastic cultural and behavioral changes under the guise of "choice" and patriotism.

This invocation of a threat to US military supremacy echoes the Moynihan Report, which describes the military as a general solution to societal racism and black family pathology. Moynihan asserts that "the ultimate mark of inadequate preparation for life is the failure rate on the Armed Forces mental test," noting that the failure rate for potential black recruits is almost four times that of whites, perpetuating their inequality (Moynihan 1965). If only more Black Americans passed the test, the unemployment rate would decline, they would have greater access to social services. Military discipline could even be the solution for Moynihan's emasculated black male—given the "matrifocal" family life common in the black community, the military is the place where "you get to know what it means to feel like a man" (Moynihan 1965).

Nation and the Cult of True Womanhood

Michelle Obama painted a picture of America on the brink of collapse. If our most essential institution, the patriarchal heterosexual nuclear family, fails, on what foundation can the nation rest? What can save us from this terrible fate? Cue Obama—the nation's symbolic mother and moral compass, modern champion of the cult of true womanhood. Obama's *American Grown* continues the tradition of cookbooks and housewife instruction guides, coaching women not only on the practical matters of running a household and raising a family, but also on appropriate gender performance. Barbara Welter describes these instruction manuals as part of cultivating the image of the "true woman" in an unstable world where virtuous womanliness is the only thing keeping society from crumbling (Welter 1966). Drawing from Victorian cookbooks, ladies' magazines, and etiquette books offering helpful tips and suggestions for cultivating the "true woman," Welter's analysis provides a classic recipe for a maternal respectability performance. Ingredients include nursing, nourishing, and housekeeping as key occupations for a "true" woman. For example, Welter writes that popular Victorian cookbooks and parenting guides associated with the cult of true womanhood contained information on home remedies for illness, gardening tips and tricks, instruction on "the angelic art of managing properly the sick," as well as recipes for treats like pound cake and currant wine (Welter 1966, 164). Even exceptionally intelligent women—not unlike Michelle Obama—were expected to conform to these standards. One Victorian cookbook read, "As for genius, make it a domestic plant. Let its roots strike deep in your house" (Welter 1966, 167). Though over time the "true woman" transformed into a "new woman," Welter concludes, the old stereotypes lived on. Michelle Obama's cultivated image as FLOTUS and "mother-in-chief" can be understood as a "new woman"–style performance of the cult of true womanhood. When viewed through this lens, *Let's Move!* can be seen as the ultimate in highly visible "true womanhood"–style nursing, where nursing is defined as feminine caregiving, healing, and culinary skill. *Let's Move!* literally puts Obama back in the kitchen, focusing on food, fitness, and fun for America's children and families.

Evelynn Hammonds notes that the "cult of true womanhood" was never intended to include the black woman of the Victorian era (Hammonds 1999). She illustrates how black women were, and continue to be, imagined as less than ladylike. By virtue of their black womanliness, they were excluded both from the category of respectable "lady" in white society and from positions of power within masculinist black civic communities, where they were encouraged to adopt the traditional womanly roles from which they were excluded elsewhere (Hammonds 1999). Under the shadow of racist society, black families were as a rule destroyed and split apart, men denied strong father and husband breadwinner positions, women denied the womanly tasks of keeping their own homes and raising their own children under the protection of respectable husbands. Harris-Perry sees Michelle Obama's rebellious choice to wear sleeveless tops and dresses as a departure from the "prim" club women (Harris-Perry 2011). Thus, black female adoption of the respectability framework can be seen as an act of resistance (Hammonds 1999). Likewise, Harris-Perry suggests that Obama's "mom-in-chief" performance was a successful act of resistance against old racialized gender stereotypes. Indeed, as many have noted, black women are generally seen as incapable of raising their own children, lacking a maternal instinct (Roberts 1997; Jordan-Zachery 2008; White 1999). As such, Harris Perry asserts, "When a black woman claims public ownership of her children, she helps rewrite this ugly history" (Harris-Perry 284, 2011).

However, Hammonds is quick to point out that the respectable twentieth-century club women, elite black women who were able to appropriate the "true womanhood" performance, used their position to silence and police the behavior of other less affluent and "respectable" black women (Hammonds 1999). So, while it must be noted that even from her lofty position, Michelle Obama remains vulnerable to racialized and gendered attack and scrutiny, the analysis cannot rest there. An analysis that designates the first lady as the ultimate in black womanhood fails to substantively acknowledge the image of a successfully assimilated feminine black woman behaving respectably in a "tilted room." Harris-Perry's metaphor describing systemic inequality assumes that this is the upright position toward which black women ought to strive (Harris-Perry 2011). Such an analysis does little to question why the room is tilted in the first place, assumes a universal tiltedness which all black women experience in the same way, offers no possibility for escape from the tilted room, and takes a neoliberal, individualist approach to achieving uprightness. Alexander-Floyd writes that Harris-Perry's metaphor "is an implicitly conservative, phallogocentric one, suggesting that the price of political recognition before the paternal, racial state is alignment with a discernable set of appropriate norms" (Alexander-Floyd 2011, 1077). Michelle Obama is an attractive, stylish woman. She appeared on the cover of *Vogue* twice and taught Dr. Oz and Jimmy Fallon how to "Dougie." ("Michelle Obama Teaches Dr. Oz How to Dougie"). She is a modern, fresh version of the respectable club woman, demonstrating an updated version of the "true womanhood" performance at the expense of poor black women and their apparently insatiable appetites.

Implications and Conclusion

Michelle Obama's position as first lady was indeed remarkable, but her noteworthiness can be used, at least rhetorically, against the majority of black women who are unable or perhaps even unwilling to conform to her version of what constitutes legitimate and "successful" black femininity. Her ability to juggle so many activities, all while maintaining her physique and setting fashion trends, was only made possible by her elite position. There were many people working to support the woman who supported the man who ran the country. Undoubtedly, some women looked at the "Mom-in-Chief" and thought, "This woman is redecorating the White House, trying to raise two children and backseat driving the nation . . . She seems to have time to keep her arms toned, so why can't I?" (Park 2009) Thus, while Michelle and the Obama campaign found a way to reframe the first lady performance to be more politically tenable, women and families who were unable to conform to the dictated respectability model were further marginalized. This political strategy demonstrates the gendered nature of deracialization strategies. Though often focused on the strategies of men in political office and election campaigns, black women can draw on the stigmatized tropes of their sex and gender to gain credibility with white voters. In this way, the multiple oppressions that black women must navigate in the political realm may actually provide multiple opportunities to gain political support—working from the angles of race, gender, and race-gender. Though careful navigation is still necessary for a successful political performance, the payoff in Michelle Obama's case was evident, as she often surpassed her husband in approval ratings.

While community gardening is a practical, perhaps even radical, solution to some of these disparities, when the suggestion comes from a person in an elite institutional position, even if their position was as institutional wife and mother, it rings more paternalistic than radical. Obama's silence about systemic inequalities in access to food and health may very well have been due exclusively to the need to distance herself from black pathology stereotypes. After all, how could the campaign recover if a black first lady prioritized or highlighted public nutrition assistance? So Obama chose the safer narrative—the one with the bootstraps. When coupled with the language of personal responsibility and the implication that parents who do not follow her advice are bad parents, threatening national security, her message rang strikingly similar to the language that has created, maintained, and revamped the black family pathology time and again, now having co-opted the language of community organizing.

To Obama's credit, nutrition and exercise are very important sociopolitical issues. The *Let's Move!* program was not, in and of itself, completely damning. Access to nutritious, fresh, affordable food, medical care, and leisure time for playful exercise has a tremendous impact on the quality of people's lives. It is important to ask, however, what work is being done by masking these systemic injustice and deprivation issues under the guise of an excessive-weight crisis caused by laziness, overindulgence, and declining family values. By establishing herself as the literal embodiment of moral uplift and personal responsibility, Obama was able to perform her own benevolent maternal authority, designating obesity—and as such, poor black families—as a national security threat. By focusing the obesity conversation on personal responsibility, good mothering, and family values, Obama was able to distance herself from the image of the sexually depraved, insatiable, lazy Welfare Queen, while her focus on good nutrition for children, the family dinner table, and leisure gardening allowed her to perform the traditional domestic first lady role—a national symbol that gave a degree of True (white) American wholesomeness to the Obama administration.

Michelle Obama was most certainly politically constrained by racist and sexist respectability norms, but her ability to conform to an upper middle class, "traditional" family model ought to be viewed as more than "post–civil rights," "post-feminist" success. Though Obama's choices were heavily constrained by raced and gendered stereotypes and expectations, these were, nonetheless, her choices—strategic and authentic choices that she publicly defended. By using a campaign against illegitimate appetites as a deracialization strategy, to dodge and deflect racist attacks on her womanhood, Obama confirmed the claim that widespread unemployment, poverty, illness, and substance abuse are the fault of individual broken families, "loose" women, emasculated men and obese children. She replaced the need for welfare expansion, if not a complete overhaul of our economic and political institutions, with the need for family restoration, and perpetuated the fantasy of the American dream while blaming others for their inability to conform, all under the guise of care and progressive values. Moreover, this menacing behavior-dictation ultimately rested on the following premise: that if you fall short of ideal, you are not only responsible for your own ruin and exclusion, but your very existence constitutes a security breach, a threat to the rest of us.

References

Alexander-Floyd, Nikol. 2012." 'But I Voted for Obama' ": Melodrama and Post-Civil Rights, Postfeminist Ideology in *Grey's Anatomy, Crash,* and Barack Obama's 2008 Presidential Campaign." *NPSR* 13: 23–40.

Alexander-Floyd, Nikol. 2007. *Gender, Race, and Nationalism in Contemporary Black Politics.* New York: Palgrave Macmillan.

———. 2012. "Review of Melissa Harris Perry's *Sister Citizen: Shame, Stereotypes, and Black Women in America." Perspectives on Politics* 10: 1076–78.

"Evolution of Mom Dancing With Michelle Obama." 2012. *The Tonight Show with Jimmy Fallon.* http://www.nbc.com/the-tonight-show/segments/946.

"First Lady Michelle Obama Launches Let's Move: America's Move to Raise a Healthier Generation of Kids." 2010. *The White House.* Accessed April 5, 2010. https://www.whitehouse.gov/the-press-office/first-lady-michelle-obama-launches-lets-move-americas-move-raise-a-healthier-genera.

Friedman, Thomas. 1993. "Hillary Clinton To Head panel on Health Care." *New York Times,* January 25.

Guerrero, Lisa. 2011. "(M)Other in Chief: Michelle Obama and the Ideal of Republican Womanhood." In *New Femininities: Postfeminism, Neoliberalism and Subjectivity,* edited by Rosalind Gill and Christina Scharff, 68–82. New York: Palgrave Macmillan.

Hammonds, Evelynn M. 1999. "Toward a Genealogy of Black Female Sexuality: The Problematic of Silence." In *Feminist Theory and the Body: A Reader,* edited by Janet Price and Margrit Shildrick, 93–105. New York: Routledge.

Hancock, Ange-Marie. 2004. *The Politics of Disgust.* New York: New York University Press.

Haney, Lynne, and Miranda March. 2003. "Married Fathers and Caring Daddies: Welfare Reform and the Discursive Politics of Paternity." *Social Problems* 50: 461–81.

Harris-Perry, Melissa. 2011. *Sister Citizen: Shame, Stereotypes, and Black Women in America.* New Haven: Yale University Press.

Jaco, Charles. 2012. "The Jaco Report: Full Interview with Todd Akin." *Fox 2 Now, St. Louis.* August 19, 2012. Accessed May 28, 2016. fox2now.com/2012/08/19/the-jaco-report-august-19-2012/.

Jordan-Zachery, Julia S. 2008. *Black Women, Cultural Images, and Social Policy.* New York: Routledge.

Let's Move. "Eat Healthy." Accessed April 4, 2015. http://www.letsmove.gov/eat-healthy.

Mayer, Tamar. 2000. "Gender Ironies of Nationalism: Setting the Stage." In *Gender Ironies of Nationalism: Sexing the Nation,* edited by Tamar Mayer. New York: Routledge.

McClintock, Anne. 1993. "Family Feuds: Gender, Nationalism and the Family." *Feminist Review* 44: 61–80.

McCormick, Joseph P., II, and Charles E. Jones. 1993. "The Conceptualization of Deracialization: Thinking Through the Dilemma." In *Dilemmas of Black Politics: Issues of Leadership and Strategy*, edited by Georgia A. Persons, 66–84. New York: HarperCollins College Publishers.

McGinley, Ann C. 2009. "Hillary Clinton, Sarah Palin, and Michelle Obama: Performing Gender, Race, and Class on the Campaign Trail." *Denver University Law Review* 86: 709–25.

"Michelle Obama." Accessed October 15, 2012. http://www.beyonce.com/news/michelle-obama.

"Michelle Obama Teaches Dr. Oz How to (VIDEO)." 2012. *Huffington Post.* September 10, 2012. http://www.huffingtonpost.com/2012/09/10/michelle-obama-teaches-dr-oz-dougie_n_1872274.html.

Moynihan, D. P. 1965. "The Negro Family: The Case for National Action." Office of Policy Planning and Research, United States Department of Labor.

"National Responsible Fatherhood Clearinghouse." 2012. U.S. Department of Health and Human Services. Accessed April 5, 2012. https://www.fatherhood.gov/.

Park, Madison. 2009. "How to Get Michelle Obama's Toned Arms." CNN, February 26, 2009. http://articles.cnn.com/2009-02-26/health/toning.obama.arms_1_arms-strength-training-first-lady?_s=PM:HEALTH.

Parry-Giles, Shawn J., and Diane M. Blair. 2002. "The Rise of the Rhetorical First Lady: Politics, Gender Ideology, and Women's Voice, 1789–2000." *Rhetoric & Public Affairs* 5: 565–600.

Persons, Georgia A. 2004. "National Politics and Charitable Choices as Urban Policy for Community Development." *The Annals of the American Academy of Political Science* 594: 65–78.

Roberts, Dorothy. 1999. *Killing the Black Body: Race, Reproduction, and the Meaning of Liberty.* New York: Vintage.

Shaw, Gina. 2013. "Michelle Obama Takes on Childhood Obesity." WebMD. Accessed April 4, 2013. http://www.webmd.com/parenting/features/michelle-obama-intervew?page=3.

"Transcript: Michelle Obama's Convention Speech." 2012. NPR, September 4, 2013. http://www.npr.org/2012/09/04/160578836/transcript-michelle-obamas-convention-speech.

Welter, Barbara. 1966. "The Cult of True Womanhood: 1820–1860." *American Quarterly* 18: 151–74.

Williams, Verna L. 2009. "The First (Black) Lady." *Denver University Law Review* 86: 709–25.

Wilson, Jules. 2012. "Barack Obama Tucks Flotus into Bed at Night, Their Most Adorable PDA Moments (PHOTOS)." *Huffington Post*, May 5, 2012. http://

www.huffingtonpost.com/2012/05/30/barack-obama-tucks-flotus_n_1556530.html.

White, Deborah Gray. 1999. *Ar'n't I a Woman?: Female Slaves in the Plantation South*. New York: W. W. Norton & Company.

White, E. Frances. 1990. "Africa on My Mind: Gender, Counter Discourse and African-American Nationalism." *Journal of Women's History* 2: 73–97.

Yuval-Davis, Nira. 1997. *Gender & Nation*. London: Sage.

———, and Floya Anthias, eds. 1989. *Woman-Nation-State*. Jo Campling, consultant ed. Houndmills, England: Macmillan.

11

"We Always Resist: Trust Black Women"

Black Women's Reproductive Justice Activism in the Wake of Health Care Reform

TONYA M. WILLIAMS
Johnson C. Smith University

Introduction

Despite the contentious political milieu that foregrounded the enactment of the Affordable Care Act and continues to obfuscate implementation, health care reform presented a political opportunity for reproductive justice activists to articulate a radical vision for reform that reimagined the prevailing health care system. Their broad vision for reform would ostensibly call for a set of intersectionality informed policy interventions that situated the reproductive and sexual health experiences, perspectives, and broader health needs of intersectionally disadvantaged groups in the forefront of the political process. The principles that reinforced those policy interventions would promote provisions that included universal access, nondiscrimination, comprehensive coverage, and a holistic approach to health. Although reform to the nation's health care delivery system ultimately reinforced a market-oriented approach to providing health care insurance coverage, the political opportunity structure prompted coordinated collective action from reproductive justice organizations vested in representing the policy prerogatives of "intersectionally marginalized subgroups," such as Black women, who have been underserved by the health care system and underrepresented in political decision-making institutions. Drawing inspiration from what Zenzele Isoke refers to as a "black feminist intersectional analysis" (Isoke 2013, 1), this chapter chronicles the intersectional activism of "black women's reform efforts" (S. L. Smith 1995) in the reproductive justice movement as they navigated and continue to negotiate the complex polemical tapestry of health care reform.

To date, the preponderance of scholarship on Black women and women of color, more broadly, involved in what we may refer to as reproductive justice activism is located in the academic disciplines of history, sociology, and interdisciplinary projects tethered to women's/gender studies. Contributing to this evolving body of knowledge, Black feminist legal scholars have produced a complementary set of research interventions that have been particularly attentive to the ways in which the carceral state is perpetuated through the relationship between state regulation of Black women's reproduction, the promulgation of punitive social welfare policies, and the criminal legal system (Goodwin 2008; Jefferson 1989; Lee 2000; Roberts 1997). However, political science research has yielded significantly fewer studies on reproductive politics within discrete domains of inquiry. This chapter represents a scholarly intervention that seeks to link the nascent body of Black gender politics research, where reproductive politics is an underdeveloped subject of political inquiry, to the "absented presence of Black political women as subjects of research" (Alexander-Floyd 2014, 4) in the extant literature on interest group politics. The purpose of this research is to interrogate the representational activism of Black women–directed reproductive justice organizations that prioritize the political interests of intersectionally marginalized subgroups in their advocacy work, set against the backdrop of health care reform. Although this type of representational behavior is largely unaccounted for, it remains nonetheless significant for communities whose political interests are often treated as peripheral in the legislative agendas of progressive formations claiming to advocate for the subjective and objective policy prerogatives of populations traditionally underserved in the political process. Observing this proclivity in interest group behavior, Dara Strolovitch, in *Affirmative Advocacy: Race, Class, and Gender in Interest Group Politics*, observes that "the political response to oppression and disadvantage in the United States, with few exceptions has been to organize interest groups and to pursue public policies that are dedicated to addressing single axes of oppression—gender or race or poverty" (Strolovitch 2007, 26). However, I argue that investigating the reproductive justice activism practiced by Black political women (and other women of color, more broadly) represents a significant departure from the representational behavior documented by interest group scholars given whom they advocate for—populations experiencing structural oppression—and warrants further investigation by Black gender politics researchers interested in the ways in which reproductive politics has been and continues to be shaped by the lived experiences of these same populations.

The study unfolds as follows: Part I discusses reproductive justice as an intersectionality-informed analytical framework and social justice movement, highlighting the involvement of a distinct set of movement architects, that is, activist-intellectual Black women in health reform activism. Part II summarizes the Patient Protection and Affordable Care Act, accentuating gender-responsive provisions within the law in addition to bureaucratic rule making focused on the reproductive health provisions. Additionally, I briefly discuss divisive executive action involving financing abortion coverage, state legislative policy responses and federal judicial interventions centered on reproductive health provisions and Medicaid expansion. Next, a summation of the methodology that informs the study, followed by an analysis of the primary data accumulated in the research, will be considered. Finally, in the third and concluding section, I lay out the study's findings, implications, and areas of future research.

The Political Activism of Black Women in the Domain of Reproductive Politics

Pathologizing Black women's bodies, biological and cultural reproductions, sexual behavior, and mothering and coupling practices have often justified the endorsement and subsequent proliferation of punitive social welfare policy interventions ranging from coercive population control practices to welfare reform measures that have sanctioned childbearing or prospective childbearing (Jordan-Zachery 2009; Roberts 1997; Ross 1998; Rousseau 2009; Silliman et al. 2004). Documenting the degree to which interlocking systems of racism, sexism, classism, heterosexism, and myriad ancillary oppressions have shaped the nature of reproductive politics and Black female subjectivity and positionality within the US body politic, Dorothy Roberts (1997), in her widely cited *Killing the Black Body: Race, Reproduction, and the Meaning of Liberty*, deduces that "regulating Black women's reproductive decisions has been a central aspect of racial oppression in America" (Roberts 1997, 6). The location of Black women within these matrices of structural oppression presumably situates them as marginalized political subjects whose political interests are frequently rendered immutably peripheral within the political terrain of US politics. However, it is not merely that reproductive oppression experienced by Black women is inextricably linked to our understanding of the perpetuation of gendered racialized hierarchies in the United States, but also that everyday Black women and Black feminist activists have a long history of political resistance to myriad manifestations of reproductive oppression. Thus, one should resist locating Black women as insignificant political actors or one-dimensional victims of reproductive oppression, capitulating to a power structure and political system where their empowerment is perpetually circumscribed by their social, political, and economic position (Isoke 2013). Highlighting the rich legacy of subversive political action orchestrated by Black women opposing racialized patriarchy in the provision of health care in the United States, Deborah R. Grayson (1999) observes,

> It is Black women's culture of resistance, their refusal to internalize their own oppression by rejecting ideological justifications, that enables, indeed demands that Black women work for political and social change. In the history of their health activism in particular, Black women have taken the narrow spaces of opportunity available to them and expanded them. (135)

Whether through individual acts of subversion, grassroots activism and alliance formation, interest group litigation, agenda-setting priorities while serving in elective office, or through other forms of political resistance practices, Black women have sought to wrestle power and resources from the state (and private actors) to exercise control over their bodies, genders, sexualities, and reproduction for themselves, their families, and their communities (Davis 1983; Luna 2009; Silliman et al. 2004; Springer 1999). In fact, the trajectory of Black feminist health activisms are enshrined in the American body politic through the establishment of Black women's health centers (such as the National Black Women's Health Project, now the Black Women's Health Imperative, founded in 1984), and subsequent proliferation of symposia, workshops, programs, and reproductive justice organizations tethered to the interests, experiences, and activist practices produced by Black women (Ross 2015; Silliman et al. 2004). Perhaps one of the most meaningful articulations of Black feminist sentiments linking the legacy of gendered racism, injustice, and violence; and political demands for (reproductive) self-determination, including the right to abortion, to the history of reproductive violence experienced by Black women can be found in a statement published by a group of political Black women referring to themselves as African American Women for Reproductive Freedom. The statement, titled "We Remember," was published in 1989 on the heels of the Supreme Court decision in Webster v. Reproductive Health Services, a precedent-setting case that laid the groundwork for the establishment of elaborate state-regulatory regimes that circumscribed women's access to abortion (African American Women Are for Reproductive Freedom 1989; Springer 1999). Authored by Marcia Gillespie of *Ms.* magazine with the endorsement of some of the most prominent Black women scholars, activists, and politicians in American politics, "We Remember" formulates a set of pioneering foundational principles that ultimately shaped the meaning of reproductive freedom and foregrounded prescriptions for social justice interventions (Springer 1999). Faithful to a liberatory politic around bodily autonomy whereby individuals and communities have the resources and power to make self-determining decisions about their reproductive lives, the statement also included what remains a radical political prerogative then and now: the right to abortion cannot exclusively be proscribed as a matter of choice, but is a question inextricably tethered to structural intersectional oppression that produces qualitatively different reproductive realities for Black women (and women of color, more broadly).

The formation of the reproductive justice movement is illustrative of the disruptive possibilities of a political project whose theoretical groundings, grassroots organizing practices, resource allocation, and claims-making interventions are informed by the lived reproductive realities of communities experiencing intersectional oppression. Coined in 1994 by a group of progressive Black feminist activists with deep roots in social movement work, during a reproductive rights conference in Chicago, reproductive justice is a political expression illuminating the symbiotic relationship between reproductive rights, social justice, and human rights principles (Price 2010; Ross 2015). The motivation for this radical rearticulation of reproductive politics was precipitated by Black women activists' political opposition to the particular ways in which reproductive experiences, pervasive health inequities, and subsequent disparities in health suffered by Black women in addition to their favored policy prescriptions were marginalized and/or excluded from President Clinton's health care agenda–setting priorities and reform deliberations. Loretta Ross (2015), one of the most prolific Black feminist activist scholars on reproductive politics and principle architect of the reproductive justice movement, reflects on the origin of perhaps what may be the most significant theoretical innovation and intervention in reproductive politics in the last three decades, which was precipitated, in part, by health care reform:

> We recognized that health care reform debates about privacy, women's rights, fetuses, religion, and the law isolated abortion from other social justice issues like economics, violence against women, and child sexual abuse. This exceptionalizing of abortion failed to accurately analyze how a pregnant girl or woman actually decides whether or not to have a baby. Her logic chain may be based on considerations such as available health care, housing, violence, age, finances, child-care, her partner, education, or the access to, safety of, and affordability of abortion services. These other considerations are far upstream of her decision whether to become a parent, and in fact, determine whether the pregnancy is continued or terminated. Failure to consider these social justice—or human rights—issues frustrated those of us in Chicago strategizing on influencing health care reform policymaking. (Ross 2015, 5)

On August 16, 1994, the *Washington Post* and *Roll Call* published a public statement of principles authored by a coalition of Black feminist activists operating under the designation Women of African Descent for Reproductive Justice (WADRJ). Articulating a radical vision of health care reform, the declaration, directed toward members of Congress, endorsed a set of policy prescriptions based on nondiscrimination, universality, comprehensive health coverage (including the full range of reproductive and sexual health services, including abortion care), access and affordability, and meaningful inclusion of underrepresented groups and their interests in the political process. Their support for health care reform would ultimately be determined by the degree to which these governing principles were substantively included in the legislative agenda (Women of African Descent for Reproductive Justice 1994). In a statement titled "Black Women on Universal Healthcare Reform," WADRJ (1994) affirms:

> Reproductive freedom is a life and death issue for many Black women and deserves as much recognition as any other freedom. The right to have an abortion is a personal decision that must be

> made by a woman in consultation with her physician. Accordingly, unimpeded access to abortion as a part of the full range of reproductive health services offered under health care reform is essential. Moreover, abortion coverage must be provided for all women under health care reform regardless of ability to pay, with no interference from the government. WE WILL NOT ENDORSE A HEALTH CARE REFORM SYSTEM THAT DOES NOT COVER THE FULL RANGE OF REPRODUCTIVE SERVICES FOR ALL WOMEN INCLUDING ABORTION (emphasis in the original). (para. 2)

Luna and Luker (2013), observing this radical philosophical departure from rights-based claims and concomitant policy prescriptions contesting liberal democratic political thinking deeply rooted within reproductive justice activism, postulate, "RJ simultaneously demands a negative right of freedom from undue government interference and a positive right to government action in creating conditions of social justice and human flourishing for all" (328). Although the health care reform bill deliberated during the Clinton administration was ultimately jettisoned less than a month after the publication, the "black feminist intersectional analysis" that shaped the principles set forth remained intact during the political negotiations that ultimately resulted in the passage of the Affordable Care Act nearly twenty years later.

The Patient Protection and Affordable Care Act and the Ongoing Politicization of Women's Health

On March 23, 2010, President Barack Obama signed into law the "Patient Protection and Affordable Care Act" (referred to hereafter as the ACA) with the goal of addressing one of the nation's most persistent and confounding social welfare issues: guaranteeing universal access to health care insurance coverage. Without the benefit of one Republican vote in either legislative chamber on the bill's final iteration, "President Obama has, to some degree, succeeded where all of his predecessors failed, in that his healthcare legislation passed" (Rich, Cheung, and Lurvey 2013). Provisions in the new law were designed to eliminate discriminatory practices, ameliorate health inequities, and reduce disparities in health status; incentivize improvements in the quality of care and treatment; and establish greater consumer protections while containing increasingly exorbitant health care costs and public expenditures.

If implemented as originally envisioned, the expansion of public and private health insurance would move toward fostering health equity and enhanced access to coverage primarily through (a) the provision of "premium credits" for low- to middle-income individuals and families to subsidize the purchase of private health insurance coverage through health insurance marketplaces or "exchanges," (b) Medicaid expansion for non-elderly low and moderate income adults in households with incomes up to 138% of the federal poverty line (FPL), (c) mandatory provision of health care insurance coverage for eligible full-time equivalent employees by employers, and finally, (d) a requirement obligating nonexempt individuals to purchase health care insurance, popularly referred to as the "individual mandate" (Jacobs and Skocpol 2012). Additionally, ACA sought to remediate and/or prevent the onset of chronic disease through requiring health insurers to provide plans with a comprehensive benefits package including preventive services without cost sharing. Moreover, health care reform included landmark gender-responsive provisions that included the elimination of gender rating (differential pricing in the insurance marketplace based on sex), in addition to the establishment of national guidelines on comprehensive women's health services incorporating maternity care and FDA-approved family planning coverage and services, annual well-woman exams, HIV/STI screenings, and myriad health screening services, at no cost, for the first time in all new private health insurance plans (Sonfield and Pollack 2013).

Although there was relatively limited partisan interest on the Democratic side of the aisle in either chamber to wrangle over abortion coverage in the health care reform deliberations, regulatory determinations over women's reproductive decision making materialized as a subject of intense political contestation and nearly thwarted health reform at the last minute. Women's and reproductive rights and justice advocates and their allied issue coalitions vociferously resisted amendments to the bill that perpetuated what Loretta Ross (2015) refers to as "exceptionalizing of abortion" (5; just as Black women activists had done during the Clinton health care reform deliberation). However, the precarious political coalition that existed between anti-abortion and abortion rights Democrats, accentuated by zealous political opposition mounted by congressional Republican and anti-abortion issue coalitions, mitigated their appeal of abortion as reproductive health care. Highlighting the contestation over reproductive politics that characterized health care reform in the waning phase of the political process, Janet L. Dolgin and Katherine R. Dieterich postulate in "The 'Other' Within: Health Care Reform, Class, and the Politics of Reproduction":

> The political process of health care reform seemed to displace concern about the matter actually at issue—health care coverage—with concern about abortion and family planning services for poor women. Cliff-hanging negotiations about abortion coverage shaped the final Congressional vote on the Act, and the law's passage depended on President Obama's executive order, which restricted the use of funds made available pursuant to the law for abortion coverage. (2011, 378)

Ultimately, the perpetuation of abortion exceptionalization in the legislative deliberation presented advocates with a Faustian bargain: health care reform with additional regulatory burdens on abortion coverage or the demise of reform altogether. Certainly, neither option met the issue priorities enshrined in their legislative agendas. Ultimately, the least unfavorable course of action desired by reproductive rights and justice advocates eventually came to fruition—health care reform, promulgated through executive action, perpetuated abortion exceptionalization, resulting in further erosion of abortion protections at the federal level and, ultimately, inspiring further limitations at the state level as well (Guttmacher Institute 2016; Salganicoff and Sobel 2015). Notwithstanding the ideological fragmentation over abortion coverage and legislative concessions perpetuating abortion exceptionalization negotiated by the Democratic leadership in Congress and the White House to appease the anti-abortion wing of the party, Adam Sonfield and Harold A. Pollack postulate that the enactment of the Affordable Care Act was nevertheless historic in that it "may be the most important measure ever passed to expand access to evidence-based reproductive health services in the United States. The structures and policies put in place through health reform—should they survive—will define the reproductive health battleground for many years to come" (Sonfield and Pollack 2013, 387).

Notwithstanding the impetus for and merits of reform, the enactment of the ACA produced deeply partisan and ideological divisions that marred the legislative deliberation leading up to its enactment and that continue to complicate the operationalization of the law. Thus, unsurprisingly, a proliferation of interest group litigation and anti-reform legislative responses at the state and federal levels that sought to alter, repeal, obstruct, and/or otherwise delay the law's implementation shadowed reform (Redhead and Kinzer 2014). The most fervent political opposition hinged on the mandate provisions—employer, individual, contraceptive services coverage, and Medicaid expansion—in addition to restrictions on federal financing of abortion coverage in private insurance plans on the health care exchanges. The first case, *National Federation of Independent Business (NFIB) v. Sebelius*, challenged the constitutionality of the individual mandate and compulsory Medicaid expansion provisions. The Supreme Court resolved these two constitutional disputes stemming from *NFIB v. Sebelius*, upholding Congress' authority to require individuals to purchase health care insurance pursuant to its taxing power while deferring to states' discretionary authority as to whether or not to expand Medicaid coverage (Rich et al. 2013). In the second landmark case, the Supreme Court in a 5-4 ruling held in *Burwell v. Hobby Lobby Stores, Inc.*, that the government violated the "Religious Freedom and Restoration Act" by requiring for-profit corporations with sincerely held religious beliefs to provide contraception coverage and services in employer-sponsored health insurance plans. Additionally, the bureaucratic decision *not to* exempt privately held corporations with religious objections from the "birth control" mandate prompted at least five states to contravene the "contraception mandate" through resolutions, legislation, or ballot measures objecting to the regulation (Guttmacher Institute 2013).

Data and Methods

Drawing from in-depth, semistructured elite interviews, participant observation, and supplemented by additional primary and secondary research, this case study analyzes the representational behavior of Black women–directed reproductive justice organizations within the political milieu of health care reform. This study offers a window into the sets of (reproductive) health concerns experienced by their constituencies that informed and animated their political activism throughout the political process, the unfavorable political contexts that shaped the operational implementation of reform, and, most significantly, the impact of reform on their constituents from their perspectives and situational contexts. Conditions for participation in the study included (a) participants were located in southern states, specifically Georgia, Louisiana, and Texas;[1] (b) reproductive justice was identified as the analytical framework that foregrounds their mission, vision, and/or program work; and (c) organizations held nonprofit status at the time of the study.

Although most studies analyzing interest group/nonprofit behavior draw information from databases such as the National Center for Charitable Statistics (NCCS) and movement-specific directories to compile their sample populations, reproductive justice organizations in the South constitute a relatively small and exceptional constellation of interest groups operating in the United States given the breadth and scope of their constituencies, issue niches, and intersectional approach to claims making and movement building. However, SisterSong Women of Color Reproductive Justice Collective, a membership-based coalition of local, state, and national reproductive justice organizations, provides perhaps the most dependable repositories. A snowball sample followed the preliminary identification of participants and establishment of interview protocols. These two sampling methods yielded five organizations, two in Georgia, two in Louisiana, and one in Texas.[2] Although the sample may appear insignificant, the participants (and organizational affiliates) involved in this case study constitute four of the five subnational reproductive justice organizations operating in these three southern states. Interviews with current and former members of SisterSong staff were also undertaken.

Semistructured interviews were the primary qualitative method employed given their value in permitting the researcher to collect data, in the form of a narrative, on a social phenomenon that may not be widely available, may be unavailable, or may be unlikely to be captured exclusively through the use of quantitative methods. In this case, interviews were an indispensable qualitative method given that the prevailing literature on reproductive justice activism nearly focuses exclusively on the political behavior of national organizations, with few systematic studies examining the representational behavior of subnational organizations on (reproductive) health policy interventions at the national or subnational level. Interviews ranged from thirty to sixty minutes, were taped, and were then transcribed. The interview questions were intended to elicit in-depth responses pertaining to reproductive health policy concerns of women of color and Black women in particular, types of policy advocacy activities, if any, in which respondents participated during the various stages of the policy process (2009–2013), and at what level of government (state and/or federal level), in addition to respondents' perceptions of intended impact of reform on their constituents. Finally, respondents were queried about the political and administrative implementation of the law in their respective state and local contexts. Informed by the work of Berry and Arons (2003), the types of policy advocacy activities examined in this study were limited to demonstrations, dissemination of petitions, educating elected officials, testifying at legislative hearings, working in planning or advisory groups, meeting with elected officials, independent research, and encouraging members and/or constituents to write, call, fax, or email policy makers. Elite interviews with organizational leadership, defined as the executive director/president or their designee, using a seventeen-item survey, were conducted between November 2013 and March 2014. Verbal and/or written consent was secured, and interviews were conducted via telephone and in person. Themes and representative quotes were examined and incorporated into the analysis.

Findings

The preliminary findings in this study offer a broad overview of institutional characteristics, constituencies, issue niches and political interests, activist practices, and perspectives on health care reform through the lens of Black women–directed reproductive justice organizations. Although each organization operated at the state and/or local level, there was significant variability in institutional size and resources. In one case, an organization only had one staff member, the executive director, while the largest organization had a professional staff of eighteen. Unsurprisingly, organizational budgets varied significantly, ranging from less than $50,000 to more than $1.5 million. Three organizations received funding from one or more levels of government to deliver social services to their constituents during the time period under investigation. Additionally, the organizations shared very similar characteristics in terms of membership structure (non–membership based), issue priorities, and constituencies prioritized. Although the vast majority of interest groups prioritize the political interests, and ultimately the policy prerogatives of the most privileged members of their constituencies (Strolovitch 2007), reproductive justice organizations operate in stark contrast to their interest group peers in that they serve and are often guided by constituencies that are subject to intersectional marginalization (as evidenced in table 11.1), who often go underrepresented and/or altogether ignored in the political process.

While the interview questions were intended to elicit in-depth responses about the implications of health care reform for their constituents, I was also interested in the types of political activities, if any, in which respondents participated, at what level of government, including specific questions concerning the conditions relating to implementation within their respective state and local contexts. Given the federalist construction of the American political system, in addition to state-level discretion assigned in the implementation of the law through federal statute and judicial fiat, reproductive justice advocates in the South encountered dramatically dissimilar political environments depending on the level of government and the phase of the

Table 11.1. Reproductive Justice Organizations' Constituents and Issue Niches (N=4)

Organization	Constituents Served/ Represented	Issues
Georgia		
SisterLove, Inc.	Women and their families, especially women of African descent	HIV/AIDS and STIs Prevention Sexual and Reproductive Justice Health, and Rights Stigma, Discrimination, and Structural Violence Bodily Autonomy and Interpersonal Violence
Louisiana		
Institute for Women and Ethnic Studies	Women of color and their families, especially those who are socioeconomically disadvantaged	Reproductive and Sexual Health Youth Sexual Health Mental Health and Wellness
Women with a Vision	Women and Communities of Color LGBTQ Communities	Sex Worker Rights HIV/AIDS Drug Policy Reform Harm Reduction Reproductive Justice LGBTQ Advocacy
Texas		
Afiya Center for HIV Prevention and Reproductive Justice	Black Women and Women of Color	HIV/AIDS and STI Reproductive Health Reproductive Justice

Source: Data obtained from organizational websites and interviews.

political process. Although advocates encountered sympathetic Democratic majorities in Congress and in the White House amenable to their agenda-setting priorities (except on financing abortion coverage), they operated in an explicitly more hostile political milieu back home, where GOP-controlled political institutions opposed the implementation of significant reform provisions that would disproportionately benefit constituents they represented. Additionally, these states also enacted further regulatory burdens on abortion coverage in private insurance health plans administered on the health care exchanges (Guttmacher 2016). Table 11.2 illustrates the extent of their political activism at the federal level in the year leading up to the enactment of the ACA in March 2010.

During perhaps the most volatile phase of the health care reform negotiations, reproductive justice advocates were presented with at least two significant political opportunities (outside the traditional behind-the-scenes political brinksmanship between lawmakers and interest groups with shared ideological or political commitments) to amplify the objective political interests of their constituencies and to coordinate political action at the federal level: the coincidental convening of the SisterSong Women of Color Reproductive Justice Collective National Membership Conference during health care reform deliberations on November 7, 2009, followed by the Stop Stupak Rally that took place nearly a month later on December 2. Seizing on the historic opportunity to amplify the (reproductive) health experiences, needs, and political interests of their constituencies, two organizations joined in political demonstrations and lobbied members of Congress leading up to the enactment of health care reform. The first day of the SisterSong national convening was disrupted by legislative proposals

Table 11.2. Political Activities of Reproductive Justice Organizations before Enactment of the ACA (N=4)

Political activities	Number of organizations that employed specific tactic
Demonstrations	2
Disseminate petitions and/or other information concerning reform to constituents	2
Educating your elected officials	2
Testifying at legislative hearings	—
Working in a planning or advisory group or coalition	2
Independent research	—
Encouraging constituents to write, call, fax, or email policymakers	2

Source: Individual interviews with reproductive justice activists, December 2013–March 2014.

in the House to restrict federal subsidies in private plans on the exchanges that offer abortion coverage in addition to perpetuating existing exclusionary practices that restricted some authorized and all unauthorized immigrants from participating in health care reform (SisterSong Collective 2009). Activists resoundingly opposed both practices and amendments, instead advocating for comprehensive reproductive health care that included abortion coverage and full inclusion of all sectors of society in reform, including the millions of undocumented individuals and families that remain in the shadows, uninsured and underserved by the nation's health care system. National Coordinator of the Collective Loretta Ross lamented the promulgation of these policy exceptionalizations. "We are not going to protect Congress from the anger of Women of Color when they bargain away our human rights, and when they fail to protect the rights of immigrants to healthcare access" (SisterSong Collective 2009). Coordinated by the Coalition to Pass Healthcare Reform and Stop Stupak, the latter political demonstration and National Week of Action was orchestrated to oppose the enactment of the Stupak-Pitts amendment, a provision passed in the House that would have ultimately continued the practice of abortion exceptionalization originally established by the Hyde Amendment by prohibiting the use of federal funds in private health insurance plans that offered abortion coverage (Planned Parenthood Federation of America 2014).

Notwithstanding the political activities undertaken by these organizations prior to the enactment of the ACA, one respondent whose organization did not participate in either of the demonstrations or lobbying efforts expressed deep anxiety about how political activism could impact his organization's nonprofit status in addition to funding it received from governmental agencies. The commonly held belief that nonprofits relinquish their right to participate in the political process given their nonprofit status is not unusual. While organizations registered as 501(c)(3) tax-exempt, charitable organizations under the IRS tax code are not strictly prohibited from engaging in political activities intended to influence political decision making, their political behavior is subject to a complicated and often ambiguous maze of regulation and bureaucratic discretion that frequently leaves nonprofits unwilling, uncertain, or unlikely to participate in the political process (Frumkin 2005). However, other participants in the study did not express this perception or trepidation. In addition to participating in demonstrations, respondents indicated that their organizations disseminated information about the reform deliberations to their constituents and participated in coalition work to advance the specific interests of their constituents prior to the enactment of health care reform (2009–2010). During the time period under consideration, participants did not participate (i.e., submit testimony to congressional committees) in federal hearings on health care reform or publish independent research analysis exclusively produced by the organization. Given the disparate range of resources, institutional time and size, professional staff, and ongoing organizational commitments independent of ACA advocacy associated with generating independent research on health care reform, this development was unsurprising.

As illustrated in table 11.3, participants increased the trajectory of their political activism after the enactment of the ACA at the state level in terms of disseminating information to their constituents about the implications of reform and engaging in coalition-building work. Additionally, respondents indicated that their organizations served as intermediaries between health care navigators and their constituents to ensure they were provided assistance negotiating the complexities of the coverage options in the health care exchanges. Participants from two organizations stipulated that they continued to encourage their constituents to contact state lawmakers, participated in political demonstrations, and engaged in strategic lobbying opportunities at their respective state capitols during the implementation phase. In fact, participants generally maintained a consistent level of political activism even in unfavorable political environments at the state level.

Table 11.3. Political Activities of Reproductive Justice Organizations after Enactment of the ACA (N=4)

Political activities	Number of organizations that employed specific tactic
Demonstrations	2
Disseminate petitions and/or other information concerning reform to constituents	4
Educating your elected officials	2
Testifying at legislative hearings	1
Working in a planning or advisory group (coalitions)	4
Independent research	—
Encouraging constituents to write, call, fax, or email policymakers	2

Source: Individual interviews with reproductive justice activists, December 2013–March 2014.

Findings from the interviews indicated that although reproductive justice advocates supported health care reform, they remain frustrated and disappointed that the aforementioned shortcomings of the law and ultimately its implementation or lack thereof continue to obstruct efforts to ensure optimal impact on their respective constituents. Although a majority of states (28) and Washington, DC, have expanded Medicaid, none of the southern states under consideration in this study have done so at the time of this writing.[3] The failure to expand Medicaid for low-income adults who qualify for public health benefits and thus are ineligible for premium support in the private insurance marketplace produces a coverage gap where access and care remain unresolved within the current health care insurance reform framework. Presumably this state-manufactured health care dilemma could actually exacerbate the prevailing crisis in coverage and care for vulnerable populations, such as Black women living with HIV/AIDs, whose lives are already encumbered by a complex web of social determinants of health that adversely affect access to preventive and treatment services (National Women's Network, Positive Women's Network USA, & SisterLove, Inc. 2015). In addition to state-level political factors that impede maximization of health care reform, participants expressed trepidation about the degree to which health care reform would result in ameliorating disparate health outcomes, quality of care, treatment, and access experienced by their constituencies. Participants conveyed consternation about pervasive social determinants of health and structural barriers further moderating the impact of reform, including low levels of health literacy, lack of community health infrastructure in their respective neighborhoods (particularly in post-disaster settings for those based in New Orleans), and low levels of cultural competency among providers who have not traditionally been responsive to the particular health care needs of vulnerable populations (such as trans people of color, low-income people of color, and Black women living with HIV/AIDs). Assailing the persistent issues associated with access to health insurance coverage for Medicaid-eligible constituencies, one respondent explained that the ACA did not go far enough, proclaiming that it largely benefited insurance companies and that a system that included universal health insurance coverage would have been optimal. In a telephone interview with the author in February 2014, a reproductive justice advocate replied with tremendous candor, when asked, "What, if any, are the specific challenges your organization must confront in regards to the implementation of the Affordable Care Act in your state?":

> Education. Literally, the biggest challenge is getting everybody to even be informed and to have the right information so that they can go to the right resources and then make the right decisions . . . So, really raising health literacy and the level of education about the policy, about the law, about the access are really critical issues for our communities. I think that people don't know what's in it then they don't know what's not in it. If you don't know what's in it, you don't know what to fight for and you don't know what to protect. That's really our biggest charge right now. (personal communication, Reproductive Justice Advocate, phone interview, February 2014)

Another activist, in a phone conversation with the author in March 2014, conveyed a similar sentiment:

> My concern with black women in women's health is sometimes just access. This is not all black women but the black women that I serve. I serve that group of women that are marginalized not only because they are black but because of poverty, environment, and all of the other things that poverty causes . . . and they are women who feel disenfranchised . . . They have not historically accessed the healthcare system as much as other women [have] . . . They tend to lack . . . the health literacy to stay healthier and be more proactive about their health . . . So, if we are not addressing those things with black women, affordable healthcare or anything else is not going to change their overall health outcomes. We have to address health literacy. We have to address why these women are out of care all the time. (personal communication, Reproductive Justice Advocate, phone interview, March 2014)

Given that "[i]ndividuals with low levels of health literacy are least equipped to benefit from the ACA" (Somers and Mahadevan 2010, 4), informants' analyses of the pitfalls of reform provide further insight about the degree to which intersectionally marginalized constituencies in the health care system prior to reform likely will remain so.

The vociferous political resistance mounted in opposition to health care reform demanded robust coalitional partnerships throughout the political process, particularly for those organizations with objective political interests in the domain of reproductive health policy. Coalitions are perhaps even more meaningful for organizations operating at the subnational level, which routinely represent the interests of intersectionally marginalized groups in state legislative settings on reproductive health policy, including safeguarding abortion access, and will bear the responsibility for advocating for operationalization of reform on behalf of these same constituencies. Additionally, formal coalition memberships have the benefit of maximizing political influence in legislative decision making, shaping prospective policy options, and creating strategic openings to negotiate policy compromises, ideally resulting in favorable (or at the very least cultivating the least unfavorable) policy outcomes. Evidence from interviews, participant observation, and publicly available documents illuminates the extent to which participants allied themselves with national initiatives, working groups, and lobbying coalitions at the federal and subnational levels, leveraging their collective expertise, political influence, and knowledge of local political environments to pursue a set of policy priorities and implementation strategies that prioritized the interests of their shared constituencies. These political formations, operating under a common set of social justice principles prioritizing gender and reproductive justice protective policies, included the Coalition to Pass Healthcare Reform and Stop Stupak, Raising Women's Voices, Campaign to End AIDS and the 30 for 30 Campaign, the Positive Women's Network, Harvard Law School's Health and Policy Law Clinic, and the Treatment Access Expansion Project, in addition to a variety of state-level coalitions advocating for effective implementation in states across the South. Furthermore, respondents indicated that coalition partners, at the state and national levels, shared technical expertise, facilitated initiatives, and generated political education resources such as tool kits, policy briefs, fact sheets, campaign materials, and press releases, seeking to inform and empower their respective constituencies throughout the myriad stages of healthcare reform (30 for 30 Campaign 2012a, 2012b; Killelea, Cohen, and Greenwald 2011; National Women's Network et al. 2015). Additionally, participants indicated that national coalition partners offered technical expertise and resources, aiding partner organizations in the dissemination of pertinent information about health care reform to their constituent networks.

Conclusion and Implications for Future Research

"We Always Resist: Trust Black Women" refers not only to the title of a documentary chronicling the reproductive justice activism of Black women in the socially conservative political milieu of Georgia politics, but it also serves as a literal representation of Black political women who have resisted state-sanctioned actions resulting in the marginalization of everyday Black women's political interests in the province of (reproductive) health policy and reproductive politics, more broadly. The acrimonious political processes that beget the passage and subsequent implementation of health care reform were no different. Nevertheless, the operationalization of Black women's reproductive justice activism, in stark contrast to conventional single-issue axis of oppression formations, has resulted in further amplification of the lived realities, political claims making, and objective policy interests of communities subject to intersectional discrimination. Moreover, findings from this study reveal that even when confronted with adverse political conditions where implementation of reform provisions that would benefit their constituencies were not favored in a given political jurisdiction, political opposition was met with resistance and did not constrain political activism. In fact, although there was variability in political activism observed between organizations prior to enactment, there was an increase in political action as the implementation phase commenced and political environment became more hostile. While the findings of this study cannot be generalized beyond this unique constellation of political actors, Black women's reproductive justice activism at the institutional level represents a significant departure from conventional political representation discourse found in studies of interest group behavior, given their attentiveness to prioritizing the objective political interests and policy prerogatives of those most often excluded and/or marginalized by the health care system and similarly underrepresented in the political process. These findings will be unsurprising to Black women in politics scholars writing in sister disciplines that have documented the ways in which Black women activists have sought to resist systems, institutions, practices and policies and even movements, whether on the right or left, that have been unresponsive, neglectful, and/or outright hostile to addressing the health needs of Black women and other intersectionally marginalized groups they represent.

There is still much we do not know about the intersectional advocacy practices of Black women during health care reform. Notwithstanding "the political coming of age of the (reproductive justice) movement" during the health care reform deliberations (Price 2010, 61), the representational behavior of Black women in this policy domain at the national and the subnational levels has mostly gone unaccounted for in the extant bodies of literature (Luna and Luker 2013). Thus, future research on Black women's reproductive justice activism, particularly in the South, where a majority of these organizations operate, might consider embarking on a more in-depth state-level case study analysis of political jurisdictions resistant to optimization of implementation of the Affordable Care Act. Shadowing the reproductive justice activism of particular Black women–led organizations, these state-level case studies (and perhaps comparative case studies) should shed further light on the subnational political environments that condition implementation, highlighting the representational policy goals and concomitant advocacy strategies, political utility of subnational coalitions, and ultimately the operational implications of reform on their constituencies. There likely will be exceptional variability between states, even those exercising political resistance to reform, in terms of policy adoption and implementation at the state and local levels, producing qualitatively different health reform experiences and outcomes for the constituencies that reproductive justice organizations prioritize in their political advocacy. Moreover, given the privileged political positionality designated to states with regard to implementation of health care reform, subnational organizations may be best positioned to represent their constituents' political interests even in an adverse or unfavorable political climate. The next few years and future research should reveal the extent to which that is true.

Notes

1. Southern states were prioritized in this investigation given that half of the Black population in the United States resides in the region, and the majority of subnational Black women-directed reproductive justice organizations are located there as well.

2. One organization, SPARK Reproductive Justice NOW, was excluded from the study because the author served as a program director for the nonprofit from 2009 to 2011 in addition to serving as a member of the board of directors at the time of this study. However, a rigorous case study analysis documenting the representational activism of this organization also merits further investigation.

3. Although Medicaid expansion had not been implemented during the data-collection phase, Louisiana Governor John Bel Edwards (D) signaled his intention to do so through an executive order, representing a substantive political departure from his neighbors in other southern states and from his predecessor.

References

30 for 30 Campaign. 2012. "Affordable Care Act Priorities and Opportunities for Addressing the Critical Health Care Needs of Women Living with and at Risk for HIV." Accessed January 6, 2014. http://www.chlpi.org/wp-content/uploads/2013/12/30-for-30-ACA-Exec-Summary.pdf.

30 for 30 Campaign. 2012. "Making HIV Care and Treatment Work for Women." Accessed January 6, 2014. http://www.hivlawandpolicy.org/sites/www.hivlawandpolicy.org/files/30for30_care_Tx%26wo_final.pdf.

African American Women Are for Reproductive Freedom. 1989. "We Remember." Accessed January 6, 2014. http://www.trustblackwomen.org/2011-05-10-03-28-12/publications-a-articles/african-americans-and-abortion-articles/36-african-american-women-are-for-reproductive-freedom.

Alexander-Floyd, Nikol. 2014. "Why Political Scientists Don't Study Black Women, but Historians and Sociologists Do: On Intersectionality and the Remapping of the Study of Black Political Women." In *Black Women in Politics: Identity, Power, and Justice in the New Millennium*, edited by Michael Mitchell and David Covin, 3–19. New Brunswick, NJ: Transaction.

Berry, Jeffrey, and David F. Arons. 2003. *A Voice for Nonprofits*. Washington, DC: The Brookings Institution.

Davis, Angela Y. 1983. "Racism, Birth Control and Reproductive Rights." In *Women, Race & Class*, 202–21. New York: Vintage.

Dolgin, Janet L., and Katherine R. Dieterich. 2012. "The 'Other' Within: Health Care Reform, Class, and the Politics of Reproduction." *Seattle Law Review* 35, no. 2: 377–425. http://digitalcommons.law.seattleu.edu/cgi/viewcontent.cgi?article=2066&context=sulr.

Frumkin, Peter. 2005. *On Being Nonprofit: A Conceptual and Policy Primer*. Cambridge: Harvard University Press.

Goodwin, Michele. 2008. "Prosecuting the Womb." *The George Washington Law Review* 76 (6): 1657–746. http://www.gwlr.org/goodwin/.

Grayson, Deborah R. 1999. "'Necessity Was the Midwife of Our Politics': Black Women's Health Activism in the 'Post'-Civil Rights Era (1980–1996). In *Still Lifting, Still Climbing: African American's Women's Contemporary Activism*, edited by Kimberly Springer, 131–48. New York: New York University Press.

Guttmacher Institute. 2012. "Laws Affecting Reproductive Health and Rights: Trends in the First Quarter of 2012." Last modified 2017. Accessed January 6, 2014. http://www.guttmacher.org/statecenter/updates/2012/statetrends12012.html.

Guttmacher Institute. "Restricting Insurance Coverage of Abortion." Last modified 2017. https://www.guttmacher.org/state-policy/explore/restricting-insurance-coverage-abortion.

Isoke, Zenzele. 2013. *Urban Black Women and the Politics of Resistance*. New York: Palgrave MacMillan.

Jacobs, Lawrence R., and Theda Skocpol. 2012. *Health Care Reform and American Politics: What Everyone Needs to Know*. New York: Oxford University Press.

Jefferson, Laurie-Nsiah. 1999. "Reproductive Laws, Women of Color, Low-Income Women." In *Reproductive Laws for the 1990s*, edited by Sherril Cohen and Nadine Taub. New Brunswick, NJ: Rutgers University Press.

Jordan-Zachery, Julia S. 2009. *Black Women, Cultural Images and Social Policy.* New York: Routledge.

Killelea, Amy, Devin Cohen, and Robert Greenwald. 2011. "Texas State Report: An Analysis of the Successes, Challenges and Opportunities for Improving Healthcare Access with a Focus on the Texas Medicaid Program." Accessed September 17, 2014. http://www.taepusa.org/wp-content/uploads/2017/01/SHARP-Texas-Report_compressed-file.pdf.

Lee, Melanie M. 2000. "Defining the Agenda: A New Struggle for African-American Women in the Fight for Reproductive Self-determination." *Washington and Lee Journal of Civil Rights and Social Justice* 6 (1): 87–102. http://scholarlycommons.law.wlu.edu/cgi/viewcontent.cgi?article=1088&context=crsj.

Luna, Zakiya. 2009. "From Rights to Justice: Women of Color Changing the Face of US Reproductive Rights Organizing." *Societies Without Borders: Human Rights and the Social Sciences* 4 (3): 343–65. doi:101163/187188609X12492771031618.

Luna, Zakiya, and Kristin Luker. 2013. "Reproductive Justice." *Annual Review of Law and Social Science* 9: 327–52. doi:10.1146/annurev-lawsocsci-102612-134037.

National Women's Network, Positive Women's Network USA, and SisterLove, Inc. 2015. "Ryan White and the Affordable Care Act: Advocating for Public Healthcare for Women Living with HIV." Accessed March 13, 2016. https://pwnusa.files.wordpress.com/2015/03/nwhn_pwn_sl_rw_brief_final.pdf.

Planned Parenthood Federation of America. 2014. "Advocacy Groups Form Coalition to Pass Healthcare Reform and Stop Stupak!" Last modified 2017. https://www.plannedparenthood.org/about-us/newsroom/press-releases/advocacy-groups-form-coalition-to-pass-health-care-reform-and-stop-stupak.

Price, Kimala. 2010. "What Is Reproductive Justice?: How Women of Color Activists Are Redefining the Pro-Choice Paradigm." *Meridians* 10 (2): 42–65. https://muse.jhu.edu/.

Redhead, C. Stephen, and Janet Kinzer. 2017. "Legislative Action to Repeal, Defund, or Delay the Affordable Care Act." Accessed April 18, 2017. http://fas.org/sgp/crs/misc/R43289.pdf.

Rich, Robert F., Eric Cheung, and Robert Lurvey. 2013. "The Patient Protection and Affordable Care Act of 2010: Implementation Challenges in the Context of Federalism." *Journal of Health Care Law & Policy* 16 (1): 77–140. http://digitalcommons.law.umaryland.edu/cgi/viewcontent.cgi?article=1290&context=jhclp.

Roberts, Dorothy. 1997. *Killing the Black Body: Race, Reproduction and the Meaning of Liberty.* New York: Pantheon.

Ross, Loretta. 1998. "African American Women and Abortion." In *Abortion Wars: A Half Century of Struggle, 1950–2000*, edited by R. Solinger, 161–207. Berkeley: University of California Press.

———. 2015. "Reproductive Justice Theory and Black Feminism: A Manifesto for Activism." Accessed March 13, 2016. http://take-root.org/wp-content/uploads/2015/06/RJ-Theorizing-RJ-Public-Version-by-LR-for-May-2015.docx.

Rousseau, Nicole. 2009. *Black Woman's Burden: Commodifying Black Reproduction*. New York: Palgrave MacMillan.

Salganicoff, Alina, and L. Laurie Sobel. 2016. "Women, Private Health Insurance, and the Affordable Care Act." *Women's Health Issues* 26 (1): 2–5. doi:10.1016/j.whi.2015.10.008.

Silliman, Jael, Marlene Gerber Fried, Loretta Ross, and Elena R. Gutierrez. 2004. *Undivided Rights: Women of Color Organize for Reproductive Justice*. Cambridge, MA: South End Press.

SisterSong Collective. 2009. "SisterSong No on Stupak and Anti-Immigrant Amendments—From National Membership Meeting." Press release. Accessed March 13, 2016. https://www.facebook.com/notes/sistersong/sistersong-no-on-stupak-and-anti-immigrant-amendments-from-national-membership-m/200355245008/.

Smith, Susan L. 1995. *Sick and Tired of Being Sick and Tired: Black Women's Health Activism in America, 1890–1950*. Philadelphia: University of Pennsylvania Press.

Somers, Stephen A., and Roopa Mahadevan. 2010. "Health Literacy Implications and the Affordable Care Act." *Center for Health Care Strategies, Inc.* Accessed March 13, 2016. https://www.chcs.org/media/Health_Literacy_Implications_of_the_Affordable_Care_Act.pdf.

Sonfield, Adam. 2012. "Federal Contraceptive Coverage Requirement Emerges as Major Political Issue, Despite Accommodation for Religiously Affiliated Employers." *Guttmacher Policy Review* 15 (1): 2–8. https://www.guttmacher.org/sites/default/files/article_files/gpr170102.pdf.

———. 2016. "Learning from Experience: Where Religious Liberty Meets Reproductive Rights." *Guttmacher Institute* 19 (1): 1–8. https://www.guttmacher.org/sites/default/files/article_files/gpr1900116.pdf.

Sonfield, Adam, and Harold A. Pollack. 2013. "The Affordable Care Act and Reproductive Health: Potential Gains and Serious Challenges." *Journal of Health Politics, Policy and Law* 38 (2): 373–91.

Springer, Kimberly. 1999. *Still Lifting, Still Climbing: African American Women's Contemporary Activism*. New York: New York University Press.

Strolovitch, Dara Z. 2007. *Affirmative Advocacy: Race, Class, and Gender in Interest Group Politics*. Chicago: University of Chicago Press.

Women of African Descent for Reproductive Justice. 1994. "Black Women on Universal Healthcare Reform." Accessed September 17, 2014. https://bwrj.wordpress.com/category/wadrj-on-health-care-reform/.

Contributors

Nikol G. Alexander-Floyd is associate professor of women's and gender studies and political science at Rutgers, New Brunswick. She is the author of *Gender, Race, and Nationalism in Contemporary Black Politics* (Palgrave MacMillan 2007), and her articles have appeared in leading journals such as *Feminist Formations*; the *International Journal of Africana Studies*; *Frontiers: A Journal of Women's Studies*; *Meridians: Feminism, Race, Transnationalism*; the *National Political Science Review*; *Politics & Gender*; *PS: Political Science & Politics*; and *Signs*. She is a recognized leader, having been asked to serve for two years as co-chair of the Annual Meeting of the National Women's Studies Association, and serving as chair of the American Political Science Association's Committee on the Status of Women and the Profession. Her next book project, *Liminal Subjects*, will investigate the implications of post-feminist, post–civil rights ideology and melodrama for Black and US gender politics.

Professor **Keisha N. Blain** teaches history at the University of Pittsburgh. She is a historian of the twentieth-century United States with broad interdisciplinary interests and specializations in African American History, the modern African Diaspora, and Women's and Gender Studies. Her research interests include Black internationalism, radical politics, and global feminisms. She completed a PhD in history from Princeton University in 2014. She is the author of *Set the World on Fire: Black Nationalist Women and the Global Struggle for Freedom* (University of Pennsylvania Press, 2018). The book analyzes an array of primary sources to uncover the crucial role women played in building Black nationalist and internationalist protest movements in the United States and other parts of the African Diaspora from the early twentieth century to the 1950s.

Jenny Douglas is a senior lecturer in health promotion in the Faculty of Wellbeing, Education and Language Studies at the Open University. She has a PhD in women's studies from the University of York, an MA in sociological research in Health Care, an MSc in environmental pollution control, and a BSc in microbiology and virology. Her research is both varied and wide ranging spanning thirty years on issues of race, health, and ethnicity. The key theme unifying her research and activism is intersectionality—exploring how "race," class, gender, and other axes of difference affect particular aspects of African-Caribbean women's health.

K. Melchor Hall is a transnational Black feminist scholar-activist, whose work focuses on education in the US and rural development in Honduras. Currently, she is both a Visiting Scholar at Brandeis University's Women's Studies Research Center and core faculty in Fielding Graduate University's School of Leadership Studies. During Fulbright-funded dissertation fieldwork in 2011 and 2012, she developed deep bonds of solidarity with farmers, academics and professionals of the Black indigenous Garifuna community of Honduras. Since then, she has continued to explore opportunities for collaborative projects that challenge the multinational and transnational forces that oppress Black people throughout the Americas and beyond. She is indebted to the community of people who do the difficult work of cultivating cassava to make ereba (or cassava bread). They have taught her about connecting to the land, honoring one's ancestors, strengthening bonds among women, and building community.

Grace E. Howard is an assistant professor of Gender Studies at the University of Southern Indiana and is an American Fellow with the American Association of University Women. She has a Ph.D. in Political Science from Rutgers University. Her dissertation, "The Criminalization of Pregnancy: Rights, Discretion, and the Law" examines the criminal prosecution of pregnant women for crimes against the fertilized eggs, embryos and fetuses they gestate as a form of what she refers to as *pregnancy exceptionalism*. Grace's areas of research include reproductive politics and law, civil rights, criminal justice, critical race and gender theory, bioethics, and deviant mothering. Grace has several published works, including "Informed or Misinformed Consent? Abortion Policy in the United States," "The Limits of Pure White: Raced Reproduction in the Methamphetamine Crisis," and a co-authored book entitled *The Gender of Crime*, 2nd ed.

Julia S. Jordan-Zachery is professor of public and community service studies and director of the Black studies program at Providence College (RI). Her interdisciplinary research focuses on African American women and public policy. Jordan-Zachery has authored a number of articles including "Blogging at the Intersections: Black Women, Identity, and Lesbianism," "The Female Bogeyman: Political Implications of Criminalizing Black Women," and "Let Men Be Men: A Gendered Analysis of Black Ideological Response to Familial Policies." She is also the author of the award-winning book *Black Women, Cultural Images and Social Policy* (2009, Routledge) and *Shadow Bodies: Black Women, Ideology, Representation and Politics* (2017, Rutgers University Press). Additionally, she is the coeditor, with Nikol Alexander-Floyd, of a special issue of the *National Political Science Review* on Black women and politics.

Keesha M. Middlemass is an associate professor in the Department of Political Science at Howard University (Washington, D.C.), where she teaches courses in American politics, urban politics, and public policy. Her published research examines issues found at the intersection of race, institutions, and public policy, and is published in *Aggressive Behavior*, *Criminal Justice & Behavior*, and *Social Science Quarterly*. Middlemass's book *Contemporary Outlaws* will be published by New York University Press; Middlemass analyzes policies to conceptualize a felony conviction as a social disability to demonstrate how policies hinder the efforts of formerly incarcerated men and women to reenter society successfully. Middlemass is a former Andrew Mellon Post-Doctoral Fellow on Race, Crime and Justice at the Vera Institute of Justice in New York City and a former American Political Science Association Congressional Fellow. She earned an MA (American politics) and a PhD (public policy and American politics) from the School of Public & International Affairs at the University of Georgia.

Judylyn S. Ryan is an interdisciplinary scholar and Associate Professor of English at Ohio Wesleyan University. She is the author of *Spirituality as Ideology in Black Women's Film and Literature* (University of Virginia Press, 2005), and of articles published in *Signs*, *Modern Fiction Studies*, *Studies in the Literary Imagination*, and other venues. The current essay is excerpted from a forthcoming book, *Morrisonian Democracy: The Literary Praxis of a Cultural Philosophy*.

Maziki Thame teaches in political science at Clark Atlanta University. Her research is focused on the postcolonial Caribbean and the place of race, violence, identity, and gender in political life. She is currently working on two books, the first on race, citizenship and the politics of identity in Jamaica, Brazil, and Barbados; and the second on the political Left of Jamaica in the 1970s.

Tonya M. Williams is an assistant professor of political science in the Department of Social and Behavioral Sciences at Johnson C. Smith University. Dr. Williams's research is anchored in the study of gender, race, public policy, and reproductive politics and women of color in politics at the elite and grassroots levels. In addition to her teaching and research portfolio, Tonya has nearly ten years of nonprofit experience in program development, grant writing, and policy advocacy, and has held leadership positions in reproductive justice and human rights organizations in Atlanta, Georgia.

Index

30 for 30 Campaign, 255
1996 Personal Responsibility and Work Opportunities Act, 223
2008 Presidential Election, 1
2012 Presidential Election, 1, 105, 217, 222

ABC approach, 103
abortion, 244–46
Affordable Care Act (ACA): abortion and, 244–46; constitutional disputes of, 246; contraceptives and, 245–46; critques of, 253; HIV/AIDS testing and, 244, 253; passage of, 245–46, 251; political demonstrations and, 250–52; quality health care and, 243–44; reproductive health and, 237, 239, 243–46; reproductive justice organizations and, 246–250, 257
Afiya Center for HIV Prevention and Reproductive Justice, 249
Africa, 165–66, 176–180
African American Women for Reproductive Freedom, 241
African-Caribbean women: absence in research of, 61–62; as activists, 59–60, 63; categorization of, 63n1; community and, 52–53; discrimination and, 51–52, 56, 58–60; diversity within, 60; education and, 49; emigration of, 50–51; employment and, 49, 51–54, 56–60; financial status of, 53; gang violence and, 55–56; health care and, 49–50, 54–58; housing and, 49, 54; identity and, 55; invisibility of, 50, 54, 56; mental health and, 56–57; National Health System and, 54, 58–59; nurse training programs and, 51–52, 58–59; perceptions of, 53–54, 56–58; population in UK of, 52, 56; poverty and, 59; racism and, 52, 58–59; as research subjects, 61–62; return migration of, 51; settlement patterns of, 51–53; as single parents, 53, 55, 58; social capital of, 53; social care services and, 49; social exclusion of, 52; social mobility of, 53
African Diaspora, xv, xx, xxii, 17, 19, 118–19, 160, 167–69, 175
agency, xx, xxiii, 46, 76, 168, 192, 199, 201, 212
Aiken, Todd, 222
Allen, Edith, 174, 177
A Mercy, 202, 206–12
American Disabilities Act (ADA), 106

American Dream, 233
American Grown: How the White House Kitchen Garden Inspires Families, Schools, and Communities, 222, 225–28
American studies, 21
Anderson, Karen Tucker, 168
Angelou, Maya, 196
"Arise," 179
Army Nurse Corps, 170
Ar'n't I a Woman, 20
Association for the Study of African American Life and History (ASALH), 18–19
Association of Black Women Historians (ABWH), 18–19

Bacon's Rebellion, 206, 208
Bailey, Martha J., 168
Baldwin, James, 196
Bambara, Toni Cade, 196
Barriteau, Eudine, 15, 143–44, 146, 150
Batiste, Stephanie, 179
Bay, Mia, 20
Beloved, 205–6, 210
Berger, Michele, 98, 101
Bilbo, Theodore G., 177–78
Black Cultural Pathology Paradigm, 217, 223, 225, 227
Black feminism: as activists, 242; analyses of, 38; benefits in using, 17–19; black superwoman and, 58; Black women as centered subjects by, xxxii; Black women in politics and, xxi; Black women's labor and, xv–xvi; canonical texts of, xix–xx; challenges to, 5; contributions of, 74, 144, 160; definition of, 101, 119–120, 144; description of, 31; examinations within, 23; focus areas of, 45–46, 50, 56, 99–100, 137, 143, 240–41; goals of, xxiv, xxxiii, 41, 122, 138; identity and, xxxiii, 48, 108; impact of, 23; importance of, 7, 14–15, 23; intersectionality and, xv–xvi, xviii, xx, 2, 29, 37, 61, 143; invisibility of Black women and, xxvi; methodology of, xxv, 62, 238; perceptions of, 22; political engagement and, 195–97, 201, 207–8; within research, 8–13; research of, 14–15; *Their Eyes Were Watching God* and, xiii; Toni Morrison and, xxxi; "Truth" and, xxiii
Black feminist intersectional analysis, 238
Black Feminist Policy Analyst, 192
Black HIV/AIDS orphans: assistance for, 106–8; health status of, 97–98, 100, 106–7; invisibility of, 98–99, 105–6; marginalization of, 107; mothers of, 102–3; neglect of, 107; policy gaps and, 97, 106–8; stigmas and, 98; as undeserving, 102
Black men: class and, 149–150; fatherhood and, 57, 149–150, 181, 223–25; gender norms and, 171; gender roles and, 171; hierarchy within, 160; as leaders, 171, 181; *New Negro World* and, 166–67; patriarchy and, 149–150; perceptions of, 57, 149–150, 181, 223–24; police and, 71–72; as strong, 171–72, 181; World War II and, 169
Black nationalism: African Diaspora and, 168–69; Black history and, 179; Black liberation and, 181; Black women and, 153–54, 168, 181; colonialism and, 178–79; definition of, 183n1; gender and, 168–69; gender norms and, 181–82; gender roles and, 153–54, 181–82;

goals of, 166–67, 183n1; in Jamaica, 150; masculinism and, 181–82; militant leanings of, 165; newspapers of, 167; Pan-Africanism and, 114, 178–79; patriarchy, 168–69, 172; as public forum, 182
Black orphans: absence in research of, 47; boundaries of, 46
Black Power, 183
Black Studies, 21–22
black superwoman, 58
Black womanhood: definition of, xxiii; ideology and, xvi
Black women: absence in research of, 14, 18–19, 22–23, 29–30, 34, 61–62; absence of power and, 144; African Diaspora and, xv; agency of, xxiii; as angry, 33, 40; Black nationalism and, 153–54; bodies of, xx; cinema of, 198–99; citizenship issues of, xxiii, 148–49, 153; cult of true womanhood and, 230; Democratic National Committee and, 1; discrimination and, 61–62, 74–75, 103; discrimination of, 49; as domestics, 174; as elected officials, xxii, 22–23; employment and, 75; as felons, 47; femininity and, 232–33; gender norms and, 149, 151, 159–160, 171, 181–82; gender roles and, 171, 181–82; geographies of, 12, 17, 19; health care and, 54–58, 61–62, 103, 192–93, 254; *The Help* and, 1–3; hierarchy within, 160; historical research and, 9; history of, 167; HIV/AIDS and, 100, 102–3, 253; HIV/AIDS infection rates of, 99, 104; housing and, 75; identity and, 46–48, 87, 103, 122, 191; imprisonment of, xxv, 49; incarceration of, 72; intersectionality and, 2–3, 23, 28–30, 37–38; invisibility of, xxiii, xxv–xxvi, 1–4, 6, 9, 12, 14, 23, 28–29, 46, 56, 107–8; labor of, xiii–xv, 3, 32–33, 168; as Mammy, 31; marginalization of, xv–xvi, xxiv, 108, 150, 237–38; masculinism and, 181–82; as menace, 218; Michelle Obama and, 226; motherhood and, 55, 98–99, 102–3, 107–8, 153–54, 218; as mules, xiii–xv, xxiii–xxiv; as needing protection, 171; nonconformity by, 45–46; obesity and, 218, 224–26; oppression of, xx, 33, 41, 74–75, 115, 191; perceptions of, xiv, 14, 31, 33, 40–41, 55, 102–3, 180, 192, 217–18, 223–25; personal responsibility and, 193; police and, 71–72; policy making and, 108; as political, xv–xvii, xix–xxi, xxiii–xxiv, 3, 17, 22–23, 28–29, 46, 137–38, 169, 238–39; political resistance by, 239–243; political science and, 6, 9, 15–16, 38–39; politics and, 34, 46; power and, 28–29, 33, 41, 108; race and, 103; representation of, 33, 40–41, 47–48; reproductive health and, 246–48; reproductive justice organizations and, 255–57; reproductive politics and, 239–243; reproductive rights of, 192–93; as research subjects, 34, 36, 38–39, 61–62; resistance and, 113–14; resistance by, 191; resistance of, 17; respectability and, 147, 149, 153–54, 180; self-actualization of, xiii, xx; self-definition of, xiii–xiv, xx; sex work and, 103; silencing of, xxiii–xxvi, 28–29, 31–36; as single parents, 53, 55, 99, 104; social justice and, xxv; sociological research and, 9; stereotypes and, 221–22;

Black women *(continued)*
stereotypes of, xvi; stigmas and, 103–4; substance abuse and, 103; true womanhood and, 180; U.S. democracy and, 212–13; violence against, 69, 76, 87–88; voice of, 135; voting rates of, 1; in the work force, 169–170; World War II and, 169–170
Black women bodies, 89
Black Women's Health Imperative, 240
Black Women's Initiative, 19
Black women with felony convictions: access to public assistance and, 71–73, 75, 79, 88–91; discrimination and, 74–75; education and, 79–81, 84; employment and, 80–81, 83–85; food insecurity and, 86; health care and, 82–84, 87; housing and, 75–76, 79–80, 83–86, 90; identity of, 89; incarceration rates of, 71–72, 89; invisibility of, 72, 86, 90; labels and, 70–71, 74–75, 80–81, 89; mental health and, 82, 87, 91n14; motherhood and, 77–78, 80–81, 87–88; oppression of, 74–75; othering of, 70–71, 90; poverty and, 71, 76, 80; reentry of, 73–74, 81, 83, 85–86; reoffense by, 82–84, 86; resilience and, 86–88; silencing of, 74, 89; social capital of, 86, 88; spaces for, 73; stigmas and, 75–76, 86; substance abuse and, 76, 79, 81, 83–85; violence against, 76, 79
Blatt, Jessica, 16–17
Blyden, Edward Wilmer, 175, 177
Bogues, Anthony, 147
Brooks, Gwendolyn, 196
Burgess, John W., 16
Burwell v. Hobby Lobby Stores, Inc., 246
Butler, Johnella, 21–22

Campaign to End AIDS, 255
Campbell, Eustace G., 175–76
Campbell, Grace P., 174
Caribbean: gender system of, 146–47; patriarchy and, 146–150. *See also* African-Caribbean women
cassava plant, 117–18, 124–25, 129
Cheney, Charise, 168
childhood obesity, 228
Chisholm, Shirley, 213
Civil Rights Movement, 32, 169, 183, 196
Clifton, Lucille, 196
Clinton, Bill, 241
Clinton, Hillary, 105, 219–220
Coalition to Pass Healthcare Reform, 251, 255
Collins, Ethel M., 175–76, 179–182
Collins, Patricia Hill, xix–xx, 22, 30–31, 99, 168
Collins, William J., 168
colonialism, 169
Combahee River Collective, xix–xx
Communist Party, 174
"Community Cassava," 125, 128, 130
community feminism, 180–81
Congress of Racial Equality (CORE), 169
contraceptives, 221, 245–46
Cooper, Brittney, xviii
Cooper, Elaine, 177
Crenshaw, Kimberle, xix–xx, xxvi, 74, 113
Creole nationalism, 150–52
cult of true womanhood, 229–232
cultural studies, xx

Davis, Angela, 50
Delany, Martin, 177
democracy, 174, 195

Democratic National Committee, 1
Descartes' Error, 202
Dieterich, Katherine R., 244–45
Dill, Bonnie Thornton, xvii
divorce, 148
Dolgin, Janet L., 244–45
"Double V' campaign, 169
Du Bois, W. E. B., 176

economics, 5–6
Edwards, John Bel, 257n3
Eliot, T. S., 196
Ellison, Ralph, 196–97
empathy, 200–205
ereba: description of, 117–18; importance of, 117–18, 129–130, 133, 137–38; politics and, xxiv–xxv; processing of, 125, 130; as resistance, xxiv–xxv; sale of, 126–27
Ethiopianism, 179–180
eugenics, 16

FDR's Executive Order 8802, 174
femininity, 148
feminism, xvi, xxiii, 29, 45
First Ladies, 219
"Fish to Cassava," 125–26
Fluke, Sandra, 222
food deserts, 225–26
food insecurity, 225–26, 232–33
foster care system, 69–70, 77, 81–82
Foucault, Michel, 70
Frasure, Lorrie, 2, 7–8

gang violence, 55–56
gardening, 226–28, 232
Garifuna: classification of, 118–120, 123; collective labor and, 126; communal lands of, 122–24; farming methods of, 121–22, 125; gender and, 122, 130–31; gendered division of labor and, 130, 135; geographic location of, 117; health outcomes and, 135–36; history of, 118–19; kinship system of, 127; land grabs from, 121–29, 135; land ownership and, 122–24; land policies and, 121–29, 135, 137–38; land use by, 126–27, 129, 131; as matrifocal, 120–24, 131–32; motherhood and, 132–33; perceptions of, 123; political resistance by, 118; political status of, 134, 136; poverty and, 124; preserving culture of, 125, 129, 131; race and, 121–22; redistribution of wealth and, 128; resistance and, 122–23; resistance by, 124, 134, 136–38; self-definition of, 118–120; as single parents, 127; social capital of, 128, 134; societal strictures of, 131–32, 137–38
garretting, xxvi, xxx, 3, 6–7, 17–19, 22, 24n4
garrison politics, 154, 161–63n3
Garvey, Marcus, 166, 169–170, 175, 180–81, 183n2
Gender Studies, xx, 6, 15, 21, 41
General Consumption Tax (GCT), 157
geographies, 12, 17, 19
Global South, 47, 97
Goat Islands, 158
Grayson, Deborah R., 240
Great Depression, 170, 178
Greater Liberia Bill, 177–78
Green, Zebedee, 183n3
Greene, Joshua, 203–4, 213n2
group muted theory, 30, 35–36, 39–40
Guinier, Lani, 198–99

Hancock, Ange-Marie, 224, 227
Hansberry, Lorraine, 196
Harris-Perry, Melissa, 231

health care: access to, 255; African-Caribbean women and, 49–50, 54–58; Black women and, 54–58; inequalities within, 50; racism and, 53; reform of, 232–33, 238, 241–42, 257; reproductive health and, 239; reproductive rights and, 241–43
health insurance, 244, 253
Heritage Foundation, 224
Higginbotham, Evelyn Brooks, 147
Hine, Darlene Clark, 20
historical thinking, 203, 205–7
history, 5–6, 9–13
HIV/AIDS: Affordable Care Act (ACA) and, 244, 253; as a civil rights issue, 103; hot spots of, 98; as a human rights issue, 103; public opinion of, 105; research on, 46; risk factors for, 98, 102–3; stigmas and, 103–4; treatment of, 105
Holness, Andrew, 152, 155
Holocaust, 175
"Home," 198
Home, 211
homosexuality, 150, 155–56, 171
Honey, Maureen, 168
hooks, bell, xiv
Hughes, Langston, 196
Hurston, Zora Neale, xiii, xxiii–xxiv, 193, 196

identity: African-Caribbean women and, 55; Black feminism and, xxxiii, 48, 108; Black women and, 46–48, 87, 103, 122, 191; Black women with felony convictions and, 89; construction of, 39; intersectionality and, xviii, 5, 14, 114; policy making and, 29, 45–46; politics of, 28, 32–33
imprisonment: discrimination and, 49; impact of, 49
Incidents in the Life of a Slave Girl, 17
indentured servitude, 209
Institute for Women and Ethnic Studies, 249
International Women's Day, 154–55
intersectionality: applications of, 1–2; benefits of, xx–xxi; Black feminism and, xv–xvi, xviii, xx, 2, 29, 37, 61, 143; Black women and, 2–3, 23, 28–30, 37–38; critques of, xviii–xix, 34; definition of, xv–xvi, 37, 71; description of, 100–101; discrimination and, 61–62; expansion of, 28–30; health care and, 61–63; history of, 34, 61; identity and, xviii, 5, 14, 89, 114; as a legal theory, 61; misunderstandings of, xviii–xix; nature of research of, 19–20; oppression and, 100–101; origins of, xvi–xvii; policy analysis and, 45; policy making and, 101; political science and, xx–xxi, 1–2, 5, 19; popularity of, xvii–xviii, 29–31; power relations and, 100–101; race and, xvii–xviii; social justice and, xvi–xviii; stigmas and, 75, 98–101; study of, 1–2; types of, 61–62; use of, 37–38, 45
intersectionality based policy analysis, 98, 101–2
intersectionality-informed policy analysis approach, 45
intersectional stigma framework, 75
Ireland, Adelia, 179, 181
Isoke, Zensele, 238

Jackson, Esther Cooper, 174
Jacobs, Harriet, 17, 22

Jacques Garvey, Amy, 178–79
Jamaica: Black nationalism and, 150; China and, 158; colonial history of, 147; colonialism and, 147; employment in, 157; gender norms and, 155; gender system of, 147, 149; labor of, 158; marriage and, 148–49; overtime work, 158; patriarchy, 146–150; personal responsibility and, 156–58; political organizations of, 156; respectability and, 156–57
Jamaica Emergency Employment Programme (JEEP), 157
Jamaican political system: class and, 144–45; development of, 144; gender and, 144–45; inner city and, 146; paternalism and, 154; Portia Simpson-Miller and, 146, 151, 154–55; violence and, 154
James, Charles, 183n3
James, C. L. R., 145
Janie Crawford, xiii–xiv, xxiii–xxiv
Jazz, 211
Jefferson, Thomas, 228
Jezebel, 224
Jim Crow laws, 166, 169
Jones, Charles E., 222
Jones, Claudia, 174
Jordan, June, 196
Junn, Jane, 1

Kelley, Robin D. G., 175
Kennedy, Jackie, 219
Killing the Black Body: Race, Reproduction, and the Meaning of Liberty, 239

"Last Hired, First Fired: Black Women Workers during World War II," 168
League of Colored Peoples, 178
Leeds, Asia, 180
Lemelle, Sidney J., 175
Let's Move: as act of resistance, 230–31, 233; critques of, 226; as a deracialization strategy, 233; food insecurity and, 225–26, 232–33; gardening and, 226–28; goals of, 225; Michelle Obama and, 230; obesity and, 229
Let's Move: Black Cultural Pathology Paradigm and, 224–25; class and, 217–18; family values and, 223; reproductive health and, 192, 217–18; sexuality and, 217–18
Lewis, Linden, 147
Lewis, Rupert, 145
"Liberty," 177
Lift Every Voice: Turning a Civil Rights Setback into a New Vision of Social Justice, 198–99
Lorde, Audre, xiv, 196
Lubiano, Wahneema, 171, 179
lynching, 173

Mammy, 31, 224
Manley, Michael, 144
Manley, Norman, 144
"Man's Inhumanity," 171
March of Washington, 169
Marianao Division of the Universal Negro Improvement Association, 176
marriage, 148–49
Marshall, Paule, 196
masculinism: gender power and, 145; *New Negro World* and, 171–72
Matrimonial Causes Act of 1988, 148
May, Vivian, xvii
Mayer, Tamar, 223
McCormick, Joseph, Jr., 222
Medicaid expansion, 239, 244–46, 252, 257n3

Monticello, 228
Moody, Harold, 178
Moody, Josephine, 165–66
moral imagination, 201–2
moral reasoning, 202–4, 213n2
Morrison, Toni: class oppression and, 211; historical thinking and, 205–6, 209–10; impact of, 196; moral foundations and, 211–12; myths of innocence and, 211–12; narrative knowledge and, 200; as teacherly, 197; trauma and, 209, 211
Moynihan Report, 223, 229
mule, xiii–xiv
Mullenbach, Cheryl, 168
"My Race," 173

Narcotics Anonymous, 85
narrative knowledge, 199–200, 205–7
National Agrarian Institute, 121–22
National Association for the Advancement of Colored People (NAACP), 168, 170
National Black Women's Health Project, 240
National Center for Charitable Statistics (NCCS), 246
National Conference of Black Political Scientists, 19, 21
National Federation of Independent Business (NFIB) v. Sebelius, 246
National Health System, 54
National Responsible Fatherhood Clearinghouse, 223
National Urban League (NUL), 168
Neita-Hedley, Natalie, 155
"New Negro Movement," 165
New Negro World: Black female writers in, 172–73, 182; Black men and, 166–67; critques of, 172; democracy and, 173–74; discrimination and, 174; distribution of, 170–71; diverse readership of, 172–73; Ethel M. Collins and, 183n4; frustration in, 172–74; gender norms and, 171–72, 182; gender roles and, 171–72, 182; history of, 181–82, 183n4; importance of, 166–67; James R. Stewart and, 170; masculinism and, 171–72; patriarchy and, 172; praise for, 172–73

Obama, Barack, xviii–xix, 105–6, 119, 219, 232, 243
Obama, Michelle: 2012 Presidential Election and, 222; anti-obesity campaign of, 192; Barack Obama and, 217; criticisms of, 220–21, 231; cult of true womanhood and, 229–232; education of, 221; fashion sense of, 219–220, 231; health care reform and, 219; image of, 220, 223, 230–33; legal career of, 219; Let's Move and, 230; as model, 218–19; as Mom-in-Chief, 218, 222, 230, 232; patriarchy and, 221; perceptions of, 220–21; personal responsibility and, 227; political power of, 221; respectability and, 225, 230–31, 233; scrutiny of, 220–21, 231; self-regulation and, 227; speeches of, 219–221; stereotypes and, 221–22
obesity, 192, 218, 224–26, 228–29
ODECO, 133–34, 137
OFRANEH, 133–34, 137
oppositional political geographies, 12, 17
otherness, 35, 40–41

Pan-Africanism: Black nationalism and, 178–79; Black nationalist women and, 114; goals of, 167; redemption of Africa and, 180

patriarchy, 146–150
Patton, Nathaniel C., 171–72
Peoples National Party (PNP): fiscal policies of, 156–58; history of, 144–45; leadership of, 151–53; Portia Simpson-Miller and, 144, 151, 153, 156, 159–160
"Peril," 213
personal responsibility, 156–58, 223, 228–29
Petry, Ann, 196
police, 71–72
policy making, 100, 202–3
political intersectionality, 61, 113–15, 133
political science: alternative research in, xx–xxi, 12–13; Black women and, 9, 38–39; critques of, 6–7; history and, 7–11; history of, 16; as interdisciplinary, 20–21; intersectionality and, 1–2, 5; journals of, 7–13, 22–23, 36–38; purpose of, 15–16; racism and, 12, 16; sociology and, 7–11
politics of space, 6, 9, 17, 22, 23n2
Pollack, Harold A., 245
Positive Women's Network, 255
Possing, Dorthe, 6
postintersectional, xviii–xix
Prestage, Jewel, xvii, 15, 23n1, 118
PROMISE program, 83, 91n14
Putbey, Martha S., 168

racial violence, 166, 169, 174
Raising Women's Voices, 255
Remember: The Journey to School Integration, 207
representational intersectionality, 61
reproductive justice organizations, 246–250, 255–57
research, politics of, 30, 33
River, Aaron, 180
Robinson, Dean E., 178
Robinson, Tracy, 153
Romney, Mitt, 105, 222
Ross, Loretta, 241–42, 244, 251
Ryan White Care Act, 103, 106–7

Sanchez, Sonia, 196
Sasuma, 135–38
Scott, Anne Firor, 20
Second Wave of the Great Migration, 169
sexual abuse, 69, 87, 211
Sexual Offences Act, 149
Shange, Ntozake, 196
Shockley, Megan Taylor, 168
Simpson-Miller, Portia: criticisms of, 159; early career of, 146, 150–53, 160; English language and, 152; fall from power of, 158–160; fiscal policies of, 156–58; garrison politics and, 154–55; gender norms and, 149; Jamaican political system and, 146, 151, 154–55; masculinism and, 146, 161; Peoples National Party (PNP) and, 144, 151, 153, 156, 159–160; perceptions of, 144, 152, 154, 160; poor and, 146, 153–54, 156–58; presidential bids of, 152, 156, 159–160; respectability and, 149, 151, 160; silencing of, 159; support for, 152–53; violence and, 154–55
SisterLove, Inc, 249
SisterSong Women of Color Reproductive Justice Collective, 247, 250
slavery, 40, 208–9, 211–14. *See also* Harriet Jacobs
socialization, 202–4
social justice, xvi–xvii, xx, 29, 47–48, 108, 241
sociology, 5–6, 9–13, 18, 21

Sonfield, Adam, 245
SPARK Reproductive Justice NOW, 257n2
Special Economic Zone Act, 158
"spirit of manliness," 171–72
Starling, Ruben, 183n3
Stewart, James R., 166, 170, 173–74, 181–82
Stewart, Maria, 213
Stop Stupak Rally, 250–51, 255
Strolovitch, Dara, 238
structural inequality, 113
structural intersectionality, 61, 113–15, 123
structural racism, 124

Taylor, Ula, 168, 172
Telling Histories, 20
The Bluest Eyes, 201–2, 205, 209
The Heart of the Race: Black Women's Lives in Britain, 54
The Help: critques of, 27; invisibility of Black women and, 1–3; marketing campaign for, 31–32; popularity of, xxiv, 27, 31–32
Their Eyes Were Watching God, xiii–xv, xxiii–xxiv, 2, 193
"The Negro Woman Domestic Worker in Relation to Trade Unionism," 174
"The Novel as a Function of American Democracy," 196
"The Real Solution," 174
"The Site of Memory," 207
tilling (metaphor), xv, xx, xxiii
Todd, Joseph A., 173
tough on crime, 72, 90
Treatment Access Expansion Project, 255
Trump, Donald, 105
Truth, Sojourner, 213
Turner, Henry McNeal, 177
United Nations Educational, Scientific and Cultural Organization, 117
Universal Negro Improvement Association (UNIA): Ethel M. Collins and, 175; Marcus Garvey and, 170, 183n2; origins of, 170, 183n2
U.S. democracy: agency and, 199; the American Dream and, 233; Black women and, 212–13; health care reform and, 198; health of, 206, 213; historical thinking and, 203, 205–7; homelessness and, 198; human rights and, 199; immigration and, 198; myth of self invention, 209; novels and, 196–97, 212–13; othering and, 199; participation in, 199; perils of, 197–201; prisons and, 198; racism and, 197–98; risk aversion of, 210–11

Vassell, Linnette, 147
victory gardens, 227–28

Wabagari Distribution, 135–36
Walker, Alice, 196
War on Drugs, 38, 75, 89
War on Women, 217, 221
Webster v. Reproductive Health Services, 241
Welfare Queens, 192, 224–25, 227
Wells-Barnett, Ida B., 173, 213
"We Remember," 241
"We Want to Set the World on Fire," 165
White, Deborah, 20, 224
White, E. Frances, 168, 178
White, Elinor, 181
White imperialism, 169
White supremacy, 114, 147, 165, 167, 170, 175, 182, 213n1

Wilkes, Florine, 173, 179, 181
Williams, William Carlos, 196
Wilson, David, 172
Wilson, Ernest, III, 2, 7–8
Women of African Descent for Reproductive Justice (WADRJ), 242
Women's Army Corps (WAC), 170
Women's Studies, xx, xxii–xxiii, 6, 15, 21
"Women's Traditions," 125
"Women Warriors," 126, 128
Women with a Vision, 249
World War I, 16, 166
World War II, 51, 166, 169, 182, 227
Wright, Richard, 196

Young, Theresa E., 174, 177, 183n4

Zionist movement, 175

www.ingramcontent.com/pod-product-compliance
Lightning Source LLC
LaVergne TN
LVHW040200080826
844660LV00001B/47

* 9 7 8 1 4 3 8 4 7 0 9 3 1 *